DATE DUE

FEB 1 0 2009	
FEB 2 2 2009	
MAY 0 7 2009	
OCT 2 2 2009	
SEP 0 5 2013	
DEC 0 5 2013	
FEB 1 0 2016	

THE
RESPONSIBILITY
TO PROTECT

Advance Praise for
THE RESPONSIBILITY TO PROTECT

The responsibility to protect is the most important and imaginative doctrine to emerge on the international scene for decades. No one is better placed than Gareth Evans to lead the debate about its scope and application to contemporary crises, such as Darfur, Myanmar, and Zimbabwe. And no one could have done it better than in this comprehensive and sophisticated book.

> LOUISE ARBOUR, UN High Commissioner for Human Rights, 2004–08; Chief Prosecutor, International Criminal Tribunals for the former Yugoslavia and Rwanda, 1996–99

I strongly endorse Gareth Evans's eloquent argument, urging the international community to strategically operationalize R2P in all its facets and to build the necessary political will to act. This call to prevent terrible crimes against humanity like those I witnessed in Rwanda is one we must answer.

> GENERAL ROMEO DALLAIRE, author of *Shake Hands with the Devil: The Failure of Humanity in Rwanda*

R2P is one of the most powerful and promising innovations on the international scene, and, more than anyone else, Gareth Evans has been at the forefront of its development and promotion. This book is a major contribution, one which no one interested in the responsibility to protect and the prospects for its realization can afford to miss.

> FRANCIS DENG, UN Special Adviser on the Prevention of Genocide; coauthor of *Sovereignty as Responsibility: Conflict Management in Africa*

A tour de force. . . . Gareth Evans, more than anyone, has persuaded leaders to accept their responsibility to protect the vulnerable and convinced us that we can no longer be passive bystanders. This book is indispensable in this noble struggle.

> JAN EGELAND, UN Emergency Relief Coordinator, 2003–06; Director, Norwegian Institute of International Affairs; author of *A Billion Lives: An Eyewitness Report from the Frontlines of Humanity*

The responsibility to protect is part of Gareth Evans's legacy as a politician, and, as this volume demonstrates, there is no better author for explaining the crucial challenge that it presents to the formulation of foreign and security policy today. His book is both a passionate plea for R2P and a comprehensive guide to its implementation.

JOSCHKA FISCHER, Foreign Minister of Germany, 1998–2005

Gareth Evans has a rare combination of diplomatic and scholarly experience. This book is rich in information, ideas, and proposals for conflict resolution, violence prevention, and the strengthening of human rights. It will long be useful for the international community.

DAVID HAMBURG, Chair, UN Secretary-General's Advisory Committee on Genocide Prevention; author of *Preventing Genocide: Practical Steps toward Early Detection and Effective Action*

In *The Responsibility to Protect*, Gareth Evans establishes a historical and intellectual framework for preventing the worst of humankind's self-inflicted tragedies. It is both powerful and persuasive.

LEE H. HAMILTON, President and Director, Woodrow Wilson International Center for Scholars

In 2005 the United Nations General Assembly voted unanimously in favor of a major new concept: the responsibility to protect. But did they mean it—and what did they really mean? Now Gareth Evans, one of its principal creators, has written the first major work on this noble, important, and elusive concept. Anyone interested in international affairs should read this book on what is certain to be a continuing debate.

AMBASSADOR RICHARD HOLBROOKE, U.S. Permanent Representative to the United Nations 1999–2001; Assistant Secretary of State, 1977–81 and 1994–96; author of *To End a War: Sarajevo to Dayton: The Inside Story*

In taking a step further the idea of "humanitarian intervention" that I developed, the General Assembly's adoption of the responsibility to protect was a major paradigm shift for the protection of victims worldwide. Gareth Evans's book will be vitally important in ensuring that R2P is understood and accepted.

BERNARD KOUCHNER, Foreign Minister of France

We can no longer ignore atrocities beamed into our living rooms. Our conscience demands that we react whenever people suffer, from Rwanda to Srebrenica, from Darfur to Gaza. Gareth Evans's volume could not be more timely or relevant.

> KISHORE MAHBUBANI, Dean, Lee Kuan Yew School of Public Policy, Singapore; author of *The New Asian Hemisphere: The Irresistible Shift of Global Power to the East*

Gareth Evans is the best possible guide to what this hugely important development in international affairs means. A terrific book which should be required reading for every foreign minister, and anyone else wanting a better and more peaceful world.

> CHRIS PATTEN, European Commissioner for External Relations, 1999–2004; Chancellor, Oxford University; author of *What Next? Surviving the Twenty-first Century*

The UN's adoption of the Responsibility to Protect was a red-letter day for human rights. Our greatest failure is the inability to deal effectively with egregious human rights violations, such as in Darfur. This authoritative work explains why the concept is so vital. It is both timely and needed.

> MARY ROBINSON, UN High Commissioner for Human Rights, 1997–2002; President of Ireland, 1990–97

We have been shamed so often by our failure to protect the victims of mass atrocity crimes. Gareth Evans's book is a passionate, lucidly argued, and immensely well-informed guide to how the world can do better. I hope it gets the readership in high places, not least in Africa, it deserves.

> DESMOND TUTU, Archbishop Emeritus of Cape Town; Chair, South African Truth and Reconciliation Commission, 1995–98

THE
RESPONSIBILITY
TO PROTECT

Ending Mass Atrocity Crimes Once and For All

GARETH EVANS

BROOKINGS INSTITUTION PRESS
Washington, D.C.

ABOUT BROOKINGS

The Brookings Institution is a private nonprofit organization devoted to research, education, and publication on important issues of domestic and foreign policy. Its principal purpose is to bring the highest quality independent research and analysis to bear on current and emerging policy problems. Interpretations or conclusions in Brookings publications should be understood to be solely those of the authors.

Library of Congress Cataloging-in-Publication data
Evans, Gareth J., 1944–
   The responsibility to protect : ending mass atrocity crimes once and for all / Gareth Evans.
       p.   cm.
   Includes bibliographical references and index.
   Summary: "Explains Responsibility to Protect (R2P), a new international norm to protect the peoples of the world. With real-world examples, current events analysis, and assessments from personal experience, shows how R2P is better equipped to end mass atrocity crimes than is 'the right to intervene' or other 'humanitarian intervention' doctrines"—Provided by publisher.
   ISBN 978-0-8157-2504-6 (cloth : alk. paper)
   1. Atrocities—Prevention. 2. Genocide—Prevention. I. Title.
   HV6322.7.E93 2008
   363.34—dc22   2008033229

Typeset in Minion and Univers

Composition by Pete Lindeman, OSP Inc.
Arlington, Virginia

Printed by R. R. Donnelley
Harrisonburg, Virginia

To the staff and board members, past and present, of the
International Crisis Group.
Superb professionals, and optimists all.

Contents

PART II
Operationalizing the Responsibility to Protect

Acknowledgments

My first debt is to my cochair and fellow members of the International Commission on Intervention and State Sovereignty (ICISS), without whose commitment and creativity the idea of the responsibility to protect would never have been given birth: Mohamed Sahnoun, Gisele Côté-Harper, Lee Hamilton, Michael Ignatieff, Vladimir Lukin, Klaus Naumann, Cyril Ramaphosa, Fidel Ramos, Cornelio Sommaruga, Eduardo Stein, and Ramesh Thakur. The Commission was the brainchild of then Canadian Foreign Minister Lloyd Axworthy, who gave us a dream staff with which to work, led by Jill Sinclair and Heidi Hulan, and on the research side, Tom Weiss and Don Hubert.

The ICISS report would have had little resonance without being picked up in the recommendations of the UN Secretary-General's High-Level Panel on Threats, Challenges, and Change, for which I am deeply grateful to all my colleagues on that panel, and its chair, Anand Panyarachun, but in particular to Gro Harlem Brundtland, David Hannay, Satish Nambiar, Sadako Ogata, Qian Quichen, Salim Salim, and Brent Scowcroft. The panel was served by an outstanding secretariat, led by research director Stephen Stedman and his deputy Bruce Jones, who both also played crucial roles in the subsequent follow-up, including the drafting of the Secretary-General's own report to the 2005 World Summit. Kofi Annan himself was a wonderful source of inspiration and encouragement throughout this whole enterprise and has remained so since, while his successor Ban Ki-moon has maintained, professionally and personally, all the continuity of commitment to R2P for which one could possibly wish.

A third group keeping the flame of my own optimism burning on ending mass atrocity crimes once and for all has been the Advisory Committee on Genocide Prevention, established by the UN Secretary-General in 2006 under the admirable leadership of David Hamburg and comprising among others Desmond Tutu and Romeo Dallaire, along with the former and current special advisers on genocide prevention, Juan Méndez and Francis Deng. I owe a particularly long-standing personal and intellectual debt to David Hamburg, who by inviting me in the mid-1990s to join the Carnegie Commission on the Prevention of Deadly Conflict, which he co-chaired with Cyrus Vance, first really stirred my passion on this whole subject, and opened my eyes to the utility of blue-ribbon international panels supported by strong professional research teams in marrying the world of ideas to the world of policy action.

No group of colleagues could have been more supportive throughout my evolving commitment to R2P than my fellow Board members—led by Chris Patten and Tom Pickering as cochairs—and staff of the International Crisis Group, to whom this book is dedicated. Crisis Group has been my professional home now for nine years, since leaving Australian politics and government. If it has become the leading independent source of analysis and advice to global policymakers on conflict prevention and resolution, that is above all else because of the superb quality of its research, advocacy, and support teams. In writing these chapters I have constantly drawn on Crisis Group reports and briefings—of which more than 800 have now been published—and on oral advice and information from my colleagues in the field, and in our advocacy offices in Brussels, New York, Washington, and elsewhere. I am indebted to them all—and to the government, foundation, and private sector donors who have made it all possible! The Crisis Group family has made more bearable my many absences, during the nearly nine years I have been working from Brussels, from my own now extending family in Australia, for whose love and support I remain forever grateful.

For direct help in the preparation of this book, my most immediate debt of gratitude is to my senior Crisis Group colleagues Don Steinberg (for reading and commenting on every draft chapter) and Alain Deletroz,

Nick Grono, Fabienne Hara, and Carrie Flintoft (for help on particular topics); to my successive research assistants on this project, Helene Wolf and Kate Carey, who performed heroic feats over long hours against constantly pressing deadlines, with a good deal of help along the way from other staff and interns, notably Marijan Zumbulev, Zachary Vertin, and Darren Lim; and to Neil Campbell, former staffers Dan Vexler and Charles Emmerson, and a long procession of junior staff and interns who worked with them over recent years in developing our in-house conflict prevention and management "toolbox" on which I have significantly drawn in chapters 4, 5, and 7.

Outside Crisis Group I have been helped, with comment and input on various drafts and ideas, by NGO and academic colleagues associated with the recently established Global Centre for the Responsibility to Protect, including Tom Weiss, Ramesh Thakur, Nicole Deller, Jim Traub, Bill Pace, Jan Egeland, Rama Man, and Ken Roth; by Heidi Hulan, now at the Canadian mission in New York; by former Australian colleagues Ken Berry (who was executive assistant to the cochairs of ICISS) and John Dauth (head of mission in New York at the time of the 2005 World Summit); and particularly by Dr. Connie Peck, with whom I worked closely in the 1990s on various conflict prevention projects, and who gave me here, in detailed comments and suggestions, the benefit of her many years experience as a leading figure in UN diplomatic training. Of course no one but me bears any responsibility for the shortcomings still evident in the final product.

This book has drawn on some writings of my own in print, or about to be, and I acknowledge and thank in this respect the publishers of *Cooperating for Peace* (Sydney: Allen and Unwin, 1995); "When Is It Right to Fight?" *Survival* 46, no. 3 (2004); "From Humanitarian Intervention to Responsibility to Protect," *Wisconsin International Law Journal* 24, no. 3 (2006); "The Responsibility to Protect: An Idea Whose Time Has Come . . . and Gone?" *International Relations* 22, no. 3 (2008); and "The Responsibility to Protect: From an Idea to an International Norm," in *The Responsibility to Protect: The Global Moral Compact for the XXIst Century*, edited by Richard Cooper and Juliette Voinov Kohler (Basingstoke, England: Palgrave Macmillan, forthcoming).

I am grateful, finally, for the support given by Strobe Talbott, Carlos Pascual, and Ivo Daalder of Brookings, and the senior staff at Brookings

Institution Press—including, in particular, Bob Faherty, Mary Kwak, Chris Kelaher, Larry Converse, Susan Woollen, Susan Soldavin, and my extremely patient editors, Janet Walker and Starr Belsky—in getting this book conceived, written, promoted, and published in close to record speed. A pleasure to work with them all.

Brussels/Melbourne
July 2008

THE
RESPONSIBILITY
TO PROTECT

Introduction:
A Personal Journey

For me the journey, emotionally and intellectually, began in Cambodia in 1968. I was a young Australian making my first trip to Europe, to take up a scholarship in Oxford. Inexhaustibly hungry for experience, like so many of my compatriots before and since, I spent six months wending my way by plane and overland through a dozen countries in Asia, and a few more in Africa and the Middle East as well. And in every one of them, I spent many hours and days on student campuses and in student hang-outs, and in hard-class cross-country trains and ramshackle rural buses, getting to know in the process—usually fleetingly but quite often enduringly, in friendships that have lasted to this day—scores of some of the liveliest and brightest people of their generation.

In the years that followed, I have often come across Indonesians, Singaporeans, Malaysians, Thais, Vietnamese, Indians, Pakistanis, and others that I either met on the road on that trip, or who were there at the time and had a store of common experiences to exchange. But among all the countries in Asia I visited then, there is just one, Cambodia, from which I never again, in later years, saw *any* of those students whom I had met and befriended, or anyone exactly like them—not one of those kids with whom I drank beer, ate noodles, and careered up and down the dusty road from Phnom Penh to Siem Reap in child-, chicken-, and pig-scattering share taxis.

The reason, I am sadly certain, is that every last one of them died a few years later under Pol Pot's murderous genocidal regime—either targeted for execution in the killing fields as a middle-class intellectual enemy of the state or dying, as more than a million did, from starvation and disease after forced displacement to labor in the countryside. The knowledge, and the memory, of what must have happened to those young men and women is something that haunts me to this day.

That memory certainly was a core motivation during the long and grueling years in the late 1980s and early 1990s that I worked as Australian Foreign Minister, along with my Southeast Asian, Chinese, American, and UN colleagues, to find and implement a sustainable basis for peace in Cambodia. It was a recurring motif as I watched, impotently and from a distance, the tragic events in Central Africa and the Balkans work themselves out through the mid- to late 1990s.

And it was what made me accept with alacrity the offer of the Canadian government in 2000 to jointly lead a distinguished international commission charged with the task of trying to find, once and for all, a conceptual and practical answer that would unite, rather than continuing to divide, the international community in preventing and responding to mass atrocity crimes. The answer we came to—the concept of "the responsibility to protect"—is what this book is about.

* * *

Few contemporary events have seared the consciences of so many around the globe as much as two events just a year apart in the mid-1990s. In Rwanda in 1994, 800,000 men, women, and children were slaughtered over a few short weeks while the world's policymakers found reasons to do absolutely nothing in response. And in Srebrenica in Bosnia in 1995, 8,000 young and old men were massacred within a few days, taken from a UN "safe haven" while the troops deployed to protect them stood and watched.

How could we have said "never again" with so much conviction and confidence after the Holocaust of the Second World War, and then again after the revelation of the horror of Cambodia, when up to two million died in four years of tyrannical Khmer Rouge rule from 1975 to 1979? Now here we were, less than twenty years later, with the Genocide Convention in place and with all our accumulated historical experience, saying it again—and again. How, we asked ourselves with varying degrees of incomprehension, horror, anger, and shame, could we possibly have let this all happen again?

This book is about the way in which the world has at last started to answer that question and to take the steps necessary to ensure that we will never again have to say "never again." The decade of the 1990s was the watershed; the report of the International Commission on State Sovereignty in 2001, coming up with the new concept of "the responsibility to protect," was the immediate catalyst; and the unanimous decision by the World Summit in 2005 to embrace the concept was the crucial formal endorsement. As the chapters that follow make clear, much remains to be done to bed down this new international norm and ensure its effective practical application, but we are on our way, and none too soon. Part I is about understanding the responsibility to protect, how the concept emerged, and what it does and does not embrace, while Part II is about what is necessary to operationalize the new norm, to make it work effectively in practice.

The 1990s saw not only the catastrophes of Rwanda and Srebrenica but also the debacle of the attempted intervention in Somalia in 1993 and the inability of the UN Security Council to agree on a response to the killing and ethnic cleansing that broke out in Kosovo in 1999. There were other cases—northern Iraq, Haiti, Sierra Leone, Timor-Leste—where the performance was a little better. But the enduring memory of the decade is hesitation and incapacity to act, or act quickly and effectively enough, in case after case where civilian lives were massively at risk—and of an endemic lack of consensus among decisionmakers as to what was the right thing to do.

Throughout the decade, a fierce argument raged between, on the one hand, advocates of "humanitarian intervention"—the doctrine that there was a "right to intervene" militarily in these cases, against the will of the government of the country in question—and, on the other hand, defenders of the traditional prerogatives of state sovereignty, who insisted that internal events were none of the rest of the world's business. There was ample room, conceptually, to find common ground between these extremes, but no one seemed able to locate or articulate it: the verbal trench warfare, in the UN General Assembly and elsewhere, became ever more intense, and the inability to agree on an appropriate response to each of these situations as they arose became ever more frustrating and damaging.

The breakthrough came with the emergence in 2001 of the concept of the responsibility to protect and its subsequent unanimous embrace by the General Assembly, meeting at head of state and government level, in 2005. This turned "right to intervene" language on its head, focusing not on any rights of the great and powerful to throw their weight around but rather on the responsibility of all states to meet the needs of the utterly powerless. In the first instance, the responsibility to protect a country's people from mass atrocity crimes lay with its own government; but if it proved unable or unwilling to do so, a wider responsibility lay with other members of the international community to assist preventively and, if necessary, react effectively. Military intervention—the centerpiece of the earlier argument about "the right of humanitarian intervention"—remained an option in extreme cases, but only as a last resort and if the Security Council agreed. "The responsibility to protect" was about much more: the responsibility to prevent before a crisis and to rebuild after it, as well as to react during it, and in all cases, with the emphasis on nonmilitary action.

* * *

Just like in the past when Columbus in 1492 and Vasco da Gama in 1498 came with the Bible and the sword, the likes of Gareth Evans now come in 2007 with R2P.
—Lankaweb, Colombo, October 17, 2007[1]

My own direct role in the emergence of the new international norm was as cochair—with my distinguished Algerian colleague Mohamed Sahnoun—of the Canadian government–sponsored International Commission on Intervention and State Sovereignty (ICISS), which first articulated the concept in its 2001 report entitled *The Responsibility to Protect*. The commission was an extraordinarily lively group of very able and strong-willed personalities, and although our yearlong consultations and deliberations across four continents were conducted with great good humor throughout, it was something of a miracle that Mohamed and I were able to extract from our colleagues a final report that had in it not a single line of recorded dissent. Along the way, though, everything was contestable—and contested.

Congressman Lee Hamilton, I hope he won't be unhappy to recall, was the very last to join the consensus, in the last hour of our last meeting. His "Alamo" issue was the exceedingly difficult one—not least for a very public U.S. figure acutely attuned to the public mood of the time—of whether coalitions of the willing should be able to bypass the Security Council if a veto blocked action that most of the world thought appropriate and defensible. Our colleagues thought the two former politicians among us should fight it out in a private back room, and the extended arm wrestle Lee and I had to find a formula with which we each could live left us both a little misty eyed for our previous careers. All that was missing was the smoke.

The name of the report and its sustaining theme was no exception to the contestability rule. At the first of the commission's five meetings, in Ottawa in November 2000, I remember suggesting that what we needed was a strong new phrase: one that would capture the flavor of what we probably all wanted to say about the moral imperative of responding to atrocity crimes, be succinct and memorable, and, while having some continuity with the debate of which we had all been part over the last decade, also mark an escape from its sterility and divisiveness. So far, so good. But then—having spent a few mornings under the shower in the lead-up to our meeting toying with a score or more of different word combinations—I was adventurous enough to suggest that maybe, just maybe, there was a phrase—"the responsibility to protect"—we could agree met those criteria and perhaps even work as the title of the report. But to suggest the report's title before we had even begun to discuss its content, let alone taken any soundings in the dozen consultations that were scheduled to take place around the world, was considered a little presumptuous, even for an Australian. "Well, we'll have to think long and hard about *that*," was the hardly unreasonable general response. My handwritten notes of that meeting, incidentally, use "RtP" as shorthand for the phrase under discussion; it wasn't until rather later that the generally accepted summary form became "R2P" (no doubt under the universal cultural influence of *Star Wars* and its engagingly determined little droid R2-D2).

The ICISS report had the misfortune to be published in the immediate aftermath of the tragedy of September 11, and with public and professional foreign policy attention naturally now wholly focused on the issue of international terrorism, the report seemed likely to disappear without a trace. That it did not was partly a function of my serendipitous appointment in 2003 to the UN Secretary-General's High-Level Panel on Threats, Challenges, and Change, which was charged with generating input on geopolitical and security issues into the preparations for the 2005 World Summit. With a little help from another wonderful group of fellow panelists drawn from around the world, who proved equally willing—although not without a few bumps along the way—to tolerate my obsession with this issue, our 2004 report, *A More Secure World: Our Shared Responsibility*, explicitly picked up the ICISS recommendations and urged that the embrace of the responsibility to protect concept be a major Summit objective. However, what mattered even more than the High-Level Panel report in ensuring that the issue came before the World Summit was the willingness of the secretary-general to run with it in his own agenda-setting report, *In Larger Freedom*. If R2P does prove to be an enduring and influential new norm, its success will have many fathers, Kofi Annan very prominent among them.

Since 2001 I have been actively engaged in speaking and writing about the concept in many countries, with many different reactions, not all of them quite as extravagant as the Sri Lankan columnist cited above. A good deal of this advocacy has been as president of the International Crisis Group, whose mission it is to seek to prevent and resolve deadly conflict—including mass atrocity crimes—worldwide. The situations in Darfur, Burundi, Sri Lanka, Zimbabwe, and Kenya are among those in which Crisis Group is actively involved and where R2P has had prima facie application.

Most recently, Crisis Group joined with a number of other major international nongovernmental organizations—Human Rights Watch, Oxfam International, Refugees International, and the WFM–Institute of Global Policy—to establish, with the financial support of a number of governments, foundations, and individuals, the Global Centre for the Responsibility to Protect, a research and advocacy body with a strong North-South character. Its general aim is to ensure that R2P will be effectively implemented in practice, but the immediate focus is on consolidating acceptance of the concept around the world, particularly in those countries and regions where support for the concept has retreated somewhat since the high-water mark of the 2005 World Summit. In this respect, a great deal of work remains to be done by a good number of people who will need to sustain their own enthusiasm for the R2P norm for a good time to come.

* * *

For all of us in the policy world for whom the responsibility to protect concept has been more than just a matter of abstract, intellectual commitment, there has invariably been some personal experience that has touched us deeply. For many that will be bound to be scarifying family memories of the Holocaust; for others the experience of personal loss or closely knowing survivors from Rwanda or Srebrenica or any of the other mass atrocity scenes of more recent decades; for others still, perhaps, the awful sense that they could have done more, in their past official lives, to generate the kind of international response that these situations required. For me, as I have indicated, it was my visit to Cambodia in the late 1960s, just before the genocidal slaughter that killed up to a quarter of its people.

One of the things that has most sustained me over forty years of public life, more than twenty of them working in international affairs, is a fairly unquenchable sense of optimism: a belief that even the most horrible and intractable problems are soluble; that rational solutions for which there are good, principled arguments do eventually prevail; and that good people, good governments, and good governance will eventually prevail over bad.

When it comes to international relations, and in particular the great issues of war and peace, violence, and catastrophic human rights violations with which we are concerned here, there is a well-established view that anyone who approaches things in this kind of generally optimistic frame of mind must be incorrigibly naïve, if not outright demented. Certainly in the case of genocide and atrocity crimes—either directly committed by a government against its own people, or allowed to happen by a government unable or unwilling to stop it—it is hard for even the incorrigibly naïve to remain optimistic.

In this world we inhabit—full of cynicism, double standards, crude assertions of national interest, high-level realpolitik, and low-level maneuvering for political advantage—it is very easy to believe that ideas do not matter very much. But I believe as passionately now as I ever have in my long career—starting and finishing in the world of nongovernmental organizations, but with much time between in politics and government—that ideas matter enormously, for good and for ill. And for all the difficulties of acceptance and application that lie ahead, there are —I have come optimistically, but firmly, to believe—not many ideas that have the potential to matter more for good, not only in theory but in practice, than that of the responsibility to protect.

Understanding the
Responsibility to Protect

CHAPTER ONE

The Problem: The Recurring Nightmare of Mass Atrocities

China has used tanks to kill people on Tiananmen Square. It is Myanmar's sovereign right to kill their own people, too.
—Professor Shen Dingli, Shanghai, *USA Today*, October 2, 2007

It has taken a desperately long time for the idea to take hold that mass atrocities are the world's business: that they cannot be universally ignored and that sovereignty is not a license to kill. Massacres of the innocent, forced displacement of populations, large-scale sexual violence and humiliation, and the wanton destruction of civilian property have been going on since the dawn of civilization. Efforts gradually evolved over the centuries, then rapidly accelerated after the Second World War, to more effectively protect people against the commission of such atrocities, both in peace and war. But, for the most part, those horrors were met with indifference, cynicism, or deep disagreement about how to respond to them. As the twenty-first century began, there was still no universally accepted and effective response mechanism in place. This chapter traces that sad history, defining the problem to which, hopefully, the new international norm of "the responsibility to protect" will prove to be the solution.

Defining Mass Atrocities

It may be useful at the outset to clear an initial path through the often very confusing jungle of terminology involved in this debate. Throughout this work, the expressions "mass atrocities" or "mass atrocity crimes" are used more or less interchangeably to refer to what is now embraced by the description "genocide, war crimes, ethnic cleansing, and crimes against humanity," which in turn defines the scope of "the responsibility to protect" as embraced by the UN General Assembly meeting at the head of state level during the 2005 World Summit.[1] Choosing between the terms "mass atrocities" and "mass atrocity crimes" is a matter not so much of style as it is context: it would be, for example, anachronistic to refer to "crimes" for periods of history before any system of international law had evolved to label certain behavior this way. "Mass" is not a legal term of art, and many kinds of war crimes and crimes against humanity can, as a matter of law, be committed without large numbers of victims being involved. But this adjective is used here as shorthand to reflect the political reality that the kinds of atrocity crimes around which the responsibility to protect debate actually revolves are essentially those committed on a large scale And what, in turn, counts as "large scale" will always be a matter of context.

What of the four specific elements contained in the UN World Summit description? They are not mutually exclusive, and issues arise with respect to the meaning of each of them. "Genocide" has a very precise and quite narrow legal definition, spelled out in the 1948 Genocide Convention and repeated in the 1998 Rome Statute of the International Criminal Court.[2] Because it applies only to "acts committed with intent to destroy, in whole or in part, a national, ethnical, racial or religious group, as such," not even the Cambodian slaughter—directed at those of exactly the same nationality, ethnicity, race, and religion—would qualify as genocide. And even if the population in question meets the criteria, the required element of intent is notoriously difficult to prove.

"War crimes" and "crimes against humanity" are now fully, and helpfully, defined in the Rome Statute of the International Criminal Court and are much easier to apply, but the scope of each overlaps not only with that of genocide and ethnic cleansing but also with each other (for example, crimes against humanity can be committed in wartime, and most war crimes can be committed in armed conflict situations "not of an international character"). The range of conduct potentially covered by both war crimes and crimes against humanity is extremely wide, and in the case of war crimes, the responsibility to protect debate has focused primarily, as does this book, not on traditional cross-border conflicts but rather civil wars, that is, those occurring within the boundaries of a particular sovereign state.

In contrast with the other elements, "ethnic cleansing" has no formal legal definition but can be regarded, like genocide, as subsumed within the scope of both war crimes and crimes against humanity. It can be accomplished in a number of ways, including outright killing, expulsion, acts of terror designed to encourage flight, and rape when perpetrated either as another form of terrorism or as a deliberate attempt to change the ethnic composition of the group in question.

For nearly all policymaking, political, and operational purposes, it is not necessary to distinguish between these categories and give apparent crimes particular labels. Worse, labeling can be counterproductive, particularly regarding allegations of genocide, which can be very tempting rhetorically but—after lawyers have split legal hairs—can also give utterly unearned propaganda victories to those with heavy cases against them for war crimes or crimes against humanity. This is exactly what happened in 2005 in relation to Darfur, when Khartoum triumphantly claimed vindication after a UN commission found that for want of evidence of genocidal intent, charges of genocide probably could not be sustained against the Sudanese government—but charges of major crimes against humanity and war crimes certainly could![3] David Scheffer has long argued, sensibly, that for all policy discussion purposes one should just use the generic expression "atrocity crimes" and leave it to the prosecutors and judges in international courts, or courts exercising international jurisdiction, to work out which tag is most legally appropriate for particular cases.[4] That general approach is adopted here.

The Premodern Age: Centuries of Indifference

Through prehistoric, ancient, and medieval times (that is, before the age of modern sovereignty), rape, pillage, and massacre—whether perpetrated by warring tribes, conquering khans and princes, or kings and emperors against their own people—were essentially a matter of indifference to all but their victims. That was not because the scale of these atrocities was in any way trivial. For all the horrors of the last hundred years, deadly violence on a massive scale is not peculiar to modern society, nor is it a function of the technology of modern warfare. By piecing together evidence ranging from the incidence of axe injuries in prehistoric skulls to the proportion of battle deaths in contemporary foraging tribes, anthropologists estimate that rates of death in early tribal warfare were in fact some twenty times higher than was the case for all the wars and violence of the twentieth century. In terms of absolute numbers, the last century was by far the bloodiest on record, but if its wars had killed the same *proportion* of people that died in those ancient conflicts, there would have been not 100 million deaths, but two billion.[5]

What we would now call civilians—noncombatants, women, children, the old, and sick—were, so far as we can judge, no more exempt from the violence of the age in early tribal times than they have been through the whole of subsequent recorded history. The Bible, as Steven Pinker points out, "contains numerous celebrations of genocide, in which the Hebrews, egged on by God, slaughter every last resident of an invaded city, occasionally sparing the virgins so the soldiers could rape them."[6] The city-states of classical times and the Roman Empire, the first large-scale organized system of governance in the Western world, may have had some internalized formal restraints on how rulers should treat their own citizens (or at least free, male ones), but they set little or no constraint, legal or otherwise, on how, in war, either wounded or captured combatants or enemy civilians should be treated. [7] When the Romans sacked Carthage at the end of the third Punic War in 146 B.C., they went from house to house, killing or enslaving all 50,000 inhabitants before burning down the entire city.

In the decentralized, feudal, fractious, and fragmented world of the European Middle Ages—for all the residual authority of the church; for all the evolution of "just war" doctrine during this period, with its emphasis on proportionality, discrimination, and limiting damage to civilians; and for all the restraints supposedly associated with the institution of chivalry—there was little practical inhibition when it came to the treatment of civilians. For knights, indeed, "the protection of . . . the knight's horse was considerably higher on the agenda than protection of commoners, including civilians."[8] Christians did not remain immune from the temptation to tear each other apart, the worst examples in the premodern age probably being the massacre of scores of thousands of Protestant Huguenots by French Catholics during the religious wars of the sixteenth century.[9] However, when it came to non-Christians, there seemed to be no effective constraints at all. The First Crusade at the end of the eleventh century set the tone for those that followed, with the massacre of thousands of Jews in the Rhineland en route to the Holy Land, and then of many more thousands of Jewish and Muslim men, women, and children in Jerusalem. "Jews were burnt inside their synagogue. Muslims were indiscriminately cut to pieces, decapitated, or slowly tortured by fire. . . . The city's narrow streets were clogged with corpses and dismembered body parts. . . . Many of the surviving Muslim population were forced to clear the streets and carry the bodies outside to be buried in great pyres, whereat they themselves were massacred."[10] Elsewhere in the world during this period, few stories are more harrowing than that of Genghis Khan and his Mongol successors in the thirteenth century as they swept through East and Central Asia and then Europe as far west as Poland and Hungary, routinely massacring the populations of villages and whole cities along the way.[11]

In all of these cases, not only was there no external force powerful enough to constrain the scale of inhumanity perpetrated, but there also appears to have been no internalized constraint either. In the main non-Western religious and intellectual traditions, scholars have identified many parallels to evolving Christian theory in relation, for example, to the treatment of noncombatants and the obligations of rulers to their own people. Confucius, for example, while insisting on rigid hierarchical order, accompanied this with an equally strong insistence on responsibility and obligations to others. Early Islamic thought, as expressed in the Koran and elsewhere, set bounds to the caliph's absolute power and limits to the conduct of war, including the treatment of prisoners, and prohibited the killing of the old, women, and children.[12] But neither of these currents of thinking had any discernible impact on Genghis Khan and those who followed him, any more than Christian doctrine inhibited those slaughtering Huguenots three centuries later.

From Westphalia to the Holocaust: Institutionalizing Indifference

Before the seventeenth century, it makes no particular sense to view mass atrocities in terms of the responsibility of states, individually or collectively. There were clearly identifiable rulers in different territories and multiple different forms of governance, but no sovereign states existed in the modern sense. All that changed with the Peace of Westphalia in 1648, a pair of treaties arising from the gradual emergence of strong, consolidated, royalty-based states in Europe and from the need to settle a long period of bloody war among them.[13] To make peace, to make clear that the supranational writ of the Holy Roman Empire had run its course, and to achieve a firmly secular basis for ongoing state authority, the treaties of Westphalia created the key elements of the modern system of sovereign states: states legally equal to each other, not subject to the imposition of supranational authority, and, above all, not intervening in each other's internal affairs.[14]

For present purposes, the significance of the Westphalian principles, which steadily expanded beyond Europe and over time became the accepted worldwide norm, is that for all their undoubted utility as a stabilizing element in international relations, they effectively institutionalized the long-standing indifference of political rulers toward atrocity crimes occurring elsewhere, and also effectively immunized them from any external discipline they might conceivably have faced for either perpetrating such crimes against their own people or allowing others to commit them while they stood by.[15] Thus sovereignty—the possession by a country of the recognized trappings of independent statehood—meant immunity from outside scrutiny or sanction: what happened within a state's borders and its territorial possessions, however grotesque and morally indefensible, was nobody else's business. In the history of ideas, there have been few that have prevailed to more destructive effect.

The result was a long and unhappy litany of further massacres and other atrocity crimes perpetrated in the centuries that followed. Among them, to take some examples from the first half of the twentieth century, were the deaths of nearly 50,000 women and children from disease and hunger in British Boer War concentration camps in 1901; German suppression of the Herero rebellion in the neighboring colony of South West Africa by a deliberate policy of tribal extermination through relocation, resulting in over 60,000 deaths; the Turkish killing of some 1.5 million Armenians in 1915–16 by direct massacre and forced marches under appalling conditions; Stalin's orders for forced relocation, starvation, execution of members of particular targeted economic groups and minorities, and brutal occupations of neighboring countries, which killed some 62 million people from 1917–54; similar strategies of group-targeted violence by the Chinese nationalists under Chiang Kai-shek (killing some 10 million from 1927 to 1949) and the communists under Mao Zedong (believed to have killed under his leadership from 1934 onwards some 7 million in purges and by other more direct means, and tens of millions more who died in the famine of the insanely conceived Great Leap Forward of 1958–61 and in the violence of the only marginally less pathological Cultural Revolution of 1966–76); the many atrocities perpetrated during the course of the Spanish Civil War, including the aerial bombardment of Guernica in 1937, which was the forerunner—like the earlier Italian bombardment of Ethiopia—of the horrifyingly destructive saturation bombing of cities by Germany and the Allies during the Second World War; and the Japanese rape of Nanking in 1937, where some 300,000 Chinese were slaughtered and which anticipated many more atrocities against civilians throughout Asia in the world war that followed.[16]

Although other atrocity crimes have involved even larger numbers than the killing of six million Jews in the comprehensively and meticulously organized industrial-scale extermination program of the Nazi Holocaust, none has been more grotesque or has more fundamentally demeaned our sense of common humanity.[17] The basic story, and the scale of the horror and iniquity it involved, remains thankfully well known. The library shelves now full of detailed accounts, the films and television series that have won distribution and major attention worldwide, and the sensitive Holocaust memorials and museums in many countries, with their education and outreach programs, have seen to that. But of all those accounts, the hardest to bear in some ways are the stories, still not well enough known, of those grief-stricken and almost insanely frustrated witnesses to the genocide, or bearers of testimony as to its reality, who were, at a time when it could really have mattered, utterly unable to persuade British and American decisionmakers to recognize the scale of the unfolding catastrophe and take some direct action in response. For instance, there is the story of Szmul Zygielbojm, who committed suicide in 1943, crushed by his failure to persuade anyone who mattered to "believe the unbelievable."[18] The parallels with the events in Rwanda fifty years later and the lesson as to how much still remains to be done when apparently unbelievable new situations arise (as they surely will) are all too painfully obvious.

Throughout the nearly 400 years of more or less untrammeled operation of Westphalian sovereignty principles, it is hard to find examples where states looked beyond their own territorial and colonial borders, beyond their own immediate economic and security interests, to demonstrate—by acting to halt or avert new or continuing atrocity crimes—that they indeed had, in Hedley Bull's evocative phrase, "purposes beyond themselves."[19]

Britain's central role in the ending of the slave trade, through negotiating and enforcing suppression treaties throughout the nineteenth century, serves as one example.[20] There were three other nineteenth-century indicators that some kind of collective conscience was stirring on atrocity issues. First, there were the provisions in the Vienna Final Act of 1815, settling the Napoleonic Wars, which offered protection in some contexts for political and national minority rights, as well as religious rights. Another example is the Congress of Berlin of 1884–85, which attempted to set some minimal standards of commitment, among powers claiming rights to the Congo, "to watch over the preservation of the native tribes, and to care for the improvement of the conditions of their moral and material well-being" (though the result was conspicuously unsuccessful).[21] And, thanks to the campaigning of Swiss banker and founder of the Red Cross movement Henri Dunant, there was the agreement during the First Geneva Convention in 1864 that explicitly obliged states to give certain protections to the citizens of other states in time of war.[22]

In the early twentieth century, after the First World War, three more such indicators of an emerging international conscience can be identified, all associated with the newly established League of Nations: establishment of a mandate system for the governing of territories, framed in a way that recognized that the development and well-being of subject peoples was a "sacred trust of civilization"; efforts to defend and promote minority rights in Central Europe; and significant moves to address the issue of refugees, including the league's appointment of a high commissioner for refugees.[23] All these steps signaled an approach to international relations that did, to some extent, acknowledge the rights and claims of individuals and groups, as distinct from states.[24] But the Paris Peace Conference at Versailles, which gave birth to the League of Nations, was in most ways a profound disappointment to those who had hoped for a really significant change of direction. It was overwhelmingly statist in its approach, rejected the incorporation of human rights standards in the league's covenant, and—in the face of particularly strong lobbying by the United States—made no effective provision for the trial of war criminals, accepting the principle of sovereign immunity for high officials. Secretary of State Robert Lansing went so far as to say that the "essence of sovereignty [is] the *absence* of responsibility."[25]

None of the small normative advances made during this whole period from Westphalia to the Holocaust translated into much in the way of activism by states when confronted with the reality of mass atrocities occurring outside their own national or colonial borders. The only examples of state action that would come to be recognized as "humanitarian intervention" were, successively, the military incursion mounted by England, France, and Russia into Greece in 1827 to stop massacres by Turkey; the French incursion into Syria in 1860 to stop attacks on Maronite Christians, which killed more than 11,000 and made 100,000 homeless in a single month; and military action by different combinations of European powers in defense of Christians in Crete in 1866–68, the Balkans in 1875–78, and Macedonia in 1903–08. These various responses to the plight of Christians in different parts of the Ottoman Empire were all expressly justified in terms of protecting the safety of citizens of another state, although certainly driven significantly by strategic interest as well. They led some jurists to argue by the end of the nineteenth century that a doctrine of humanitarian intervention now existed as a matter of customary international law; but the prevailing view has remained that state practice was hardly consistent enough then (nor is it now) to justify such a conclusion.[26]

The Cold War Years: Cynicism and Self-Interest

One might have thought Hitler's Holocaust would have laid to rest once and for all the notion that whatever happens within a state's borders is nobody else's business. Certainly major gains were made in the immediate postwar period. With the drafting of the Charter of the Nuremberg Tribunal in 1945 came the recognition in international law of the concept of "crimes against humanity," which could be committed by a government against its own people, and not necessarily just during wartime. Individual and group human rights were recognized in the UN Charter of 1945 and, more grandly and explicitly, in the Universal Declaration of Human Rights of 1948 (which was supplemented—after eighteen years of painful further negotiation—by the two 1966 covenants on civil and political rights and on economic, social, and cultural rights).[27] And 1949 saw agreement on the Third and Fourth Geneva Conventions, regarding the treatment of prisoners of war and of civilians under occupation, respectively, providing in each case for state parties to exercise universal jurisdiction.[28] All these charters and agreements set the foundation for the development of the modern human rights movement, both domestically and internationally.

Beginning in the 1970s, UN human rights bodies became more assertive in making fact-finding visits, issuing reports, interceding with offending governments, and generally seeking to make the domestic violation of human rights a legitimate concern of the international community. But there is little evidence that any of this—with the possible exception of the sustained focus on apartheid in South Africa—did much to make any less bloody the dreadful record of continuing mass atrocity crimes.

Not even the signing of the Convention on the Prevention and Punishment of Genocide of 1948 made much difference, despite its apparently explicit override of the nonintervention principle for the most extreme of all crimes against humanity. The concept of genocide—developed in 1944 by the legal scholar and campaigner Raphael Lemkin, yoking together the Greek noun for family, tribe, or race and the Latin verb for massacre—was an important development in the history of ideas. It captured some of the momentous quality of actions that are aimed not just at destroying individuals but whole national, racial, ethnic, or religious groups—targeting, as Lemkin put it, the essential foundations of their life as such groups.[29] But it was almost as if, with the signing of the Genocide Convention, the task of addressing man-made atrocities was seen as complete. It took the major powers years (in the case of the United States, forty years) to ratify it, it was rarely invoked, and has never been effectively applied in practice either to prevent or punish actual atrocities.

The long-awaited test case in the International Court of Justice (ICJ), *Bosnia* v. *Serbia*, decided that Serbia had not itself committed genocide in Srebrenica—though it did have some culpability for failing to prevent it. But no compensation or reparation was to be paid, and in its ruling, the court simply decided that Serbia "shall immediately take effective steps to ensure full compliance with its obligation to punish genocide . . . and to transfer individuals accused of genocide" to the International Criminal Tribunal for the Former Yugoslavia.[30] Although the case was important for its affirmation that, as a matter of international law, there was indeed a duty of sovereign states to prevent and punish genocide to the extent of their capability, it also showed all too clearly what lawyers have long feared: that the legal definition of genocide as provided in the Genocide Convention is so narrow in scope that there are very few kinds of behavior, by either individuals or governments, that will be actually caught by it.

And so it was that during the first half century of the UN's existence, the early flurry of norm-setting activity and hope gave way to a collective state of mind that not even the Cambodian killing fields were any of the world's business. Three overarching explanatory factors were at work. The first was the persistence of the core idea, going all the way back to the Peace of Westphalia in 1648, that sovereignty means, above all else, control of a state's territory, unfettered by external constraints. This remained an incredibly tenacious belief in the minds of the UN's key players. Article 2(7) of the UN Charter states that "nothing contained in the present Charter shall authorize the United Nations to intervene in matters which are essentially within the domestic jurisdiction of any state."[31] The UN founders were overwhelmingly preoccupied with the problem of states waging war against each other, and—with the establishment of a Security Council able to authorize military enforcement measures—they took unprecedented steps to limit freedom of action in that respect. But, notwithstanding all the genocidal horrors inflicted during the Second World War, they showed no particular interest in the question of what constraints might be imposed on how states dealt with their own populations.

A second factor was the large increase in UN membership during the decolonization era, which reinforced this very traditional view of sovereignty. From 1945 to 1989, UN membership grew from the original 51 member states to 159, and the states that joined were all newly proud of their identity and conscious, in many cases, of their fragility. They generally viewed the nonintervention norm as one of their few defenses against threats and pressures from more powerful international actors seeking to promote their own economic and political interests. In the nations of the developing world, there was a widespread and perfectly understandable perception that the involvement of developed countries in their internal affairs had not always been principled or consistent in the past and was not likely to be any better in the future.

The dynamics of the cold war constituted a third factor, dominating the UN system almost from the start and hamstringing the organization when it came to dealing with mass atrocities. The two major superpowers rapidly became very focused on what was needed to keep their respective alliance blocs functioning, and were reluctant to impose any significant constraints on misbehaving partners: the "he-may-be-a-son–of-a-bitch-but-he's-*our*-son-of-a-bitch" syndrome.[32] The superpowers were largely indifferent, rhetoric aside, to what happened inside the other bloc and were incapable anyway of doing much about atrocity crimes that might be perpetrated there because of the inevitable application of the Security Council veto. Although in the immediate aftermath of the Holocaust the world had started to institutionalize its collective conscience, during the cold war decades that followed cynicism trumped conscience every time the major powers faced a serious choice.

All this meant that, during this period, a great many serious crimes against humanity were perpetrated, either actively by states or in the face of their unwillingness or inability to intervene, without any effective action being taken or even attempted by any outside power. Among these mass atrocities were the Indonesian massacres of up to 500,000 or more Communist Party members, suspected sympathizers, and others caught up in the mayhem from 1965 to 1966;[33] the hunting down and killing of more than 100,000 Hutu in Burundi between April and September 1972;[34] tens of thousands of forced "disappearances" of political dissenters during the "Dirty War" in Argentina of 1976–83 and Pinochet's Operation Condor during the mid-1970s;[35] the massacre in Guatemala from 1981 to 1983 of some 150,000 Mayans and the destruction of over 400 villages in government counterinsurgency operations;[36] the series of mass murders perpetrated in Zimbabwe's Matabeleland from 1982 from 1987, believed to have killed over 10,000 and as many as 30,000;[37] and the poison gas attack by Saddam Hussein's Iraqi air force on the Kurdish town of Halabja in March 1988, in which some 5,000 perished.[38]

Other crimes were committed on a less gigantic scale but were still large enough to shock the world's conscience—for example, the My Lai massacre by U.S. forces in 1968, in which over 500 men, women, and children were murdered in three Vietnamese villages;[39] and the bloody crackdowns on domestic dissent by the military regime in Burma in 1988, and by the Chinese government against protesters in Tiananmen Square and elsewhere in Beijing in 1989, with many hundreds, and almost certainly several thousands, killed in each case, although exact numbers will never be known.[40]

All that said, the cold war period was notable for the quite large number of coercive military interventions of one kind or another that did occur for purported, and sometimes real, humanitarian reasons. On examination, these interventions fall into two broad classes: those where a quite weak humanitarian or quasi-humanitarian motive was claimed, other motives were manifestly in play, and international condemnation was strong; and those where a humanitarian motive was not claimed, although a strong humanitarian justification was in fact potentially available, and where international condemnation was still strong.[41]

In the first category were a series of interventions where the claimed humanitarian justification that was given was primarily the protection of the intervening country's own nationals (normally thought to be less a matter of disinterested humanitarianism than of national self-interest), and where there were invariably other strategic or economic interest motives in play: Belgium in the Congo in 1960; Belgium and the United States in the Congo rebel stronghold of Stanleyville in 1964; the United States in the Dominican Republic in 1965; France and Belgium in the rebel-held Shaba Province of Zaire in 1978; the United States in Grenada in 1983; and the United States in Panama in 1989. These cases all attracted significant condemnation in the UN, regional organizations, or both. One exceptional case was France's intervention in the Central African Empire in 1979 to overthrow the friendless, brutal, and poverty-stricken Bokassa regime on entirely justified human rights grounds (after its murder of more than 150 demonstrating school children), which attracted very little international censure.

In the other category were three major cases where intervention could plausibly have been justified on strong humanitarian grounds, since it protected people seriously at risk from the behavior of their own governments, but instead was largely justified by flimsy arguments about self-defense due to the intense international hostility to intrusions on sovereignty for any other reason.

EAST PAKISTAN

The first instance was India's invasion of East Pakistan in 1971, in the context of West Pakistan's extraordinarily brutal response to the self-determination struggle of the Awami League that led to the creation of independent Bangladesh. The intervention was ostensibly (and not entirely incredibly) a self-defense response to a preemptive air strike by Pakistan; but, in fact, the action was taken primarily to ensure that mass murder and displacement, especially of the Hindu population, would not continue. While India had strategic interests in ensuring a weaker Pakistan, its humanitarian justification and motive were both quite strong, but neither was offered as an explanation. Regardless, whatever reasons Delhi provided, they were not enough to allay the sustained diplomatic censure it received for tearing up the sovereignty rulebook.[42]

CAMBODIA

The second case was Cambodia, where Vietnam's invasion in 1978 stopped the Khmer Rouge in its tracks and yet was again universally condemned, not applauded, even though it ended one of the worst sustained mass murders of the twentieth century.[43] Pol Pot's unbelievably brutal three-year "purification" reign of terror from 1975 to 1978 had resulted in the direct killing of hundreds of thousands of Cambodians, and the deaths from malnutrition and disease of many hundreds of thousands more, producing a total death toll of up to 2 million. The scale of the horror was well enough known by the time of Vietnam's invasion, and most of Hanoi's opponents acknowledged the human rights issues involved. But this reality did not in any way diminish the ferocity of the attacks on Vietnam for violating Cambodia's sovereign rights. Condemnation was widespread, from the United States, United Kingdom, and their NATO allies; every member state of the Association of Southeast Asian Nations (ASEAN); Australia; most Latin American countries; and many others as well. Vietnam's own motives were no doubt less than high-minded, and it did not help its cause by dissimulating about the invasion before claiming self-defense (on the basis of Khmer Rouge aggression on the Cambodia-Vietnam border since early 1975), but it was a sign of the times that it could muster support only from the Soviet bloc.

UGANDA

The remaining case was Tanzania's 1979 overthrow of Uganda's Idi Amin, whose eight-year rule had deteriorated into an increasingly random despotism that had devastating consequences for the country. Amnesty International estimated the murder of at least 100,000—possibly as many as half a million—people under the Amin regime. Tanzania's military intervention was based, in this case, on a credible claim of self-defense—Amin having announced his intention to annex a border region of the country into which some of his mutinous soldiers had fled—and the international reaction to it was accordingly very muted. The human rights case was also extremely strong, and given President Julius Nyerere's respectable reputation against that of the notoriously mad, bad, mendacious, and dangerous Amin, one might have expected him to rely on it to justify Tanzania's intervention, at least to some extent. He did not—another reflection of the absolute primacy of sovereignty claims during this period.[44]

The cynicism of the great powers about major human rights violations in their own and each other's backyards was understandable enough in purely realist terms, and it was even more understandable that, for defensive self-interested reasons, sovereignty should have continued to be a very sensitive subject indeed with the many states who gained their independence during the decolonization era. But the trouble with these reactions, like most things taken too far, is that they had a terrible downside, which came to a head in the 1990s in the international response to the series of man-made catastrophes that erupted in many parts of the world, but to most deadly effect in the Balkans and Africa.

The 1990s: The Clash of Competing Imperatives

It was not until the 1990s that the tension burst into the open between the high ideals of the international treaties and declarations, and the low realpolitik of the actual behavior of governments and intergovernmental organizations. With the breakup of various cold war state structures, most obviously in Yugoslavia, and the removal of some superpower constraints, conscience-shocking situations repeatedly arose. But old habits of nonintervention died very hard. Even when situations cried out for some kind of military response, and the international community did react with UN authorization, it was too often erratically, incompletely, or counterproductively. And when states chose to act completely outside the framework of the UN, as in Kosovo, this raised anxious questions about the integrity of the whole international security system.

In all, through this decade, there were nine significant military operations mounted that, unlike all but a tiny handful in the past, were essentially both humanitarian and coercive. Each had an overt and credible humanitarian justification, addressing real civilian protection concerns, although sometimes there were other motives in play as well (for example, larger regional security, as in Liberia, and the restoration of democracy, as in Haiti). And in each case, these interventions took place either expressly against the wishes of the government concerned (as in northern Iraq, Bosnia, and

Rwanda) or in circumstances where the issue of consent was irrelevant (because no government existed, as in Somalia), controversial (usually because of the absence of de facto control by the regime representing the state, as in Liberia, Haiti, and Sierra Leone), or ambiguous (as in Timor-Leste, where the consent was given only under immense international pressure and by a power generally regarded as in illegal occupation).[45]

Five of these operations generated less strident objections than the others, although each had its opponents. Liberia from 1990 to 1997 saw the first intervention of this kind by an African subregional organization (the Economic Community of West African States [ECOWAS], acting with UN Security Council endorsement, albeit five months after the event), with a Nigerian-led force landing there in 1990 to stop a bloody civil war from descending into total anarchy, with mixed results. Northern Iraq in 1991, in the aftermath of the first Gulf War and in response to a brutal campaign of repression by Saddam Hussein against the Kurds, saw the United States and its allies successfully imposing a safe haven, relying on the authority (albeit somewhat uncertain) of an earlier Security Council resolution. Haiti from 1994 to 1997 was a case of the Security Council authorizing (after initial reluctance) a multinational force to "facilitate the departure" of the military junta that had overthrown President Aristide; although that transition was successfully managed, the necessary nation-building efforts had barely started when the force left. Sierra Leone in 1997 experienced another Nigerian-led ECOWAS intervention—again with post-event endorsement by the Security Council—to restore constitutional order after a coup and prevent further bloodshed. That conflict continued to flare out of control periodically, and the ECOWAS force struggled to contain it, as did its successor UN missions, which were generally seen as poorly armed, ill-disciplined, and ineffective. The fifth operation took place in Timor-Leste in 1999, after terrible Indonesian-supported violence had predictably followed the successful independence referendum. A Security Council resolution authorized a multilateral force under Australian leadership to restore peace and security: this was successfully accomplished but only after much foot dragging by Indonesia and a good deal of international arm twisting of Jakarta.

The other four instances of military intervention each raised many more problems. Together, Somalia, Rwanda, Bosnia, and Kosovo throw into stark relief every one of the conceptual, operational, and political will issues with which this book wrestles.

SOMALIA

Somalia erupted into clan-based civil war when President Siad Barre was overthrown in January 1991 after losing, with the end of the cold war, the protection he had successively enjoyed from the Soviet Union and the United States. As a result, hundreds of thousands of Somalis were displaced in the ensuing turmoil. Although a small UN peacekeeping force was dispatched there in April 1992 to support humanitarian relief operations, six months later, the UN secretary-general was telling the Security Council that 1.5 million Somalis were immediately at risk of death, and many more threatened, by starvation and disease and that a fully empowered peace enforcement operation was required. By the end of the year, 28,000 U.S.-led troops were on the ground, with the full support of the Non-Aligned Movement and even China casting its first affirmative vote for an enforcement resolution. The justification for the intervention was unequivocally humanitarian, as were the motives of the interveners, and the mission succeeded in its basic objective to the extent that assistance in one form or another did reach the entire population of five million, and less than 100,000 of those threatened actually died. But whatever good was done by the U.S.-led force—and by the new UN mission that replaced it with an even more expansive enforcement mandate—was completely undermined by subsequent events. There was the misconceived attempt to wage war against militia leaders, followed by the "Black Hawk Down" debacle in Mogadishu in October 1993, in which eighteen Americans died. Subsequently U.S. troops were pulled out, and the UN mission was finally withdrawn in April 1995, with most of its objectives unachieved and a nasty taste in the mouths of a number of troop contributors about their humanitarian intervention experience.[46]

RWANDA

The "Mogadishu effect" was critical in explaining the reluctance of the major powers, particularly the United States, to respond to events unfolding in Rwanda in 1994. On April 6, a plane carrying Rwandan president Juvenal Habyarimana was shot down. Shortly thereafter, reports started to flow into UN headquarters and into Washington about the massive ethnic-based violence that was unfolding there, and the desperate need to mount a fully empowered military enforcement operation to stop it.[47] Against the background of anti-Tutsi massacres in the 1960s and 1970s, those reports were highly credible and cried out to be taken seriously. But they were not, when it mattered, taken seriously enough as a result of systemic and personal failures by those most immediately responsible—including the then head of peacekeeping operations Kofi Annan, whose scarifying sense of personal responsibility subsequently drove him so hard to ensure that no Rwanda ever happened again.[48] Canadian general Romeo Dallaire, who commanded the light peacekeeping mission established a year earlier to monitor recently signed peace accords, made heroic attempts to save those he could and argued fiercely that just 5,000 well-armed and trained troops—together with measures such as the external jamming of hate-radio frequencies—could stop hundreds of thousands of murders.[49] But he was ignored, with Belgium withdrawing its contingent entirely, and the Security Council initially actually drawing down troops already on the ground. When French troops eventually did arrive in late June with an enforcement mandate, their impact was at best cosmetic (and some judgments are even less generous). In the event some 800,000 Tutsis and moderate Hutus were slaughtered in less than four months, an unequivocal case of genocide in any lawyer's language and by far the worst since the Holocaust. To read eyewitness accounts of what happened—graphically captured in the title of Philip Gourevitch's book, *We Wish to Inform You That Tomorrow We Will Be Killed with Our Families*—is to weep.[50]

Bosnia

The disintegration of the former Yugoslavia has occupied the Security Council since the end of the cold war, with multiple resolutions passed, many UN missions coming and going, and unfinished business continuing to this day. The central and most problematic mission of the 1990s was the UN Protection Force (UNPROFOR), initially established in early 1992 as a peacekeeping operation with the consent of the Former Republic of Yugoslavia and other governments. As the situation worsened, UNPROFOR's mandate was extended to include more complex security operations, protection of aid workers and convoys in Croatia and Bosnia, and, in May 1993, protection of five specifically identified "safe areas" around Sarajevo and five Bosnian towns, including Srebrenica. The catastrophe that followed was born of several elements. First, there were ambiguities in the language of the protective mandate. Second, there was the required "dual key" agreement between the force commander and the secretary-general's special representative before there could be any coercive response. And then there was the still-prevailing culture of impartiality in peacekeeping operations (a recipe for disaster when there is no peace to keep and spoilers are abroad, as the Brahimi Report later agreed).[51] In July 1995, Bosnian Serbs under the command of General Ratko Mladic seized Srebrenica, brushing past the 400 Dutch UNPROFOR defenders by threatening to kill hostages if there were air strikes and no surrender, loaded 8,000 men and boys into trucks and buses, drove them to nearby fields and forests, and shot them in cold blood—by far the largest mass murder in Europe since the Second World War.[52]

Kosovo

In 1998 Serbian president Slobodan Milosevic began making good on his long-foreshadowed determination to crush ethnic Albanian separatist sentiment once and for all, using police units as a tool for murder. However, with the memory of Srebrenica reversing the "Mogadishu effect" in Rwanda, the NATO allies were only too determined to ensure that no new massacres or ethnic cleansing occurred. A complex minuet was danced between NATO and the Security Council for many months, with allegations and counterallegations about Serb and Kosovo Liberation Army behavior, but neither Russia nor China would agree to any resolution clearly authorizing the use of force. In March 1999—after the massacre of forty-five Kosovo Albanians in Racak and the breakdown of subsequent last minute Rambouillet negotiations for an independence referendum— the United States and its NATO allies decided to go it alone and commenced a campaign of air strikes against the Former Republic of Yugoslavia. The seventy-eight days of destructive bombing produced a flood of refugees and internal displacements, and a surge of further killings—some thousands in all—by the Serbs, but a settlement was reached only when NATO finally threatened the insertion of ground troops.[53] The Kosovo intervention continues to generate some opposition on its merits, with claims that Serb atrocity crimes were exaggerated and matched by those of the Kosovo Albanians, and, in particular, that NATO sacrificed any moral high ground by bombing from 15,000 feet rather than exposing its servicemen to risk. But the balance of international opinion generally favors the intervention's justifiability in all the circumstances. Where international opinion remains much less favorable to the NATO action is on the question not of the legitimacy but rather the legality of the intervention, which bypassed the authority of the Security Council.

The 1990s was the decade in which every one of the central questions surrounding humanitarian intervention was, for the first time, exposed with real clarity. But it ended with absolutely no consensus on any of the answers. Every general discussion in the UN General Assembly and other international forums, and nearly every difficult individual case that arose, became a political battlefield with two warring armies. On the one side were those, mostly from the global North, who, in situations of catastrophic human rights violations, could not see beyond humanitarian intervention, "the right to intervene" with military force. On the other side were those, mostly from the global South, who were often prepared to concede that grave rights violations were occurring but were resolutely determined to maintain the continued resonance, and indeed primacy, of the traditional nonintervention concept of national sovereignty. Battle lines were drawn, trenches were dug, and verbal missiles flew. The debate was intense and very bitter, and the twentieth century ended with it utterly unresolved in the UN or anywhere else.

The Solution:
From "The Right to Intervene" to
"The Responsibility to Protect"

If humanitarian intervention is indeed an unacceptable assault on
sovereignty, how should we respond to a Rwanda, to a Srebrenica—to gross
and systematic violations of human rights that offend every precept of our
common humanity?

—Kofi Annan, *Millennium Report of the Secretary-General*
of the United Nations, 2000

The twenty-first century began with no agreed answer to Kofi
Annan's troubling question. A number of efforts had been made during
the 1990s to set international thinking on a new path, in particular
Bernard Kouchner's assertion of "the right to intervene," but none of them
won broad support. The breakthrough came in late 2001 when the International Commission on Intervention and State Sovereignty (ICISS)
introduced into the debate the concept of "the responsibility to protect,"
which described the obligations of states to prevent and respond to these
human rights catastrophes in a potentially much more acceptable way.
Less than four years later, "R2P" was formally and unanimously embraced
by the UN General Assembly meeting at the head of state and government
level at the 2005 World Summit. This was a remarkably short time—just a
blink of an eye in the history of ideas—when measured against the
decades, or sometimes centuries, it usually takes for new concepts to take
hold to this extent. But euphoria would be premature: on any assessment
of the progress made since then in consolidating and implementing the
new international norm, it is clear that much unfinished business
remains.[1]

Initial Attempts to Build Consensus

The most important contributions to the 1990s debate were those made by Bernard Kouchner and Tony Blair, with their new twists on the old humanitarian intervention theme; by those advocating the new overarching concept of "human security"; by Francis Deng and his Brookings Institution colleagues with their insistence on "sovereignty as responsibility"; and by UN Secretary-General Kofi Annan with his idea of "individual sovereignty" to be weighed against the traditional state variety. But, for all the creativity and commitment involved in each of these efforts, none of them succeeded in generating any kind of broad international consensus as to when and how the international community should respond to mass atrocity crimes.

Bernard Kouchner and "The Right to Intervene"

The French physician Bernard Kouchner—cofounder of both Médecins Sans Frontières and the breakaway Médecins du Monde, government minister, and globally prominent humanitarian activist—did not invent the concept of, or even the expression, "humanitarian intervention." That terminology was first used—and in pretty much its modern sense of military force deployed across borders to protect civilians at risk—as early as 1840.[2] And it has been the subject of perennial discussion in international law literature since the early twentieth century.[3] But what Kouchner did was give it a new lease on life by inventing and popularizing the expression "*droit d'ingérence,*" the "right to intervene" (or, by extension, "*droit d'ingérence humanitaire*"), which had real resonance in the new circumstances of the post–cold war world, when both the need and the opportunity to take protective action repeatedly arose. In the recurring debates of the 1990s, the banner call from those demanding forceful action in the face of catastrophe was invariably, echoing Kouchner, "the *right* of humanitarian intervention," the right to intervene. In making the response to mass atrocities the single most debated foreign policy issue of the decade, rather than one that could be comfortably ignored by policymakers, his contribution was outstanding.

Kouchner had first wrestled with the policy issues involved as a young doctor working for the International Committee of the Red Cross in Biafra, Nigeria, in the 1960s, where he felt constrained by that organization's policy of strict neutrality. He and law professor Mario Bettati launched the concept of *droit d'ingérence* in 1987—at a conference, typically, aimed at energizing everyone in the French intellectual and political establishment, from Mitterrand and Chirac down. But it was not until a few years later that the expression first came into real prominence, at the time of the U.S.-led intervention in Somalia in 1992, when just about all major French newspapers, struggling to find a way of capturing the apparently self-contradictory idea of a "humanitarian invasion," at Kouchner's urging uniformly headed their editorials "*Le droit d'ingérence.*"[4]

As the 1990s wore on, however, it became more and more apparent that while "the right to intervene" was a noble and effective rallying cry with a particular resonance in the global North, around the rest of the world, it enraged as many as it inspired. The problem was essentially that the concept remained so inherently one-sided, not in any way acknowledging the anxieties of those in the global South who had all too often been the beneficiaries of *missions civilisatrices* in the past. That concern was compounded, in the French-speaking world, by the fact that *ingérence* conveyed the sense not just of "intervention" but "interference."

THE BLAIR DOCTRINE

In a much-quoted speech to the Chicago Economic Club in April 1999, made in the context of defending the NATO air strikes on Kosovo that were then in full operation, U.K. Prime Minister Tony Blair sought to articulate a "doctrine of international community," designed to address "the most pressing foreign policy problem we face . . . to identify the circumstances in which we should get actively involved in other people's conflicts," and to do so by bringing together a "more subtle blend of mutual self-interest and moral purpose in defending the values we cherish." He characterized the Kosovo conflict in this context as "a just war, based not on any territorial ambition but on values." The most specific contribution of Blair's speech was to identify five major considerations, not "absolute tests" but "the kind of issues we need to think about in deciding in the future when and whether we will intervene." They were first, "Are we sure of our case?" Second, "Have we exhausted all diplomatic options?" Third, "Are there military operations we can sensibly and prudently undertake?" Fourth, "Are we prepared for the long term?" And fifth, "Do we have national interests involved?"[5]

There was much in this that captured the mood of the time, and Blair was certainly onto something important in trying to identify, in a way that had not been part of the debate until then, specific criteria for military intervention that would focus on the complex mix of issues that decisionmakers needed to take into account. But looked at more closely, the Chicago speech—like that which followed it—was not much more than a hodgepodge of sound bites. The checklist was incomplete and lurched back and forth between conceptual, evidentiary, and political considerations. Its perspective was national—not international—decisionmaking, reinforcing the perception (despite Blair's call "to find a new way to make the UN and its Security Council work") that, for the United Kingdom, the UN mattered less than its most powerful members. Prevention was neglected, the focus being reactive, after the event, and entirely military (albeit only after diplomacy failed) rather than including less extreme coercive options. Finally, the description of a "just war" simply as one "based on values" was guaranteed to stir the anxieties of the developing world about the selective way in which the West had commandeered values to justify its adventures in the past and might do so in the future.[6] Like Kouchner before him, Blair knew how to rally the North, but his doctrine fell on very deaf ears in the South.

HUMAN SECURITY

A very innovative attempt to bridge the gap between North and South views of the world came with the launch by the United Nations Development Program (UNDP) of the *Human Development Report 1994*, with its subtitle *New Dimensions of Human Security*. Mahbub ul Haq and his team saw the need, conceptually and politically, to link together in a single coherent framework what had hitherto been the quite separate preoccupations of developed countries with national boundaries and institutions, and military threats and responses, and of developing countries with feeding, clothing, sheltering, healing, and educating their populations. The idea was that whereas issues of *state* security had dominated international discourse in the past, what really ultimately mattered was how all this affected individuals' lives. The concept of *human* security was broad enough to advance both freedom from fear and freedom from want. For the UNDP authors, it was the summation of seven different dimensions of security: economic, food, health, environmental, personal, community, and political. As they put it, in what became in various forms a much-chanted mantra in many subsequent reports and discussions, "Without peace, there may be no development. But without development, peace may be threatened."[7]

The concept of human security has since become a thoroughly accepted and familiar part of international public policy vocabulary, spawning a large literature of its own and some significant efforts at institutional coordination.[8] It has helped policymakers see the interconnectedness of their narrow specialties and to capture some of the widespread mood that looking at even traditional "hard" security issues through wholly state-centered lenses is to miss much of what is happening in a fluid, globalizing world—one in which nonstate actors are increasingly important and in which deadly conflict is much less likely than in the past to involve states waging war against each other. Some national governments even made "human security" the leitmotif of their whole external policy—conspicuously Canada's under Lloyd Axworthy's creative stewardship as foreign minister, when issues as disparate as land mines, the development of international criminal law, child soldiers, governance, human rights, peace operations, and peacebuilding all flew under this banner.

The trouble with the concept of human security in the present context is not that it has produced too little consensus but rather, if anything, too much: so many different issues and themes nestle comfortably under its wings that it is difficult to extract any prescriptions about how to deal with any of them other than to look at problems in a "people first" kind of way. That perspective, of course, is an extraordinarily valuable one and has helped to mobilize global campaigns around issues such as the establishment of the International Criminal Court that might otherwise have struggled to find a voice. Academics and others who have been inclined to dismiss human security as more a matter of hot air than serious intellectual innovation have been deftly put in their place by the Canadian scholar and diplomat Don Hubert as rejecting an idea that "worked in practice, but not in theory."[9] As a way of framing issues and mobilizing concern, human security will always have resonance, but in answering questions as to who should do precisely what and when in response to an emerging mass atrocity situation, it seems destined to never have immediate operational utility.

Francis Deng and "Sovereignty as Responsibility"

A concept that, by contrast, does have some immediate operational utility in its own terms is that which grew out of the experience of the distinguished scholar and former Sudanese diplomat Francis Deng as the Representative of the UN Secretary-General on Internally Displaced Persons (IDP) from 1992 to 2004, which he articulated in a series of books and articles written with other colleagues at the Brookings Institution, most comprehensively in *Sovereignty as Responsibility: Conflict Management in Africa* in 1996. The IDP issue, as Deng had to constantly confront it on the ground, was by its very definition an internal affair, usually arising wholly in the context of domestic conflicts, and as such, lending itself almost invariably to a reluctance to engage with international officials by the governments concerned. But as Deng describes it, he was more often than not able to defuse that reflex antagonism within the first few minutes by saying to his interlocutors, "I realize this is an internal matter. I am wholly respectful of your country's sovereignty, but the essence of being a sovereign country these days is not just protection from outside interference—rather it's a matter of states having positive responsibilities for their own citizens' welfare, and to assist each other. So on that basis, let us engage together to see how we can solve this problem."[10]

The articulation of "sovereignty as responsibility" in this way had a considerable pedigree, beginning with the work of the Refugee Policy Group in Washington, a pioneer in the internal displacement field, and in particular Roberta Cohen. Cohen, who later joined Brookings to work extensively with Deng, appears to have been the first to spell out, in 1991, that "sovereignty carries with it a responsibility on the part of governments to protect their citizens."[11] The logical corollary of this, hinted at in a number of their joint publications, most explicitly in a 1998 *Foreign Affairs* article was that a failure to exercise that responsibility carried international consequences.[12] However, the principle was not developed much further than this, and—as is the fate of many such ideas—had no obvious impact on policymakers at the time. What did gain more recognition was the actual work in the field not only of Francis Deng but also his colleague Sadako Ogata, UN High Commissioner for Refugees, in what she described in her memoir as "the turbulent decade" from 1990 to 2000.[13] During that period, Ogata significantly expanded her agency's operations to cover not only traditional refugees but also IDPs and other internally affected populations, and in so doing, she contributed a great deal in practice to the growing acceptance that sovereign states were not completely free agents when it came to the protection of their own people.

The conceptualization of sovereignty as responsibility—and not just in terms of the traditional preoccupation with sovereignty as control of territory—gained traction from all the post–Second World War institutional developments associated with the establishment of the United Nations, membership of the UN, and in particular, accession to its human rights instruments, which necessarily entails the voluntary acceptance of sovereignty-limiting obligations or responsibilities, both internally and externally. The formulation of Deng and his colleagues—although it received none of the wider attention that was focused on *droit d'ingérence* or human security, or the ideas of Tony Blair or Kofi Annan, became, more than any of these other contributions of the 1990s, a central conceptual underpinning of the responsibility to protect norm as it finally emerged.

Kofi Annan and "Individual Sovereignty"

Toward the end of the 1990s, UN Secretary-General Kofi Annan made a major attempt to resolve the conceptual impasse at the heart of the sovereignty-intervention debate by arguing that there was not just one kind of sovereignty in play here but two: in these cases, *national* sovereignty had to be weighed and balanced against *individual* sovereignty, as recognized in the international human rights instruments. He spelled out the argument most clearly in an article in *The Economist*, published just before the opening of the 1999 General Assembly:

> State sovereignty, in its most basic sense, is being redefined—not least by the forces of globalization and international cooperation. States are now widely understood to be instruments at the service of their peoples, and not vice versa. At the same time individual sovereignty—by which I mean the fundamental freedom of each individual, enshrined in the Charter of the UN and subsequent international treaties—has been enhanced by a renewed and spreading consciousness of human rights. When we read the Charter today, we are more than ever conscious that its aim is to protect individual human beings, not to protect those who abuse them.[14]

If he had hoped this approach would defuse the controversy, the secretary-general was to be sadly disappointed. Quite unmoved by the elegance of his formulation, the debate, in the General Assembly and elsewhere, continued as vigorously, and in some cases as viciously, as before. Even those trying hard to defuse the controversy and come up with a consensus solution felt that the "two sovereignties" approach did not so much resolve the dilemma of intervention as simply restate it. This was something that Kofi Annan was quite graciously prepared to concede a few years later, saying that he rather wished that he himself had thought to cast the issue in the way it subsequently emerged, because it would have given him rather more feathers with which to fly.[15]

The Birth of "The Responsibility to Protect"

Kofi Annan's heartfelt challenge to the Millennium General Assembly in April 2000, quoted at the head of this chapter, was the stimulus for what proved to be, at last, the long-awaited conceptual breakthrough.[16] The Canadian government, on the initiative of Foreign Minister Lloyd Axworthy, appointed an international commission tasked "to wrestle with the whole range of questions—legal, moral, operational and political—rolled up in this debate, to consult with the widest possible range of opinion around the world, and to bring back a report that would help the secretary-general and everyone else find some new common ground."[17] The International Commission on Intervention and State Sovereignty was launched in September 2000 and just over a year later, in December 2001, published its 90-page report and a 400-page supplementary volume of research essays, bibliography, and background material, all under the title *The Responsibility to Protect*.

The pace throughout was punishing. The commission met five times and hosted eleven regional roundtables and national consultations across five continents: in Beijing, Cairo, Maputo, New Delhi, and Santiago in the global South, and Brussels, Geneva, London, Ottawa, Paris, St. Petersburg, and Washington in the North. Skepticism abounded, from governments, academics, and some foundations, as to whether anything worthwhile could possibly emerge from such a "forced march," which drew an early wry comment from our secretariat head, Jill Sinclair—one that also describes well how we actually saw our task: "Governments are not usually accused of moving too quickly, so I am always intrigued by the reactions to our timetable. . . . This is not an intellectual, academic exercise but rather a political effort to catalyse a debate, drawing on reams (and centuries) of existing erudite thought and writing on the subject, supplemented by some current research and analysis."[18]

The commission members certainly proved equal to the enterprise. I was joined as cochair by the Algerian diplomat and veteran UN Africa adviser Mohamed Sahnoun, extraordinarily knowledgeable on the issues from his years of field engagement in Somalia, the Great Lakes region of East Africa, Ethiopia and Eritrea, and elsewhere, and a great leavening influence on, among others, sometimes overly exuberant antipodeans. We had with us what could reasonably be described as a cast made in heaven for a panel of this kind—needing, as it did, to be visibly representative of the whole world, in command of the issues, creatively minded, and highly tolerant of each other's foibles. From the global South there were former Philippines president Fidel V. Ramos, African National Congress head Cyril Ramaphosa from South Africa, Guatemalan foreign minister Eduardo Stein, and Indian scholar Ramesh Thakur. From the North there were former U.S. congressman Lee Hamilton, German NATO general Klaus Naumann, and Canadian human rights and conflict specialists Michael Ignatieff and Gisele Côté-Harper, with Russian diplomat and parliamentarian Vladimir Lukin and former long-serving president of the International Committee of the Red Cross Cornelio Sommaruga (whom we liked to describe as "a Northerner with Southern characteristics") making up the balance.

In writing the report—a process in which Michael Ignatieff and Ramesh Thakur were particularly closely engaged with the cochairs—a good deal of attention was paid to keeping the core messages straightforward and simple, while ensuring that there was enough detailed analysis and argument in the rest of the text and in the supporting volume to satisfy those hungry to understand their underpinnings. In this spirit, the "Core Principles" we were espousing were extracted in a short synopsis, which remains probably the most useful quick introduction to the ideas we were presenting (see box 2-1).[19]

The ICISS report made four main contributions to the international policy debate that seem likely to have a lasting impact. The first, and perhaps ultimately the most useful politically, was inventing a new way of talking about "humanitarian intervention." We sought to turn the whole weary—and increasingly ugly—debate about "the right to intervene" on its head and recharacterize it not as an argument about the "right" of states to do anything but rather about their "responsibility"—in this case, to protect

Box 2-1. R2P in the 2001 ICISS Report: Core Principles

1. BASIC PRINCIPLES

A. State sovereignty implies responsibility, and the primary responsibility for the protection of its people lies with the state itself.

B. Where a population is suffering serious harm, as a result of internal war, insurgency, repression or state failure, and the state in question is unwilling or unable to halt or avert it, the principle of nonintervention yields to the international responsibility to protect.

2. FOUNDATIONS

The foundations of the responsibility to protect, as a guiding principle for the international community of states, lie in:

A. obligations inherent in the concept of sovereignty;

B. the responsibility of the Security Council, under article 24 of the UN Charter, for the maintenance of international peace and security;

C. specific legal obligations under human rights and human protection declarations, covenants and treaties, international humanitarian law, and national law;

D. the developing practice of states, regional organizations and the Security Council itself.

people at grave risk. The relevant perspective, we argued, was not that of prospective interveners but of those needing support. If any "right" was involved, it was of the victims of mass atrocity crimes to be protected. The searchlight was swung back where it should always be: on the need to protect communities from mass killing and ethnic cleansing, women from systematic rape, and children from starvation.

Another reason for wanting to sideline the humanitarian intervention terminology was that it had become irretrievably linked to the use of military force, and *only* military force, as the way to respond to actual or impending mass atrocities. Although the phrase was, as a matter of ordi-

3. ELEMENTS

The responsibility to protect embraces three specific responsibilities:

A. *The responsibility to prevent:* to address both the root causes and direct causes of internal conflict and other man-made crises putting populations at risk.

B. *The responsibility to react:* to respond to situations of compelling human need with appropriate measures, which may include coercive measures like sanctions and international prosecution, and in extreme cases military intervention.

C. *The responsibility to rebuild:* to provide, particularly after a military intervention, full assistance with recovery, reconstruction, and reconciliation, addressing the causes of the harm the intervention was designed to halt or avert.

4. PRIORITIES

A. *Prevention is the single most important dimension of the responsibility to protect:* prevention options should always be exhausted before intervention is contemplated, and more commitment and resources must be devoted to it.

B. The exercise of the responsibility to both prevent and react should always involve less intrusive and coercive measures being considered before more coercive and intrusive ones are applied.

Source: ICISS, *The Responsibility to Protect,* p. xi.

nary language, capable of being used in a perfectly neutral way to describe the active engagement of humanitarian relief organizations in addressing catastrophic situations (analogous to doctor-patient "medical intervention"), it overwhelmingly had come to mean the application of nonconsensual military force to achieve a humanitarian objective. And this was a matter of deep unhappiness for the Red Cross movement and many other relief organizations, who found inherently abhorrent the association of "humanitarian" with any form of military action, however elevated the motives in question might be. So throughout the report, when military action is what is being referred to, the terminology used is "military intervention for human protection purpose": something of a mouthful, which has not won quite the slavish following among commentators to which we (Cornelio Sommaruga in particular) aspired.

The commission's hope, above all, was that using "responsibility to protect" rather than "right to intervene" language would enable entrenched opponents to find new ground on which to more constructively engage. We very much had in mind the power of new ideas, or old ideas newly expressed, to actually change the behavior of key policy actors. And the model we looked to in this respect was the Brundtland Commission, which a few years earlier had introduced the concept of "sustainable development" to bridge the huge gap that then existed between developers and environmentalists.[20] With a new script, the actors have to change their lines and think afresh about what the real issues in the play actually are.

The second big conceptual contribution of the ICISS commissioners, very much linked with the first, was to insist upon a new way of talking about sovereignty itself: building squarely on Francis Deng's formulation, we argued that its essence should now be seen not as "control," in the centuries-old Westphalian tradition, but, again, as "responsibility." The starting point is that any state has the primary responsibility to protect the individuals within it. But that is not the finishing point: where the state is unable or unwilling to meet its own responsibility, through either incapacity or ill will, a secondary responsibility to protect falls on the wider international community to step in, by whatever means is appropriate to the particular situation. Most of the subsequent discussion of R2P has focused on the second of these two elements, external engagement. But the first—the emphasis on the state's *own* responsibility to protect its own people—is equally important. It marks a very sharp break, substantively as well as presentationally, with previous humanitarian intervention discourse, and was seen by the commission as a crucial aspect of R2P's potential role as a bridge builder between North and South on mass atrocity issues.

The third contribution of the commission was to spell out very clearly what the responsibility to protect should mean in practice, both for the sovereign state itself in meeting its primary responsibility to its own people, and then, if it could not do so, for the responsibility of the wider international community to assist. We tried hard to make it clear beyond argument that "the responsibility to protect" was about much more than military intervention. It extended to a whole continuum of obligations: the responsibility to *prevent* mass atrocity situations arising; the responsibility to *react* to them when they did, with a whole graduated menu of responses from the persuasive to the coercive; and the responsibility to *rebuild* after any intrusive intervention.

Of these three layers of responsibility, the commission insisted that over-whelmingly the most important to pursue was the responsibility to pre-vent, through means such as building state capacity, remedying grievances, and ensuring the rule of law. We also insisted that whatever means are cho-sen in exercising any of these responsibilities—whether political and diplo-matic, legal, economic, or security-sector related—the process "should always involve less intrusive and coercive measures being considered before the more coercive and intrusive ones are applied" (see box 2-1).

The fourth and remaining contribution of the commission was to address the unavoidable question of when the most extreme form of coer-cive reaction, military action, *would* in fact be appropriate, however much we might hope to avoid that necessity arising. We sought to identify a set of guidelines—rather more focused than those spelled out by Tony Blair in 1999—that could be adopted by the Security Council and would prove of real utility to decisionmakers. The first criterion was obviously *legality*, and here we saw our task not as trying to find alternatives to the clear legal authority of the Security Council but rather as making it work better, thus lessening the chance of it being bypassed altogether. That was followed by five criteria of *legitimacy*, designed as a set of benchmarks that, while they might not guarantee consensus in any particular case, would make its achievement much more likely. These were, in short, the seriousness of the harm being threatened (which would need to involve large-scale loss of life or ethnic cleansing to prima facie justify something as extreme as military action), the motivation or primary purpose of the proposed military action, whether there were reasonably available peaceful alternatives, the proportionality of the response, and the balance of consequences—whether more good than harm would be done by the intervention.

From ICISS to the World Summit

As many blue-ribbon commissions and panels have discovered over the years, it is one thing to labor mightily and produce what looks like a major new contribution to some policy debate, but quite another to get any policymaker to take any notice of it. The ICISS *Responsibility to Protect* report looked headed for that fate, and more rapidly than most of its kind, when it was almost suffocated at birth by being published in December 2001, in the immediate aftermath of September 11, with the massive international preoccupation with terrorism, rather than internal human rights catastrophes, which then began. But after a slow start, the report did eventually gain traction and by 2005 was setting the terms of the international policy debate.

The R2P concept was first seriously embraced in the doctrine of the newly emerging African Union, created in 2002, which unlike its predecessor, the Organization of African Unity, placed the emphasis, when it came to catastrophic internal human rights violations, not on "noninterference" but on "nonindifference."[21] Over the next two to three years, the idea also won quite a constituency among academic commentators and international lawyers—an important development, given that international law, unlike its domestic counterpart, is capable of evolving through practice and commentary as well as through formal instruments and judicial decisions.[22]

But the really big step forward in terms of formal acceptance of R2P came with the UN Sixtieth Anniversary World Summit in September 2005, and with the two major peace and security reports prepared in the lead-up to it. The critical link between the ICISS report and the summit outcome document was the work of the UN Secretary-General's High-Level Panel on Threats, Challenges, and Change. The panel, of which I had the good fortune to be appointed a member, was established in late 2003 to "recommend clear and practical measures for ensuring effective collective action, based upon a rigorous analysis of future threats to peace and security," and its 130-page report, *A More Secure World: Our Shared Responsibility,* was released in December 2004.[23]

The panel's report was far more wide-ranging in scope than the ICISS report, following a human security approach that linked together poverty, disease, and environmental degradation with conflict both within and between states, terrorism, proliferation of weapons of mass destruction, and transnational organized crime. Thus it had rather more substance, coherence, and bite than almost anyone expected, with its 101 recommendations making serious reform proposals right across that whole policy spectrum, including on the vexed question of UN—and particularly Security Council—structural reform. On R2P, the crucial recommendation was expressed in these terms: "The Panel endorses the emerging norm that there is a collective international responsibility to protect, exercisable by the Security Council authorizing military intervention as a last resort, in the event of genocide and other large-scale killing, ethnic cleansing or serious violations of humanitarian law which sovereign governments have proved powerless or unwilling to prevent."[24]

This was supplemented by a further detailed recommendation spelling out the "five basic criteria of legitimacy" for the use of force, drawing very directly on the language in the ICISS report, which it was proposed be embodied in declaratory resolutions of both the Security Council and General Assembly. There was also language on the issue of legal authority for the use of force, again reflecting a key ICISS theme, that the "task is not to find alternatives to the Security Council as a source of authority but to make the Council work better than it has."[25]

For an issue raising as many sensitivities as R2P, and in a sixteen-member panel that was very broadly representative of global sentiment, with more than half its members from the global South, there was remarkably ready acceptance of the vitality and utility of the basic principle. Those most immediately engaged on this issue were former Norwegian prime minister Gro Harlem Brundtland, U.K. diplomat David Hannay, U.S. National Security Adviser Brent Scowcroft, High Commissioner for Refugees Sadako Ogata (who brought, as always, a sturdily practical cast to the debate—I can still hear her asking, "What does all this language actually mean for suffering people on the ground?"), former Organization of African Unity secretary-general Salim Salim, and the Indian UN force commander Satish Nambiar. But in retrospect, the support that mattered most for the future of our recommendations—fairly passive though it was at the time—was probably that from the former vice premier and foreign minister of China, Qian Qichen; without his immense prestige back in Beijing, it is difficult to believe that, given the traditional strength of its concerns about nonintervention, China would have been quite as relaxed on this issue as it proved to be at the World Summit.[26]

The crucial next step was for the High-Level Panel's recommendations to be picked up in the secretary-general's own report to the summit, designed to bring together in a single coherent whole all the credible UN reform proposals in circulation, in particular from our panel and the huge Jeffrey Sachs–chaired project report on the implementation of the Millennium Development Goals.[27] In his eighty-eight-page report, *In Larger Freedom: Towards Development, Security and Human Rights for All,* published in March 2005, Kofi Annan duly obliged, saying that "while I am well aware of the sensitivities involved in this issue . . . I believe that we must embrace the responsibility to protect, and, when necessary, we must act on it."[28] He formally urged heads of state and government to

> embrace the "responsibility to protect" as a basis for collective action against genocide, ethnic cleansing and crimes against humanity, and agree to act on this responsibility, recognizing that this responsibility lies first and foremost with each individual State, whose duty it is to protect its population, but that if national authorities are unwilling or unable to protect their citizens, then the responsibility shifts to the international community to use diplomatic, humanitarian and other methods to help protect civilian populations, and that if such methods appear insufficient the Security Council may out of necessity decide to take action under the Charter, including enforcement action, if so required.[29]

This language touched even more ICISS direct bases, with its emphasis on initial state responsibility and, in particular, the importance of non-military responses being explored first, and was enormously helpful in setting the scene for the World Summit debate. It was accompanied by a further recommendation on principles for the use of force, which again almost exactly mirrored ICISS language, as had the High-Level Panel recommendation.[30] The significant difference here, though, was that the R2P and force recommendations appeared in different sections of the Annan report ("Freedom to live in dignity" and "Freedom from fear," respectively), resulting in them being seen as quite separate, rather than inherently linked, proposals when they came to be debated at the World Summit. From one point of view that may have helped on the R2P side, in disengaging it from a military context, but from another perspective, it did not much help the prospects of the already somewhat controversial criteria for legitimacy.

When the more than 150 heads of state and government—presidents, prime ministers, and princes—finally convened as the World Summit to commemorate the sixtieth anniversary of the UN in September 2005, it was after intense months of in-house wrangling in New York about nearly every one of Annan's sixty or so recommendations. The atmosphere was not helped by the late arrival on the scene of the famously ideological and combative new U.S. ambassador to the UN, John Bolton—a man for whom, in Sir Brian Urquhart's dry assessment, "arguments and even rows" are something "which he appears to enjoy in a joyless kind of way"—with some 700 spoiling amendments designed to throw the whole painfully evolving negotiating process into chaos, many of them evidently more his own work than anything directed from Washington.[31] In the event, the whole summit proved to be a major disappointment to all those who had hoped it would result in a major overhaul of the UN system and global policy, with very little of substance agreed on anything. But, remarkably, the secretary-general's R2P recommendation (although not his proposals for agreed criteria to govern the use of force) survived almost unscathed, with the final summit Outcome Document devoting a special section to it (box 2-2).

The language of the relevant paragraphs, 138 and 139, of the Outcome Document differs a little from all the previous formulations in the ICISS, High-Level Panel, and secretary-general's reports, but it does not vary from core R2P principles in any significant way—despite the disposition of some commentators to argue otherwise.[32] The unanimous agreement on this language at the World Summit was an enormous achievement by the many diplomats who worked to craft it, and should be seen absolutely as an occasion for celebration rather than disappointment by supporters of the responsibility to protect norm. There are straightforward responses to all the concerns that have been raised. First, the slight change in the description of the particular mass atrocity crimes of concern is not significant at all. Second, the more explicit emphasis on the threshold responsibility of states to protect their own people—"we accept that responsibility and will act upon it"—is a plus, helping to consolidate support for the norm in the global South. Third, it is wholly desirable that emphasis is placed on assistance being given to societies under stress by others in the international community: this was not given sufficient attention in the original ICISS report. Fourth, it is also a plus that there is an even stronger emphasis in paragraphs 138 and 139 than in the earlier reports on prevention, and on the responsibilities of states to assist each other in building preventive capability. Fifth, when it comes to reaction,

---

Box 2-2. R2P in the UN General Assembly 2005: World Summit Outcome Document

Heads of state and government attending the 60th session of the UN General Assembly 14–16 September 2005 agreed as follows:

· · ·

RESPONSIBILITY TO PROTECT POPULATIONS FROM GENOCIDE, WAR CRIMES, ETHNIC CLEANSING, AND CRIMES AGAINST HUMANITY

138. Each individual State has the responsibility to protect its populations from genocide, war crimes, ethnic cleansing, and crimes against humanity. This responsibility entails the prevention of such crimes, including their incitement, through appropriate and necessary means. We accept that responsibility and will act in accordance with it. The international community should, as appropriate, encourage and help States to exercise this responsibility and support the United Nations in establishing an early warning capability.

139. The international community, through the United Nations, also has the responsibility to use appropriate diplomatic, humanitarian, and other peaceful means, in accordance with Chapters VI and VIII of the Charter, to help to protect populations from geno-

---

it is again a positive feature of the summit document that more emphasis is placed on reactive measures falling short of military action, while Chapter VII enforcement action is still very expressly envisaged "should peaceful means be inadequate and national authorities are manifestly failing to protect their populations." Finally, the insistence on the central role of the UN in all theses matters—and the necessary role of the Security Council when it comes to military enforcement measures—is certainly wholly consistent with all the earlier recommendations. The only disappointing omission from the Outcome Document is the failure to adopt any criteria for the use of military force, leaving the argument for such guidelines to be made another day.

cide, war crimes, ethnic cleansing, and crimes against humanity. In this context, we are prepared to take collective action, in a timely and decisive manner, through the Security Council, in accordance with the Charter, including Chapter VII, on a case-by-case basis and in cooperation with relevant regional organizations as appropriate, should peaceful means be inadequate and national authorities are manifestly failing to protect their populations from genocide, war crimes, ethnic cleansing, and crimes against humanity. We stress the need for the General Assembly to continue consideration of the responsibility to protect populations from genocide, war crimes, ethnic cleansing, and crimes against humanity and its implications, bearing in mind the principles of the Charter and international law. We also intend to commit ourselves, as necessary and appropriate, to helping States build capacity to protect their populations from genocide, war crimes, ethnic cleansing, and crimes against humanity and to assisting those which are under stress before crises and conflicts break out.

140. We fully support the mission of the Special Adviser of the Secretary-General on the Prevention of Genocide.

Source: UN General Assembly, "World Summit Outcome 2005," Resolution A/RES/60/1 (October 24, 2005); available at www.un.org/summit2005/documents.html.

That this endorsement happened was anything but inevitable. Not only was little else of any significance agreed upon by the summit participants—despite all the preparatory buildup and high expectations—but a fierce rearguard action was fought almost to the last by a small group of developing countries, joined by Russia, who basically refused to concede any kind of limitation on the full and untrammeled exercise of state sovereignty, however irresponsible that exercise might be. And consistent support for R2P from both the United States and United Kingdom—reasonably strong from Washington (though opposed outright to criteria for the use of force, and less than fulsome on R2P itself, at least in the case of Ambassador Bolton, who called it "the High Minded *cause du jour*"), much more so from London—was not particularly helpful in allaying the familiar sovereignty concerns of the South, against the background of the deeply unpopular coalition invasion of Iraq in 2003.[33]

What carried the day in the end was persistent advocacy by sub-Saharan African countries, led by South Africa, and supplemented by a clear—and historically quite significant—embrace of limited-sovereignty principles by the key Latin American countries. There also was some very effective last minute personal diplomacy directed toward leaders of major wavering countries—including in Asia, and India in particular—by the Canadian Prime Minister Paul Martin, a passionate supporter of the ICISS report, whose involvement demonstrates the importance of seriously committed follow-through by countries commissioning reports of this kind, which does not always happen.[34]

After the Summit: A Race Still Not Won

For supporters of R2P there has been, since the 2005 World Summit, a reasonably steady trickle of good news, in terms of formal endorsement of the concept by the Security Council and its increasing take-up in international policy debate. But that has been matched by some less good news, in terms of continuing—and in some cases enhanced—resistance to both the language and substance of R2P in parts of the global South.

THE GOOD NEWS

The Security Council adopted in April 2006 a thematic resolution on the Protection of Civilians in Armed Conflict, which contains, in an operative paragraph, an express reaffirmation of the World Summit conclusions relating to the responsibility to protect.[35] And this was followed by a further resolution in August 2006 specifically invoking this in the context of the ongoing conflict in Darfur.[36] A General Assembly resolution may be helpful, as the World Summit's unquestionably was, in identifying relevant principles, but the Security Council is the institution that matters when it comes to executive action. And at least some toeholds there have now been carved.

There was further reason for optimism in the very enthusiastic embrace of R2P by the new secretary-general, Ban Ki-moon, who succeeded Kofi Annan in January 2007. From the outset, in both his public and private statements, he made clear that he understood very clearly the significance of the conceptual shift involved (and the risks to his own and the UN's reputation if anything remotely like Rwanda or Srebrenica ever happened again), and there has been no sign of any distancing of himself from the new norm as being his predecessor's legacy, not his own. On the contrary, as for example when he addressed the African Union Summit on January 31, 2008, he said: "I am fully committed to keeping the momentum that you the leaders have made at the 2005 World Summit and will spare no effort to operationalize the responsibility to protect."[37] And the secretary-general took some steps toward operationalization when he appointed a special adviser to work on institutional process issues, and when he replaced the retiring special adviser on the prevention of genocide with an impeccably credentialed candidate—but not, as will be noted below, without eliciting a degree of controversy in both instances.

A further encouraging indication that R2P continued to resonate in the post–World Summit period was the way in which it was publicly invoked to describe the response required to the alarming situation in Kenya, where very overtly ethnic-related violence exploded after allegations of a rigged national election in the last days of 2007. Over 1,000 people were killed—including dozens in a church-burning incident horribly reminiscent of Rwanda thirteen years earlier—and some 300,000 were displaced within a few weeks until a mediation team led by Kofi Annan was able to negotiate a political settlement that dampened the violence and, hopefully would prove sustainable.[38] They did so against the background of Secretary-General Ban being very quick to characterize the situation as an R2P one and his newly appointed genocide adviser, Francis Deng, urging Kenyan political and community leaders to "meet their responsibility to protect the civilian population," specifically warning them that they could be held accountable for violations of international law committed at their instigation.[39] And, in a widely published opinion article, Archbishop Emeritus Desmond Tutu very explicitly stated that "what we are seeing in Kenya is action on a fundamental principle, the Responsibility to Protect."[40]

The Less Good News

That, unfortunately, is about where the good news on the embrace of R2P stops. It had seemed beyond argument that the unanimous decision of the General Assembly, sitting at head of state and government level, to endorse paragraphs 138 and 139 of the World Summit Outcome Document actually meant something. After all, the first of these paragraphs begins with the words, "Each individual state has the responsibility to protect its populations," and the second, "The international community, through the United Nations, also has the responsibility . . . to help to protect populations." And that section of the document does have a heading of its own, does it not, that reads, "Responsibility to protect populations from genocide, war crimes, ethnic cleansing and crimes against humanity." Surely, with this kind of international endorsement, R2P now had the pedigree to be described, at the very least, as a broadly accepted international norm, and maybe even as one with the potential to evolve further into a full-fledged rule of customary international law.

Not so, it seems, in the minds of a number of governments who joined in this endorsement, or at least their representatives in New York. It never takes much more than a few days around the corridors and meeting rooms of the UN to learn that absolutely nothing there is beyond argument. The prevailing mood in at least some quarters was captured early in 2008 by the way in which, with evidently perfectly straight faces, Latin American, Arab, and African delegates to the UN's budget committee took the floor to say, variously, that "the World Summit rejected R2P in 2005," "the concept of the responsibility to protect has not been adopted by the General Assembly," and "the responsibility to protect itself . . . was not accepted or approved as a principle by the General Assembly."[41] The occasion for this nonsense, of a class that Jeremy Bentham would have described as "nonsense on stilts," was the approval process for the appointment of the highly qualified scholar Edward Luck—vice president of the International Peace Academy (now Institute) and former head of the UN Association of the United States—to a newly created position intended by the secretary-general to be designated "Special Adviser on the Responsibility to Protect."

The argument, in essence, was that the World Summit paragraphs were just about the protection of civilians from specific crimes, not the endorsement of the concept of the responsibility to protect; so if R2P was never adopted, how could the secretary-general have the effrontery to seek approval for a special adviser on it? In any event, the secretary-general decided to abandon the unequal struggle and accept Mr. Luck as a special adviser, but without either a specific job description in his title or much prospect of tenure longevity. In a similar spirit, the Office of the Secretary-

General abandoned under fire its initial decision—made, sensibly, to avoid unproductive legal squabbles about the scope of his mandate—to add to Francis Deng's title as "Special Adviser on the Prevention of Genocide" the phrase "and Mass Atrocities." Deliberately debilitating, such squabbles will no doubt continue to be part of the natural order.

The atmosphere in New York on these kinds of issues is often a little more heightened, and ideologically colored, than it is in capitals, but supporters of R2P ignore these warning signs at their peril. For whatever reason—embrace of the concept but concern about its misuse, ideological association of any intervention with neo-imperialism or neocolonialism, or, in some cases, simply embarrassment about their own behavior—there is a recurring willingness by a number of states to deflate or undermine the new norm before it is fully consolidated and operational. There has been a falling away of overt commitment to the norm in sub-Saharan Africa (although in substance it still remains a significant theme in the doctrine of the African Union and some of the sub-regional organizations), and some increased skepticism in the Arab-Islamic and Latin American worlds. And in Asia there has never been much enthusiasm, although not everywhere is as overtly hostile as in nationalist governing and media circles in Colombo, where I was told by a columnist during a visit in July 2007 that "the so-called responsibility to protect is nothing but a licence given by the white man to himself [to] intervene in the affairs of dark sovereign countries, whenever the white man thinks it fit to do so."[42]

If the unanimous adoption of the R2P principles by the 2005 World Summit and the UN Security Council is not to be the high-water mark from which the tide recedes, then serious, ongoing diplomatic and other advocacy efforts have to be made—in which civil society organizations must play a key role—to explain and defend the norm. Such efforts must be sustained over a number of years with the goal not only of enshrining R2P principles in the language of relevant international, regional, and national institutions and forums beyond the UN, but also of institutionalizing their practice. The immediate objective must be to get to the point where, when the next conscience-shocking case of large-scale killing, or ethnic cleansing, or other war crimes, or crimes against humanity comes along—as is all too unhappily likely—the immediate reflex response of the whole international community will be not to ask *whether* action is necessary but rather *what* action is required, by whom, when, and where.

There have been encouraging signs—for example, the swift and supportive diplomatic and political response to the crisis in Kenya early in 2008—that this may be beginning to happen, but there are still three big challenges that need to be addressed if R2P is indeed to become the accepted international reflex in principle, and if it is to be put effectively into practice on the ground as new cases arise.

The first challenge is essentially *conceptual*: to ensure that the scope and limits of the responsibility to protect are fully and completely understood in a way that is clearly not the case now. In particular, it is to ensure that R2P is seen not as a Trojan horse for bad old imperial, colonial, and militarist habits but rather as the best starting point the international community has—and may ever be likely to have—in preventing and responding to genocide and other mass atrocity crimes. This is the challenge taken up in chapter 3. The four that follow after it, on the responsibility to prevent, to react, and to rebuild are primarily designed to show how the core components of the responsibility to protect can and should be applied operationally; they should also be helpful in consolidating an understanding of just how rich, and above all multidimensional, a concept R2P is, and what it does and does not embrace.

The second challenge is *institutional* preparedness: to build the kind of capacity within international institutions, governments, and regional organizations that will ensure that, assuming that there is an understanding of the need to act—whether preventively or reactively, and whether through political and diplomatic, or economic, legal, or policing and military measures—there will be the physical capability to do so. Chapters 8 and 9 explore what is necessary in this respect.

The third challenge, as always, is *political* preparedness: how to generate that indispensable ingredient of will—how to have in place the mechanisms and strategies necessary to generate an effective political response as new R2P situations arise. To suggest how that challenge might be met will be the task of the concluding chapter in this volume.

CHAPTER THREE

The Scope and Limits of the Responsibility to Protect

The concept of the responsibility to protect does not exist except in the minds of Western imperialists.
—Head of UN mission of a major G-77 country, New York, 2007

Why is there so much continuing resistance to a principle that so many accept as an important breakthrough, capable of resolving an age-old debate in a practical and principled way? A good part of the answer seems to lie in some serious misunderstandings which continue to exist about the intended scope and limits of the responsibility to protect norm.

It is not uncommon in public policy debates, as in life itself, for as much trouble to be generated by the misdirected enthusiasms of one's admirers as by the misguided hostility of one's opponents, and there are three kinds of self-described friends of R2P whose attentions have, for good reason, been less than entirely welcome. There are those who play into the hands of the ideological critics by being far too ready to think and talk of the application of R2P only in military terms; those who have simply misapplied the norm to justify military intervention in circumstances where this was plainly wrong, most conspicuously with Iraq in 2003; and those who, at the other extreme, view R2P not in narrow military terms at all but far more broadly, as a way of referring to most of the world's ills, from climate change to HIV/AIDS.

If the R2P norm is to win genuinely universal consensus and to become effectively operational in practice, more needs to be done, with both friends and skeptics, to describe exactly what it is about, what are the kinds of situations to which it applies, and what are the appropriate policy responses at different stages in the evolution of a situation of concern. This chapter, and those that follow, try to respond to that need.

Five Major Misunderstandings about R2P

The five biggest and most commonly encountered conceptual misunderstandings about the responsibility to protect are that this is just another name for the much unloved doctrine of humanitarian intervention; that, at least in extreme cases, R2P always means the use of military force; that R2P applies only to weak and friendless countries, never strong ones; that R2P is about the full range of human protection issues that cry out for international attention, not just mass atrocity crimes; and, possibly most damaging of all, that the invasion of Iraq in 2003 was an example of the proper application of R2P and a foretaste of things to come. Sometimes these misunderstandings are cynically and deliberately fostered by those with other axes to grind or interests to protect, but more often they are real and the product of quite genuine misapprehension as to what R2P is all about. Either way, they each need to be seriously addressed.

ONE: "R2P IS JUST ANOTHER NAME FOR HUMANITARIAN INTERVENTION"

This is absolutely not the case: they are very different concepts. The very core of the traditional meaning of "humanitarian intervention" is coercive military intervention for humanitarian purposes—nothing more or less. But "the responsibility to protect" is about much more than that.

Above all, R2P is about taking effective *preventive* action, and at the earliest possible stage. It implies encouragement and support being given to those states struggling with situations that have not yet deteriorated to the point where genocide or other atrocity crimes are a reality, but where it is foreseeable that they *could* so deteriorate if effective preventive action is not taken, with or without outside support. It recognizes the need to bring to bear every appropriate preventive response, be it political, diplomatic, legal, economic, or in the security sector—but falling short of coercive action (for example, a "preventive deployment" of troops, as in Macedonia in 1995).[1] The responsibility to take preventive action is very much that of the sovereign state itself, quite apart from that of the international community. And when it comes to the international community, a very big part of *its* preventive response should be to help countries to help themselves.

All this is abundantly clear in the successive formulations of R2P, from the ICISS report to the World Summit Outcome Document. In the original ICISS formulation, it is emphasized that R2P has three different dimensions—to prevent mass atrocity crimes occurring in the first place; to react appropriately when they are occurring or imminently about to, but considering military action only in the most extreme cases; and to rebuild afterward, addressing the root causes of the harm in question. And in all of this, it is stated explicitly, "Prevention is the single most important dimension of the responsibility to protect."[2]

The World Summit Outcome Document language is even clearer in its noncoercive, nonmilitary, preventive emphasis. Paragraph 138 says that each individual state's responsibility to protect its populations from the mass atrocity crimes in question "entails the prevention of such crimes, including their incitement, through appropriate and necessary means." In this context, it adds that the role of the international community is to "as appropriate encourage and help States to exercise that responsibility." Paragraph 139 drives home that same point even more forcefully, focusing strongly on the use of "appropriate diplomatic, humanitarian and other peaceful means, in accordance with Chapters VI and VIII of the Charter," and concludes with the assembled world's leaders saying, again unanimously, "We also intend to commit ourselves, as necessary and appropriate, to helping States build capacity to protect their populations from genocide, war crimes, ethnic cleansing and crimes against humanity and to assisting those which are under stress before crises and conflicts break out."[3]

Of course, there will be situations when prevention fails, crises and conflicts do break out, and reaction becomes necessary. But reaction does not have to mean military reaction: it can involve political, diplomatic, economic, and legal pressure, measures that can each cross the spectrum from persuasive to intrusive, and from less coercive (for example, economic incentives and offers of political mediation or legal arbitration) to more coercive (for example, economic sanctions, political and diplomatic isolation, or threats of referral to the International Criminal Court)—which is true of military response as well. As the ICISS commissioners insisted, "The exercise of the responsibility to both prevent and react should always involve less intrusive and coercive measures being considered before more coercive and intrusive ones are applied."[4] Coercive military action is not excluded, in either the ICISS or World Summit formulations, as a last resort option in extreme cases, when it is the only possible way to stop large-scale killing and other atrocity crimes, as nobody doubts was the case, for example, in Rwanda or Srebrenica. But it is an absolute travesty of the R2P principle to say that it is about military force and nothing else.

With all this so clear from the language of the source documents, it is not immediately obvious why the claim that R2P is only about military action maintains such a tenacious hold. But three explanations suggest themselves. The first is, unhappily, cynical self-interest. As much as we might wish it otherwise, there are a number of countries that continue to have something to hide or be ashamed about in terms of their own internal behavior and who are deeply reluctant to acknowledge, as a result, any limitations at all on their sovereignty: while they felt unable to hold out against the final consensus at the World Summit, they will remain alert to any opportunity to puncture or undermine the new norm.

The second explanation is that there are a number of critics who oppose the whole idea of R2P, and the constraints on absolute state sovereignty it entails, not for any crudely self-interested reason but for high-minded and ideological ones: those who retain a strong aversion to imperialism, or perceived neo-imperialism or neocolonialism, in any shape or form, and who remain instinctively unwilling to concede in principle that any form of external intervention could ever wholly avoid having that character. This is a recurring theme in a good deal of academic literature that continues to have some influence—for example, in recent articles by Alex de Waal and Mahmood Mamdani.[5] What is intriguing about these and other such pieces is that they continue to hammer away at humanitarian intervention as the target, and only incidentally mention R2P, flailing away at the old straw man without acknowledging that the debate has moved on and the extent to which their concerns have already been conceptually accommodated.

A third explanation, it has to be acknowledged, is that supporters and promoters of the responsibility to protect norm have not done nearly so good a job as we should have in explaining the multifaceted character of R2P and the central role that prevention, rather than just reaction—let alone coercive military action—plays in it. The best way to make this point is perhaps to identify clear examples where the international community has been engaged in exactly this kind of preventive support but without, until now, labeling it as an "R2P" exercise.

Burundi, in Central Africa, is as clear a case study of this as one could wish for. With its long history of earlier atrocity crimes and continuing ethnic tensions, the country could very easily have followed Rwanda's path in

1994, and it remains extremely fragile to this day. But multiple international players have been working hard and long to ensure that the situation did not so deteriorate. These efforts have included Nelson Mandela's initial political mediation; the deployment, essentially preventively, of peacekeeping troops, particularly by South Africa; the detailed analysis and recommendations, for a decade now, by my own International Crisis Group as to what is necessary to achieve sustainable peace; and the attention being given to Burundi as one of the first two cases taken up by the UN's new Peacebuilding Commission.[6]

TWO: "IN EXTREME CASES R2P ALWAYS MEANS THE USE OF COERCIVE MILITARY FORCE"

This is not so, although it is a misunderstanding very often shared by even the most enthusiastic supporters of the responsibility to protect norm. Leaving aside for present purposes the practical question of whether military forces will actually be provided by anyone, and focusing just on whether they should be available, it is important not to confuse necessary and sufficient conditions. It is necessary for a case to be really extreme for coercive military force to be an option, but the fact that it is extreme is not in itself sufficient to conclude that such force *should* be applied.

As was made abundantly clear by ICISS in its 2001 report, the High-Level Panel in its report to the UN before the 2005 World Summit, and UN Secretary-General Kofi Annan in his pre–World Summit report, military intervention for human protection purposes is a desperately serious, extraordinary, and exceptional matter that must be judged by not just one prudential criterion but a whole series of them. The first of those criteria is certainly the seriousness of the threat, and the ICISS commissioners spelled out what they thought this "just cause threshold" meant in very specific terms: it required either large-scale loss of life, actual or apprehended, or large-scale ethnic cleansing, again actual or apprehended, and whether carried out by killing, forced expulsion, acts of terror, or rape.[7] The High-Level Panel report formulated a little differently its first "criterion of legitimacy" (because it was addressing the use of force generally, not only in R2P mass atrocity situations), but it was to similar effect, asking, "In the case of internal threats, does it involve genocide and other large-scale killing, ethnic cleansing, or serious violations of international humanitarian law, actual or imminently apprehended?"[8]

But it is not just a matter of saying that if a threshold of seriousness is crossed in one or other of these ways, then it is time for the invasion to start. There are another four criteria of legitimacy, all more or less equally important, that also have to be satisfied if the case is to be made for coercive, nonconsensual military force to be deployed within another country's sovereign territory: the motivation or primary purpose of the proposed military action (whether it was primarily to halt or avert the threat in question, or had some other main objective); last resort (whether there were reasonably available peaceful alternatives); the proportionality of the response; and, not least, the balance of consequences (whether overall more good than harm would be done by a military invasion).[9]

One of the many disappointments of the World Summit is that although guidelines for the use of force of just this kind were advocated in all the lead-up reports mentioned, in the hope that this would lead to their adoption by the Security Council, they were not adopted by the summit. The issue was caught in a diplomatic pincer movement between the United States (supported, though less overtly, by other Permanent Five members), who wanted no such restrictions to affect any decision to use force, and some in the South who argued, in a way that they at least found convincing, that to adopt guidelines purporting to limit the use of force would, in fact, by recognizing its legitimacy in at least some cases, on the contrary encourage it. Had the proposed criteria been accepted and made part of the summit outcome document, it would have been very much clearer that in applying the R2P norm, the extreme nature of a particular conscience-shocking situation and the failure of preventive attempts to resolve it are only the beginning of the argument about the use of military force, not the end of it.

Darfur is the clearest contemporary example of this misunderstanding at work, with the debate about how the international community should react tending to polarize into a choice between, as Lee Feinstein put it, "the stark options of 'Doing Nothing' and 'Sending in the Marines,'" without acknowledging the many way stations in between.[10] There is no doubt that the "seriousness of threat" criterion has been satisfied: since 2003, in this region of Sudan, more than 200,000 have died from outright violence or war-related disease and malnutrition, and well over 2 million have been displaced. And, at the time of this writing in mid-2008, peacekeeping efforts have proved manifestly inadequate, peace negotiations are going nowhere fast, humanitarian relief is faltering, the conflict is spilling over into neighboring countries, and the overall situation remains desolate. But the argument is very strong—and accepted by most governments and relief organizations on the ground—that a nonconsensual military intervention (even assuming that the troops could be found anywhere to sustain it) would almost certainly be disastrously counterproductive, in terms of its impact on current humanitarian relief operations and the very fragile north-south peace process.[11]

Darfur still remains, on any view, an "R2P situation," and one, moreover, where the responsibility to react has shifted to the international community because of Khartoum's manifest abdication of its own sovereign responsibility. The inability here to use coercive military measures does not mean that this is a case of "R2P failure"; it just means that the international response to the Sudan government's ill-will or incapacity has to take other forms, including the application of sustained diplomatic, economic, and legal pressure to change the cost-benefit balance of the regime's calculations. If the concept of R2P is not to be eroded, it is important that its friends apply it, here and elsewhere, in an appropriately nuanced way. The international community has so far failed dismally in its responsibility to protect the people of Darfur from mass atrocity crimes, but that failure has been in the application of other measures, not the non-application of coercive force.

THREE: "R2P APPLIES ONLY TO WEAK AND FRIENDLESS COUNTRIES, NEVER THE STRONG"

This is a very frequently heard objection to the R2P norm, and one that must be taken seriously because it has prima facie plausibility. How could, after all, a coercive military intervention ever seriously be contemplated against China or Russia, let alone the United States, whatever terrible situation might internally unfold? And with the Security Council as ultimate arbiter, how could an adverse finding ever be made against those wielding the power of the veto, or any country that any one of the Permanent Five might choose to protect?

But the ability to apply coercive military force in extreme cases is not and cannot be the yardstick by which the success or failure of the R2P principle is measured. The first misunderstanding involved here is a variation on that addressed immediately above. Situations will arise where such military action is just not a realistic or acceptable option because one or more of the five criteria of legitimacy have not been satisfied, even though lesser measures have not produced the results hoped for, and the military option seems very attractive. In the case of Darfur, just discussed, the "balance of consequences" problem remains that any such action would be likely to trigger an even greater humanitarian disaster, both in Darfur itself and across a much wider area of Sudan.

Moreover, in the case of any proposed military action against a Permanent Five member or any other major power, this particular criterion would always be a showstopper, whatever other factors (including the possible exercise of veto power in the Security Council) were in play. The ICISS commissioners were deeply conscious of this issue and of the "double standards" criticism that it would inevitably invite. It is worth spelling out in full how we answered it:

4.41 Military action can only be justified if it stands a reasonable chance of success, that is, halting or averting the atrocities or suffering that triggered the intervention in the first place. Military intervention is not justified if actual protection cannot be achieved, or if the consequences of embarking upon the intervention are likely to be worse than if there is no action at all. In particular, a military action for limited human protection purposes cannot be justified if in the process it triggers a larger conflict. It will be the case that some human beings simply cannot be rescued except at unacceptable cost—perhaps of a larger regional conflagration, involving major military powers. In such cases, however painful the reality, coercive military action is no longer justified.

4.42 Application of this precautionary principle would on purely utilitarian grounds be likely to preclude military action against any one of the five permanent members of the Security Council even if all the other conditions for intervention described here were met. It is difficult to imagine a major conflict being avoided, or success in the original objective being achieved, if such action were mounted against any of them. The same is true of other major powers who are not permanent members of the Security Council. This raises again the question of double standards—but the Commission's position here, as elsewhere, is simply this: the reality that interventions may not be able to be mounted in every case where there is justification for doing so, is no reason for them not to be mounted in any case.

4.43 In relation to the major powers, there are still other kinds of pressure that can be applied, as happened, for example, in the case of Indonesia and East Timor. And other types of collective action—including sanctions—could and should still be considered in such cases as part of the responsibility to protect.[12]

The reality that there will always be some countries too militarily powerful for military action against them to be likely to do more good than harm does not mean that the rest of the world is totally impotent when it comes to applying the R2P norm against them. The commission gave the example, in the last paragraph just quoted, of Indonesia, a large and important regional power with over 230 million people, the largest Islamic population in the world, and armed forces 300,000 strong, succumbing to strong collective international pressure to allow—much against its instincts and initial will—the Australian-led intervention to protect the people of Timor-Leste (as East Timor is now known) in September 1999. The pressure in question was essentially diplomatic, applied very directly and personally by President Clinton and other presidents and prime ministers in the margins of the Asia Pacific Economic Cooperation (APEC) heads of government meeting, which happened, very fortuitously, to be meeting in Auckland just at the time the situation in Timor-Leste was exploding.

No major country in the world, however big and powerful, is today wholly immune from peer group pressure. Even China, much criticized for many years for its tolerant accommodation of various unlovely regimes abroad, including those of Sudan and Burma/Myanmar (reminiscent though this may have been of much American and Russian behavior during the cold war years), has shown many signs recently of being far more concerned about its international image and being willing to play a much more constructive problem-solving role behind the scenes.[13] The picture is more mixed regarding internal dissent, the intolerance of which has led to many brutal crackdowns in the past in Tibet, Xinjiang, and, of course, in Beijing itself with the Tiananmen massacre of 1989. The present generation of leaders remains extremely cautious about any move toward greater domestic democracy and political freedom, and is wholly resistant to any independence sentiment anywhere within the country—as became clear in early 2008 in Beijing's reaction to the efforts of Tibetans to use the forthcoming Olympics as a vehicle to draw international attention to their cause. But the Chinese leadership is much more conscious of international censure and has been more restrained in its responses than it would have been in earlier years.

The point is that the R2P norm is, and must remain, universally applicable. It must be seen as imposing a strong internal discipline on both great and small countries, the strong and the weak, the protected and the friendless alike, and as requiring an even-handed approach by all members of the international community in analyzing and criticizing behavior that may be offensive to that norm going on elsewhere. But that does not preclude some variation of approach when it comes to the practical application of stronger measures. And there will be some countries for whom such measures will never be a practical option—a fact of life with which we simply have to live in many different international contexts. This does not mean that we should abandon the R2P norm, any more than (as discussed further in chapter 6) we should give up on the Security Council as the only legal source of authority (self-defense aside) for the use of force, just because it can be bypassed in practice by the world's most powerful countries: that way lies the abandonment of a rules- and principles-based international order.

Four: "R2P Covers All Human Protection Issues"

This misunderstanding is at the other end of the spectrum from those which take it that R2P is only about the application of military force. The concern is that to use the responsibility to protect too broadly, in non-mass-atrocity contexts, is to dilute to the point of uselessness its role as a mobilizer of instinctive, universal action in cases of conscience-shocking killing, ethnic cleansing, and other such crimes against humanity.

Of course, one can argue, linguistically and as a matter of good public policy, that the international community has the responsibility to protect people from the ravages of HIV/AIDS worldwide; the proliferation of nuclear weapons and other weapons of mass destruction; the ready availability of small arms and the use of land mines and cluster bombs; the impact of dramatic climate change, particularly on specific groups like the Inuit of the Arctic Circle; and much more besides. But if one is looking for umbrella language to bring these issues and themes together, it is much more appropriate to use a concept like "human security" than to say these are proper applications of the new international norm of "the responsibility to protect."

It is not just a matter here of making the formal point that these cases are clearly not intended to be subsumed under the various descriptions of mass atrocity crimes that appear in the World Summit Outcome Document and the relevant lead-up reports. The argument is a more practical one: if R2P is to be about protecting everybody from everything, it will end up protecting nobody from anything. The whole point of embracing the new language of "the responsibility to protect" is that it is capable of generating an effective, consensual response to extreme, conscience-shocking cases in a way that "right to intervene" language simply could not. We need to preserve the focus and bite of "R2P" as a rallying cry in the face of mass atrocities.

A further problem with stretching the R2P concept to embrace what might be described as the whole human security agenda is that this immediately raises the hackles of those who see it as the thin end of a totally interventionist wedge—as giving an open invitation for the countries of the North to engage to their hearts' content in the *missions civilisatrices* (civilizing missions) that so understandably anger those in the global South, who have experienced it all before. That trouble is compounded when it is remembered that coercive military intervention, while absolutely not at the heart of the R2P concept, as has been already made clear, is nonetheless a reactive response that cannot be excluded in really extreme cases. So any understanding of R2P as a very broad-based doctrine, which would open up at least the possibility of military action in a whole variety of policy contexts, is bound to give the concept a bad name.

This issue was thrown into stark relief by the dilemma facing the international community when, in May 2008, the ruling military regime of Burma/Myanmar dragged its feet appallingly in responding to offers of international aid following the catastrophic Cyclone Nargis with its tidal surge that devastated the Irrawaddy delta, directly killing over 130,000 people and putting scores of thousands more at risk from disease, starvation, and exposure. Was this, or was it not, an R2P case of a kind that would conceivably justify coercive military intervention for the explicit purpose of delivering the necessary aid? The short answer is that natural disasters, as such, are not R2P situations, but they *can* be if mass atrocity crimes are also involved, and this may have been the case here. It was not unreasonable, accordingly, for some countries to raise the issue in these terms, although there was a high risk for a time that doing so would be counterproductive both in terms of winning the generals' cooperation and for the longer term acceptance of the R2P norm.

The Burma cyclone case raised many difficult and complex issues, and it is worth spelling out this short answer a little more fully. Of course, terrible natural catastrophes like this one, or the Chinese earthquake that followed it a few days later, cry out for a humanitarian, protective response by the country's own government and by anyone else in a position to offer assistance. But they are not normally, on the face of it, about protecting people from "genocide, war crimes, ethnic cleansing, and crimes against humanity." If the language of R2P (and in particular the sharp military end of it) is invoked when such mass atrocity crimes are not involved, then that will mean the evaporation of any remaining international consensus in favor of the new norm. And that means that when the next case of genocide or ethnic cleansing comes along we will be back to the same old depressing arguments about the primacy of sovereignty that led us into the horrors of inaction in Rwanda and Srebrenica in the 1990s. That is one of the reasons why, when French Foreign Minister Bernard Kouchner made an initial statement arguing that the generals' dilatory response justified coercive intervention under the "responsibility to protect" principle and proposing that the Security Council pass a resolution which "authorises the delivery and imposes this on the Burmese government," he generated a storm of controversy.[14] (The other reason was the fear that this threat would be counterproductive in winning any still-possible cooperation from the generals.) But what if man-made mass atrocity crimes *were* also involved, and Kouchner had put the argument expressly in these terms (as he and others in fact later did)? What made the Burma/Myanmar case such a difficult, borderline one is that the Burmese military regime, in initially resisting all external help in the way that it did—even though such help was immediately available in large quantities—appeared to be so recklessly indifferent to the fate of its own people that it was arguable it *was* committing crimes against humanity. The definition of such crimes (in the Rome Statute establishing the ICC, as well as in customary international law) embraces, along with widespread or systematic murder, torture, persecution, and the like, "other inhumane acts of a similar character intentionally causing great suffering, or serious injury to body or to mental or physical health." That leaves plenty for the lawyers to argue about—starting with whether "intentionally" covers harm caused by reckless negligence or indifference—but at least a prima facie case could be made. Further complicating the Burma/Myanmar story is that, even if such a prima facie case could have been made, that would not have been in itself enough to justify a military intervention: as always, R2P allows the use of military force only with Security Council endorsement, and only as a last resort, after prevention has failed, when it is clear that no less extreme form of reaction could possibly halt or avert the harm in question, that the response is proportional to that harm, and that on balance more good than damage will be done by the intervention. Even if the military intervention had taken the form only of helicopter air drops and boat landings of supplies, it may have been practically ineffective, in the absence of a supporting relief operation on the ground, and—by generating a response from the Burmese military—may have ignited a full-blown conflict that, quite apart from its other impacts, could only have added further to the misery of the cyclone victims.[15]

In the event, enough assistance was delivered by local nongovernmental organizations, foreign relief organizations with personnel already in-country, the military itself, and external relief organizations it finally allowed—mainly through Asian intermediaries—to deliver substantial supplies, for the feared post-cyclone disaster to be avoided. And the affair did generate a serious international debate about R2P that appears to have advanced, if only a little, international understanding of the scope and limits of the norm along the lines here suggested.[16] It was always going to be difficult to win agreement that the scale of the government's default (involving acts of omission more than commission and indifference more than hostility to those suffering) was such as to constitute a crime against humanity; or that a military operation conducted without any local consent or cooperation (even one limited, as proposed here, to the delivery of relief supplies by foreign military aircraft or boats) could possibly succeed in its immediate objectives; or that such an intervention would not (for example, by provoking military retaliation) make the overall situation even worse for those on the ground. But none of this meant, any more than in the case of Darfur, that the R2P norm was proven valueless. Certainly many raised anxious concerns as to what its application actually meant in this situation, and many opposed outright the question of military intervention being even considered. But almost no one was to be heard saying that the Burma/Myanmar cyclone disaster, and the generals' response to it, was none of the rest of the world's business. On the contrary, the regime's behavior—particularly when compared with China's welcoming of international support to cope with its own catastrophic Szechuan earthquake, occurring at the same time—came under immense and sustained international condemnation, including from most of the country's regional neighbors. And the pressure that was applied—not least from those countries like France and the United Kingdom that were willing to squarely raise the issue in R2P terms, and in particular to open up the question as to whether crimes against humanity might be involved—can reasonably be argued to have been the main reason the regime opened its doors to any international support at all.[17]

There is a variation on the general misunderstanding being discussed—"that R2P covers all human protection issues"—that deserves a little more attention. This is the notion that "every kind of *conflict* or *human rights abuse* is a potential R2P situation." The problem here is not so much R2P being stretched to deal with all the world's ills, from HIV/AIDS to climate change, but being too indiscriminately applied to a narrower group of them—those that are conflict or human rights related. Of course, people do need protection from the horror and misery of any violent conflict and from the ugliness of tyrannical human rights abuse; again, one can easily see how, linguistically, the R2P principle could be seen as having ready application. But, again, R2P situations must be more narrowly defined.

If they are perceived as extending across the full range of human rights violations by governments against their own people, or all kinds of internal conflict situations, it will be difficult to build and sustain any kind of consensus for action. If this wide reach is accepted, we will rapidly return to an environment where governments with the capacity to assist or intervene will find themselves trying to explain to their voters about how, if they do so engage in a particular mass atrocity case, this won't mean a potential multitude of further foreign entanglements. And, of course, it will be an environment in which vulnerable governments will be massively reinforced in their concern about their sovereignty being at risk from interventionary overreach, and much more inclined, as a result, to throw cold water on the whole R2P enterprise.

Of course, it is very tempting to broaden R2P's application beyond the actual or feared commission of mass atrocity crimes: it is the case that issues of civilian protection (from loss of life, injury, economic loss, and assaults on human dignity) are always involved in any deadly conflict, whatever its cause and whatever its scale, and in any significant human rights violation. And, of course, it is true that some full-fledged R2P mass atrocity situations evolve out of less extreme human rights violations, or out of general conflict environments. But, again, to widen the focus too much is dangerous from the perspective of undermining R2P's utility as a rallying cry. If too much is bundled under the R2P banner, we run the risk of diluting its capacity to mobilize international consensus in the cases where it is really needed.

FIVE: "IRAQ 2003 WAS AN EXAMPLE OF THE APPLICATION OF THE R2P NORM AND A FORETASTE OF THINGS TO COME"

Few misunderstandings have been more persistent, or have done more to undermine global acceptance of R2P, than the perception that the coalition invasion of Iraq in 2003 was a good example of the responsibility to protect principle at work. It was in fact nothing of the kind, and—quite apart from its botched implementation—stands rather as a classic example of how *not* to apply the R2P norm. In the first place, in the absence of Security Council authorization—and any credible claim of self-defense against actual or imminent attack—the invasion was simply illegal under international law. Second, the invasion had none of the redeeming mitigating factors that in some cases (as discussed in chapter 6) may work to soften, if never eliminate, that illegality: it was not only illegal but illegitimate.

Why, then, does the notion that Iraq in 2003 was a proper case of R2P in action—and, as such, gives good grounds for criticizing the whole norm—have such a tenacious hold? This is due, more than anything else, to the enthusiasm with which, in explaining why a military invasion was necessary, some of the coalition partners, the United Kingdom in particular, came to hang their hats on the tyrannical and murderous character of the Saddam Hussein regime. That was not the explanation of choice for President Bush, who preferred to focus on the issue of weapons of mass destruction or Iraq's alleged connection with the al Qaeda terrorists responsible for September 11. But as these rationales crumbled away for want of any serious supporting evidence, the human rights argument was the only one left with any shred of credibility and was embraced accordingly—although, to be fair to Prime Minister Blair, his instinctive distaste for the undoubtedly brutal and ugly Saddam regime, and desire to enable a better life for the Iraqi people appears to have been his primary motive from the outset.

The truth of the matter is that Iraq in 2003 would have been, applying the kind of criteria discussed below, on anyone's R2P country watch list and a suitable candidate for a variety of preventive and reactive responses from the international community designed to improve the human rights environment. But it was simply not a case for coercive military intervention, applying the criteria of legitimacy that the ICISS commissioners, the High-Level Panel, and Secretary-General Annan have all argued to be necessary ingredients of R2P decisionmaking. The problem arises right at the threshold level, when one is weighing the gravity of the threat involved. Although there were clearly significant human rights violations continuing to occur (which justified international concern and response, for example, by way of censure and sanctions), and although mass atrocity crimes had clearly occurred in the past—against the Kurds in the late 1980s and the southern Shiites in the early 1990s—which justified close international attention to a whole variety of preventive strategies to ensure that they did not occur again, such crimes were neither actually occurring nor apprehended as being likely to occur when the coalition invaded the country in early 2003.

The argument for coercive military intervention would have been a very strong one a decade and more earlier, when the Iraqi regime was slaughtering large numbers of Kurds and Shiites—while the world in both cases deliberately turned its gaze away. But for a number of years before 2003, the Iraqi regime's behavior, for all its brutality, was not much worse than that of a score or two of other countries. If countries could be a suitable case for military treatment on the basis of their past behavior, when their current or likely future behavior, however bad, could not justify it, any prospect of international consensus around R2P would evaporate. Robert Mugabe's Zimbabwe, for one, would be fair game, not on the basis of his recent onslaughts on democracy and human rights and the immiseration of his entire country, but rather because of the massacres perpetrated by his supporters in Matabeleland in the mid-1980s. It might, at first sight, be thought attractive to have any rationale at all to deal with a regime so discredited, but this is not the way to mobilize international consensus. To be able to pluck rationales off the shelf in this way is simply to undermine the whole R2P norm, and ensure that when the time comes to respond to mass atrocity crimes happening here and now, or imminently feared, no one will be listening.[18]

The irony is that while Iraq in 2003 was not an R2P situation of a kind justifying military intervention, it may well have become one subsequently. With more than 2 million people displaced and scores of thousands killed in postinvasion sectarian violence, the situation remains eminently capable of generating ethnic cleansing and genocide on a scale even greater than that witnessed in the Balkans. At the time of this writing, in mid-2008, despite some improvements in both the security and political environment in recent months, there is every reason to fear that—particularly if there were to be now a precipitate withdrawal of foreign forces from the center of the country—the present situation will rapidly deteriorate into massive further outbreaks of communal and sectarian violence beyond the capacity of the Iraqi government to control, and from which it would be unconscionable for the wider world to stand aloof.

Identifying Countries of R2P Concern

The crucial need, to repeat a recurring theme of this book, is to ensure that when the next extreme, conscience-shocking situation stares us in the face—as one surely will—the reflex response will not be to ask whether the international community should act at all, but only when and how it should act. Viewed in this way, there will always be many fewer countries in the world of explicitly R2P concern than there are of more general conflict or human rights concern. How should we go about identifying them?

THE NEED FOR SELECTIVITY

Around the world, at any given time, there are some seventy different situations that can reasonably be described as ones of actual or potential deadly conflict—the International Crisis Group documents them each month in its *CrisisWatch* bulletin—and there are at least as many countries, not all the same ones, where significant human rights violations are occurring, as documented by Human Rights Watch and Freedom House surveys, among others.[19] But applying fairly strict criteria, for all the reasons stated in the above discussion, there are perhaps no more than a dozen countries at any one time, not 70 or 100 or more, that can reasonably be classified as R2P situations.

What are those criteria? What is it that makes an "R2P situation" or makes a country one of "R2P concern"? The short answer is that R2P situations are those where mass atrocity crimes—involving genocide, ethnic cleansing, or other war crimes or crimes against humanity—are actually occurring or imminently about to occur, or where the situation could deteriorate to this extent in the medium or longer term unless appropriate preventive measures are taken. They are situations, actual or reasonably foreseeable, that should engage the attention of the international community simply because of the particularly conscience-shocking character of the conduct actually or potentially involved.

More than just a short answer is really needed here, however, because there will always be differences of view—often strongly and honestly held—about how to characterize particular cases. It should be easy enough, on the face of it, to identify situations where mass atrocity crimes are actually occurring, but evidence of the requisite quality is not always immediately available, and even when it is, characterizations may differ. For example in Darfur, the question arises whether what is happening, at the time of writing in mid-2008, is properly described as a continuation of the atrocity crimes that unquestionably occurred in 2003–04, or whether rather, while the country is still bearing all the scars of those days and the problem still requires immense international effort to resolve, the situation has changed into a kind of conflict much less distinguishable from many others. And what of Zimbabwe? Has Robert Mugabe's despoliation of his own people—extending in mid-2008 to the winning of a further election by unleashing a campaign of murderous violence against his political opponents which left him as the only candidate—approached a level we could reasonably call mass atrocity crimes, or does it still fall a little short of that?

Again it should not, prima facie, be all that difficult to identify situations where mass atrocity crimes are very imminently likely to occur, but the case of Kenya at the end of 2007 showed just how quickly and comparatively unexpectedly some situations can explode. And what of the temporary emergence of some apparently ethnicity-manipulating hate speech in Côte d'Ivoire in 2004: was it an indicator of imminent catastrophe—an alarming reminder of what resulted from the broadcasts of Radio Milles Collines immediately before and during the Rwandan genocide—or rather just a product of irresponsible political leadership, which demanded censure on human rights grounds but needed to generate no particular wider anxiety?[20]

The much more difficult task is to identify those cases where the risk of mass atrocity crimes is in the medium or longer term. Is the situation in Kosovo, with its independence still strongly contested by Serbia, Russia, and others, capable of deteriorating back into the large-scale killing and ethnic cleansing that prompted military intervention, unhappily without Security Council approval in 1999? Is Sri Lanka best understood as a particularly bloody and intractable separatist conflict, or, does it—given its ethnic dimension and the kinds of atrocities that have occurred in the past— count as the kind of R2P situation in the making that demands preventive action, by the Sri Lankan government and with the support of the wider international community, to ensure that further deterioration does not occur? Is the current political situation in Burma/Myanmar, leaving aside the separate issue of its lamentable response to the May 2008 cyclone as discussed above, best characterized and responded to as a human rights and democracy problem, requiring whatever mix of pressure and persuasion will best work, or as an R2P situation in the making?

And what of the situations in Russia and China? As mentioned earlier in this chapter, Beijing has certainly had an ugly record in past decades of violently suppressing separatist dissent in Tibet and Xinjiang and domestic protest elsewhere, and the crackdowns of early 2008 in Tibet and elsewhere in the context of sensitivities unleashed by the Olympic torch relay, give some reason for concern that those days may not be over. But there are also grounds for believing that, as China's participation and stature in global institutions grows, and as its governance becomes increasingly sophisticated, its leaders simply will not see the commission of mass atrocity crimes as a remotely permissible option. But no one can be completely sure. Similarly with Russia: for all the advances since the collapse of communism, the Kremlin's insouciant response to international criticism under President Putin, and the numerous abuses that have occurred in the course of the Russian suppression of the Chechen independence movement since the mid-1990s, including the massacre of scores of civilians in Grozny in February 2000 and thousands of enforced disappearances from

1999 until at least 2005, have not done a great deal to win international confidence.[21] Which way will things move in the period ahead?

WATCH LIST CRITERIA

All these questions point to the need for some further criteria to be developed and properly applied if any kind of credible "R2P watch list" is to be prepared. While a great deal of work has been done on early warning signs, particularly in the case of conflict generally, with some attempt to build complex quantitative models as well as lists of qualitative indicators, this enterprise remains for the most part an art rather than a science.[22] My own long experience as a government minister and head of a nongovernmental organization working in these areas, constantly trying to make these essentially seat of the pants judgments, is that there are five factors in particular that one should take into account in making the call that a particular country, in situations where mass atrocities are not obviously occurring right at that time, is indeed one of "R2P concern."

The first relevant consideration is whether the country in question has a past history of mass atrocities perpetrated by repressive governments or different groups in the population against each other or both. We know that one of the best single indicators of future conflict is past conflict, and unhappily the same seems to hold true for atrocity crimes.

The second is whether tensions of a kind that have given rise to conflict in the past, even if falling short of the perpetration of full-scale mass atrocities, still persist. One thing to look for here are formally articulated and credible grievances, about constitutional and legal status, political representation, group or individual discrimination, economic wealth and opportunity, repressed cultural identity, and the like. But these are not the only indicators of relevant tension. As Paul Collier has pointed out in the large body of work, now brilliantly summarized in his recent book *The Bottom Billion*, "grievance" is often an overworked term in analyzing the causes of conflict, and very often more direct factors are at work, in particular low income and low economic growth, which generate a pervasive sense of hopelessness, especially among young men, creating thereby a ready pool of recruits for almost any cause or for power seekers pursuing no credible cause at all.[23]

The third factor is the strength of the country's coping mechanisms when it comes to resolving grievances and tensions. Conflict of a nonviolent kind is endemic in all societies: different interests and perceptions of interest will always ensure that. What matters is how good that society's institutional structures are for resolving that conflict peacefully, as distinct from being inadequate to the task or, worse, counterproductive—in particular, in the present context, the political system, the legal system, and the policy and army security infrastructure.

The fourth factor is the receptivity of the country or society in question to external influence, either positively, in the form of welcoming assistance to solve its problems, or negatively, in the sense of being susceptible to economic, political, diplomatic, legal, and—in the last resort—military pressure. Closed societies, or those wholly indifferent to what anyone else thinks of them, are more likely to be equally indifferent to how their own people are treated.

And the final factor, here as so often elsewhere, is good leadership. Countries with such leadership tend to be able to solve almost any problem—including a past history of atrocities, continuing tensions, and even very weak institutions of governance. Bad leaders, by contrast, can make any problem worse and—as with Mugabe—create catastrophe out of a hitherto almost problem-free environment.

Everything depends on case-by-case analysis, and these factors are by no means exhaustive of what would need to be taken into account in any full risk evaluation. Moreover, like all such criteria (including those for the use of force discussed in chapter 6), they are not inherently capable of being applied with push-button precision, even where quantifiable matters are involved. To the extent they involve nonquantifiable and subjective judgments, these criteria certainly will not be applied the same way by every observer and will not all point in the same direction at the same time. But they may at least help to narrow and focus the argument in particular cases, and certainly should help reinforce the general case that R2P situations are and should be seen as relatively few and far between, and not nearly as common as cases of conflict or human rights concern.

Trying to apply these factors, and also taking into account the very detailed analysis of many countries of conflict concern over the years by my own International Crisis Group, it would seem that there is a good case for regarding a number of them as "countries of R2P concern," not so much, in most instances, because of what is happening in each of them right now but more because of the risk of them deteriorating over time into situations where mass atrocities do occur. Opinions are bound to differ, but as of this writing in mid-2008, the clearest prima facie candidates that might be considered for inclusion in a current watch list (in alphabetical order, not by degree of seriousness or imminence of risk or anything else) are Burma/Myanmar, Burundi, China, Congo, Iraq, Kenya, Sri Lanka, Somalia, Sudan, Uzbekistan, and Zimbabwe.

It should hardly need to be said, after addressing earlier in this chapter all the most common misunderstandings about R2P, that this is, most emphatically, *not* a list of countries being suggested as suitable cases for coercive military intervention. It is, rather, a list of countries that are vulnerable, where situations are delicately poised and could further deteriorate, and whose people—or certain groups among them—are at significant risk of becoming victims of new mass atrocity crimes if efforts are not made to put in place, or sustain, appropriate preventive measures. The responsibility for such preventive effort remains, as the 2005 World Summit Outcome Document makes clear, primarily with the governments of the sovereign states concerned, but with such assistance and support from neighbors and the wider international community as is appropriate. The toolbox of available preventive measures is the subject of the next chapter.

*Operationalizing the
Responsibility to Protect*

CHAPTER FOUR

Before the Crisis:
The Responsibility to Prevent

Prevention is the single most important dimension of the responsibility to protect.

—ICISS, *The Responsibility to Protect*, 2001

Wars can be prevented just as surely as they can be provoked, and we who fail to prevent them must share in the guilt for the dead.

—General Omar Bradley, June 1948

Had the world but eyes to see them, early warning signs were abundant for just about every one of the world's worst cases of genocide and mass atrocity. Hitler's Germany, Rwanda, and the former Yugoslavia had all for some years been characterized by growing repression, abuse of human rights, and, especially, hate speech directed at often vulnerable groups blamed for a country's troubles.[1] But the signs were not heeded by those in a position to make a difference, and the necessary action was not taken in time. Experience has constantly taught us that effective prevention is far less costly in blood and treasure than cure—than reacting only after many lives have been lost, a lust for revenge aroused, and reconciliation made that much harder.[2]

Recognition of these realities—that prevention is the single most important dimension of the responsibility to protect—is at the heart of the 2005 World Summit's conclusions, as it was of the reports leading up to them. The unanimously agreed outcome document could not have been clearer in ascribing the responsibility to *prevent* to both individual member states and the wider international community. The relevant language, with emphasis added, reads as follows:

138. Each individual State has the responsibility to protect its populations from genocide, war crimes, ethnic cleansing and crimes

against humanity. This responsibility entails the *prevention of such crimes, including their incitement,* through appropriate and necessary means. *We accept that responsibility* and will act in accordance with it. *The international community should,* as appropriate, *encourage and help States to exercise this responsibility* and support the United Nations in establishing an *early warning capability.*

139. The international community, through the United Nations, also has the *responsibility to use appropriate diplomatic, humanitarian and other peaceful means, in accordance with Chapters VI and VIII of the Charter,* to help to protect populations from genocide, war crimes, ethnic cleansing and crimes against humanity. . . . We also intend to commit ourselves, as necessary and appropriate, to *helping States build capacity to protect* their populations from genocide, war crimes, ethnic cleansing and crimes against humanity and to assisting those which are under stress *before crises and conflicts break out.*[3]

For good measure, the heads of state and government also agreed, in paragraph 140, to "fully support the mission of the Special Adviser of the Secretary-General on the Prevention of Genocide."

The basic principle of conflict prevention is firmly based in Chapter VI of the UN Charter, which identifies a catalogue of preventive measures for parties to stop and settle conflict by peaceful means, including "negotiation, enquiry, mediation, conciliation, arbitration, judicial settlement" and (as provided for more fully in Chapter VIII) "resort to regional agencies or arrangements."[4] But it was not really until the 1990s, in the post–cold war era, that conflict prevention assumed any kind of prominence in the discourse or institutional behavior of UN member states. Secretary-General Boutros Boutros-Ghali's pathbreaking 1992 *Agenda for Peace* emphasized the UN's role "to try through diplomacy to remove the sources of danger before violence results," identifying preventive diplomacy as "the most desirable and efficient' tool.[5] But it was the Carnegie Commission on Preventing Deadly Conflict, cochaired by David Hamburg and Cyrus Vance, with its 1999 report, and more specifically the seventy-five associated books, reports, and monographs to which it gave birth, that gave most enduring momentum to an emerging "culture of conflict prevention."[6] The commission's work was prominently cited in Secretary-General Kofi Annan's comprehensive and warmly received 2001 report on the *Prevention of Armed Conflict*, the leitmotif of which was the need "to move from a culture of reaction to a culture of prevention."[7]

Effective conflict prevention, and by extension the prevention of mass atrocity crimes, depends on three major factors. First, it requires detailed knowledge of the countries and regions at risk: strong analysis and good early warning are essential preconditions. Second, policymakers have to fully understand the comprehensive "toolbox" of policy instruments potentially available to them, long and short term, for prevention of the outbreak, continuation, or recurrence of conflict.[8] Third, as for almost every public policy area, conflict prevention requires the availability in practice, not just theoretically, of capability to deliver the appropriate responses and the necessary political will to apply those resources. Early warning and the toolbox available to prevent the outbreak of conflict and mass atrocities are the subject of this chapter. Subsequent chapters address the toolboxes of reactive (chapters 5 and 6) and postconflict measures (chapter 7), and the questions of institutional capability (chapters 8 and 9) and political will (chapter 10).

Analysis and Early Warning

IDENTIFYING THE CAUSES OF CONFLICT AND MASS ATROCITIES

If any kind of prevention is to be effective, everything starts with identifying those situations that have the potential to generate mass atrocity crimes. What makes analysis so difficult is that there appear to be so many of them, including—to take just one recent catalogue—"historical grievances and enmities; recent or bitterly rankling social traumas; arrogant elites prospering in the midst of widespread poverty; poor governance; poor education (including strong prejudice); rapid political, social, or economic dislocation; colonial occupation; war; and revolution."[9] Because so many mass atrocity crimes occur under the cover of war, either between states or within states, it is important, at least in the first instance, to look at the potential for conflict generally and not to cast one's exploratory net too narrowly.[10] But any kind of prediction in this area is neither easy nor uncontroversial, and however one approaches the task, there is bound to be disagreement: the task for analysts is to reduce that to manageable bounds.

General analyses of the causes of war are legion, and a very large body of explanatory and argumentative literature now exists just on violent conflict within states, a good deal of it supported by excellent empirical research. Initially the work on internal conflict tended to focus on broadly political factors, with much attention given in the early post–cold war period to the competition to fill power vacuums caused by the collapse of external support for repressive regimes.[11] Much emphasis has also been placed on violence generated by groups defined by their ethnicity, religion, class, or region, resentful at social discrimination against them or their exclusion from a proper share of governing power.[12]

Subsequent attention turned to more specifically economic factors, with a lively debate on the role of "greed" rather than "grievance" in fostering and sustaining violence. Oxford's Paul Collier has been the most prominent skeptic of justifications advanced by rebel movements in terms of repression, exploitation, and exclusion (not to mention those of "politically motivated academics . . . with their own hobbyhorse which usually cast rebels as heroes").[13] In his earlier formulations of the "greed theory," it was argued that loot seeking rather than grievance or justice seeking was the key factor in the onset of violent rebellion, with resources pursued for their own sake rather than to sustain war.[14] More nuanced subsequent formulations focused more on the opportunity for violence than its motivation, emphasizing the role of access to lucrative natural resources and diaspora networks, and of high numbers of poorly educated youth, in making rebellion more feasible.[15]

More recently, it seems to have become generally accepted, as case studies have multiplied, that one-dimensional general explanations of any kind are bound to be unsatisfactory, and that we are condemned to acknowledging that "most of today's conflicts are a complex amalgam of economic, political, ethnic and security dynamics, in which contests over resources intersect with and often reinforce contests over identity and power."[16] Interplaying economic, political, social, and cultural factors vary from place to place and often over time within a particular place: Angola is as clear an example as any, with characterizations of its four-decade-long conflict changing from a struggle for national liberation (1961–74), to cold war proxy conflict (1975–91), to a resource-based civil war (1992–2002).[17] At the end of the day, general analyses of the kind just discussed may be extremely helpful in getting us to ask the right *questions*, but it is a mistake to think that in any given situation they can provide answers. As Collier himself says of his own model: "It cannot be used for prediction. It can tell you what typically are the structural factors underlying proneness to civil war . . . and from this it can tell you the sort of countries that are most at risk. But it cannot tell you whether Sierra Leone will have another civil war next year. That depends on a myriad of short-term events."[18]

"Objective" versus Field-Based Early Warning

Recognizing the multiplicity of variables involved and their tendency to change over time—but at the same time the hunger of policymakers for *some* kind of predictive tools to make their lives easier when it comes to preventing mass atrocities and conflict generally—a large and growing academic and governmental cottage industry has arisen devoted to creating objective "early warning" models. To reduce to its bare essentials—perhaps a little unfairly—an activity that has occupied an inordinate number of highly capable people for an inordinate amount of time, the idea is to identify and give comparative weightings to those variables that seem to have most causal relevance for the problem at hand, accumulate quantifiable data relevant to each of them, set the computer program running, and wait for the appropriate alarm bells to ring. Part of the attraction of such objective models is that their conclusions may appear less biased by analyst judgment, and in that sense be easier to sell to countries otherwise reluctant to acknowledge that there is a problem.

There are at least thirty such models, of varying degrees of complexity and ambition, currently publicly accessible. They include at the national government level C/FACTS in the United States and CIFP in Canada; at the international organization level, the UN Development Program's CDA and the World Bank's CAF; at the academic-NGO-think tank level, FEWER and Swisspeace's FAST; and at the private level, CRG ratings and Standard and Poor's Ratings Group.[19] The trouble with all of them is that, for all the effort invested and whether the focus is on predicting long-term trends or near-term crises, the "objective" indicators tell us no more—and in many cases rather less—than we already tend to know from good qualitative analysis, and there is a deep reluctance, accordingly, among practitioners to rely upon them. A recent study by the Center for Strategic and International Studies in Washington, D.C., found that they are seen by decision-makers as having "minimal value beyond confirming what is commonly known": the main reasons are summarized as continuing disagreement as to what are the relevant variables and how they should be weighted, the unreliability of much baseline data, and the inherent difficulty of expressing much relevant data in metric terms at all.[20]

As was suggested in the last chapter, there may be some utility—if one is trying to put together some kind of watch list of countries most likely to require preventive attention—in developing general checklists of the kinds of factors that are most likely to put countries at risk of conflict and mass atrocities. The one offered there focused on five general factors, none of them readily quantifiable: past history, continuing tensions, availability of coping mechanisms, receptivity to external influence, and quality of leadership. But the bottom line is that if one is seriously in the business of understanding how close to the brink is a particular situation, and the kind of policy responses that need to be deployed to avert some serious harm occurring, there is absolutely no substitute for case-by-case field-based analysis.

Every conflict, or potential conflict or mass atrocity situation, does have its own dynamic, and there has to be a comprehensive understanding of all the factors at work. Everything starts with having an accurate take on what is happening on the ground, the issues that are resonating, and the personalities and local dynamics—political, economic, social, cultural, and personal—that are driving them. For a variety of reasons, mainly security and budgetary, traditional diplomats are not performing this assessment with as much breadth and depth as they traditionally have—it is hard to get out and about when you are locked up in a fortress or have minimal staff resources—and both early warning and effective conflict prevention capacity are more at risk as a result. Filling this gap, providing the kind of detailed field-based analysis that is absolutely critical for effective conflict prevention and resolution, has been the primary rationale for the creation and work of my own International Crisis Group, now widely seen as the leading organization in this field.[21]

FROM ANALYSIS AND WARNING TO EFFECTIVE RESPONSE

It is obvious enough, but needs saying, that good analysis is not only a critical precondition for getting early responses from those in a position to deliver them but is critical for getting the *right* policy response. How an emerging conflict or mass atrocity situation is characterized, in terms of its causes, both underlying and immediate, will make or break the effectiveness of the action then taken. If, for example, an emerging conflict is characterized more in terms of criminal greed than the failure to resolve real underlying political grievances, not only might opportunities be missed for effective political mediation or constitutional accommodation but commodity embargoes might be imposed that have the effect of raising the value of the targeted activity—thus either creating incentives that may not have been there before for unscrupulous profit seekers, or adding new layers of economic misery to reinforce other genuine grievances, or both.[22]

The timeliness of the response is again crucial. If early warning alarm bells do not generate an early response they might as well not be rung at all. "Wishful thinking," as David Hamburg has put it, citing the awful warning of Rwanda among others, "can lead to catastrophic missteps. It encourages widespread denial, avoidance of serious problems, and delay in facing them. When necessity finally forces leaders to cope with such problems later, the costs and risks are inevitably much greater."[23] An example, little known but compelling, of timely and appropriate action bearing possibly very large fruits indeed was the response of Juan Méndez, in his then role as the UN Secretary-General's Special Adviser on the Prevention of Genocide, when he learned in the course of a visit to Côte d'Ivoire in November 2004 that hate speech, reminiscent of that spread to such devastating effect over Rwanda's Radio Mille Collines a decade earlier, was beginning to be heard on certain media outlets: he issued a statement making clear that such behavior was potentially subject to prosecution in the International Criminal Court and calling upon the national authorities to put an immediate end to it, which they then did.[24]

Making the transition from effective analysis and early warning to timely and effective response demands effective institutional capability, a theme that will be taken up again in chapter 8. But that means not just having people in place with resources and influence at their disposal. It means those on the front line of policy reaction having a very clear understanding of the policy measures available to them and which are most appropriate to the particular situation with which they are confronted. As with understanding what might trigger deadly conflict and mass atrocity crimes, so with applying the right preventive solutions. The crucial thing is to recognize not only that each situation has its own characteristics and that one-size spanners don't fit all, but that each situation is likely to require a complex combination of measures, with the balance between them bound to change, and to have to change, over time as circumstances evolve. Conflict prevention is a business for the fleet of foot, not the plodders—but unfortunately in international affairs, as in life itself, the latter usually have the numbers.

As a result of the much more systematic focus on conflict prevention since the early 1990s, we now have a much better understanding not only of the causes of deadly conflict and mass atrocities but of the preventive and reactive measures available to deal with these problems. There are many different ways of categorizing and classifying them, and there is a voluminous literature on the subject.[25] But the simplest way of getting one's head around the options available in the preconflict situations with which this chapter deals is to think of a toolbox with two main trays: for structural prevention measures (which tend to be more long-term and "root cause" oriented) and more direct operational measures (which tend to be more responsive to short-term crises), respectively: see box 4-1. Each tray has four basic compartments for, respectively, political and diplomatic measures, legal and constitutional measures, economic and social measures, and security sector measures; and each compartment has as many subcompartments as necessary to house the kinds of measures available— for example, "direct economic measures" would have separate slots for positive and negative incentives (sanctions), respectively. Similar (though more narrowly specialized) toolboxes are available for the reaction and rebuilding stages of the R2P response continuum; these are addressed in subsequent chapters. The elements of all three toolboxes are charted together in appendix B.

It is important to appreciate, in the discussion of different preventive measures that follows, that the primary focus is on what states at risk can do for themselves, by their own national effort and with their own national capacity, and what they can do voluntarily for each other by way of offering support. The prevention of mass atrocity crimes, like the prevention of conflict more generally, should start, and if possible finish, with the minimum of intrusion. The World Summit Outcome Document was clear about that, but in doing so did no more than reflect the spirit and letter of the reports leading up to it, all of which emphasized that, at all stages of the conflict cycle, less intrusive measures were to be preferred to more intrusive ones, and that persuasion was always to be preferred to coercion if it could produce the necessary results.

BOX 4-1. THE PREVENTION TOOLBOX

Structural
- Promote good governance
- Promote membership in international organizations

Structural
- Support economic development
- Support education for tolerance
- Community peacebuilding

Direct
- Preventive diplomacy
- Threat of political sanctions

Direct
- Aid conditionality
- Threat of economic sanctions
- Economic incentives

Political/Diplomatic Measures

Economic/Social Measures

Structural
- Promote fair constitutional structures
- Promote human rights
- Promote rule of law
- Fight corruption

Structural
- Security sector reform
- Military to civilian governance
- Confidence-building measures
- Small arms and light weapons control

Direct
- Legal dispute resolution
- Threat of international criminal prosecution

Direct
- Preventive deployment
- Nonterritorial show of force
- Threat of arms embargo or end of military cooperation programs

Constitutional/Legal Measures

Security Sector Measures

Political and Diplomatic Strategies

STRUCTURAL AND LONGER-TERM POLITICAL MEASURES

Achieving *good governance* in all its manifestations—representative, responsive, accountable, and capable—is at the heart of effective long-term conflict and mass atrocity prevention. Some conflicts that may appear at first sight to be clear-cut examples of loot seeking or a contest over resources—in Sierra Leone and the Democratic Republic of the Congo, for example—were more fundamentally driven by failures of basic governance: decades of misrule and corruption by parasitic state elites and associated socioeconomic deterioration and institutional decay. These made their ruling regimes extremely vulnerable to both general popular discontent and the specific ambitions of rebels and various external actors, with poor governance not only fueling political and economic grievances but reducing the risk and cost of mounting violent challenges to it.[26]

Both individual states themselves and the wider international community have mutually supportive roles to play in developing the institutions and processes—legislative, executive, and judicial—of effective government. While development assistance programs from donors the world over are devoting ever-increasing attention to capacity building of this kind—as distinct from the earlier focus on immediate poverty alleviation programs—and that support has proved extremely important in helping stabilize a number of potentially volatile situations (with Burundi being, here as elsewhere, a good example), it is important to recognize just how much of the responsibility must fall on the shoulders of the states themselves.[27] It is true that a great many simply do not have the physical or financial capacity by themselves to deliver material well-being to their people. But what every state *does* have, at the very least, is the capacity to deliver political and civil rights—giving everyone a direct say in how they are governed and the ability to talk and act freely, including through the media, subject only to reasonable respect for the rights of others—and distributive justice (ensuring, through taxation and related policies that gross inequalities of wealth and income are minimized).[28] The willingness to accept strong civil society organizations is both a measure of the quality of existing governance and a means of ensuring its improvement in the future, and no state should be immune from pressure to encourage their growth.

Part of the process of building up preventive structural safeguards is to encourage states to join and participate actively in *international organizations and regimes* (that is, global, regional, and bilateral treaties and arrangements) designed to minimize threats to security, promote confidence and trust, and create institutional frameworks for dialogue and cooperation. Isolated and insulated states like Burma/Myanmar are among those least likely to be sensitive to the needs and aspirations of their people, and achieving any shift toward a more open and internationalist perspective is worth the effort.[29] At another level of engagement entirely, it remains worth saying that the establishment of the European Union has been perhaps the most effective structural conflict prevention measure in history, imposing a multitude of good governance disciplines not just on its existing members but more particularly its aspiring ones. That said, it has to be acknowledged that Serbia and perhaps Macedonia and Bosnia remain test cases for anyone inclined to be too optimistic about the attractions of EU membership making quarrels about ethnicity and territory in the Balkans a thing of the past, while the tensions emerging in recent times over new members joining both the EU (in the case of Turkey) and NATO (in the case of Macedonia, Georgia, and Ukraine) have made it a little more difficult to argue that greater international organizational engagement is always a net positive. Here, as elsewhere, it is a matter of case-by-case evaluation.

DIRECT POLITICAL MEASURES

All diplomacy is in a sense preventive: managing differences, addressing potential disputes, and resolving real conflicts before they become violent is what diplomats *do*. But the concept of *preventive diplomacy* has acquired real resonance since the end of the cold war created a much more promising environment for all the tools of this trade, including the direct "good offices" role of the UN secretary-general and his staff, fact-finding missions, friends' groups, eminent persons' commissions, conciliation and mediation, and nonofficial "second-track" dialogue.[30] The 2005 Human Security Report calculated that, notwithstanding continuing weaknesses in UN infrastructure, there had been a sixfold increase between 1990 and 2002 in the number of UN diplomatic missions aimed at stopping wars before they started; its authors plausibly claim that this is one of the reasons for the very significant decline over that period in the number of wars, genocidal and other mass atrocities, and number of people dying violent deaths as a result of them.[31]

The techniques mentioned are equally applicable at both the preventive and reactive stages of the conflict cycle but usually more visible in the latter, when actual conflict resolution is involved (and will be discussed again in that context in the next chapter). By contrast diplomacy to prevent the merely threatened initial outbreak of conflict or mass violence is most successful when nothing happens, and practically nobody notices. There have been many such successful but largely unsung efforts over the years, for example, the sustained effort mounted in Burundi (in which South Africa played a particularly important role) to hold together after 1994 a situation that was almost as perilous as that in its neighbor Rwanda; the rapid mobilization of international pressure at the UN (in which the International Crisis Group played a key part) to stop what in November 2007 looked to be the imminent resumption of a major war between Ethiopia and Eritrea; and perhaps above all the heroic efforts of the Organization for Security and Cooperation in Europe (OSCE) high commissioner on national minorities over many years, particularly during the volatile early–cold war period when Max van der Stoel held the post, to quietly stop as many as a dozen major ethnic and language-based conflicts from breaking out across Central and Eastern Europe, from the Baltics to Romania.[32]

Direct preventive diplomacy is normally thought of as a "soft" technique, but it does have a harder end. *Threats of political sanctions*—that is, diplomatic isolation, suspension of organization membership, travel and asset restrictions on targeted persons, "naming and shaming," or other such actions—are part of the diplomatic toolkit and have their place if, but only if, softer approaches fail. The Commonwealth has been more ready than most international organizations to apply these kinds of measures—for example, in its suspension from membership at different times of South Africa, Nigeria, Pakistan, and Zimbabwe for various kinds of egregious rights-violating behavior.[33] But the African Union (AU) and its subregional organizations have also been showing a gradually increasing willingness to impose peer group pressure on misbehaving colleagues. For example, at its annual summit in January 2007, the AU refused to give its revolving chairmanship to Sudanese leader Omar al-Bashir as a result of the deteriorating situation in Sudan, allocating it instead to Ghana's John Kufuor, whose country had emerged well from the application of the African Peer Review Mechanism.[34]

Economic and Social Strategies

STRUCTURAL AND LONGER-TERM ECONOMIC MEASURES

Economic development matters. Certainly it is hard to argue that severe economic deprivation is, as such, a direct cause of conflict or mass atrocities—if it were, the world, with a billion people still living on around a dollar a day, would be much more alarmingly violent than it is now.[35] But there is every reason to accept that economic decline, low income, and high unemployment are contributing conditions, either directly by fueling grievances among particular disadvantaged or excluded groups, or indirectly by reducing the relevant opportunity costs of joining a violent rebellion—or quite probably both.[36] As Paul Collier puts the recruitment point, "Low income means poverty and low growth means hopelessness. Young men . . . come pretty cheap in an environment of hopeless poverty."[37]

More generally, it is now universally acknowledged, as the 2005 World Summit Outcome Document puts it, that "development, peace and security and human rights are interrelated and mutually reinforcing."[38] Development cannot be achieved without security—as the recent history of Iraq and Afghanistan makes clear beyond argument—and security cannot be confidently guaranteed without development. So there is every reason, from a conflict and mass atrocity perspective, to make a major effort to dramatically close the income and opportunity gap between rich and poor countries, and to dramatically reduce levels of both absolute and relative deprivation within countries that are struggling. Achieving the Millennium Development Goals is not just a humanitarian aspiration but a rational security one as well.[39]

The policy measures available to achieve this are well enough known: development assistance and cooperation to address inequities in the distribution of resources or opportunities; encouragement and technical assistance to adopt institutional reforms and internal policies that will increase government efficiency, reduce corruption, generate investment, promote growth and reduce inequality; specific assistance to develop transport and communications infrastructure and improve the management of natural resources; acceptance of trade regimes that will permit greater access to external markets for developing economies and better terms of trade for them; and encouragement of regional and larger economic integration strategies. Development assistance continues by its nature to be based on specific projects, but policymakers have a variety of other tools of external financial support, such as direct budgetary support or debt relief, to shore up a state's financial position before, during, or after conflict in order to prevent it from collapse and promote investment.

There is of course a major continuing debate—no discussion of development assistance would ever be complete without one—on what particular policies, or combination of policies, are likely to work best in achieving commonly shared objectives. Jeffrey Sachs and William Easterly are seen as the major protagonists, with Sachs passionately committed to the Millennium Development Goals and to major additional financial commitments from the developed world to achieve them, and Easterly arguing that most of that money has been and will continue to be wasted and that the primary effort should go into building efficient and accountable organizations.[40] This is not a contest capable of resolution here, or perhaps ever. Most policymakers will see merit in both positions and limp along with strategies wandering uncertainly between the two. But most countries in the global North are at least making a greater effort than they have in the past—incomplete, erratic, and self-serving as that may often be—to address the huge underlying economic problems of large numbers of developing countries, particularly in Africa, and that is to be applauded.

What would justify some more explicit applause would be greater national and international support for what David Hamburg—the doyen of analysts and advocates in this area—calls *education for tolerance,* a crucial item in any agenda addressing the underlying causes of mass atrocity crimes.[41] We know something now about how much damage education for hate can do when practiced in certain Pakistani *madrasas* and elsewhere.[42] But we could usefully pay much more attention to the kinds of formal education and media dissemination programs and strategies that have been devised to cut across ethnocentric divides and stereotypes, and increase positive attitudes and interaction between members of previously hostile or suspicious groups.

More generally, there is a strong case for supporting *community peace-building* programs of the kind run by a great many civil society organizations, both national and international, working with local actors at the grassroots level to dispel the fear, mistrust, and prejudice so often at the heart of intractable conflicts. Examples abound, such as Seeds of Peace, an initiative established in 1993 to bring together Arab and Israeli teenagers between the ages of thirteen and fifteen in a neutral setting to share their experiences, argue about their beliefs, and learn how to cooperate. The program's premise, that "interaction breeds understanding" is based not on the belief that both sides have to like one another but that both sides have to learn to respect each other. [43] It has now expanded its network to encompass over 3,500 young people from several conflict regions around the world including South Asia, Cyprus, and the Balkans.[44] Other forms of community peacebuilding emphasize the need to strengthen sustainable economic development, democracy and respect for human rights, viable political structures, and healthy environmental and social conditions, with the goal of increasing capacity to manage change without resort to conflict.[45] Search for Common Ground, for instance, adopts an integrative approach to resolving what can seem like intractable differences: in Sierra Leone it has set up the Talking Drum Studio (TDS)—a multimedia studio that produces national and district-level radio programs for distribution to radio stations across the country—and the Community Peacebuilding Unit, which organizes solidarity events, builds local and national coalitions, facilitates community dialogue, performs live drama, and offers training to those previously marginalized from the decisionmaking process, specifically women, children, and youth.[46] Swanee Hunt's Initiative for Inclusive Security—incorporating the Women Waging Peace Network—is at the forefront of highlighting the critical role of women in averting violent conflict at all levels; in its first two years alone, the organization conducted more than forty consultations in countries as diverse as Afghanistan, Colombia, Guatemala, Liberia, Rwanda, and Sudan.[47]

DIRECT ECONOMIC MEASURES

Aid conditionality means targeting development assistance so as to achieve particular policy responses from the recipient—for example, the holding of proper elections or the cessation of some more direct human rights abuse. Used this way, aid is not so much a structural measure to address root cause problems but a kind of functional equivalent of broad-based economic sanctions.[48] Conditionality of this kind is controversial. Whether it is ever very useful in changing behavior is a matter for doubt; so too is it contentious whether the denial of aid to people suffering under a recalcitrant regime is ever likely to do more good than harm. In the case of Burma/Myanmar, my own International Crisis Group, after long agonizing and in the face of some criticism from human rights organizations, concluded (before the May 2008 cyclone disaster changed the terms of this debate) that humanitarian assistance concerns should outweigh whatever limited impact the denial of aid might have in concentrating the mind of the military regime on its own iniquity, and that in the continuing effort to avoid a deterioration of the situation into renewed atrocity crimes, other strategies should take precedence.[49]

Direct broad-based economic sanctions—or at least the *threat of economic sanctions*, as a preventive measure—are equally controversial. Including such measures as comprehensive or selective trade embargoes, the freezing or dissolution of trade agreements, capital controls, the withdrawal of investment, and the withdrawal of IMF or World Bank support, they have traditionally been seen as one step, albeit a very significant one, in a graduated process of international pressure falling short of war.[50] If sanctions are to have binding force on the whole international community, they must be authorized by the Security Council under Chapter VII (Article 41) of the UN Charter, but there is no inhibition as a matter of international law on individual countries, or groups of countries, threatening or applying their own. The real question, again, is their utility in achieving legitimate policy objectives and the cost-benefit equation when it comes to assessing the good or harm they involve. This issue is taken up in the next chapter, when the role of economic sanctions as a reactive measure is considered.

Economic incentives, by contrast, are winning more sympathetic interest as a conflict prevention tool. Positive inducements can take such forms as the promise or delivery of better trade terms, new investment, more favorable taxation treatment, access to technology, and lifting existing negative sanctions. Over many years they have been used frequently in diplomatic negotiations, including on such major strategic issues as the Egypt-Israel Camp David accords in 1978, the relinquishment by Ukraine and other former Soviet entities of their nuclear arsenals in 1991, and the nuclear negotiations with North Korea in the early 1990s (and in their current reprise).[51] Although sometimes less popular with critical domestic audiences, who would often prefer to bludgeon perceived bad guys into submission than reward their actual or potential wrongdoing with taxpayer-funded handouts, incentives have the great attraction for policymakers that they actually tend to work—albeit probably best with some sticks in reserve as well.[52] David Cortright identifies what is probably, at the end of the day, the major advantage of incentives over sanctions: their greater sensitivity to some of the basic realities of human psychology. "Incentives foster cooperation and goodwill, whereas sanctions create hostility and separation. Threats tend to generate reactions of fear, anxiety and resistance, whereas the normal responses to a promise or reward are hope, reassurance and attraction. Threats send a message of 'indifference or active hostility'. . . whereas promises 'convey an impression of sympathy and concern.'"[53]

Constitutional and Legal Strategies

Structural and Longer-Term Legal Measures

A sense of security for many people begins with confidence that they live under *fair constitutional structures* not inherently hostile to their interests. In Sudan, for example, the conflict in Darfur in the west is best understood as part of a larger problem in that country: the concentration of power at the center under the Islamist ruling party, the National Congress Party (NCP), and the attendant desire for greater political autonomy and share in national wealth by the major outlying regions—a problem that also lies at the heart of the long-running, appallingly destructive, and still barely resolved civil war between Khartoum and the south, of continuing tensions in the east, and of emerging new tensions in the north.[54] In Somalia, amid all the other problems besetting the country, no sustainable peace will be achievable unless the Somaliland independence issue—with its own complicated history—is resolved, with the African Union capable of playing a decisive role.[55] In Sri Lanka a central reason for the continuation of the bloody conflict that has wracked the country for most of the last quarter century has been the inability of Tamils and Sinhalese, despite the efforts of moderates on both sides, to agree on new constitutional arrangements giving significant autonomy, but falling short of independence, to the Tamil-majority areas of the north and east of the country.[56] In all these cases, and many others like them, enormous domestic sensitivities are involved, and in most there are limits to what outsiders can do apart from offering creative technical assistance in devising possible power- and wealth-sharing solutions, drawing on the vast array of different models already in existence.

There are other ways, however, of addressing group grievances and winning underlying protections for minority rights—and in so doing helping prevent the outbreak of violent conflict—than making fundamental changes to a state's system of internal governance. *Human rights protections* can take many forms: for a start, constitutional or legislative guarantees of freedom of expression, association, religious practice, use of language, and nondiscrimination in employment, and the creation of effective human rights commissions and other such institutional mechanisms both inside and outside the court system. While sensitivities obviously abound in all these areas as well—as attendance at any meeting of the Human Rights Council in Geneva makes quickly and painfully clear—it is remarkable, looking back over the last few decades, how much progress has been made at least in making countries defensive about their shortcomings in group and individual rights protection. The Helsinki Process had its own dramatic long-term impact in unwinding the cold war and the repression associated with it; but also beginning in the 1970s, as already noted in chapter 1, international activity intensified on a much broader front, and not just in the context of southern Africa and the Israeli-occupied territories.

Remedial action has been slow to follow in many cases, and none of this activity made much difference, as also noted earlier, when it came to preventing or responding to the really catastrophic mass atrocity crimes of the cold war years and immediately after. But the momentum is evident, and states do feel themselves under constant international pressure to avoid more egregious violations. That pressure should be maintained by all available means, including attention regularly being drawn to divergence of domestic practice from agreed international standards. Over the long term, promoting respect for human rights is likely to help prevent conflict in a number of ways. [57] Governments that use their security forces to stifle dissent through arbitrary imprisonment and torture may be actually creating the seeds of violent rebellion: Uzbekistan and Azerbaijan are recent examples of repressive government responses to Islamist movements contributing to the radicalization of such groups. [58]

The promotion of human rights requires a multifaceted approach, including investigating and documenting human rights abuses; funding and assisting in the creation of sustainable local institutions capable of defending human rights and monitoring violations; training and educating local human rights advocates; training and educating local police and judicial officials; assisting in setting up appropriate judicial bodies to prosecute violations; and assisting in tracking down suspected human rights abusers. The Geneva-based Office of the High Commissioner for Human Rights has become an increasingly important player across many of these areas of activity in a large number of volatile locations, and deserves further and better resourcing by the UN system and donor governments. And global NGOs like Human Rights Watch and Amnesty International play a major role in spotlighting abuses and campaigning for redress. When donors, public and private, contemplate, however, extending their support beyond organizations of this kind to locally based groups and individuals, a word of caution is required. There is a need for well-meaning outsiders to be guided by well-meaning insiders as to how best to deliver support and encouragement. While in some cases civil society actors have found the perception of their connection with powerful internationals a source of protection, in others there is a real risk that perceived external financial support for internal reform groups will prove counterproductive, exposing their members (as happened in Iran recently) to charges of treachery, and at the very least significantly diminishing their domestic influence. It is for the locals to call, but the most productive momentum for change is likely to be that driven, and seen to be driven, from within.

The broader need is to promote, in those many states at risk of conflict, a much more fundamental respect for *the rule of law* generally—which, reduced to its basic conceptual essentials, means the nonarbitrary exercise of state power, in accordance with laws that are clear and non-retrospective, the subjection of the institutions of the state themselves to law, and the application of the law to all persons equally: these are the essential ingredients, irrespective of the system of government a country has and the particular policy content of its laws.[59] In too many countries the law is systematically abused, ignored, or manipulated, no more than an instrument of power and oppression in the hands of ruling groups, with access to justice for most people a sham, and with an evident crying need to protect the integrity and independence of the judiciary, promote honesty and accountability in law enforcement, and strengthen local institutions and organizations, including the legal profession, that are working for improvement. The essential practical needs are for adequately resourced courts with effective administrations, with well-trained, honest, and independent judges and legal professions, and procedural systems that allow matters to be dealt with quickly, fairly, and justly; access to and affordability of basic legal remedies; and clear and reasonable legal rules, not least those governing commercial transactions. No one should be in any doubt about the magnitude of the reform task in many countries, but equally there should be no doubt about its utility, and the need for donor governments to make offers of assistance in this area a very high priority.[60] Although some policymakers in the West were slow to appreciate the real significance of Pakistan President Pervez Musharraf's assault on the independence of the judiciary in 2007, this was the critical factor in mobilizing the country against him—in the lawyer-led "black revolution"—and setting it back on a democratic and less conflictual path.[61]

No single rule of law issue is more important than the *eradication of corruption*. It has a bad impact on economic growth, undermines the smooth inflow and effectiveness of foreign aid, and destroys trust in government and public institutions. Deeply ingrained corruption can ultimately push states to the edge of state failure and precipitate conflict. In Macedonia widespread corruption in state structures and collusion in police malpractice thwarted democratic development and undermined the legitimacy of institutions, contributing to the Albanian minority's rejection of the governing institutions and the spread of organized crime, which in turn funded the secessionist forces of the National Liberation Army.[62] Fighting corruption, particularly in resource-rich countries where the problem tends to be at its most acute, is a major task, requiring integrated in-country effort by government, judiciary, and civil society, with support from the international community, including major business players. Transparency International is a formidably effective nongovernmental organization working in this area—primarily as a global network of national organizations—that deserves continuing support, along with companion exercises such as Revenue Watch, the Publish What You Pay campaign, and Extractive Industries Transparency Initiative, all of which have built strong working coalitions of governments, NGOs, and private sector leaders.[63]

DIRECT LEGAL MEASURES

Various avenues are available for the direct *legal resolution of disputes* before they realize their potential to become violent, although there is no international equivalent to a properly functioning domestic judicial system. In addition to less formal processes of mediation or arbitration, the International Court of Justice is established by the UN Charter as the UN's principal judicial organ (Article 92), but member states are only bound to comply with its decisions to the extent that they voluntarily submit to its jurisdiction (Article 94) and only a third of UN members—sixty-five at last count—have signed a declaration recognizing the jurisdiction of the court as compulsory.[64] That said, its adjudications of vexed issues between states (often involving boundary delimitation, as with the recent *Cameroon* v. *Nigeria* case) and its capacity to offer advisory opinions (as with the recent *Bosnia* v. *Serbia* case, making much clearer the obligations imposed on states by the Genocide Convention to prevent and punish genocide) have from time to time played a significant role in the prevention of conflict and mass atrocity crimes, and the court deserves more commitment from states than it has received.[65]

In the present context, a more significant legal weapon has in recent years emerged in the international preventive armory: the *threat of international criminal prosecution*. It is now possible, in a way that was not the case before, to ensure that those minded to commit mass atrocity crimes know that there is a real prospect of them being tried and punished. Three separate developments have, or should have, concentrated the minds of potential perpetrators on the risks they run of international retribution. First, there has been the establishment of specialist tribunals to deal with war crimes committed in specific conflicts—for the former Yugoslavia, Rwanda, and Sierra Leone in particular. Second, there has been the establishment of the International Criminal Court—after surviving a baptism of fire from the Bush administration in the United States—creating a new jurisdiction over a wide range of established crimes against humanity and war crimes, some of which are described in greater detail in the statute than in existing instruments, such as the categories of sexual violence constituting crimes against humanity, and some of which are new, such as the prohibition on the enlistment of child soldiers: the latter provision has already formed the basis for the court's first trial, of a leader of the Ituri rebels in the Democratic Republic of the Congo.[66]

Third, there have been some significant applications in recent years of "universal jurisdiction": this is available for certain crimes committed under the Geneva Conventions and Protocols, the Convention against Torture, and, under customary international law, for genocide and crimes against humanity, and means that any state party (if it has legislated to give its courts this jurisdiction) can bring to trial any person accused of such crimes, irrespective of any connection of the accused or the crime with the state in question. The prosecution and conviction in 2001 in a Belgian court of Rwandan nuns charged with complicity in the Rwandan genocide was an important demonstration of this option. So too was the British House of Lords decision in 1998–99 in the General Pinochet extradition case, which went a long way to void the sovereign immunity of at least former government leaders for crimes against humanity committed while they were in office.[67] And more recently there has been the decision to try in Senegal, at the request of the African Union, Chad's ex-President Hissène Habré, accused of crimes against humanity, war crimes, and torture committed during his rule from 1982 to 1990.[68]

One of the big problems in having the threat of international criminal justice as a *preventive* tool is that not enough convictions have yet accumulated to give potential perpetrators any real sense that impunity for mass atrocity crimes really is a thing of the past. The existing specialist tribunals for the former Yugoslavia, Rwanda, and Sierra Leone by definition have no application for future situations arising outside these countries, and their expense and uneven record makes it not especially likely that any of them will be replicated elsewhere. Not many countries—only around a dozen—have legislated to allow their courts to apply universal jurisdiction, or have shown much inclination to do so. And the International Criminal Court, with its jurisdiction only prospective from July 2002, is finding it quite difficult to apply that jurisdiction to ongoing rather than completed conflicts, an issue that will be considered further in the next chapter when the use of criminal justice as a reactive tool is discussed.

Security Sector Strategies

Structural and Longer-Term Security Measures

Supporting *security sector reform*—ensuring that armed forces, police, and intelligence services are competent and democratized—is a significant conflict prevention tool, vital to enhancing governance, promoting stability, and ensuring greater public trust in the state. Undisciplined, poorly structured, or otherwise ineffective security forces can aggravate tensions and create environments where conflict can prosper: Congo and Timor-Leste are just two examples among many that could be cited.[69] Reforming military and police structure is particularly important in a postconflict peace-building context and is discussed further, accordingly, in chapter 7.

The biggest security sector reform of all is managing a *transformation from military to civilian-controlled government*. This requires, to be successful, not only formal constitutional and political mechanisms that embody that change but new habits of routine deference to civilian authority and fully transparent civilian financing. Indonesia is the best example of a major country successfully managing that transition process—not an easy one when, among other considerations, only one quarter of the army's budget has been covered by central government funds, with the remainder requiring to be raised by a variety of legal and illegal economic activities.[70] Many sensitivities remain, with the military still enjoying substantial immunity from punishment for its past excesses—not least in the bloody attempted suppression of Timor-Leste's independence aspirations—but the recent successful Aceh peace process, in which traditional military positions yielded to a civilian-driven negotiation, is evidence of how far and fast things are moving.[71] So much so that Indonesia's capacity to be a significant regional model for Burma/Myanmar, demonstrating that fundamental change is possible without the life or liberty of military leaders being in any way put at risk, is now widely recognized.[72]

In potential conflict situations, particularly of a cross-border character, a significant longer-term military contribution to prevention can be made by embracing *confidence-building measures*.[73] These involve tools such as reciprocal information exchanges and military-to-military programs. The basic idea is to reduce high levels of mistrust about security threats between parties to a dispute and achieve transparency both in security policy and in the physical disposition of military, paramilitary, or police forces. Reciprocal information exchanges provide each party with a better understanding of the capabilities and intentions of the other: they might include exchange of information on troop strengths and dispositions, exchange of information about weapons acquisition, advance notification of troop movements, joint military exercises, reciprocal military placements and training courses, prior notification of a declaration of civil emergency or martial law, or the existence of hotlines between political leaders. Reciprocal information exchanges, ideally on a formal basis, are crucial in cases such as Kashmir where strategic asymmetry means that any misunderstanding of the potential belligerents' actions could rapidly escalate into a nonconventional confrontation. Military-to-military confidence-building programs can also be used to assist in professionalization and training of the military.

At a different level, a significant structural or longer-term contribution to conflict prevention can be made by encouraging states to adhere to the full range of arms control, disarmament, and nonproliferation regimes, including—of particular significance in internal conflict situations—*controls over light weapons and small arms*. The scale of the small arms and light weapons problem is staggering: more than 640 million such weapons and 16 billion rounds of ammunition are estimated to be in circulation worldwide today, with an additional 8 million new weapons entering the market each year, altogether causing more than half a million deaths each year, including some 300,000 in conflict situations.[74] The main policy emphasis to date has been on the supply side, trying to reduce illicit transfer by increasing accountability and government regulation in production, transfer, sale, and end user certification, and those efforts must continue. But even the most heroic international achievements here—and those to date have been rather less than that—would leave an extraordinarily large number of weapons in circulation, creating a huge continuing problem for those trying to curb the number of weapons in the hands of antagonists in actual or potential conflict areas.

DIRECT SECURITY MEASURES

When it comes to more direct and immediate conflict prevention strategies of a military character, the most interesting innovation of recent times has been *preventive deployment*. This involves, where there is an emerging threat of conflict but it has not yet broken out, the positioning of troops either within or across state borders, with the consent of the government or governments involved, for the primary purpose of deterring the escalation of that situation into armed conflict; associated objectives may be to calm communities in the area by monitoring law and order and general conditions, and offering other forms of assistance to local authorities. The clearest example of such a deployment—and a very successful one—was the UN Preventive Deployment Force (UNPREDEP), placed on the Former Yugoslav Republic of Macedonia's borders with Serbia (now Kosovo) and Albania, at Macedonian request, from 1992 to 1999: with around 1,000 military personnel, plus military observers and civil police, designed to deter any possibility of intervention from the former Yugoslavia, the presence of the force also contributed to the stabilization of the very fragile internal situation there, involving major tensions between ethnic Macedonians and ethnic Albanians.[75] The deterrent utility of this kind of deployment—particularly when, as here, it is approved by the Security Council—lies not in the numbers on the ground but in the demonstration of high-level international interest and concern in the situation: it puts all the parties under close international scrutiny, and there is at least an implication of willingness to take further action if there is any resort to violence.

Another category of preventive military response involving the deployment of troops is *nonterritorial shows of force*—what might have been called in an earlier age "gunboat diplomacy" but are more elegantly described in the ICISS report as situations where

> military resources are deployed without an actual intervention on the territory of the targeted state, and accordingly the question of consent does not arise. Such operations may be intended as a show of force to give added weight to diplomatic initiatives, or perhaps serve as instruments to monitor or implement non-military enforcement actions such as sanctions and embargoes. . . . A robust and decisive deployment may help to deter trouble, but can also provide a rapid response capacity should trouble arise.[76]

Shows of this kind have been a familiar part of the U.S. repertoire in the Gulf, with Iran the most favored audience. The closest recent example of this kind of deployment in response to immediately threatened internal violence was probably the positioning of U.S. warships, with substantial detachments of marines, offshore from Monrovia, Liberia, in 2003, in an exercise designed—without actually putting any American boots on the ground—to concentrate the mind of potential spoilers pending the arrival of a UN peacekeeping mission.[77]

Remaining military tools of some preventive utility, both quite commonly applied, are *threatened arms embargoes or withdrawal of military cooperation* programs. Arms embargoes are a familiar tool of the Security

Council and the international community generally when conflict arises or is threatened, and also have quite a history of informal application by trade unionists and others, a recent example, in April 2008, being the turning away, at least from South African and Mozambique ports, of a Chinese ship carrying arms intended for delivery to the Mugabe government in Zimbabwe.[78]

CHAPTER FIVE

During the Crisis: The Responsibility to React

The exercise of the responsibility to . . . react should always involve less intrusive and coercive measures being considered before more coercive and intrusive ones are applied.

—ICISS, *The Responsibility to Protect*, 2001

Doing nothing is not an option.

—Congressman Lee H. Hamilton, 2005[1]

When prevention fails, conflict breaks out within a state, and mass atrocity crimes are occurring or imminent, it is not an option for the world to stand by and do nothing: that way lies, yet again, the horror of Rwanda and Srebrenica. But who should do what, when, and how?

The primary responsibility to react, to halt or avert the harm in question, is—as always—that of the state itself where the crisis is erupting. But if that state is unable to act, or unwilling to do so, perhaps because it is the government itself that is doing the major damage, the responsibility to take appropriate action falls on the wider international community. The 2005 World Summit Outcome Document makes this clear beyond doubt, identifying the broad options available, in a sequence moving—appropriately—from less to more intrusive and from less to more coercive:

139. The international community, through the United Nations, also has the responsibility to use appropriate diplomatic, humanitarian and other peaceful means, in accordance with Chapters VI and VIII of the Charter, to help to protect populations from genocide, war crimes, ethnic cleansing and crimes against humanity. In this context, we are prepared to take collective action, in a timely and decisive manner, through the Security Council, in accordance with the Charter, including Chapter VII, on a case-by-case basis and in cooperation

with relevant regional organizations as appropriate, should peaceful means be inadequate and national authorities are manifestly failing to protect their populations from genocide, war crimes, ethnic cleansing and crimes against humanity.[2]

But this all leaves a lot still unsaid. How, in practice, is the responsibility to react to situations of compelling need for human protection actually to be operationalized? There are, as with the responsibility to prevent, four broad sets of tools available—political, economic, legal, and security—and a multitude of actors potentially available to apply them: see box 5-1. In this chapter the focus is on all those measures falling short of the coercive use of military force. The hardest and most sensitive question of all—when is it right to fight, against the will of the state in question—is addressed separately, in chapter 6.

Political and Diplomatic Strategies

DIPLOMATIC PEACEMAKING

Kenya in early 2008 is the best recent example of the early, and effective, mobilization of political and diplomatic resources to bring back under control an explosive mass atrocity situation—the postelection violence, largely interethnic in character, leaving within a matter of days 1,000 dead and 300,000 displaced—that could have quickly become, without this intervention, very much more catastrophic in scale. An African Union–mandated Panel of Eminent African Personalities, led by former UN secretary-general Kofi Annan and including former Tanzanian president Benjamin Mkapa and former first lady of Mozambique and South Africa Graça Machel, managed by their presence to calm the situation and eventually mediate a settlement between incumbent Mwai Kibaki and opposition leader Rail Odinga, who most observers reasonably believed had won a majority in the December 2007 presidential election. The agreement was built around a power-sharing cabinet, agreement for ongoing negotiations on underlying root cause issues (especially land, economic disparity, and the constitution), and the establishment of formal commissions to review electoral law and practice, investigate postelection violence, and set in place a truth and reconciliation process. Although doubts persist as to the solidity of the arrangements reached, and intense efforts will

BOX 5-1. THE REACTION TOOLBOX

Direct
▮ Diplomatic peacemaking
▮ Political sanctions and incentives

Political/Diplomatic Measures

Direct
▮ Application of economic sanctions
▮ Economic incentives

Economic/Social Measures

Direct
▮ Criminal prosecution

Constitutional/Legal Measures

Direct
▮ Peacekeeping for civilian protection
▮ Safe havens and no-fly zones
▮ Arms embargoes
▮ Jamming of radio frequencies
▮ Threat or use of military force

Security Sector Measures

have to be sustained, by the AU in particular, to hold the process together, it was an ideal "R2P reaction" outcome in the sense that an alarming situation was defused by the key national players themselves, with external diplomatic support, but no more intrusive or coercive measures needing to be applied (although targeted sanctions and the like had certainly been under discussion in the wider international community).[3]

There are many other examples of diplomatic mediation, facilitation, or more hands-on peacemaking that have successfully resolved conflicts that have had an actual, or feared, mass atrocity crime dimension. At the more robust end of the spectrum were the Dayton peace negotiations, cajoled and pummeled to a conclusion in 1995 by the indefatigable Ambassador Richard Holbrooke, which did not satisfy any of the former Yugoslavia and international participants that they resolved all Bosnia and Herzegovina's problems but did bring a peace that has proved, for all the bumpiness of the ride, sustainable.[4] Another was the combined effort, led by NATO's George Robertson and the EU's Javier Solana, to defuse a potentially disastrous downward spiral of interethnic violence in Macedonia in 2001, culminating in the Ohrid Agreement (a success that Robertson attributes to a combination of early intervention, top level engagement, continuity of effort, interinstitutional cooperation, and implementing past lessons learned).[5] Another was the Comprehensive Peace Agreement in 2005 between the Khartoum government and the insurgent Sudan People's Liberation Movement/Army (SPLM/A)—very professionally mediated by Kenyan General Lazaro Sumbeiywo on behalf of the regional Intergovernmental Authority on Development (IGAD)—which, although it remains very fragile, formally ended Africa's longest civil war, and one of its ugliest.[6]

Successful peace negotiators, mediators, and facilitators come in all shapes and sizes, and with a variety of pedigrees. At any given time the UN secretary-general, in the exercise of his general "good offices" role, has dozens of special representatives, personal representatives, special envoys, or special advisers working on peace and security issues in all parts of the world—full time or part time, heading field-based missions, at headquarters, or acting as roving envoys.[7] Regional organizations like the EU and AU are similarly much engaged. So too, from time to time, are nongovernmental organizations like the Carter Center (which over many years has helped broker significant peace agreements and arrangements in locations as various as Liberia, Uganda, Haiti, Nepal, and Israel-Palestine), the Community of Sant'Egidio (which played a crucial role in bringing the war in Mozambique to an end in 1992), and the Geneva-based Centre for Humanitarian Dialogue.[8] The Elders, a group of former senior statesmen and -women founded in 2007, chaired by Archbishop Desmond Tutu, and including members like Kofi Annan, Jimmy Carter, and Gro Harlem Brundtland, can be expected to make a major new contribution to this scene.[9]

Former Finnish president Martti Ahtisaari is as good an example as one can find of someone who has successfully played all these roles: as UN Special Representative managing the transition to peace in Namibia in 1989; special negotiator effectively representing the EU in assisting Russia's Victor Chernomyrdin and the U.S.'s Strobe Talbott to end the fighting in Kosovo in 1999; leader—as head of his own NGO, Crisis Management Initiative—of the peace negotiations between Indonesia and the Free Aceh Movement (GAM) in 2005; and Special Envoy of the UN Secretary-General for the Future Status Process for Kosovo since 2005. Ahtisaari combines, to great effect, immense personal charm with a tough, no-nonsense, tell-it-like-it-is approach to conducting negotiations (and to chairing, as he did for a time, the International Crisis Group!). The Aceh peace negotiators were in no doubt that his personal role was indispensable: in the words of government envoy Farid Husain, "He exuded authority, like a father. . . . His method was really extraordinary. He said, 'Do you want to win, or do you want peace,'" and of the GAM representative Munawarliza Zein, "There was no chit chat, there were brief greetings and then you got down to work. . . . our respect grew. This man wasn't playing around." Strobe Talbott describes him in the 1999 Kosovo peace process as playing "Mr. Hammer to Chernomyrdin's Mr. Anvil, with Milosevic being what was beaten between the two."[10]

There is a large literature on the qualities and techniques required of good peace mediators and negotiators. Dennis Ross's summary of "twelve rules to follow in negotiations" and "eleven rules for mediation" are as sensible and useful as any of their kind.[11] But, eminently capable and experienced practitioner as he was, they didn't enable him—as chief Middle East peace negotiator in the presidential administrations of both George H.W. Bush and Bill Clinton—to make much progress in the ever-intractable Israeli-Palestinian process. And many other such enterprises have failed over the years because, among other reasons, the timing has not been optimal, the parties have been just too dug in and too far apart (as, for example, the Norwegian peace facilitators, for all their intense efforts over several years, found in Sri Lanka), or, sometimes, the effort has been just too half-hearted (as it would be fair to characterize the South African and Southern African Development Community [SADC] role in addressing the ever more alarmingly deteriorating situation in Zimbabwe through the course of 2007 and the first half of 2008).[12]

What is ultimately most crucial in any peacemaking diplomacy is to somehow find a way of persuading the key parties that their basic interests, and pride, will not suffer from an agreement. This was at the heart of the solution, for example, to the most difficult peace negotiations in which I have ever been directly engaged, those over 1989–93 bringing to an end the long-running conflict in Cambodia. The situation was extraordinarily complex, being played out at three distinct levels: first, the warring internal factions, with Hun Sen's government against a fragile coalition of non-communist Sihanoukists and Son Sann's Khmer People's National Liberation Front (KPNLF) party on the one hand, and the reduced but still dangerous Khmer Rouge on the other; second, the region, with Vietnam supporting Hun Sen and ASEAN his opponents; and third, the great powers, with China (determined to neutralize Vietnam's influence) supporting the Khmer Rouge and Prince Sihanouk, the Soviet Union supporting Hun Sen, and the United States favoring the two noncommunist resistance groups. The key to unraveling it all was China: without its willingness to step back and withdraw support from the Khmer Rouge, the latter simply could not have been isolated and marginalized, a broad-based "independent" government formed, and a sustainable peace achieved. And what finally broke the impasse was an Australian proposal to give the UN an unprecedentedly large role in the civil administration of the country during the transition period, which was expressly designed to give China a face-saving way of engaging in just that withdrawal.[13]

The period since the end of the cold war has been, for all that has continued to go wrong, a particularly productive one for peace accords, with more old conflicts being resolved by negotiation and mediation than new ones have erupted.[14] Over that period, there are perhaps five main lessons that we have painfully learned about what makes for successful diplomatic peacemaking. First, a peace accord is not an event so much as a process, and signing the agreement is not the end of it: the critical need is to generate commitment to, and ownership of, the peace by the warring parties, so that their commitments are not just formal but internalized, and will stick. Second, any peace accord must deal with all the fundamentals of the dispute, all the issues that will have to be resolved if normality is to return. Sometimes that can be done in a sequential or stage-by-stage way, applying confidence-building measures now with some key issues deferred, but the failed Oslo process for Israel-Palestine shows how risky that approach can be. Third, any successful peace accord must get the balance right between peace and justice, an issue further addressed below. Fourth, the terms of any accord, and the method of its enforcement and implementation, must be sufficiently resilient to deal with spoilers—those who would seek to undermine or overturn it. And finally, bearing in mind particularly the last point, a peace accord to be successful must have the necessary degree of international support, with all the guarantees and commitment of resources that are necessary to make it stick. It must never be forgotten that the 1994 genocide in Rwanda, taking 800,000 lives, followed a major peace deal in Arusha just a year earlier, and that in Angola the 1991 Bicesse Agreement to end the war there was followed by a relapse into bloody conflict for another decade, which cost some half a million additional lives.

POLITICAL SANCTIONS AND INCENTIVES

Political incentives are a familiar part of the repertoire of peace negotiators, and those trying to encourage improvement in countries' human rights behavior: they can include diplomatic recognition, membership in an international organization (not least, in a European context, the holy grail of the EU itself), military assistance, and measures with a more specifically economic flavor like access to aid and cancellation of debt. Sometimes it will be enough to have these potential gains put on the table as an alternative to the status quo, with the downside of no agreement being simply no new benefits.

But policymakers will sometimes want, or need, more leverage than that: to be able to signal negative consequences if no peace deal is reached or unconscionable violations of human rights continue, which brings into play the prospect of sanctions.

Most of the argument about the utility of sanctions, and the respective merits of comprehensive and targeted measures of this kind, has taken place in the context of economic sanctions, which are discussed further below. Political sanctions essentially involve withdrawal of diplomatic recognition, expulsion from international organizations, suspension of sporting contacts, "naming and shaming" through condemnation in international forums, and—in the case of influential individuals—travel bans. While measures like sporting bans, whether directed to Zimbabwe, apartheid South Africa, or various Olympic hosts, have proved notoriously ineffective, and naming shames only those familiar with that emotion, some political sanctions have a greater potential impact than may immediately meet the eye. As the ICISS commissioners pointed out, restrictions on diplomatic representation, including expulsion of staff, while often viewed in the past as primarily of symbolic significance and largely related to the battle for public opinion, have also increasingly come to be seen as a relevant and useful measure in efforts to limit illicit transactions— whether for the sale of commodities such as illegally mined diamonds or drugs, or for the purchase of arms and other military-related matériel, or with respect to the movement of funds. Again, suspension of membership or expulsion from international or regional bodies (or refusal to admit to membership) may entail not only loss of a degree of national prestige but also of the technical cooperation or financial assistance countries may receive from such bodies.[15] That said, Zimbabwe's expulsion from the Commonwealth in 2002 appears to have left Robert Mugabe profoundly unmoved, and one has a sense that the expulsion of Burma/Myanmar from ASEAN—one of the few shots left in the regional locker after its ill-advised admission in 1997 without any significant change of behavior being required as a precondition—would leave its generals equally unflustered. Generally the irritancy of political sanctions is closely correlated to the openness of the state to begin with: already isolated and insulated regimes shrug them off much more readily than more open ones.

Targeted travel bans do seem to weigh heavily when applied against specific leaders or individuals and their families, although the evidence is more anecdotal than systematic. While it may reasonably be assumed that an inability to shop at Harrods would not be a serious disincentive for an AK-47–wielding Janjaweed camel driver, visa bans for major international retail and entertainment destinations have been known to cause serious pain to a number of serially offending national leaders. And even more painful, interestingly, appear to be bans on entry to attend school or university: while it may be tough to visit the sins of the fathers upon the children, this is a form of leverage not to be neglected. What is important about all these measures is that they be imposed with some sustained seriousness of purpose and not just in order to be seen to be doing something in order to shelter from some passing media storm. An unhappy example of what not to do in this respect is the European Union's performance over the visa bans it imposed on Uzbekistan officials involved in the horrendous Andijon massacre of May 13, 2005: the day they took effect, in November that year, one of those on the list, the interior minister, was enjoying medical care at a clinic in Hanover; in 2006 the list was reduced; in 2007 the bans were suspended for six months; and in April 2008 they were suspended again, set to expire completely in October except in the unlikely event of a unanimous decision to reinstall them. And all this without any sign of either penitence or behavioral change by the Uzbek government.[16]

Economic Strategies

ECONOMIC SANCTIONS

My own initial experience of the use of economic sanctions—against apartheid South Africa—was wholly positive. Not in the case of trade sanctions, which had been applied, and avoided, for years without discernible effect, but *financial* sanctions—involving the cooperation of governments and banks in denying or limiting credit to the South African government and local companies. A sophisticated case for such measures was made in a study commissioned by me as then Australian Foreign Minister, and with the support of the African National Congress opposition widely promoted internationally, including through successive Commonwealth ministerial meetings, as a result of which, and other parallel efforts in the United States and Europe, their application quickly gained major momentum.[17] Very early in the subsequent peaceful transition to democracy—brilliantly negotiated by Nelson Mandela with F. W. de Klerk to the vast relief of all those who had feared a bloodbath—the real significance of the financial sanctions was graphically brought home to me when I visited the country in 1991 and spoke to a succession of senior ministers and officials. It was conceded outright by all of them—including the finance minister and the South African Reserve Bank governor—that it was these sanctions, more than any other form of external pressure, that had ultimately forced South Africa to the negotiating table.

Since then it has been difficult to discern any other major successes for broad-based sanctions of any kind, though the capacity of financial sanctions to do real damage—including, for example, to Iran—should never be underestimated. If sustained for a long time they can have a major negative effect on the well-being of a country's people by denying access to goods, services, or other externally provided requirements necessary or important to maintenance of a country's economic, social, or political infrastructure, even if—as was the case for Iraq in the 1990s—an attempt is made to make exception for food and medical supplies and other essentials. But the real question is whether they have made, or are ever likely to make, the same kind of compensating policy impact that occurred in the South Africa of the late 1980s on a country's leadership (who are usually perfectly capable of insulating themselves from any direct damage, or even benefiting from the situation, as happened with oil-for-food in Iraq). Policymakers worldwide appear to be becoming increasingly dubious, and it is hard to argue with them.[18]

However, there remains a need, both in terms of the UN Security Council's formal Chapter VII powers and the policy options available to states and regional organizations outside the UN framework, for a tool lying "between words and war": thus the emphasis in recent times on targeted or "smart" sanctions, and the wide interest in the work, in this context, of the Stockholm Process on the Implementation of Targeted Sanctions.[19] These are measures "directed against particular political leaders and members of their regimes whose actions constitute a threat to international peace and security": examples extend across the whole political, economic, and military spectrum, ranging from travel bans on key individuals, discussed above, to financial sanctions, to specifically focused trade sanctions, to aviation bans (denying individual targets, or target states, permission to land in, take off from, or fly over national territory) and arms embargoes. The intention is that such targeted sanctions should avoid the unintended consequences of comprehensive economic sanctions and focus sanctions on the pressure points of the regime, group, or individual to be sanctioned.

Targeted financial sanctions may be aimed at the foreign assets of a country, a rebel movement or terrorist organization, particular leaders and their families, or companies associated with any of them. One kind of sanction here might involve an asset freeze; another, a blanket restriction on dealing with companies or banks from a certain country: financial sanctions can be quite closely calibrated, adding to their policy utility. The other main category of targeted economic sanctions involves restrictions on income-generating activities such as diamonds and logging, which may be easier to get at than the funds that they generate.[20] A further attraction of targeting these latter activities is that the profits from them may be very directly related to the conflict in question, often constituting either the principal motivation for it, the means to start or sustain it, or both. Sanctions on oil production or export are often proposed but usually less easy to justify because of the difficulties of implementation involved, or their local or international price impact implications.[21]

ECONOMIC INCENTIVES

Positive economic incentives include measures such as concessions on trade access, development assistance, beneficial trade agreements, investment offers, or membership in a regional economic organization.[22] Economic incentives have been used quite successfully in connection with major political or strategic goals: for example, U.S. largesse played a major part in persuading Egypt to agree to peace with Israel in 1978 through the Camp David accords, and in encouraging Kazakhstan and Ukraine to relinquish in 1991 the major nuclear weapons arsenals they had acquired as a result of the collapse of the Soviet Union. In a more specific immediate conflict resolution situation, positive economic incentives were part of the diplomatic armory, discussed above, deployed by the EU and NATO to secure the Ohrid Agreement, in particular holding out the carrots of a comprehensive aid package and closer economic association with the EU.[23]

Legal Strategies

CRIMINAL PROSECUTION: PEACE VERSUS JUSTICE

The strongest direct legal weapon to employ against those initiating unlawful violence, and in particular threatening or perpetrating mass atrocity crimes, is to arrest, try, and, if properly convicted, punish them in a competent criminal court. If that can be done within a state's own justice system, either with the state's own resources or with international assistance (perhaps with the court in question taking, by agreement, a hybrid national-international form, like the Special Court for Sierra Leone or Extraordinary Chambers in the Courts of Cambodia), then so much the better.[24] But a further option these days, if a state is unable or unwilling to undertake this task—and if the interests of justice seem to demand it—is to seek to mount such a prosecution in some other court or tribunal, outside the state, exercising international criminal jurisdiction.

As described in the last chapter, there are three classes of such courts: the specialist or ad hoc tribunals dealing with crimes committed in specific conflicts; the International Criminal Court (ICC); and other national courts able and willing to exercise "universal jurisdiction." Historically, most international war crimes tribunals have been ad hoc bodies. The International Military Tribunal set up in Nuremberg in 1945 to try twenty-one major figures accused of crimes against peace, violations of the laws of war, and crimes against humanity was established by charter agreed by France, the Soviet Union, the United Kingdom, and the United States. Post-

1945 international war crimes tribunals (such as the International Criminal Tribunal for the former Yugoslavia [ICTY] and the International Criminal Tribunal for Rwanda [ICTR]) have been set up by resolution of the UN acting under Chapter VII of the UN Charter, and have operated under the specific statutes that have set them up.[25]

The establishment of the ICC through the 1998 Rome Statute is a significant break from this history, for a number of reasons.[26] First, unlike the ICTR and the ICTY, the ICC was established by treaty and not by UN Security Council resolution. Second, the ICC breaks with the ad hoc tradition of war crimes tribunals by setting up a permanent court to hear cases of genocide, crimes against humanity, and war crimes. As a corollary of this, the ICC does not have a time limitation on its ability to prosecute, which, particularly in cases of state obstruction, has threatened to derail ad hoc tribunals such as the ICTR.[27] Third, for previous ad hoc tribunals to be established, the international community essentially acted to suspend state sovereignty in criminal justice investigations and prosecutions for a limited time period and under a specific mandate. Under the statute of the ICC, no such special act on the part of the international community is required: the court *automatically* has jurisdiction over a violation of international humanitarian law if a state is unwilling or unable to investigate and prosecute.[28] The UN Security Council (and state parties) may choose to refer a matter to the ICC—which, in itself, may be a powerful diplomatic tool— but such a reference is not a precondition of the ICC beginning an investigation. Fourth, whereas international courts such as the International Court of Justice (ICJ) rule only on state-to-state relations, the ICC has the capacity to try individuals.

Actually exercising the prosecution option in practice before the ICC, or any of the tribunals mentioned, may be a lot easier said than done: there are a myriad of procedural and substantive difficulties to be overcome in satisfying the various jurisdictional thresholds and in getting the necessary evidence about the right indictees before the appropriate body. Not the least of the problems is in securing the arrest and physical transfer to the courts of the indictee in question, given that none of the international courts have any kind of marshals' service of their own and rely entirely on the cooperation of relevant states for this purpose.[29] Although such cooperation was recently forthcoming from the Belgian authorities in their important arrest of former DRC vice president Jean-Pierre Bemba Gombo in Brussels in May 2008, following his indictment by the ICC for war crimes and crimes against humanity allegedly committed in the Central African Republic in 2002–03, it was for a decade famously not forthcoming in the cases of ICTY indictees Mladic and Karadzic.[30] It is probably reasonable to now assume that the future of international criminal justice lies with the ICC—and the spread of universal jurisdiction in national courts—rather than with new ad hoc tribunals, but there is still a great deal to be done to make the ICC itself effectively operational.

There is a larger policy problem, however, which has dominated all these other considerations when it comes to weighing the utility of attempting criminal prosecutions against those reasonably believed to be guilty of any of the large range of atrocity crimes now within the jurisdiction of the ICC.[31] That is the so-called *peace versus justice* problem: should the demands of justice—to bring an end once and for all to the almost universal impunity that has prevailed in relation to these crimes in the past, and to create an effective deterrent to their commission in the future—ever yield, in the case of a clash between them, to the demands of peace, namely to bring an end to some conflict that has wreaked untold destruction and misery until then and which may continue to do so if a peace agreement cannot be reached?

It should not be doubted that these demands do in fact clash from time to time: not when one side or another has been clearly defeated, or has been for all practical purposes defeated and is trying to negotiate the terms of a surrender, but when there is an ongoing conflict, and the peace negotiation is attempting to reach agreement between parties capable of perpetuating it. In this context, strong views have been expressed in a number of quarters that the ICC indictments issued against Joseph Kony and other leaders of the Lord's Revolutionary Army (LRA) for atrocity crimes committed in Northern Uganda, and against senior government figures in Sudan for such crimes in Darfur, are simply misconceived and a hindrance to the achievement of peace—which, so the argument goes, will require formal amnesty, or effective immunity in practice, of the kind that has been associated with peace negotiations involving parties of some strength from time immemorial. It is not a matter of being able to fudge the issue, as some would like, and say "negotiate peace now and address the impunity issue later": potential indictees are far too conscious of their vulnerability these days to settle for that uncertainty.

The arguments for *not* giving amnesty are often more finely balanced than critics are inclined to acknowledge. In the Northern Uganda case, the ICC indictments do seem to have clearly concentrated the minds of at least the lesser LRA commanders, to the extent that there has been a dramatic improvement in the overall security situation since their issue, and do seem to have given Kony himself some sense that the net is closing in; but equally clearly, as of mid-2008, they have been a significant obstacle to the final conclusion of that deal. In the case of Sudan, it has been strongly argued that moves to prosecute senior regime figures—including, as this book was going to press, President Bashir himself—were needed to pressure the country's leadership into recalculating the costs of further defying the international community, and that any softer line, trading away justice for the hope of peace, would simply go on being ignored.[32]

All that said, we also must acknowledge that situations can arise in which the need to advance a peace process can work against the impunity principle: as much as it may shock the conscience to contemplate not pursuing prosecutions when major perpetrators of atrocity crimes are involved, this *can* be helpful in certain circumstances in ending conflict, and in saving as a result a great many more lives. The classic case is Nigeria's initial grant of asylum to Liberia's murderous Charles Taylor in 2003, not at all unreasonable given the prospect then looming of thousands more deaths in the final battle for Monrovia. The understandable joy among human rights advocates in the region and around the world when Nigeria subsequently succumbed to international pressure and handed him over, through Liberia, to be tried in the Sierra Leone Special Court should be tempered by the appreciation that this happening, in the absence of any clear evidence that Taylor had breached his asylum conditions, sent a very unhelpful message to some other serial human rights violators: Zimbabwe's Robert Mugabe, in particular, is understood to be obsessed with the Taylor case, as evidence of what might be his own fate if he succumbs to pressure to accept some kind of agreed graceful exit from office (of the kind that, as of mid-2008, had long been on offer from the opposition party).

But there are two important principles that must govern any decision to prefer peace over justice. The first is that only in the most exceptional cases, where the evidence really is clear that very major peace benefits are involved, should serious consideration be given to discontinuing investigations under way or granting formal amnesties. Justice serves too many public policy goals to ever be lightly traded away: retribution (helping channel revenge through institutional rather than freelance channels), incapacitation (physically removing from the scene potential postconflict spoilers), rehabilitation (giving some hope to offenders that they will have a post-justice future), truth telling (focusing on reality, stripping away myths, and minimizing the prospect of repetition), delegitimization (again, exposing and discrediting), institutionalization of human rights norms, and deterrence (the power of example preventing future misbehavior by others). All these benefits—and most of all deterrence—are significant over the long term. It is only when the shorter-term costs of prolonging an ongoing conflict clearly outweigh these benefits that non-prosecution of clearly prosecutable cases should be contemplated. The obvious downside risk of these situations is that the more the ICC's work is perceived as "negotiable," the more its role as a deterrent of atrocity crimes is undermined: the cases really do have to be *very* exceptional.[33]

The second principle is that if decisions to give primacy to peace over justice do have to be made in certain hard cases, those decisions are best made not by the ICC or its prosecutor but by those with appropriate political responsibility: in the case of this court, the Security Council has that power, if it chooses to use Article 16 of the Rome Statute enabling it to suspend prosecutions for renewable periods of twelve months. The prosecutor's job is to prosecute, and he should get on with it, with bulldog intensity. His task is to end impunity for the worst atrocity crimes: Article 53 gives him a certain discretion not to pursue matters if the "interests of justice" so require, but the interests of justice do not necessarily coincide with the interests of peace. Having the prosecutor make the determination as to when and how to weigh the demands of conflict resolution puts him in an impossible situation. So he has to get on with justice. If the judgment has to be made, on occasion, that the interests of peace should override those of justice, then that should be not for the ICC but the Security Council to decide—however difficult that will no doubt prove to be in practice—and the pressure and weight of expectations should be taken off the prosecutor's shoulders in this respect. There is a reluctance—particularly by those who come at these issues from a human rights rather than conflict resolution perspective—to give so central a role to Article 16, and this general balancing role is probably more than was originally contemplated for it. But the international community has to recognize that because there are competing principles of more or less equally compelling moral force involved here, there has to be some mechanism for accommodating them and that Article 16 seems to be the best available option.

Military Strategies Short of Applying Coercive Force

PEACEKEEPING FOR CIVILIAN PROTECTION

For most of the life of the UN, a clear conceptual and practical distinction has existed, even if the terminology has sometimes been variable and confusing, between peacekeeping (implicitly authorized by Chapter VI of the Charter) and peace enforcement (expressly authorized under Chapter VII). *Peacekeeping*—not contemplated by the UN's founders, and not explicitly mentioned in the Charter, but developed to the status of a full working doctrine under Secretary-General Dag Hammarskjold—involved, in what is now called its "traditional" form, blue-helmeted forces being engaged essentially in the monitoring, supervision, and verification of cease-fires and early-stage peace agreements. Operations were multinational in character, authorized by the UN Security Council, under UN command, premised on the consent of all the parties to the conflict, expected to remain completely impartial between them, and not mandated or expected to use force except in self-defense if under attack.[34] Seen essentially as a complement to diplomatic peacemaking, as described above, traditional peacekeeping operations were an extremely useful tool in helping to restore peace when the restoration process already had some momentum.[35]

But they were not much use in creating peace in crisis and conflict situations where there was no agreement among the relevant parties. For that, *peace enforcement* operations were required, not premised on consent of all sides or requiring impartiality. These were clearly anticipated in Chapter VII of the Charter, which gave the Security Council power to "take such action by air, sea or land forces as may be necessary to maintain or restore international peace and security" (and also created an elaborate—but never in practice used—mechanism, the Military Staff Committee, responsible for "the strategic direction of any armed forces placed at the disposal of the Security Council"). Intervention of this kind by the UN itself, with all forces blue-helmeted and under at least notional UN command, has been extremely rare, the clearest examples being the cold war–era operations in Korea in 1950 and, on a much smaller scale, the

Congo in 1960. In recent years the practice has been for major peace enforcement operations, where the robust use of force is integral to the mission from the outset (for example, in response to cross-border invasions or other explosions of violence), taking the form of Security Council–mandated multinational forces, the classic case being the operation against Iraq in 1991 after its invasion of Kuwait. The Report of the Panel on United Nations Peace Operations in 2000—the Brahimi Report, as it is more familiarly known, after its chairman—described the current position exactly in saying that "the United Nations does not wage war. Where enforcement action is required, it has consistently been entrusted to coalitions of willing States."[36] When and by whom, and with what authorization, such full-scale coercive force *should* be used, in responsibility to protect situations, is the subject of the next chapter.

What this familiar distinction between traditional peacekeeping and full-blown peace enforcement left unaddressed, however, was how to deal with the cases in the middle, where what was required was something less than full-scale war fighting but something rather more than traditional watching, reporting, and assisting. After the end of the cold war, more and more UN peacekeeping missions were being deployed but in circumstances where there was ever-growing pressure upon them to take action to protect civilian populations at risk, while at the same time great confusion as to whether their mandates, and in particular their traditional obligation to remain "impartial," allowed them to do so—with the catastrophes of Rwanda and Srebrenica being the worst fruits of that confusion. But it was not only there that peacekeeping operations found themselves becoming hostage to changing circumstances to which they were unable to adequately respond. Five hundred peacekeepers were literally taken hostage in Sierra Leone in 2000, in a rapidly deteriorating situation that was only resolved by the deployment of British troops in a separate operation.[37] It became increasingly obvious that peacekeepers needed to be able to respond to "spoilers," including some who may have agreed to deployment in the first place. The Brahimi Report, the first to systematically consider these issues and to make serious operational recommendations for their solution, stated the problem exactly:

Impartiality for United Nations operations must . . . mean adherence to the principles of the Charter: where one party to a peace agreement clearly and incontrovertibly is violating its terms, continued equal treatment of all parties by the United Nations can in the best case result in ineffectiveness and in the worst may amount to complicity with evil. No failure did more to damage the standing and credibility of United Nations peacekeeping in the 1990s than its reluctance to distinguish victim from aggressor.

In the past, the United Nations has often found itself unable to respond effectively to such challenges. It is a fundamental premise of the present report, however, that it must be able to do so. Once deployed, United Nations peacekeepers must be able to carry out their mandate professionally and successfully. This means that United Nations military units must be capable of defending themselves, other mission components and the mission's mandate. Rules of engagement should be sufficiently robust and not force United Nations contingents to cede the initiative to their attackers.

This means, in turn, that the Secretariat must not apply best-case planning assumptions to situations where the local actors have historically exhibited worst-case behaviour. It means that mandates should specify an operation's authority to use force. It means bigger forces, better equipped and more costly but able to be a credible deterrent. In particular, United Nations forces for complex operations should be afforded the field intelligence and other capabilities needed to mount an effective defence against violent challengers.

Moreover, United Nations peacekeepers—troops or police—who witness violence against civilians should be presumed to be authorized to stop it, within their means, in support of basic United Nations principles. However, operations given a broad and explicit mandate for civilian protection must be given the specific resources needed to carry out that mandate.[38]

As a result, something of a revolution has occurred in UN peacekeeping over the last few years, not only in the ever-increasing numbers of missions and personnel deployed (in mid-2008, seventeen missions with around 88,000 troops and civilian staff), and not only in the ever-evolving recognition that peacekeeping missions have a major postconflict peacebuilding role, requiring their expertise and capability in a wide range of civil administration functions (an issue taken up in chapter 7), but also in the recognition that such missions have an inescapable civilian protection role, which may require much more than merely the traditional mission–self-defense capability.[39] For most new missions, in fact, Chapter VII mandates have now become routine.[40] These kinds of "coercive protection" missions are still properly described as peacekeeping (albeit "peacekeeping plus" or "complex peacekeeping," to distinguish them from "traditional peacekeeping") rather than peace enforcement operations because—unlike the latter, where it is known from the outset that the primary role will be fighting—they are embarked upon with a reasonable expectation that force may not be needed at all. But the point is that it is now generally acknowledged, in a way that was not the case during the 1990s, that there is every chance that, as the High-Level Panel put it, "even the most benign environments can turn sour—when spoilers emerge to undermine a peace agreement and put civilians at risk—and that it is desirable for there to be complete certainty about the mission's capacity to respond with force, if necessary."[41]

Not all peacekeeping is done by troops operating within a UN command structure.[42] For example, when the UN's Chapter VI MONUC I mission (Mission des Nations Unies en République Démocratique du Congo) was not able to contain escalating violence in Ituri province, in eastern Democratic Republic of Congo, a UN-requested European Union mission (Operation Artemis) provided a bridge between it and the upgraded MONUC II, which had a Chapter VII mandate, updated rules of engagement, and a larger force but took time to put together.[43] Both the International Security Assistance Force (ISAF) mission in Afghanistan and the Kosovo Force (KFOR) mission are essentially NATO missions authorized by Security Council resolutions. Peacekeeping sanctioned by the UN but undertaken by regional organizations (the best-known example probably being the African Union's Mission in Sudan (AMIS) operating in Darfur, now to be subsumed in the joint United Nations–African Union Mission in Darfur [UNAMID]), individual countries, or coalitions of countries is a useful way of unburdening a stretched UN, particularly in terms of standing planning capacity; and in cases where the security risks are particularly high, albeit still falling short of full-scale war fighting (for example, Afghanistan), a UN-commanded peacekeeping mission may not be the best way of proceeding.[44] UN authorization for regional, national, or coalition action has the potential attraction of achieving more rapid deployment and gaining greater local political legitimacy and engagement.

Overall, it does seem that some serious lessons have been learned—some of them discussed here and others to be addressed further in later chapters—about what is key to the effective functioning of peacekeeping missions, UN-run or otherwise. There is the necessity for, first, a clear, comprehensible, and achievable *mandate*, to reflect the precise reality of what the mission has to perform; second, *flexibility*, recognizing that mandates may need to be changed in order for the original objectives to remain achievable; third, *robust doctrine*, because without that and effective rules of engagement, even the most appropriate mandates may not be delivered; fourth, an *effective force on the ground*, in sufficient numbers to perform its tasks, with sufficient equipment and with the right skill set, including an understanding of local languages and context; and above all, *political will*, without which, including the willingness to reassess force posture in the light of changing circumstances, peacekeeping missions risk becoming dead letters.

For all this increased understanding, it has to be acknowledged, however, that there is still not much occasion for congratulation as to the way in which many of these missions are being carried out on the ground, particularly in Africa.[45] There has been a surge of new or expanded peacekeeping operations around the continent, most with more or less credible mandates, and many of them have achieved notable successes, but that success has not been often enough where it has been needed most, in the critical area of civilian protection. For example, MONUC very competently organized the 2005 referendum and 2006 elections in the Democratic Republic of Congo, in extraordinarily difficult circumstances, but has performed very poorly indeed in saving lives, and, in particular, protecting women from assault in eastern Congo. And in Sudan neither AMIS in the past nor UNAMID as it presently evolving seems able to provide significant protection from the combined depredations of Janjaweed militias, Khartoum bombardments, and assaults by the various rebel groups.

The problem comes down, as much as anything else, to the age-old one that there is not a great deal a peacekeeping mission can do when there is no peace to keep, and that the reaction to violent conflict and atrocity crimes needs to have not only a military component but an effective political one—involving properly negotiated political settlements that are not just quick fixes but seriously tackle the roots of the conflicts and are effectively followed through. Part of the problem in eastern Congo is that the insurgency has been addressed with no agenda other than electoral victory and military containment; in Sudan it is that negotiations have stalled on issues like Janjaweed disarmament and compensation for crimes committed without addressing the core problems of Darfurian political under-representation and the need for greater wealth sharing. And neither in Chad nor Somalia, any more than in Darfur, are there—as of mid 2008—anything resembling viable peace agreements to implement. Security-focused strategies only ever take you so far: it is the broader based political ones that ultimately count most.

SAFE HAVENS AND NO-FLY ZONES

These are essentially further examples of security-focused quick fixes, which may or may not amount to effective civilian protection in crisis situations. A *safe haven* is a specific and limited form of security guarantee, often but not exclusively intended to provide for the safe delivery of humanitarian aid, but in all cases demanding a genuine commitment to protect civilians with force if necessary. Safe havens differ from demilitarized zones principally in their purpose: whereas classic demilitarized zones are generally part of a cease-fire or are intended to promote the establishment of a permanent peace, safe havens can be established in the middle of conflict with the limited aim of protecting civilians. The advantages of creating safe havens are clear. They allow a third party to intervene in a conflict where a full peacekeeping mission is politically impossible and nevertheless achieve limited goals of civilian protection.[46] In cases of potential or actual mass atrocity crimes, where speed of deployment is critical, the setting up of even limited safe havens can help to restore peace over a wider area and prevent genocide from taking place.

The most critical issue with respect to safe havens is what happens if they are threatened: the example of Srebrenica in 1995 stands as an awful warning that, ultimately, an internationally mandated safe haven is only as good as the capacity to protect it.[47] In the Bosnian war following the breakup of Yugoslavia, the UN Security Council declared six safe areas, but these were not contiguous and, being lightly manned, were essentially hostage to Bosnian Serb forces, as horrifyingly proved to be the case. The assumption of both civilian and military planners was that the havens would be respected, without there being any policy or doctrine in place to guide a response if they were not.

A lesser but still often expressed concern with safe havens is that they may create a humanitarian alibi, in the sense that a limited humanitarian mission is potentially substituted for a wider, more complex mission that would address the real root of the problem—they may mitigate conflict without resolving it. The EU intervention in Congo's Ituri province is pertinent: while the Artemis mission, essentially creating a safe haven in Bunia town, was successful within its mandate and may have prevented a wider conflagration, that mandate was very limited as to time, place, and content.[48]

No-fly zones are the aerial equivalent of safe havens. They have been used as a form of limited security guarantee, attempting—with mixed success—to prevent the use of airpower being brought to bear in a conflict, as for example in Iraq, where the United States and the United Kingdom imposed a no-fly zone over northern and southern Iraq from 1991 to 2003 intended to protect Kurdish and marsh Arab populations from reprisals, and in Bosnia, where a NATO no-fly zone was imposed in April 1993. While their role is best seen, given the limits of airpower, as designed to mitigate the impact of conflict rather than preventing or ending it, they can notionally provide meaningful and rapidly deployable protection to civilians under threat of air attack, and may, if applied seriously, have had an impact in Darfur.[49]

Both safe havens and no-fly zones obviously involve, if they are to be effective, a willingness by the protecting power to apply full-scale coercive military force in their defense if that proves necessary. To that extent, they raise all the issues about when it is right to use such coercive power and in effect to invade in the process the sovereign territory of another state, with all the issues that again raises (which are discussed in the next chapter). Neither measure should be seen as any kind of cheap or cost-free form of civilian protection.

OTHER MEASURES

Arms embargoes, described in the last chapter as a preventive measure, are also capable of being applied by individual states, regional organizations, or—under Chapter VII authority of the UN Security Council—by the whole international community as a reactive measure after violence breaks out, and have been routinely imposed, albeit to no enormous practical effect, in a large number of such situations.[50]

The *jamming of radio frequencies* is another often urged reactive measure designed to address behavior closely linked to the commission of mass atrocity crimes when stations are used to broadcast hate messages, as in the case of Radio Mille Collines in Rwanda in 1994. This means sending a disrupting radio signal that overtakes or disrupts targeted radio frequencies: a receiver finds the signal frequency of the radio station that is sending hate messages, and then a jamming signal can be tuned to either interrupt the broadcasting or replace it with a different message. Radio frequencies can be jammed in this way by trained and equipped personnel operating receivers and blocking devices from the ground in-country or in a neighboring country. If the situation on the ground is too insecure to deploy personnel and equipment, or the required strong energy source for the blocking devices is lacking, mobile units can disrupt or replace radio frequencies from the air; yet this is much more visible and intrusive as planes have to stay in the country's airspace until transmission begins before they are able to send the disrupting signal.

Free speech arguments might reasonably be expected to yield in these cases to the greater harm capable of being done by incendiary speech of this kind, and there are no other obvious legal problems inhibiting, in a Rwanda-type situation, the UN Security Council authorizing such jamming by whatever means are necessary, in the exercise of its Chapter VII powers.[51] But there can be no question that anything—like jamming from the air—that requires actual intrusion into or over a country's territory can be characterized as risk free or cost free; as with safe havens and no-fly zones, measures of this kind may also require the use of military force to protect the personnel and equipment applying them, and that again raises questions better addressed in the next chapter.

CHAPTER SIX

Reacting to Crises:
When Is It Right to Fight?

Military intervention for human protection purposes is an exceptional and extraordinary measure.

—ICISS, *The Responsibility to Protect*, 2001

All notions of sovereignty with respect to Rwanda should be completely forgotten and we should just go in and stop the killing.

—Nobel Laureate Wole Soyinka, May, 1994[1]

It is inevitable that the use of coercive military force should have dominated so much of the responsibility to protect debate, because the mass atrocity crimes that resonate most in our memory, and make this whole discussion so emotional, are the ones where we know that the timely use of military force would have saved thousands, or hundreds of thousands, of innocent lives—the cases like Rwanda in 1994 and Srebrenica in 1995. Hard as it may be for many to instinctively accept, if there is one thing as bad as using military force when we should not, it is *not* using military force when we *should*.

But it is also unfortunate that so much of the R2P discussion should have focused on this subject, because this has led many, particularly in the global South, to misunderstand R2P as being *only* about the use of force and just another way of talking about "humanitarian intervention," when in fact, as earlier chapters should by now have made clear, it is about much more than that—about prevention at least as much as, if not more than, reaction, and about many much less extreme kinds of reaction. If force is to be an option, it can only be in very narrowly defined circumstances, and it is the purpose of this chapter to spell out in detail what they are.

Use of force issues have also attracted a great deal of time and attention in the R2P debate simply because they are so hard to resolve. They are very difficult in practice because they arise most obviously in cases where people are immediately at grave risk and where speedy action is required. They are very difficult politically because the stakes are so much higher when a government is deciding whether to put on the line the lives of its own country's troops. And they are very difficult intellectually, in terms of the quality of judgment involved, because there are always multiple criteria, some of them in direct competition with each other, that have to be weighed and balanced before any kind of decision can be made that it is indeed right to fight.

No case of this kind has caused more agonized, and continuing, debate than that of Kosovo in 1999. The prevailing view internationally has been that the use of nonconsensual military force was justified, on moral and practical grounds, by the scale of the ethnic cleansing and other crimes against humanity that were already occurring and would have become much worse had NATO not forcibly intervened (although the issue is not without strong dissenting voices still, especially in the non-Western world, on the questions of both whether and how force should have been applied). But because intervention was not authorized by the United Nations Security Council, as a result of Russia's threatened veto, it raised anxious questions, which resonate to this day, about the integrity of the whole international security system.

So how should policymakers keep their balance here? What determines whether a coercive military intervention is legal, what determines when it is legitimate, and how do we resolve situations when there is a prima facie clash between these two requirements?

The Question of Legality

In the United Nations Charter of 1945, the use of force was subjected to the rule of law in a much clearer way than had ever previously been internationally attempted, including in the ill-fated League of Nations Covenant. And it was backed by a system of collective security much more potentially effective than anything that had gone before, with the centerpiece a Security Council empowered to deal forcefully with acts of aggression and threats to the peace. The sense was strong that international relations had at last emerged from a centuries-old jungle, that a new age of international law had dawned: the UN was created above all else "to save succeeding generations from the scourge of war, which twice in our lifetime has brought untold sorrow to mankind," as the Charter's Preamble put it, and the operative provisions of the Charter seemed to give real substance to this rhetoric.[2] Article 2(4) made clear that all UN member states "shall refrain in their international relations from the threat or use of force against the territorial integrity or political independence of any state, or in any other manner inconsistent with the Purposes of the United Nations." Only two exceptions were allowed: self-defense (under Article 51) and military measures authorized by the Security Council in response to "any threat to the peace, breach of the peace or act of aggression" (under Chapter VII, Article 42).

It was one thing, however, to create a new legal order and quite another to make it work The founders of this new order were not naïve, recognizing, as Adlai Stevenson said at the time, that "Everything depends on the active participation, pacific intentions and good faith of the Big Five."[3] Mutual hostility among the five permanent members did very soon emerge, was sustained throughout the cold war years, and threatened to bring the whole edifice down. For forty-four years, until 1989, states repeatedly used military force against others (by one count 200 times and by another 680 times);[4] a great many of these occasions could not begin to be explained or justified as self-defense under Article 51, although that fig leaf was regularly relied upon.[5]

But a paralyzed Security Council passed very few Chapter VII resolutions, and there was only one large-scale collective military action responding to a breach of the peace: in Korea in 1950, during the Soviet Union's misjudged period of absence from the Council. The order that prevailed was essentially a new variation on an old balance of power theme, one in which "each superpower would refrain from attacking the essential interests of the other, but would be freed to use force at will in its own sphere of influence."[6] Such force was used repeatedly, particularly in Central and Eastern Europe and in Latin America and the Caribbean.

Through all this, the UN security system managed to stay afloat, playing a reasonably significant role at least in defusing and managing conflict. "Good offices" diplomacy contributed to the peaceful abatement of some 25 percent of the post-1945 conflicts.[7] And peacekeeping—a role invented by the Secretariat involving the verification, monitoring, and supervision of cease-fire and broader peace agreements—proved crucial in reducing the risk of a number of further wars, especially in South Asia and the Middle East.[8] But it is hard to argue that the new international legal order promised by the Charter was, for the duration of the cold war, under anything but stress.

All that changed dramatically after the Berlin Wall came down in 1989. The removal of a major source of ideological and great-power conflict liberated the UN to play the global security role its founders intended, as became immediately apparent with the response to Iraq's invasion of Kuwait in 1991. Expectations were reinforced by UN-organized or -authorized military deployments in the former Yugoslavia, Somalia, and Haiti. The average number of resolutions passed in a year went from fifteen to sixty, or from a resolution a month to a resolution a week. Ninety-three percent (247 out of 267) of all Chapter VII resolutions of the Council were passed between 1990 and 2002. Before 1989 the Council applied sanctions twice; since then it has imposed them fifteen times.[9]

Whether all this activity was effective is another question, certainly in relation to interventions for human protection purposes. As already discussed in chapter 2, too often what happened—not least in Somalia in 1993, Rwanda in 1994, and Bosnia in 1995—was too little too late, misconceived, poorly resourced, poorly executed, or all of the above. And in Kosovo in 1999, in what was arguably a very strong case for intervention, a divided Security Council was bypassed completely. But there was reason to believe that step by step, painful and disappointing as so much of the process was, a new and much more responsive international legal order was falling into place.

The high-water mark, in terms of both commitment to collective security institutions and a willingness to adapt them to deal with new kinds of threats, probably came with the unanimous Security Council resolution on September 12, 2001, a day after the attacks on the twin towers and the Pentagon, accepting that Article 51 self-defense extended to using force against non-state terrorist organizations as well as "those responsible for aiding, supporting or harbouring the perpetrators, organizers and sponsors of . . . acts" of terrorism.[10] This was followed two weeks later by the adoption of mandatory global controls to prevent the financing of terrorism and the recruiting of terrorists. Confidence in the flexibility of the UN system, and its capacity to deliver, was strong.

But then the wheel turned again, with the decision of the United States and its coalition allies to go to war in Iraq in March 2003 in defiance not only of one or more threatened vetoes but of the clear and overwhelming majority of the members of the Security Council. To the extent that the invasion of Iraq was based on a claim of anticipatory self-defense more far-reaching than any previously asserted, Article 51 was stretched beyond endurance. And to the extent that the invasion was based on claims of threats to international peace and security sufficient under Chapter VII to justify Security Council authorization, but with those claims poorly argued and the Council eventually bypassed, the credibility of the whole Charter system was again frontally challenged.

In the event, the U.S.-led invasion of Iraq conspicuously failed to meet its stated objectives, the wisdom of the wider international community's initial caution about the whole enterprise was vindicated on many fronts, and the death notices served on the UN security system in the immediate aftermath of the bypassing of the Security Council in 2003 proved more than a little premature. Policymakers—even in the United States in the last years of the Bush administration—started thinking again about what could and should be achieved within the framework of that system, rather than assuming its constraints were impossible and constantly seeking to work around it.

In this context it was hoped that the World Summit in 2005, held to commemorate the UN's sixtieth anniversary, would demonstrate a new level of commitment to the institutional renewal of a UN security system badly showing its age. The most optimistic of these hopes proved to be disappointed: there was no agreement on updating the membership of the Security Council to reflect the realities of the world of the twenty-first century rather than that of 1945, no agreed language at all on how to deal with the ever-alarming issue of weapons of mass destruction, and no willingness, as will be discussed further in this chapter, to grapple with setting guidelines for the use of force generally. But at least on the issue of responding to mass atrocity crimes, the unanimously agreed Summit Outcome Document did place the UN firmly in the center of the entire response repertoire, and squarely reasserted the primacy of the Security Council when it came to authorizing the use of force.

So, as things presently stand, the traditional UN Charter rules have been reasserted. But that is only the beginning of the answer to the question of how these rules are to be applied, not least in the present context. Are they really up to meeting the challenge of mass atrocity crimes?

SECURITY COUNCIL AUTHORIZATION UNDER CHAPTER VII

If a legal foundation has to be found in the UN Charter for the authorization of coercive military force to respond to mass atrocity crimes or for any other purpose, the obvious place to start is Chapter VII, which sets out what is on the face of it a complete scheme for dealing, through the Security Council, with "any threat to the peace, breach of the peace, or act of aggression." The key provisions are Article 39, which gives the basic authority to the Security Council, saying it "shall determine the existence of any threat to the peace, breach of the peace, or act of aggression and shall . . . decide what measures shall be taken . . . to maintain or restore international peace and security"; Article 41, which makes clear that less extreme options are to be preferred, saying that the Council "may decide what measures not involving the use of armed force are to be employed . . . These may include complete or partial interruption of economic relations and . . . means of communication, and the severance of diplomatic relations"; and then the very explicit Article 42: "Should the Security Council consider that measures provided for in Article 41 would be inadequate or have proved to be inadequate, it may take such action by air, sea, or land forces as may be necessary to maintain or restore international peace and security."

All this language is as clear as it possibly could be in its application to external threats—the traditional concern with cross-border aggression and the threats this poses to international peace and security. But it is not so obvious how it relates to internal threats to civilian security of the kind with which the norm of the responsibility to protect is concerned. These situations clearly may involve a threat to, or breach of, the peace, but does addressing them involve maintaining or restoring *international* peace and security? Does the language of Article 42 anticipate collective action against a state when the only threat involved is to those within it? Does there have to be some provable external element, like cross-border refugee flows, to make a particular such case genuinely a threat to "international" peace and security? Does Article 2(7) of the Charter, which expressly prohibits intervention "in matters which are essentially within the jurisdiction of any state" (even though 2(7) itself says "this principle shall not prejudice the application of enforcement measures under Chapter VII"), mean that the Chapter VII intervention power will be interpreted very narrowly? Does the language elsewhere in the Charter and the Universal Declaration, and in the

Genocide Convention, acknowledging individual human rights, make any difference here?

Although the Article 42 power was interpreted narrowly during the cold war, in practice since then the Security Council has taken a quite expansive view of what constitutes "international peace and security" for this purpose, as it did for example in Somalia, and eventually Bosnia, in the early 1990s. In the absence of any provision for judicial review of its decisions, the Council will continue to have considerable latitude to define an "international" threat any way it likes, however limited the actual cross-border impact of a particular situation may be.[11] With no higher authority to gainsay it, threats to international peace and security are what the Security Council says they are. It does not have to give its reasons for determining a matter to be within the scope of Article 42 and does not explicitly do so. That said, the perception that, in an increasingly globalized and interdependent world, few events are ever totally local in their impact has played its part, as has the fact that clear breaches of international human rights standards, and indeed crimes against international law, are invariably involved in these cases. None of this means that, since the end of the cold war, the Security Council has always acted in the way that it should in "internal" cases—as we have seen, more often than not, even in shocking situations like Rwanda in 1994, it has declined to initiate or authorize any enforcement action at all—but it does mean that there is no longer seen to be anything preventing it authorizing military action.

Self-Defense under Article 51

Not all uses of military force under Chapter VII require Security Council authorization. Article 51, which concludes the chapter, makes clear that "nothing in the present Charter shall impair the inherent right of individual or collective self-defense if an armed attack occurs against a Member of the United Nations."[12] The nature and extent of the right to self-defense, and in particular whether it allows preemptive or preventive action, continues to be much debated, but none of that debate has suggested that Article 51 has any utility as a primary source of legal authority for cross-border military action undertaken for the purpose of protecting another country's civilians at risk.[13] This is seen as a completely different kind of enterprise, with an inherently unrelated rationale, needing a different source of authority.

It is true that, as mentioned in chapter 1, "self-defense" has on occasion been invoked in the past in circumstances where the military action in question has in fact provided some useful protection to civilians of another country. In the case of India's invasion of East Pakistan in 1971 (responding to West Pakistan's brutal suppression of Bengalis) and Tanzania's overthrow of Uganda's despotic Idi Amin in 1979, there was some credibility in each case to the claim of self-defense, but this ground was much less available in the case of Vietnam's invasion of Cambodia in 1978 (effectively halting the Khmer Rouge's genocidal brutality toward its own people), where regional strategic advantage was the more obvious rationale. In none of these cases did the reliance on Article 51, real or contrived, do anything to dilute the international criticism of the intervention at the time, but in retrospect at least the East Pakistan and Uganda cases look legally defensible.

The point, in short, is that Article 51 by its nature cannot be a direct source of legal authority for "humanitarian intervention," but it can be an indirect source—in circumstances where there is, independently, a good case to be made for relying on Article 51 self-defense, and where the military action so taken under that cover does in practice also serve a useful protective purpose for the people of another country. This is not an argument for using Article 51 artificially; it is just a matter of acknowledging that there are some cases where shelter might properly be taken under its wing.

Regional Organizations Acting under Chapter VIII

Chapter VIII of the Charter acknowledges the security role of regional and subregional organizations but expressly states that "no enforcement action shall be taken under regional arrangements or by regional agencies without the authorisation of the Security Council," and to that extent Chapter VIII is no more than a variation on the basic Chapter VII theme of Security Council preeminence. That said, there is a general willingness to allow regional organizations a fairly free hand in dealing with human protection catastrophes at least within their own defined region, and the required authorization has on occasion been given after the event, as with ECOWAS's Monitoring Group (ECOMOG) in Liberia in 1992 and Sierra Leone in 1997, suggesting scope for further such action in the future. It is rather more difficult to contemplate such tolerance being extended to a regional organization taking coercive action out-of-area against a nonmember, as with NATO in Kosovo in 1999.[14]

GENERAL ASSEMBLY AUTHORITY

It has regularly been suggested that the General Assembly may have a role in authorizing military action in the exercise of its "Uniting for Peace" procedures, developed in 1950 specifically to address the situation where the Security Council, because of lack of unanimity among its permanent members, fails to exercise its primary responsibility for the maintenance of international peace and security.[15] This involves a mechanism whereby an "emergency special session" of the General Assembly could be called either on a procedural vote in the Security Council (which cannot be blocked by the permanent members) or within twenty-four hours of a request by a majority of UN members being received by the secretary-general. Certainly, if a decision were supported by an overwhelming majority of member states, it would provide a high degree of legitimacy for a military intervention (and had the procedure been tested in the cases of Rwanda and Kosovo, it is conceivable that there would have been such support)—but, given that the General Assembly has no power to direct such action or to override the Security Council, it would not ensure formal legality.

LEGAL AUTHORITY OUTSIDE THE UN CHARTER?

A good deal of intellectual energy has been expended over the years in exploring whether, at least for the kinds of situations we are discussing here—involving mass atrocities against civilians—alternative sources of legal authority to the Security Council are available or can be devised. Arguments here fall into three broad categories: those making a case for institutional reforms to change or replace the Security Council; those suggesting that customary international law has evolved to the point that a separate source of authority already exists; and those taking the more extreme view that the whole UN-focused international security system is a chimera, and that until it can be replaced with something more appropriately representing global power realities, it should not be seen as a constraint on states doing what they feel they need to do.

There have been many relevant proposals for the reform of the institutions of global governance, ranging from removing or modifying the veto powers presently held by the five permanent Security Council members, to vesting greater authority in the General Assembly, to creating wholly new institutional structures.[16] One of the more ambitious such proposals would have states proposing the preventive use of military force either get prior Security Council approval on the basis they submit themselves afterward for evaluation by an impartial body on the accuracy of their prior statements and proportionality of their actions, or, if the Security Council blocks the proposed action, go through a similar ex ante and ex post process with a coalition of democratic states.[17] But the trouble with all such proposals is that they founder, some more heroically than others, on the rock of political reality. No permanent member is going to vote in the foreseeable future for a Charter amendment that removes or dilutes its veto power. A more modest proposal advanced by ICISS (after some indication of support from France) was that the permanent members at the very least agree voluntarily not to utilize their veto to block action for which there is otherwise a Council majority and where their own vital national interests are not engaged; but this received little support.[18] A more modest proposal still currently being advanced by the nongovernmental community in New York is that, at the very least, there be a voluntary agreement that the veto not be exercised in cases of evident mass atrocity crimes. But the trouble with all such proposals is that they tend to run into the stumbling block immortally characterized by an Australian Prime Minister of the 1940s, Ben Chifley: "The trouble with gentleman's agreements is that there are not enough bloody gentlemen." And more far-reaching proposals for wholly new decisionmaking institutions, while intellectually stimulating, are simply quixotic in the present and foreseeable international political environment.

Arguments that customary international law in fact allows military intervention for human protection purposes have been around, as mentioned in chapter 2, since the early twentieth century. But at least since the adoption of the UN Charter in 1945, any approach suggesting that unilateral interventions, without Security Council approval, might be so authorized founder at the threshold that clear treaty provisions, including those of the UN Charter, prevail over customary rules. Some attempts have been made to meet this objection by suggesting that the basic meta-rules of international law—including as to what are customary rules, and what are rules of treaty interpretation, and how they interrelate—are themselves changing as a result of state practice, but this approach is hard to accept given the lack of credible evidence that there is any widespread international movement of practice or opinion of this kind.[19]

The most extreme challenges to the authority of the Security Council are those that argue that there are simply no rules any more, that the whole UN Charter "edifice" has come "crashing down." Professor Michael Glennon, for example, took this position writing in *Foreign Affairs* in the immediate aftermath of the coalition invasion of Iraq in 2003 that occurred without specific Security Council authorization, and indeed in the face of a clear majority of members opposed to such action, at least on the state of the evidence available at that time. His argument was that the reality of U.S. power, and the failure of the Security Council structure to reflect it, should be frankly recognized and that, in any attempt in the future to recreate a body of international law governing the use of force in all its manifestations, "what the design should look like must be a function of what it can look like."[20]

This view was hardly unchallengeable, and it did not go unchallenged at the time.[21] The trouble with intellectualizing failure in this way, whether it be motivated by cynicism or genuine despair, is that it can become self-fulfilling. There is always a choice, when confronted with the unhappy reality that governments do not always behave as we hope they might, of raising one's sights or lowering them. When, as Kofi Annan described them, "the principles on which, however imperfectly, world peace and stability have rested" for the last six decades come under assault, as they did in the context of Iraq in 2003, the appropriate response would seem to be not to abandon the search for an orderly, principled system of international law and practice on conflict, which is almost as old as conflict itself, but rather to renew it.[22]

This was the approach taken by both the ICISS commissioners and the High-Level Panel. In the words of the former:

> There is no better or more appropriate body than the Security Council to deal with military intervention issues for human protection purposes. . . . That was the overwhelming consensus we found in all our deliberations around the world. If international consensus is ever to be reached about when, where, how and by whom military intervention should happen, it is very clear that the central role of the Security Council will have to be at the heart of that consensus. The task is not to find alternatives to the Security Council as a source of authority, but to make the Security Council work much better than it has.[23]

The Question of Legitimacy

Accepting that the Security Council is the right decisionmaking body to confer legal authority on a coercive military intervention does not mean that it will in fact make that decision in a particular case, or that it should. Making the Security Council work better means devoting a lot more attention to its decisionmaking processes, and in particular to ensuring that decisions about authorizing or supporting military intervention are made on solid evidentiary grounds and for the right reasons of morality or principle: in short, ensuring that they are not just legal, but legitimate.

The distinction between legality and legitimacy first came into prominence in this context with the argument of the Sweden-sponsored Kosovo Commission in 1999 that the NATO invasion may not have been legal, in the absence of Security Council approval, but it was—taking into account and balancing out some fourteen "threshold" and "contextual" principles—legitimate.[24] The distinction—if it can be operationalized, with criteria of legitimacy simplified, standardized, and commonly accepted—is an important one. The effectiveness of the global collective security system, as with any other legal order, depends ultimately not only on the legality of decisions but also on the common perception of their legitimacy: their being made on solid evidentiary grounds, for the right reasons, morally as well as legally. While it is obviously optimal for any military action to be both unquestionably legal under international law and more or less universally accepted as legitimate (as was the case, for example, with the 1991 Gulf War), it is fair to suggest that military action that is technically illegal but widely perceived to be legitimate (as with Kosovo in 1999) does far less damage than action which is generally perceived to be neither legal nor legitimate (Iraq in 2003).

A corollary of this argument is that if there is a widespread perception that action is illegitimate, making it formally legal will not do anything to change that—and may in fact do even more damage to the reputation of the legalizing body. This was very much France's argument in the context of the Iraq debate: that the credibility of the Security Council would be put even more at risk by endorsing action widely seen around the world as unjustified than it would by being ignored and bypassed altogether. A further corollary of the argument may be that legitimacy helps breed legality. If there is general confidence that Security Council decisions on the use of force *will* be made for the right reasons, giving attention to the full range of threats with which major countries are currently preoccupied, having regard to the weight of the evidence, applying appropriate threshold and prudential criteria, and with the power of veto not being exercised capriciously, then those who are currently tempted to bypass the system will be much less tempted to do so—or, perhaps equally importantly, will be at much greater risk of embarrassment if they do so act.

It is with this objective in mind that the ICISS commissioners recommended that to help achieve consensus in reaching any decision about the coercive use of military force, against the will of the state in question, the Security Council should adopt as guidelines a number of criteria of legitimacy. The particular criteria that we advocated were picked up subsequently, in almost identical terms, by the High-Level Panel on Threats, Challenges, and Change and by the Secretary-General in his own 2005 *In Larger Freedom* report, but not, unhappily, by the World Summit or, so far, by the Security Council itself. The task of identifying the right principles proved easier than anticipated. While the literature on this subject is very large, and while there are almost as many different lists of such criteria as there have been contributions to this debate, in reality there is an enormous amount of common ground to be found when one focuses on the core issues. All the relevant decisionmaking criteria seemed capable of being summarized under the following five headings, discussed in turn below: seriousness of harm, proper purpose, last resort, proportional means, and balance of consequences (see box 6-1).[25]

All of them have an explicit pedigree in Christian "just war" theory, going back to the early Middle Ages, but their themes do resonate equally, and are not inconsistent, with the other major world religious and intellectual traditions.[26] It is important to appreciate that the criteria were intended to reflect universal values and not in any way be culture or religion specific: the ICISS commissioners were hardly unaware of the Christian and Eurocentric associations of the particular language adopted, but chose to emphasize its more general application.

No one who supports these criteria of legitimacy (which are equally applicable to individual countries' decisionmaking about the use of force as they are to the Security Council's) is naïve about their utility. There is no push-button inevitability about their application, and for the Security Council to adopt them is no guarantee that the objectively best outcome

Box 6-1. The Use of Force: Criteria of Legitimacy

ONE: SERIOUSNESS OF HARM

Is the threatened harm of a kind, and sufficiently clear and serious, to justify *prima facie* the use of military force? In the case of internal threats, does it involve genocide, war crimes, ethnic cleansing or crimes against humanity, actual or imminently apprehended?

TWO: PROPER PURPOSE

Is it clear that the primary purpose of the proposed military action is to halt or avert the threat in question, whatever other purposes or motives may be involved?

THREE: LAST RESORT

Has every nonmilitary option for meeting the threat in question been explored, with reasonable grounds for believing that other measures will not succeed?

FOUR: PROPORTIONAL MEANS

Are the scale, duration, and intensity of the proposed military action the minimum necessary to halt or avert the threat in question?

FIVE: BALANCE OF CONSEQUENCES

Is there a reasonable chance of the military action being successful in meeting the threat in question, with the consequences of action not likely to be worse than the consequences of inaction?

Sources: ICISS, *The Responsibility to Protect*, pp. xii, 35–37; High-Level Panel, *A More Secure World*, pp. 66–67, 106–07; Kofi Annan, *In Larger Freedom*, pp. 43, 83.

will always prevail. The argument is that existence of agreed criteria surely would change the nature of Security Council debate; maximize the possibility of achieving Council consensus around when it is appropriate or not to go to war; maximize international support for whatever it decides; and minimize the possibility of individual member states bypassing or ignoring it. As Kofi Annan put it in his *In Larger Freedom* report to the World Summit, "By undertaking to make the case for military action in this way, the Council would add transparency to its deliberations and make its decisions more likely to be respected, by both Governments and world public opinion."[27]

CRITERION ONE: SERIOUSNESS OF HARM

This threshold "just cause" test needs to be set high and tight, for both conceptual reasons (military intervention for human protection purposes must be a measure seen as acceptable only in the most exceptional circumstances) and practical political ones (if intervention is to happen when it is most necessary, it cannot be called upon too often). The High-Level Panel expressed it in the following terms: "Is the threatened harm to State or human security of a kind, and sufficiently clear and serious, to justify *prima facie* the use of military force? In the case of internal threats, does it involve genocide and other large-scale killing, ethnic cleansing or serious violations of international humanitarian law, actual or imminently apprehended?"[28]

This drew upon the ICISS commissioners' formulation, which remains useful as a slightly more detailed guide to the kind of hurdle which needs to be jumped at the outset. It suggested that military intervention in internal civilian threat situations was justified in just two sets of circumstances, namely to halt or avert "*large scale loss of life,* actual or apprehended, with genocidal intent or not, which is the product either of deliberate state action, or state neglect or inability to act, or a failed state situation; or *large scale 'ethnic cleansing,'* actual or apprehended, whether carried out by killing, forced expulsion, acts of terror, or rape."[29]

While neither ICISS nor the High-Level Panel made any attempt to quantify "large scale," leaving this to be determined context by context, both made it absolutely clear that military action can be legitimate as an anticipatory measure in response to clear evidence of likely large-scale killing or ethnic cleansing. Without this possibility of anticipatory action, the international community would be placed in the morally untenable position of being required to wait until genocide begins before being able to take action to stop it. Both formulations are certainly wide enough to cover the deliberate perpetration of horrors such as occurred, or were anticipated, in Bosnia, Rwanda, and Kosovo. Situations of state collapse and the resultant exposure of the population to mass starvation and/or civil war (as in Somalia) would clearly be covered by the ICISS formulation, but in the High-Level Panel version, probably only if large-scale crimes against humanity, involving some element of intent, were also involved.

What are not intended to be covered by either of these formulations are three familiar situations: human rights violations (such as systematic racial discrimination or political oppression), which nonetheless fall short of large-scale killing or ethnic cleansing; the overthrow of democratically elected governments; or the rescue by a state of its own nationals on foreign territory. Although eminently deserving of external action of various kinds—including in appropriate cases political, economic, or military sanctions—these are not cases that would seem to justify military action, given the conceptual and practical need to always regard such action, as the ICISS commissioners put it, "an exceptional and extraordinary measure."

CRITERION TWO: PROPER PURPOSE

The relevant question here, formulated in almost identical terms by both ICISS and the High-Level Panel, is straightforward: is it clear that the primary purpose of the proposed military action is to halt or avert the threat in question, whatever other purposes or motives may be involved?

The primary purpose of the intervention, whatever other motives intervening states may have, must be to halt or avert human suffering. Overthrow of regimes is not, as such, a legitimate objective, although disabling a regime's capacity to harm its own people may be essential to discharging the mandate of protection, and what is necessary to achieve that will vary from case to case. One way of helping ensure that the "proper purpose" criterion is satisfied is to have military intervention always take place on a collective or multilateral rather than single-country basis. Another is to look to whether, and to what extent, the intervention is actually supported by the people for whose benefit the intervention is intended. Yet another is to look to whether, and to what extent, the opinion of other countries in the region has been taken into account and is supportive.

Complete disinterestedness—the absence of any narrow self-interest at all—may be an ideal, but it is not likely always to be a reality: mixed motives, in international relations as everywhere else, are a fact of life. Moreover, the budgetary cost and risk to personnel involved in any military action may in fact make it politically imperative for the intervening state to be able to claim some degree of self-interest in the intervention, however altruistic its primary motive might actually be. To those domestic constituencies who may actually demand of their governments, when it comes to intervention for human protection purposes, that they not be moved by altruistic "right intention," the best short answer may be that, these days, good international citizenship is a matter of national self-interest. With the world as close and interdependent as it now is, and with crises in "faraway countries of which we know little" as capable as they now are of generating major problems elsewhere (terrorism, refugee outflows, health pandemics, narcotics trafficking, organized crime, and the like), it is strongly arguable that it is in every country's interest to contribute cooperatively to the resolution of such problems, quite apart from the humanitarian imperative to do so.[30]

CRITERION THREE: LAST RESORT

The question to be asked here is again a simple one, but extraordinarily often misunderstood: has every nonmilitary option for meeting the threat in question been explored, with reasonable grounds for believing that other measures will not succeed?

This guideline was not intended by ICISS and the High-Level Panel to mean that every nonmilitary option—not only diplomatic persuasion but economic sanctions, threats of International Criminal Court proceedings, or any other conceivably relevant measure—must literally have been tried and failed. "Exploring" an option to the point of having "reasonable grounds for believing" that it will not succeed does not mean, as a matter of plain English or practical common sense, actually putting it in place and waiting around for it to fail. Given that there will often be simply no time for that process to work itself out, what is necessary is simply that there be reasonable grounds for believing, in all the circumstances, that these other less extreme measures would not have worked.

CRITERION FOUR: PROPORTIONAL MEANS

The appropriate question here, again formulated in almost identical terms by ICISS and the High-Level Panel, is whether the scale, duration, and intensity of the proposed military action are the minimum necessary to meet the humanitarian objective of the particular case. The means have to be commensurate with the ends and in line with the magnitude of the original threat. The effect on the political system of the country targeted should be limited, again, to what is strictly necessary to accomplish the purpose of the intervention. While it may be a matter for argument in each case what are the precise practical implications of these strictures, the principles involved are clear enough.

CRITERION FIVE: BALANCE OF CONSEQUENCES

The question here, again similarly framed by both ICISS and the High-Level Panel, is deceptively simple, but this final criterion of legitimacy is often in practice the most difficult to satisfy: is there a reasonable chance of the military action being successful in meeting the threat in question, with the consequences of action not likely to be worse than the consequences of inaction?

Coercive military action can only be justified if it stands a reasonable chance of success, that is, halting or averting the atrocities or suffering that triggered the intervention in the first place. It is not justified if actual protection cannot be achieved, or if the consequences of embarking upon the intervention are likely to be worse than if there is no action at all. The classic contemporary case is Darfur, already discussed in chapter 3: quite apart from the practical question of finding troop-providing countries willing to support a nonconsensual intervention, there has been huge concern among those wholly sympathetic to the Darfurians' plight that such an enterprise would make the overall situation much worse, in terms of its negative impact on current humanitarian relief operations, and the probability that it would reignite the already horribly destructive north-south Sudan conflict. In particular, a military action for limited human protection purposes cannot be justified if in the process it triggers a larger conflict. It will be the case that some human beings simply cannot be rescued except at unacceptable cost—perhaps of a larger regional conflagration, involving major military powers. In such cases, however painful the reality, coercive military action is no longer justified. None of this means that "the responsibility to protect" norm is irrelevant: just that it has to be implemented here by means falling short of full-scale coercive military intervention.

There is a further "balance of consequences" constraint on coercive military action that has to be realistically acknowledged. As the ICISS commissioners explained, application of this precautionary principle would be likely to preclude military action against any one of the five permanent members of the Security Council, even if all the other conditions for intervention described here were met.[31] It is difficult to imagine a major conflict being avoided, or success in the original objective being achieved, if such action were mounted against any of them. The same is true of other major powers who are not permanent members of the Security Council. This raises the familiar question of double standards, to which the only answer can be this: the reality that interventions may not be able to be mounted in every case where there is justification for doing so is no reason for them not to be mounted in any case.

Legality versus Legitimacy

There remains to address the problem of what exactly is to be done in a situation in which the criteria of legitimacy seem manifestly to be satisfied, yet the cloak of formal legality is not available because, for whatever reason, the Security Council fails or refuses to authorize the relevant military action.

As the ICISS commissioners expressed it, in these cases a very real dilemma arises as to which of two evils is the worse: the damage to international order if the Security Council is bypassed, or the damage to that order if human beings are slaughtered while the Security Council stands by. Their own response to this dilemma was not to try and establish some alternative basis for the legality of interventions but to opt instead for a very clear political message, in the following terms. It has to be anticipated that if the Security Council fails to discharge its responsibility in a conscience-shocking situation crying out for action, a concerned individual state or ad hoc coalition will step in. And if it does so, fully observes and respects all the necessary criteria of legitimacy, intervenes successfully, and is seen to have done so by world public opinion, then this is likely to have "enduringly serious consequences for the stature and credibility of the UN itself."[32]

Such an intervention is essentially what happened with U.S. and NATO action in Kosovo in 1999—which has been seen since as essentially well-motivated and effective by most, if not all, of the international community—and it is realistic to argue that the UN Security Council, if it is to maintain its standing, simply cannot afford to drop the ball too many times on that scale. For all the weaknesses of this essentially political response—which those of a more theoretical disposition do tend to find a little alien and discomfiting—there are not many ways of squaring the circle here. Any concession that as a matter of law (as distinct from morality or principle) there are some circumstances that justify the Security Council being bypassed is one that seriously undermines the whole concept of a rules-based international order. That order depends upon the Security Council, in the absence of a credible self-defense argument, being the *only* source of legal authority for nonconsensual military interventions.

Another way of dealing with the legality-versus-legitimacy problem, which may have a little more appeal to those whose taste runs more to legal constructs than political arguments, is to call in aid the familiar courtroom process of a "plea in mitigation," as suggested by Thomas Franck among others.[33] This would involve an acknowledgment of the illegality combined with a claim that it took place in exceptional and defensible circumstances. Michael Byers and Simon Chesterman have made the case for this approach about as strongly as it can be made:

> If the intervening state admits that it is violating international law, the intervention itself will not undermine the existing rules, while the admission of illegality may in fact serve to strengthen them. . . . Indeed the greatest threat to an international rule of law lies not in the occasional breach of that law—laws are frequently broken in all legal systems, sometimes for the best of reasons—but in attempts to mould that law to the shifting practices of the powerful.[34]

We must simply hope that over time there emerges some greater convergence between the legal and political order, that the Security Council *will* work better than it has done, and that fewer cases will arise of manifest tension between legality and legitimacy.

CHAPTER SEVEN

After the Crisis: The Responsibility to Rebuild

The responsibility to rebuild [is] to provide, particularly after a military intervention, full assistance with recovery, reconstruction and reconciliation, addressing the causes of the harm the intervention was designed to halt or avert.

—ICISS, *The Responsibility to Protect*, 2001

Any mule can kick a barn door down, but it takes a carpenter to build it back.

—Speaker Sam Rayburn, January 1953

Deadly conflict is rarely over when it's over. We understand much better now than we did even a decade ago that mass violence is much more cyclical than linear—that the best single indicator we have of the probability of future conflict is past conflict. Sustainable peace cannot be guaranteed just because a diplomatic peacemaking initiative has apparently been successful: think of the horror still to come after the Angola agreement of 1991 or the Rwanda accords in 1993. Nor can it be ensured because a clear-cut military victory has apparently been won: think of Afghanistan after the withdrawal of the Soviet Union in 1989 and the defeat of the Taliban in 2001, or Iraq after 2003. Postconflict peacebuilding is not the end of the process of conflict resolution; it has to be the beginning of a new process of conflict prevention, with the focus again on structural prevention, tackling the longer-term, root causes of the violence in question. It is a hugely complex, time-consuming, and usually very costly enterprise. But when the responsibility to rebuild is neglected, by national governments and the international governments and organizations that must stand ready to help them, it is only a matter of time before the boil will erupt again.

The responsibility to rebuild a society, in the aftermath of war or mass atrocity crimes that have torn it apart, has four interrelated but distinct dimensions, discussed successively below: achieving security, good governance, justice and reconciliation, and economic and social development. There are a great many lessons that can be drawn from our by now considerable experience of postconflict peacebuilding in the post–cold war world, but one very basic one is that these multiple objectives have to be pursued more or less simultaneously: physical security may always be the first priority, but it cannot be the only one, and, in particular, recreating—or creating—a viable justice system and respect for the rule of law, and the governance preconditions for economic development, deserves higher priority than it usually has been given. The toolbox of rebuilding measures reflects the reality that very similar kinds of structural strategies are involved here as for long-term crisis and conflict prevention: see box 7-1 and appendix B.

There are some other general lessons as well that, obvious as they may seem, appear not yet to have been fully absorbed—and certainly not yet fully acted on—by all the relevant international players. First, sort out who should do what and when—immediately, over a medium transition period, and in the longer term—and then allocate the roles and coordinate them effectively, both in relevant capitals and on the ground. Second, commit the necessary resources, and sustain that commitment for as long as it takes. Third, understand the local political dynamics and the limits of what outsiders can do. Fourth, have an exit strategy, and one that is *not* just devoted to holding early elections as soon as possible, as important as it obviously is to vest real local authority and responsibility as soon as possible. Fifth, don't confuse an exit strategy with an exit timetable; be prepared to stay, subject to local consent, as long as it takes, recognizing that more peacebuilding mistakes have been made by internationals leaving too soon and doing too little than staying too long and doing too much.[1] The new Peacebuilding Commission, agreed to at the 2005 World Summit—one of its few achievements other than the endorsement of R2P—is intended to play a major role in improving practice in all these respects, as discussed further below. It is unusual for intergovernmental organizations of this kind to do precisely what they are supposed to, and even more for them to do it well, but one lives in hope.

BOX 7-1. THE REBUILDING TOOLBOX

Structural
- **I** Rebuilding governance institutions
- **I** Maximizing local ownership

Structural
- **I** Support economic development
- **I** Social programs for sustainable peace

Political/Diplomatic Measures

Economic/Social Measures

Structural
- **I** Rebuilding criminal justice
- **I** Managing transitional justice
- **I** Supporting traditional justice
- **I** Managing refugee returns

Structural
- **I** Peacekeeping in support of nation building
- **I** Disarmament, demobilization, and reintegration
- **I** Security sector reform

Constitutional/Legal Measures

Security Sector Measures

There is one other more fundamental lesson, which should have been learned in Iraq after 2003 if nowhere else, that is worth internalizing at the outset by anyone in the peacebuilding business: *imposing* a peace settlement and democratic institutions of governance on a state and people ravaged by war and atrocity crimes is highly unlikely to work. What is crucial is to somehow win a much deeper understanding among the major parties to the conflict that they have shared interests, a common vision, and must learn to live and work in collaboration with each other. This is much easier said than achieved, even with sophisticated special programs designed for this purpose, but if it is not part of the mind-set of peacebuilders from the outset, the whole process is very likely to end in tears.[2]

Achieving Security

Peacekeeping in Support of Nation Building

It has become common, almost the norm now in the post–cold war era, for major peace operations to have a significant peacebuilding or, as more often described in this context, "nation-building" component. That is true for those conceived from the outset as "peacekeeping plus" missions, focused on supporting and consolidating peacemaking processes, stabilizing the country in question through immediate postconflict transition, and paving the way for long-term development, as with the missions led wholly, or most of the time, by the United Nations in Namibia, El Salvador, Cambodia, Somalia, Mozambique, Haiti, Eastern Slavonia, Sierra Leone, and Timor-Leste.[3] It is also true for a number of heavy-duty peace enforcement missions led by the U.S. and various combinations of allies, acting with or without an initial UN mandate, as in Bosnia, Kosovo, Afghanistan, and Iraq.[4]

A comprehensive Rand study of all these operations has concluded, interestingly, that while, for familiar reasons, the United States and its allies have been much better in recent decades than UN-led forces at mounting high-posture, large-footprint, peace enforcement, or actual war-fighting, operations—where the whole point of the enterprise is to confront an enemy, identified as such for better or worse, from the outset rather than dealing with spoilers after some kind of peace has been agreed—the UN has in fact been very much better, in terms of achieving sustainable peace and stable governance, when it comes to the use of military resources in support of nation building. This has something to do with UN-led missions usually having been less intrinsically difficult—although, as I can well personally recall, there can have been few postconflict missions more complex in their design and stressful in their implementation than Cambodia from 1991 to 1993.[5] But the UN success is also attributed to generally more modest ambitions ("American officials tend to emphasize democratization as their chief goal, whereas the UN leadership stresses the more measurable, and somewhat more achievable goals of conflict resolution and sustained peace"), and to UN staff, with more continuity and specialist expertise, doing a better job of learning from its mistakes ("Throughout the 1990s the United States became steadily better ... but the learning curve was not sustained into the current decade").[6] The Rand study concludes, "Assuming adequate consensus among Security Council members on the purpose for any intervention, the United Nations provides the most suitable institutional framework for most nation-building missions, one with a comparatively low cost structure, a comparatively high success rate, and the greatest degree of international legitimacy."[7]

As to the costs and benefits overall of devoting military resources to nation building, the quantitatively irrepressible Paul Collier has come up with what appears, if one accepts the arithmetic, a very good economic reason for supporting sustained peacekeeping operations in countries ravaged by civilian violence. Suggesting that the total cost of any given civil war to a country and its neighbors is from $60 billion to $250 billion (taking into account impact on growth and time needed to recover), he and his colleagues estimate that $8.5 billion spent on ten years of peacekeeping would reduce the risk of renewed conflict by enough to save no less than $18 billion to $75 billion.[8]

There are a variety of security tasks that peacekeeping missions in the postconflict peacebuilding stage must be prepared to perform in the general context of providing the safe environment necessary for the restoration of good governance, the rule of law, and the conditions for economic growth and development. Some are essentially a continuation of the responsibility-to-react role that was described in chapter 5 as "peacekeeping for civilian protection," in particular responding militarily, as necessary, to spoilers who may seek to violently disrupt a hard-won peace, until such time as confident and capable national forces can play that role themselves. Some tasks may be more akin to ordinary law and order maintenance, a police rather than military function but one that is crucial for stabilizing a war-torn society and, among other things, ensuring that refugees and internally displaced persons (IDPs) are willing to return home. This is a role, again, that has to be somehow exercised or led by peacekeepers until such time as effective national capability has been built or rebuilt, a process often much more protracted and difficult than planners anticipate, as experience in Afghanistan, among many other cases, bears out.[9] "Security sector reform," discussed below, is essentially the business of building that necessary local capability. Interacting with this, and also discussed separately below, is the invariably complex and troublesome process of managing the disarmament, demobilization, and reintegration (DDR) of former combatants.

In addition to these somewhat all-consuming roles, there are two other more specific tasks that peacekeepers may be called upon to perform or supervise that were identified in the ICISS report and are worth specific mention here.[10] One is *mine clearance.* Worldwide, there remain some 40 million to 50 million active land mines currently in the ground in almost every significant civil conflict area.[11] In 2006 uncleared land mines killed nearly 1,400 people and left many thousands more injured: the number of known mine injury survivors rose to 473,000, many of whom now need lifelong care.[12] Demining operations are clearly essential not only for the immediate safety of people in the areas in question but also for the return of civilians to areas previously subject to conflict. But they have to be carried out not only with great technical expertise but a care that can seem painfully slow. As former U.S. land mines expert and now International Crisis Group Deputy President Donald Steinberg has recalled,

> In the rush to see Angola's four million displaced persons return to their homes in a country where large numbers of landmines had been planted, we focused primarily on the commercial demining of major roads. Regrettably, our humanitarian demining efforts in local fields, forests, and lakes were given secondary priority. When the displaced returned to their homes and started going out to plant fields, collect firewood, and fetch water, there was a rush of tragic landmine accidents.[13]

The *pursuit and apprehension of indicted war criminals* is another task very likely to fall upon international peacekeepers during the peacebuilding phase. It is one that has tended to remain sadly incomplete, with enforcement agencies finding local intelligence often difficult to obtain and fearing violent local reactions from one side or another if their diligence should succeed. Even when, as discussed later, there is a desire on the part of the national population to place more weight on reconciliation than accountability, and even given the reality, discussed in chapter 5, that considerations of peace will occasionally trump those of justice when it comes to concluding peace negotiations, there are some crimes committed that are so unconscionable as to make their non-prosecution by national or international courts an unacceptable option. But actually apprehending indicted war criminals remains hugely difficult, with the advent of the International Criminal Court not offering any institutional solutions and, if anything, exposing even more starkly the problem of lack of enthusiasm and cooperation in making arrests. The most blatant cases were for many years the non-capture of International Criminal Tribunal for the former Yugoslavia (ICTY) Bosnian Serb indictees Radovan Karadzic and Ratko Mladic: despite various efforts by NATO forces and local authorities, and much continued international pressure on the Bosnian and Serbian governments, Karadzic was not captured until July 22, 2008, after a change of government and as this book was going to press, while Mladic, who received an army pension as late as November 2005, remains at large.[14]

Disarmament, Demobilization, and Reintegration (DDR)

This is an essential part of the postconflict peacebuilding and stabilization process, aimed at interrupting the conflict cycle and facilitating a transition of armed groups into national forces or back into civilian life. To be effective, as with so much else in postconflict peacebuilding, it requires close and effective cooperation between national authorities and the international missions assisting them. In some contexts this is much more than a straightforward security problem: in Afghanistan, for example, successful DDR will necessarily involve, by reducing the influence of warlords, a major restructuring of the political landscape, and the halting progress of these programs has been a factor holding up other political, economic, and administrative developments.[15] The overwhelming lesson from all experience is that the political will of the principal parties is essential for DDR: while pressure can be applied by international bodies and their resources used to facilitate the process, this is largely futile without clear commitment from the parties themselves.

Disarmament, aimed at the collection and destruction of existing weapons and the progressive suppression of the capacity to produce or purchase new ones, is obviously likely to be most effective when based on consent, regardless of whether any external forces involved in the process are deployed under Chapter VI or VII mandates. But achieving voluntary disarmament regularly runs into local resistance from combatants, with peacekeeping operations often then proving unable or unwilling to compel them, a recurring problem in eastern Congo among many other instances.[16] Sometimes disarmament can be more symbolic than real, in terms of seeing the actual surrender and destruction of all usable weapons, but be a useful contribution to the consolidation of the peace process notwithstanding.[17] It is not uncommon for peace operations facing complete local recalcitrance to simply acquiesce in this reality, adjust the mandate, and proceed with the "peace process" regardless: while not to be enthusiastically emulated, this is sometimes unavoidable, and was the approach taken, for example, in Angola.[18]

Demobilization, even more than disarmament, has to be handled intelligently and sensitively if there is not to be counterproductive backlash—as the mindless wholesale disbanding of the former Iraqi army after 2003 makes abundantly clear, leaving scores of thousands of former soldiers, many of whom displayed no loyalty to the regime and most of whom had played no part at all in its atrocities, without income, future, or honor.[19] In some cases, like Kosovo, the problem of former combatants has been managed, albeit not without controversy, less by demobilization than reclassification, with the creation of the Kosovo Protection Corps (KPC), perceived as a way station toward the creation of an army for a future independent country and whose command structure was essentially that of the former Kosovo Liberation Army (KLA).[20] In other cases, like Cambodia, elaborate cantonment and demobilization provisions, like much of the disarmament part of the process, simply had to be largely abandoned.[21]

Reintegration is the most costly and the most extensive element of DDR and ultimately the most complex, involving a host of issues ranging from transport arrangements to the resolution of land and property issues and finding employment for the ex-combatants.[22] Mozambique is a classic example of a slow and long-term yet very effective process, with reintegration successful politically—with RENAMO's transition from insurgent group to opposition party—as well as economically and socially.[23] While employment creation schemes may not normally be the most productive use of donor resources, and former insurgent or militia combatants may well be among the least deserving of claimants, there is a strong security imperative in many cases to, at the very least, detach the more dangerous individuals from each other enough to prevent them easily reassociating, rearming, and rethreatening.[24] Public works programs are frequently viewed as the most effective in this respect because they tend to be within the ability of donors to deliver; reconstruction of infrastructure is often, in any case, a pressing postconflict need; and involvement of ex-combatants in visible reconstruction efforts can provide a positive image of ex-combatants as contributors to society.

There is an important social as well as economic element to reintegration, which becomes nightmarishly complex and sensitive to manage in the case of children caught up in conflict, particularly as child soldiers.[25] It is also important to take into account the special needs of female ex-combatants, combatant associates, and dependents, and the special contribution that women can make, here as elsewhere, to peace processes: women should be included on demobilization design committees, and be empowered to lobby and assist in reintegration efforts by providing them with access to resources and training.[26]

SECURITY SECTOR REFORM

Reforming the security sector—ensuring the competent performance and properly accountable management of the armed forces, police, and any intelligence services—is one of the biggest challenges after a conflict, just as it is in avoiding its initial outbreak, as noted already in chapter 4. An ineffective and badly structured security system potentially fuels new tensions and violence, and reform of this sector is often an essential first step in opening up the political climate toward a democratic process.[27] The military components of international peacekeeping missions usually play an important role in efforts to professionalize existing armies or create new ones, but in the case of police reform, it is usually preferable for that input to come from civilian components. Intelligence services are something else again. There may be a need for special agencies to combat terrorism and deal with internal and external security challenges, but they must be highly professional in character, under close government policy control, open to some appropriate degree of external oversight, not in the business of undermining democratic freedoms—and produce useful information. Perhaps there may be paragons of those many virtues in the wider international community, able to pass on their expertise accordingly to frailer brethren in postconflict societies. But as someone who in the course of his earlier ministerial career had responsibility for both external intelligence gathering and internal counterespionage, and many international contacts in those capacities, I am afraid that I remain a little skeptical.[28]

On the military side, strategies for reform encompass enhanced education and training for military forces; strengthening civilian control mechanisms, including budget control; and generally encouraging efforts to ensure that security services are accountable for their actions and operate within the law.[29] The immediate object for national governments, supported by such international assistance as they can get, should be professionalization: ensuring that armed forces focus on their primary mission of external defense, restoring or achieving higher standards of personal discipline, ensuring their criminal accountability, removing them from politics and private business, or more effectively subordinating them to appropriate control by the legitimate government (most desirably a civilian and representative one).[30] Armies are frequently inappropriately involved in internal security; in a pathological case like Liberia, this led to their becoming ethnically based, wholly politicized, and effectively employed by Charles Taylor to crush his opponents.[31] Structural reform needs to be driven by the (civilian) government but also requires fairly comprehensive compliance of the entire chain of command in the armed forces. Various incentives can be employed to encourage progress: in Macedonia, for example, NATO's Membership Action Plan and Partnership for Peace program have been useful catalysts to the reform of force structures, with the reform process itself assisted, including by the successful placement of an influential British special defense adviser inside the ministry.[32]

Similar imperatives apply for police forces, where indiscipline, corruption, and incompetence are even more immediately socially destabilizing.[33] The challenges of recruiting and training local police (as well as the linked problem of reforming other elements of the justice system) have been very evident in countries from Haiti to Bosnia and East Timor but probably nowhere more seriously now than in Afghanistan and Iraq.[34] There have been a number of enthusiastic initiatives in police training and institutional support by the EU and individual member states, the OSCE and NATO, and others, as well as in the context of various UN missions with a police component, but the kindest thing that can be said about all but a handful of them is that the performance has not lived up to the billing. Capable leaders, a professional police force, subnational local oversight, police monitoring, public education on democratic policing, the introduction of professional management strategies, and adequate resourcing are the basics of building a sound and effective police system.

In ethnically or religiously polarized societies, armed forces or security services are often heavily skewed toward one ethnic or religious group, and it is important that any restructuring process seeks to redress that. Not that the task is ever easy: in Burundi the army has traditionally been dominated by the minority Tutsi military class, in Macedonia only 3 percent of the army corps have been Albanian even though they represent 40 percent of the population, while in Northern Ireland the Royal Ulster Constabulary police service, overwhelmingly dominated by Protestants, was—until effectively reformed following the 1999 Royal Commission chaired by Lord Patten—understandably accused by the nationalist community of sectarian bias in favor of unionists.[35]

Achieving Good Governance

Rebuilding Institutions of Governance

There are two distinct dimensions to this task in postconflict peacebuilding situations: the immediate restoration of government services, and the creation, or recreation, of a *system* of governance—with functioning executive, legislative, and judicial institutions—that is capable of sustaining peace in the longer term. A preoccupation with the niceties of constitution making is unlikely to win many local friends if not only law and order is in a shambles—the security issues just addressed—but energy and water supplies are erratic or nonexistent, roads are impassable or unusable, telecommunications are out, public health delivery has collapsed, and schools are not open. So much is obvious, but making governance happen at this basic level sometimes seems beyond the capacity of even the most apparently capable of interveners, as the experience of Iraq after 2003 amply demonstrates.

The first need, accordingly, is to establish a workable source of transitional authority, capable of making the necessary decisions about basic service provision and having them implemented. Depending on local circumstances there are essentially three options: for the existing national government to stay in place, relying as necessary on external advice and support, until such time as its authority can be relegitimated; for an external intervener, in the absence of any credible immediate national alternative, to govern on its own; or for the external intervener to establish an interim national government by cooption, appointment, or consultation.[36] The latter two options are obviously less desirable in principle than the first but may be unavoidable. What is absolutely crucial is that intervening international authorities get it very firmly in their heads from the outset that they will never be in a position to deliver any of the required services without relying hugely on host-country nationals and local institutions: with all the problems this may entail of choosing on whom to rely and whom to benefit with funds and power, there is no alternative but to approach basic governance with the need to maximize local ownership, discussed further below, as a central guiding principle.

There remains a certain residual nostalgia, as noted in the ICISS report, for the recreation of some kind of UN "trusteeship" framework for some of those states, particularly in a postconflict environment, that can be characterized as failing or failed or having institutions so minimally credible that even "failed" seems generous and "phantom" a more accurate description.[37] Such a framework does notionally still exist in the UN Charter, as Chapter XII, but it predated the age of decolonization and is now for all practical purposes defunct: the Charter would need to be rewritten to make it applicable to actual sovereign member states, as distinct from dependent territories, and that seems inconceivable in the contemporary age. Probably the most that can be hoped for is that the new Peacebuilding Commission, discussed further below, will evolve over time to the point where it can effectively coordinate the support of a broad range of countries and institutions to manage these extremely difficult situations—with Somalia, now seventeen years without an accepted national government, the most pressing example—in a more coherent and committed fashion than the international community has managed so far.

The bigger challenge than getting the basics of service-providing governance in place is to develop a longer-term governance structure that is not only capable in this minimal sense but is responsible and genuinely representative. It is important not to be overambitious in this respect: as the Rand study points out (in a chapter nonetheless headed "Democratization"!), the "prime objective of most nation-building missions is to make violent societies peaceful, not to make poor societies prosperous or authoritarian societies democratic."[38] I, for one, remain disappointed that Cambodia, after all the effort put into creating democratic institutions and respect for human rights, remains such a laggard on both counts but console myself with the thought that the central object of the whole peacemaking and peacebuilding exercise there in the late 1980s and early 1990s was to bring sustainable peace to a country that had suffered appallingly for nearly twenty years from massive bombing, civil war, a genocidal reign of terror, invasion, and renewed civil war, resulting overall in the deaths of some 2 million people and the destruction of the lives and hopes of many more—and that object has been overwhelmingly achieved. There is still important unfinished business left on the governance front, but Cambodia is today on nobody's conflict or mass atrocity watch list.

Most of the points that were made in chapter 4, in the context of "the responsibility to prevent," about the structural ingredients of good governance—including fair constitutional structures, effective human rights protections, promotion of respect for the rule of law in general, and the eradication of corruption in particular—are equally applicable in the present rebuilding context and do not need to be repeated. Perhaps what does need a little more attention here is the role of *elections* in legitimating governments in the postconflict stage.

The reality is that holding elections—although good for political show business and much loved as an exit benchmark for governments anxious to meet their expeditionary commitments and go home—quite often has nothing much to do with democracy. The International Crisis Group was one of the first organizations to make this point loudly and clearly, opposing as we did a rush to an early election in Bosnia in 1996, not only because the formal conditions under the Dayton Accords had not been met but also because we feared this would consolidate ethnic divisions that remained highly charged and manipulated by the ruling parties, and had not had the chance to be counterbalanced by the development of national secular political forces, or at least strong civil society institutions.[39] Since then this kind of concern has become a very commonly chanted mantra, best encapsulated in the observation by Richard Haass that "electocracy is not to be confused with democracy."[40]

We know that the period of transition to democracy is in many ways one of the most dangerous and fragile of all, especially, as Timothy Garton Ash has put it,

in countries divided along religious and ethnic lines, and where you rush to the party-political competition for power without first having a functioning state with well-defined borders, a near-monopoly of force, the rule of law, independent media and a strong civil society. That's what happened in the former Yugoslavia. That's what's been happening, in different ways, in Palestine, in Lebanon and in Iraq. Full liberal democracy contributes to peace; partial, half-baked democratization can increase the danger of war.[41]

This all leads him to conclude, appropriately, not that we should retreat from democratization but that we should rethink our priorities in the way we pursue it. As New York Governor Al Smith said in the 1920s, in a line that has application to Pakistan and Bangladesh recently, among many other societies, "The only cure for the ills of democracy is more democracy."[42]

In formal institutional terms, the most important thing to prioritize in this respect is probably the rule of law. The argument has been very well put by an experienced Australian election specialist, William Maley, drawing on his observations of East Timor, Angola, Namibia, Cambodia, Afghanistan, and Iraq:

> Elections should be preceded by concerted steps to restore a functioning judiciary and a culture of legality, and a functioning police and a culture of law-enforcement. . . . The rule of law is central to democratic civility, and without it there can be little in the way of meaningful democratic choice. Meaningful choice is free choice, and without a framework that protects citizens' freedoms, the "choices" people make should be seen as a form of theatre rather than as an exercise in popular decision-making.[43]

In less formal terms, the crucial need is for civil society—with such external support as is possible and appropriate—to have more time to develop its voice and allow new movements, forces, and potential new leaders to emerge.

MAXIMIZING LOCAL OWNERSHIP

The ICISS commissioners were clear that the aim of international actors on the ground in postconflict situations had to be to "do themselves out of a job," expressing the critical issue in the starkest of terms: "Intervening to protect human beings must not be tainted by any suspicion that [it] is a form of neo-colonial imperialism. On the contrary, the responsibility to rebuild, which derives from the obligation to react, must be directed towards returning the society in question to those who live in it, and who, in the last instance, must take responsibility together for its future destiny."[44]

Peacebuilding that is almost exclusively externally driven is usually unsustainable: the point is not that internal actors will necessarily "develop better policies than external actors, but experience shows that external domination generates resentment, inertia and resistance."[45] Minimizing external ownership is often, however, easier said than done. In Afghanistan, for example, it was decided from the outset that, while protecting the security needs of the population, and particularly certain groups at particular risk, would require fairly heavy international engagement, the UN Assistance Mission in Afghanistan (UNAMA) "should aim to bolster Afghan capacity (both official and non-governmental), relying on as limited an international presence and on as many Afghan staff as possible, and using common support services where possible, thereby leaving a light expatriate 'footprint.'"[46] Subsequent developments, not least the explosion of drug production and the weakness of economic development and certain critical sectors like policing and justice generally, have led to some anxious questioning of whether the "light footprint," attractive as it seemed, was really the right strategy.[47]

What is important is that moves toward local ownership not be token. Samantha Power describes the salutary experience in this respect of the late—and very sadly lamented by me, among a legion of others around the world—Sergio Vieira de Mello when, as the UN Secretary-General's Special Representative in East Timor, he established in 1999 the National Consultative Council (NCC), an advisory body that he hoped would make the Timorese feel as though they had more of a say in their future, and in fact from whom he did seek consensus on major decisions, like establishing a civil service. But with it evident soon enough that the Security Council had authorized only its own administrator to make law, and that the NCC could be at best only a sounding board, Jose Ramos Horta, later to be foreign minister and president, declined to serve on it, and Xanana Gusmão, later to be president and prime minister, recalled, "We felt we were being used. We realized we weren't there to help the UN make decisions or to prepare ourselves to run the administration. We were there to put our rubber stamp on Sergio's regulations, to allow the UN to claim to be consulting."

Not long after, Gusmão began to refer to the UN presence as the "second occupation."[48] That was somewhat unfair, and as events subsequently transpired, the UN and other international players engaged in the process could not have been clearer about their willingness to hand over real power to national leaders sooner rather than later, as they did in 2002. But the extent to which both real and perceived power were vested, until then, in a single international figure remained a highly sensitive issue.

Achieving Justice and Reconciliation

REBUILDING THE JUSTICE SYSTEM

There are few more urgent imperatives in postconflict societies than restoring a functioning justice—and above all, criminal justice—system in those many situations where the rule of law, and all the institutions needed to support it, have manifestly broken down. What is required is not just effective policing but functioning courts, prisons, and in some cases, where respect for a previous governing system has totally evaporated, even an acceptable body of basic substantive law. In the Cambodia case—the first really major attempt to provide in a UN peacekeeping mission support for national authorities across a whole range of civil administration functions—it became rapidly obvious, as it has been in many missions since, that simply not enough planning and resources had been devoted to these crucial needs. As the ICISS commissioners put it, "If an intervening force has a mandate to guard against further human rights violations, but there is no functioning system to bring violators to justice, then not only is the force's mandate to that extent unachievable, but its whole operation is likely to have diminished credibility both locally and internationally."[49]

The case has been made many times for "justice packages" to be a central component of all peacebuilding support missions.[50] Elements of such a package would include provision, as appropriate, for a body of criminal law and procedures drawing, in as non-culturally-specific a way as possible, on universal principles; civil police, with training as well as immediate law enforcement responsibilities; a panel of judges, prosecutors, and defenders able to work with available local professionals during the transitional period, again with an obligation to train their local successors; and adequate correctional facilities and personnel to staff them while developing local replacements. The Rand nation-building study has, here as elsewhere, made some very interesting calculations of the scale and cost of the support needed to deliver a well-functioning justice sector, taking into account not only mentoring needs that have emerged from past operations but the realities of cost constraints and the likely availability of international personnel. After comparing data from a dozen completely different systems across the world, it recommended, for example, that as a rough rule of thumb there be provided one adviser for every ten judges, one mentor for every thirty prosecutors, and one adviser for every prison. This would translate, for a country with the size and needs of Mozambique, into a commitment of around 240 personnel at an international cost of some $45 million annually.[51]

MANAGING TRANSITIONAL JUSTICE: ACCOUNTABILITY VERSUS RECONCILIATION

In postconflict societies trying to rebuild themselves after mass atrocity crimes have been committed (often, as in the case of Rwanda, by very large numbers of people, not just isolated psychopaths), both national leaders and internationals trying to advise and assist them face hugely difficult dilemmas in deciding how, on the one hand, to ensure accountability for those crimes but, on the other, somehow to achieve social reconciliation. In one society investigations of mass murder and prosecutions of those responsible for it in national, international, or hybrid courts may well be thought to contribute to a sense of political catharsis that clears the air, relaxes tensions, and opens the door to restorative justice.[52] But in another it may be seen as increasing instability and deepening hostility among adversarial groups: Mozambique and Namibia are among many examples where reconciliation was pursued to the exclusion of accountability.[53]

Between the polar extremes of emphasizing retributive justice through trial and punishment, and hoping that time itself will be sufficient to heal the wounds and memories of past atrocities, there lie several other options, a number containing elements of both approaches.[54] One is simply *postponement*, delaying the day of reckoning—as essentially Chile and Argentina did until the society was felt to be strong and cohesive enough to face its past and itself impose accountability for those crimes without fear of destabilizing consequences.[55]

A second is *lustration*, the barring, by administrative rather than judicial process, of a whole class of individuals from public employment, political participation, and the enjoyment of other civil rights—as with denazification in Germany and demilitarization in Japan (for both of which there was an administrative appeal apparatus), and de-Baathification in Iraq (where there was no such process).[56] This can work where the class in question is clearly defined and comprehensively discredited, with its members all evidently sharing some moral responsibility, but it tends to be counterproductive, generating resentment and resistance, where, as in Iraq, these conditions are not met. A more selective version of this approach may be described as *vetting*, as for example in Bosnia where, after the Dayton Peace Accords, many members of military, paramilitary, or police forces responsible for serious violations of basic rights of ethnic or minority groups were dismissed from service;[57] or in the Czech Republic, Lithuania, and post-unification Germany, where administrative purges temporarily removed those affiliated with past abuses from certain positions in the public sector, with a particular emphasis on those who are alleged to have collaborated with the former secret police;[58] or in Greece, where "accountability for abuses committed during the 1967–74 rule by a military junta, separate from the prosecution of more than 400 former officials or members of the military, involved the administrative dismissal of as many as 100,000 people."[59]

The third option is a *truth commission*, premised in its pure form on the notion of fixing responsibility without attendant punishment, in effect amnesty in return for full disclosure (thus addressing key accountability objectives such as truth telling and delegitimization of state-sponsored violence). In the familiar South African Truth and Reconciliation Commission, there was a heavy additional emphasis on forgiveness as a key to reconciliation and less in practice on the truth for amnesty trade-off.[60] In fact almost no very senior figures from the apartheid regime appeared nor were any prosecuted for their failure to do so, evidently because such prosecutions could have derailed the fragile transition.[61]

Truth commissions and court processes can also be seen as complementing each other rather than being somehow in competition. In Argentina the significant amounts of information produced by the truth commission established in 1983 were then utilized by the authorities in prosecuting members of the military junta that had ruled the country.[62] In Sierra Leone both a truth commission and a special court were established, and they were held simultaneously for a time.[63] Certainly trials as well as truth commissions may be pictured as vehicles of emotional expression and cathartic transformation: it has been argued that trials are beneficial because (among other things) they can express the community's abhorrence of the atrocities committed and because they "can placate a victim's desire for vengeance."[64]

A fourth option is to provide *reparations* to victims of human rights violations, which might be either substantive (compensatory or restitutive) or symbolic. The restitutive example most often cited, and frequently touted as a success, is of the Canadians and Americans of Japanese descent who were interned during the Second World War: in 1988 the American government gave those Japanese who had been interned USD $20,000 per survivor as a form of compensation under the Civil Liberties Act, while in the same year, the Canadian government awarded CAD $21,000 under the Japanese Canadian Redress Agreement.[65] An example of the symbolic approach is the apology offered to the indigenous peoples of Australia on behalf of all Australians by Prime Minister Kevin Rudd, in a moving address to the parliament on February 13, 2008, following the earlier institution of an annual "National Sorry Day" to encourage Australians to "participate and be involved in activities to acknowledge the impact of the policies of forcible removal on Australia's indigenous populations."[66] The key consideration for those wrestling with these options is that it must ultimately be a matter for the people of the distressed country itself to decide which, or what combination, they choose. Certainly there must be a strong presumption in favor of conducting whatever process is decided upon on local soil. As David Crane has argued in the case of the Special Tribunal for Sierra Leone:

> The tribunal is set up for the victims, their families, towns, and districts. At the end of the day they are the ones who will have to live with the result and to try to put their destroyed lives back together in some small semblance of order. A tribunal that loses that focus will drift into history under a very dark cloud indeed. That is why in the future tribunals need to be where the horrors took place, in the middle of the crime scene. The people need to see their tribunal in action.[67]

TRADITIONAL JUSTICE

Taking the point just made one step further, another option for dealing with postconflict accountability and reconciliation issues is to rely on traditional justice mechanisms—informal tribal, local, grassroots, and/or village-level justice systems that owe nothing to European-derived state-level justice. In some contexts traditional justice may be a viable complement, or alternative, to conventional state-administered justice systems, given that establishing conventional forms of governance in postconflict settings, or in countries where states are fragile, is complex and time consuming.

Rwanda provides an example of efforts made to reinvent a form of traditional justice. In an attempt to address in a manageable way the massive number of crimes committed during the 1994 genocide, the government reintroduced in 2002 a form of traditional justice known as "gacaca," with the stated intention both of easing pressure on the conventional justice system and helping bring about national reconciliation through traditional means.[68] Gacacas are state-mandated courts with legal jurisdiction, where a panel of lay judges coordinates a process in which survivors and arrested suspects confront each other without lawyers, and the community gives testimony, drawing on traditional, rural conflict resolution mechanisms normally used to settle minor village disputes. But applying this process to crimes of the scale involved here—where those found guilty of murder can receive sentences of up to twenty-five years—poses some real problems, in that the accused are denied legal representation, many judges are illiterate and have little legal knowledge, and the system's reliance on voluntary confessions encourages self-incrimination.[69]

Given the chronic shortage of judges and lawyers in Rwanda and its huge prison population, some see the gacaca courts as a pragmatic and necessary addition to the slow, expensive conventional justice system.[70] The gacaca emphasis on reconciliation may also prove a more effective means of undermining the country's culture of impunity than the distant International Criminal Tribunal for Rwanda in Arusha, Tanzania, which has itself had a number of serious problems.[71] However, benefits that arise from the gacaca courts must be weighed against their potential for abuse—the shortcomings identified are significant, and the aim cannot be to mete out summary justice or the system be allowed to undermine internationally accepted standards of fairness and human rights.[72]

A British project to restore Sierra Leone's rural paramount chiefs in 2000, with the aim of stabilizing the postconflict situation there and encouraging displaced people to resettle in their villages, pointed up another potential hazard of attempts to revive traditional justice.[73] In strengthening the customary authority of paramount chiefs—considered a major source of 1990s conflict—the conditions for renewed conflict may have been inadvertently recreated. As the International Crisis Group has pointed out in Liberia and Sierra Leone, the project's at first sight attractive reliance on the traditional may have missed an opportunity to encourage citizens to reconsider the modes of domination and governance that had been among the initial causes of conflict.[74]

These considerations are by no means applicable just to Africa, or only in a postconflict context. In a report on Pakistan's judiciary system, for example, Crisis Group argued that traditional tribal justice systems, while speedier and less expensive than formal courts, were more open to abuse and subjective, coercive forces, and unlikely to deliver justice. Women fared especially poorly under traditional justice mechanisms that condoned or prescribed punishments such as gang rape and honor killing. Since informal dispute resolution mechanisms, involving tribal or village-level councils, were unlikely to deliver justice, conventional courts (in this case district and civil courts in the subordinate judiciary) would need to remain a critical part of dispute resolution strategies.[75]

MANAGING REFUGEE RETURNS

In many postconflict peacebuilding situations, putting in place the conditions under which refugees and internally displaced persons can return to their homes is one of the highest of all priorities. For example, in Kosovo in 1999 more than half the population was displaced, with a quarter fleeing its territory, and the issue has been a particularly acute one in every Balkans postwar context: the International Crisis Group alone published between 1997 and 2002 thirteen reports solely devoted to refugee and IDP issues in that region. In Timor-Leste, fully 80 percent of the population, around 265,000 people, became refugees after the 1999 violence following the independence referendum, with some 100,000 IDPs still living in camps in 2008, causing security risks und undermining the process of reconciliation and reconstruction.[76] And low levels of return are everywhere a sure sign of continuing insecurity, as for example now in Iraq.[77]

The problem is not just one of providing the right physical, economic, and social environment to enable sustainable returns: it also has, as emphasized by the ICISS commissioners among others, a number of legal dimensions.[78] How the issue of transitional justice is handled in a country like

Rwanda, as discussed, is one aspect of this. Another dimension is unequal treatment in the provision of basic services, repatriation assistance, and employment, with administrative and bureaucratic obstacles deliberately created to send a powerful signal that returnees are not welcome: discrimination in the provision of reconstruction assistance was a major problem in Croatia, for instance, where it was enshrined in law.[79] Property laws have been a particular source of grief, either providing inadequate protection of property rights or being deliberately framed to deter potential returnees and disadvantage those who do return.[80] Other barriers, as well as straightforward obstruction by local authorities, include difficulties in establishing tenancy rights over formerly socially owned property, the main form of property holding in former Yugoslavia, for example, and the loss, in conflict environments, of legal documentation.[81]

A clear definition of property rights can prevent or mitigate grievances that may stem from property disputes arising from refugee returns and should therefore be part of any legal or constitutional reform after a violent conflict and mass atrocity crimes.[82] One possibility is to include refugee return and property issues in peace agreements, as for example in Annex 7 of the Dayton Agreement ending the war in Bosnia, which provides a legal basis for organized property claims.[83] However, evictions alone will not solve all returns issues: a sizable amount of new housing stock will usually need to be built throughout the country, and donor-funded projects are critical in meeting these needs. And beyond all that, measures have to be taken to ensure return *sustainability*, which is pivotal to the long-term success of repatriation. This is about creating the right social and economic conditions for returnees: it includes access to health, education, and basic services, and is linked to reform in other areas—eradicating corruption, promoting good governance, and long-term economic regeneration of the country.[84]

Achieving Economic and Social Development

Economic Development

There are two very big economic tasks that have to be accomplished by national postconflict peacebuilders and their international advisers and supporters.[85] The first is to stabilize the economy, creating an environment in which people can simply engage in ordinary activity, safely and profitably: not an easy task when the currency is likely to have been debased, the revenue system broken, infrastructure destroyed, and the labor market chaotic. The key challenges are to stabilize the currency (where the International Monetary Fund [IMF], for all the angst it has generated in the global South in the past, clearly remains the best equipped to lead with technical assistance and emergency financing); to reestablish some kind of revenue base, in a way that will neither generate new distortions, including in the sensitive resource sector if the country has one, nor multiple new opportunities for corruption (and at the same time hopefully make a start on distributive justice); to generate donor support (preferably pooled through World Bank or UN Development Program trust funds, to minimize the prioritizing and administrative problems associated with a multitude of separate contributors); and to start to build an effective, accountable, and non-corrupt civil service. Having international civil servants as advisers or mentors to senior, and in some cases mid-level, civil servants can help ensure that government services are delivered while local control is restored. The International Crisis Group in 2004 recommended a particularly intrusive form of international engagement in some of these areas, including, for example, the insertion of international experts with co-signature authority in key parastatals to help control revenue flows, which subsequently came to be embraced by Liberia in its Governance and Economic Management Assistance Program (GEMAP).[86]

The second big task is to move from basic stabilization to creating the conditions for sustained economic growth, with the potential for external investor rather than just donor support (for which having a general governance environment that looks respectful of the rule of law seems an indispensable requirement). This means, more specifically, bringing inflation under control, bringing budgets into some kind of balance, having a viable central banking system, having tax and regulatory systems that are transparent and readily enforceable, and getting donor or, as appropriate and possible, investor support for infrastructure reconstruction and development—not an easy set of tasks even for a fully developed conflict-free country. All of these policies and programs will usually require sustained international technical assistance and a good deal of financial support. For the quantitatively inclined, the Rand nation-building study estimates that effective assistance for reconstruction and development after a major civil conflict means providing one-third to two-thirds of a state's

GDP in the first three years, gradually reducing to around one-fifth of GDP by the seventh year (which, with expected GDP growth, should not imply any reduction in absolute levels of support).[87]

SOCIAL PROGRAMS FOR SUSTAINABLE PEACE

As emphasized in the discussion of prevention strategies in chapter 4, societies that are at risk of the occurrence or recurrence of conflict need to work hard not just at getting the commanding heights of government, security, and economic systems right but at having peacebuilding work from the bottom up as well. All that was said about the utility of community peacebuilding programs and organizations with regard to prevention is just as relevant, if not more so, to postconflict rebuilding. Women, in particular, are far more than victims in this context: they are often the key not only to preventing the reemergence of violence and resolving ongoing conflict, but to rebuilding societies once the guns go silent. International Crisis Group research in Sudan, Congo (DRC), and Uganda suggests that peace agreements, postconflict reconstruction, and governance do better when women are involved: one of the main reasons is that women tend to adopt a more inclusive approach toward security and address key social and economic issues that would otherwise be ignored. But in all three countries, they remain marginalized in formal processes and underrepresented in the security sector as a whole, and it remains important that governments and the international community do much more to support women peace activists, including through funding, training, and inclusion in assessment missions and other decisionmaking mechanisms.[88]

Education remains the other critical social underpinning for sustainable peace that must be mentioned again in this context. For countries coming out of years of mass violence, getting children back to school signifies a return to normalcy as well as an investment in the future. In settings where educational infrastructure has been destroyed, rebuilding schools, training teachers, and distributing materials—including those specifically promoting education for tolerance—must be given priority.[89] There are multiple international actors, both intergovernmental organizations and many NGOs, able to play a significant support role here. One campaign showing the way was that in Colombia in 1996, when millions of children and adults, under the auspices of the United Nations Children's Fund

(UNICEF) and in collaboration with the Movement for Peace, mobilized to put an end to violence and work for peace and social justice, eventually forcing the then-government to make this objective a priority.[90]

The Role of the Peacebuilding Commission

The Peacebuilding Commission (PBC), endorsed as a concept at the 2005 World Summit and established soon after as an intergovernmental advisory body by resolutions of the General Assembly and Security Council, was designed to address a long-standing and obvious weakness in the institutional response to postconflict situations, namely the tendency for international interest, attention, and donor resources to fall away rapidly after the immediate excitement of achieving an end to mass violence was over.[91] International commitment all too often could be expressed graphically as a bell curve heavily skewed to the left-hand end of the time scale, with a long, very skinny tail to the right. The need was clear to establish not just another body to improve the UN's own peacebuilding efforts but to address the strategic deficit in the international body as a whole when it came to follow-through.

What was required, in the view of the High-Level Panel whose report was the immediate catalyst for the PBC's creation, was a forum and supporting secretariat that would enable *all* the key actors—the national government in question, donors, regional and international organizations, and the international financial institutions—to reach agreement on strategic priorities, enable better coordination on delivery, sustain attention over time on the rebuilding problems of the country in question, and help marshal the resources required to address them.[92] It was the view of the panel members—although we did not express this quite so robustly in the text of our report—that, if nothing else, the creation of the PBC might prove to be very useful in ensuring that when commitments were entered into by international donors and others, there would be no subsequent weaseling.

The first year of the operation of the PBC—from mid-2006 to mid-2007—disappointed many hopes, if not expectations. There was endless wrangling about the composition and procedure of the umbrella body, the Organizational Committee, with much of the subtext the familiar UN food fight between the Security Council and General Assembly; not much drive from the Peacebuilding Support Office inside the Secretary-General's office, which took an inevitable age to become fully staffed and functional; not much focus in the country-specific meetings, where the real hands-on work was supposed to be done, even after the first two country cases, Burundi and Sierra Leone, were taken on; and an unseemly preoccupation with the distribution of the resources of the new Peacebuilding Fund, which was designed not to be just another source of support for worthy NGO and other projects but to fund very urgent, targeted interventions (for example, time-critical activities in the lead-up to the Sierra Leone election) that might otherwise go unfunded because they were outside traditional development assistance areas.

By early 2008, however, skepticism had turned into cautious optimism, thanks to some demonstrably positive impacts on the ground in Burundi (in particular the defusing of a looming crisis over IMF funding) and Sierra Leone (with stakeholders reaching agreement on controversial strategic framework priorities, including energy); effective engagement and leadership by country-specific meeting chairs; signs that the Support Office was finding its feet; and some cooling in the political temperature as those more entranced by procedural and ideological battles than the need to solve practical real-world problems went off to tilt at other windmills.

That said, there is still much to be done to make the PBC the central part of the landscape it has to be if there is to be a dramatic improvement in the exercise of the responsibility to rebuild. It needs to deal with many more cases, and at a rather earlier stage of the transition from immediate post-conflict to stabilization than has been the case with its country subjects so far (just Burundi and Sierra Leone, and more recently Guinea-Bissau); it has to be prepared to take on and provide significant value-added input to very large problem cases like Afghanistan and Iraq, not the much smaller and more manageable ones that have been its brief to date; it needs to do much more to improve the effectiveness of its internal procedures and support arrangements; it needs to get much more focused buy-in from many of the UN agencies and other participants who have themselves been less than optimally internally coordinated, as between field and headquarters and various fiefdoms within the latter, and not as constructively engaged in the PBC's coordination role as they should; and it needs to expand the quantity and improve the quality of its working relations with the international financial institutions.

As has been pointed out in an excellent recent analysis of its role commissioned by the government of Denmark, making these and other points, the Peacebuilding Commission does have two great strategic advantages that give it the potential to make, over time, a huge practical difference: it is the only body in the UN system that explicitly links together its political, security, and economic functions, and it is broad and balanced enough in its composition to have a chance over time of bridging some of the distracting and debilitating North-South and political-developmental divides that have inhibited such progress in the past.[93] There are grounds for hope.

CHAPTER EIGHT

Institutional Preparedness: The Actors

Blaming the U.N. for Rwanda is like blaming Madison Square Garden when the Knicks play badly.

— Ambassador Richard C. Holbrooke, 2007[1]

When it comes to actually delivering the appropriate response to responsibility to protect situations—be it preventive, reactive, or rebuilding in character—who is actually capable of doing what? There is a large cast of actors potentially available in the international community: the multiple entities that make up the UN system, other global and regional intergovernmental organizations, national governments, and nongovernmental organizations. But who among them can best do whatever job is required, by whatever means are needed—supportive, persuasive, or coercive? This chapter discusses the respective contributions, actual and potential, of the major international actors and how they might be strengthened.

The United Nations System

The UN is and should remain the natural focal point for debating and responding to R2P situations, whether the context is the long-term prevention of mass atrocity crimes, reaction to their imminent or actual occurrence, or picking up the pieces after the event to ensure there will be no recurrence. It has effectively universal membership; the worldwide legitimacy that flows both from that and from the language of its Charter; multiple theatres and stages for debate, including the General Assembly and Human Rights Council; great executive authority vested in the Security Council on matters of war and peace; and leadership of real inherent stature and moral authority in the secretary-general, who can choose to bring almost any security issue to the attention of the Security Council at any time and play a critical role in the prevention and resolution of any conflict, either directly or through appointed special representatives and envoys.

It is not widely appreciated just how many different roles are played by the multiple departments, programs, organs, and agencies within the UN system, how many of them have performed outstandingly for many decades, and how very little, comparatively, it all costs. The core functions of the UN (involving the headquarters in New York; the offices in Geneva, Vienna, and Nairobi; and the five regional commissions) engage some 37,000 people at a cost of just over $2 billion a year—about the same number of employees it takes, at rather higher cost ($3.6 billion), to run the New York Police Department, just one part of one city's administration in one of the UN's 192 member states.[2] If to the UN's core functions are added its related programs and organs (like the UNDP and UNHCR), the other specialized programs and agencies of the entire UN family (like the FAO and WHO), and also its peacekeeping activities, the total UN system cost is still no more than $15 billion—less than half the amount ($33.2 billion) paid out in Wall Street bonuses in 2007.[3] Peacekeepers aside, the whole UN system employs 98,000 people, about as many as work in Disney resorts worldwide, just over half of those who sell Starbucks coffee, and much less than a tenth of those who sell McDonald's hamburgers.[4]

In addition to these UN employees, over 88,000 international military, police, and civilian peacekeepers are currently deployed in seventeen separate UN missions, many now with strong civilian protection mandates, at a cost of around $7 billion (less than three weeks' worth of current military expenditure by the United States in Iraq).[5] There has been a dramatic increase in the number of such missions since the early 1990s, and for all that went badly wrong in Rwanda, Bosnia, and elsewhere, as fully discussed in earlier chapters, much else has gone right, particularly in postconflict "nation-building" missions where, as already noted, the Rand Corporation has assessed the success rate of UN-led missions as being significantly higher than those led by the United States.[6] It has been persuasively argued, moreover, that the great drop that has actually occurred in the number of conflicts, battle deaths, and political mass murders since the end of the cold war—and that is the statistical reality, counterintuitive though it may be—

has been largely attributable to the huge upsurge in activity in conflict prevention, conflict management, negotiated peacemaking, and postconflict peacebuilding activity that has occurred over the last decade and a half, with most of this effort being spearheaded by the much maligned UN.[7]

All that said, when it comes to performing many of its functions, not least those related to peace and security, the UN has an understandable reputation for being "slow, cautious and bureaucratic."[8] The difficult birth of the new Peacebuilding Commission has already been mentioned in the last chapter. In the critical area of analysis and early warning, successive efforts to give the Department of Political Affairs (DPA) substantial new capacity have come to naught, foundering each time on the concern of various member states that this would lead to them becoming subject to more scrutiny, and at an earlier stage, than they would find comfortable. That was the fate of a central recommendation of the Brahimi panel in 2000, to establish a modestly sized information and strategic analysis secretariat, and so far at least, in mid-2008, it has been the fate of a new plan to increase DPA staff by over 100 positions to upgrade its early warning, preventive diplomacy, and mediation support capacity (with in this instance U.S. financial opposition playing a major role as well).[9] Specifically in relation to the prevention of genocide and mass atrocities, it was an excellent initiative to create in July 2004 the position of special adviser on the prevention of genocide, initially occupied part-time by Juan Méndez and now full-time by Francis Deng. But getting agreement on the kind of staffing support that would enable this position to be really effective in practice has proved a labor of Hercules.

The problem of UN institutional effectiveness has been particularly acute when it comes to mounting peace operations, which are "typically debated at length, budgeted sparingly, manned inadequately and deployed incrementally."[10] In the case of peace enforcement, the days are long gone since the UN system had any capacity to itself mount a full-scale warfighting campaign: these operations are now universally seen as the province of specially created coalitions of the willing, operating with Security Council endorsement but without blue helmets or other direct UN connections (although it should be acknowledged that MONUC troops in the DRC in recent years have engaged regularly, with varying degrees of effectiveness, in smaller-scale offensive operations against militia groups in eastern Congo).[11] And for all the debate over many years and various attempts to improve standby arrangements, there is still little resembling the kind of instantly available "fire brigade" rapid reaction capability that could have saved the lives, among others, of hundreds of thousands of Rwandans. As to the peacekeeping operations for which there is now an almost insatiable demand—those not just with a traditional monitoring function but requiring active civilian protection capability—there have been many problems. In particular, the demand has far outstripped the supply of qualified human resources being made available and the equipment they need to perform effectively. Although nearly 120 countries contribute at least some uniformed personnel, the burden of supplying the boots on the ground for these operations has fallen ever more heavily on the countries of the global South, who would be the first to acknowledge that they have had real difficulty in training and equipping personnel to the relevant standard. And one measure of the equipment problem is that, despite having nearly 12,000 military helicopters in its global inventory, the international community has been unable to come up with the less than thirty needed to sustain the UNAMID mission in Darfur.[12]

It is worth remembering that things were not always like this, even during the cold war when multilateral action of any kind was so often paralyzed. In July 1960, when an army mutiny wracked the Congo barely a week after its long-deserved independence from Belgium, it took the Security Council just two days to authorize military assistance and another forty-eight hours for the first contingents to arrive. And over the next four years, with up to 20,000 troops in the field, along with civilians brought in to help maintain public services, the UN's main aims were achieved: Belgian forces left the country, its physical integrity was preserved, and an East-West confrontation was avoided. The process was costly and controversial, killed Dag Hammarskjold, and failed to achieve a government strong enough to resist later civil war, dictatorship, massive corruption, and foreign interference.[13] But this full-scale peace enforcement mission, and first UN nation-building one, was an extraordinary demonstration of what the Security Council, secretary-general, and secretariat, with key member states acting in unison, could actually do in response to a mass violence crisis.

Whenever "the UN," or the secretary-general or secretariat, is targeted for criticism, those really responsible as often as not are the member states. Former under-secretary-general Shashi Tharoor has made the distinction between the UN as stage and as actor, with the secretariat and agencies often being blamed as actors for staging over which they have had no control.[14] To the same effect, but more pointedly still, is Ambassador Holbrooke's comment at the head of this chapter. The need for major systemic reform to the whole UN administrative system—everything from setting and administering budget priorities to sanctions monitoring and, above all, personnel management—has been documented and advocated over and over again, but the delivery of necessary change constantly founders on the concerns of various member states, or particular groups like the G77 representing the global South, that their voice or influence will be weakened.[15] Similar problems have meant the death until now of successive attempts to make the structure of the Security Council, the most important UN entity of all, more representative of the world of the twenty-first century than that of 1945.[16] Inter- and intra-regional rivalries (as well as more disinterested concerns about the potential unwieldiness of a significantly larger body) have continued to mean that Africa remains wholly unrepresented among its permanent members, and that major powers like India, Japan, and Brazil are also denied such a voice. And specific efforts to change or modify the veto powers of the existing Permanent Five—the United States, United Kingdom, France, China, and Russia—have been met with rock-like resistance by the five themselves, all of whose votes are required by the Charter for any amendment of its terms.[17]

The difficulty of reaching agreement in the Security Council on crucial peace and security issues (with, at the time of this writing in mid-2008, the situations in Kosovo, Sudan, Iran, Burma/Myanmar, and Zimbabwe looming large in this respect), and the very divisive and often unproductive character of much debate in other key elements of the UN system—including the General Assembly and its key committees, and the Human Rights Council—have meant the emergence from time to time for calls to replace the UN, or at least to supplement the Security Council with some international structure that might enable a detour around these obstructions and frustrations.

Based on the assessment, itself not unreasonable, that countries like Russia and China may well be more autocratic than democratic for a long time to come, the current favorite such idea—advanced by Robert Kagan and embraced by Republican presidential candidate John McCain—is for a "League of Democracies" to unite on multiple global fronts the good guys against the bad.[18] This, however, is a profoundly misconceived enterprise for at least three reasons, in ascending order of seriousness. First, it would be institutionally unworkable because there are profound differences of interest and outlook within the democracy camp on most relevant issues (with, for example, the North-South divide tending to have rather more salience for countries like India and South Africa than that between democratic and authoritarian governments); this has already rendered largely impotent and invisible the much more modest attempt to establish a "Community of Democracies" to act as an informal democracy support and policy caucus within the UN and elsewhere. Second, it would be deeply counterproductive to the cause of finding solutions not only to what Kagan calls the "transcendent" threat of Islamic terrorism but to other global challenges that can only be resolved by common and cooperative strategies, including nuclear nonproliferation and disarmament, climate change, and mass atrocity crimes. Third, the institutionalization of competing ideological alliances would be simply very dangerous, directly undermining the whole premise on which world order has been founded since the catastrophes of 1914 to 1945.

To argue that the Security Council could be "supplemented," and not fatally undermined, by a League of Democracies, setting itself up as a group claiming the right above all to take military action on its own authority, is to pursue a chimera. For all its problems, the UN system—with the Security Council at its heart on issues of war and peace and civilian protection—is the only credible international institution we have, or are ever likely to have, with the necessary combination of legitimacy and authority. The task as always is not to replace or bypass what we have but to make it work better.[19]

Regional Organizations: EU, AU, NATO, and OSCE

In the post–cold war years, regional organizations have come to play a much more substantial role than previously in diplomatic peacemaking, peacekeeping, and peace enforcement, but their potential utility both in relation to peaceful settlement of disputes and enforcement action was acknowledged in a UN context right from the outset.[20] Chapter VIII of the UN Charter identifies roles for "regional arrangements and agencies," but they are not further defined there or anywhere else. Certainly they include the most active and familiar players in peace and security issues—the European Union (EU), the African Union (AU) and its subregional partners, and the Organization for Security and Cooperation in Europe (OSCE). On the face of it, they also include the North Atlantic Treaty Organization (NATO), although that organization has always preferred to describe itself, for not especially compelling reasons, as a "collective self-defense pact" rather than a Chapter VIII regional arrangement.[21] The role that each of these organizations has played, and should be capable of playing in R2P contexts, is discussed in what follows.

There are a number of other regional organizations, many with a primarily economic focus, that have sometimes become diplomatically engaged in security issues, although their potential to make a positive contribution to crisis prevention and management remains, at best, less than fully realized. They include the League of Arab States (LAS), much engaged over the years in the Israel-Palestine issue, and more recently Lebanon, but in most cases with more enthusiasm than results; the Organization of American States (OAS), gradually increasing its security role, for example, in the early 2008 Colombia-Ecuador-Venezuela contretemps; the Commonwealth of Independent States (CIS), composed of the former states of the Soviet Union and no longer seen even by its major members as having much relevance or utility; the Association of Southeast Asian Nations (ASEAN), periodically engaged in issues such as trying to improve the behavior of Burma/Myanmar, but to little conspicuous effect; the ASEAN Regional Forum (ARF), which brings together a wide range of Asia-Pacific actors, including the United States, but other than in the context of helping to defuse the conflict potential of the South China Sea, has not in its fifteen years of existence moved much beyond general dialogue; the Pacific Islands Forum, increasingly actively involved in recent years in mobilizing responses to security threats in the Solomon Islands and elsewhere; the South Asian Association for Regional Cooperation (SAARC), which India-Pakistan rivalry has long condemned to a bit-part role; and the Shanghai Cooperation Organization (SCO), bringing together China, Russia, and several Central Asian countries in a body that has yet to establish a clear identity and role but that has recently indicated a willingness to play a constructive role alongside NATO in Afghanistan.[22]

Another long-standing regional organization with a potentially relevant role to play, if not in conflict resolution at least in addressing some of its underlying causes, is the Council of Europe, founded in 1949 to work for European integration with a particular emphasis on human rights, democratic development, and the rule of law in Europe, and now with 47 member states. The European Court of Human Rights, established to enforce the European Convention on Human Rights, and its Parliamentary Assembly (PACE) has recently shown some rather overdue signs of life in overtly criticizing some of its newer members—including Armenia, Azerbaijan, and Georgia—for breaching human rights and democracy standards.[23]

In principle, the reasons are clear for both greater cooperation with regional organizations in peace and security issues, and greater delegation to those of them that can get their act together. They should have a comparative advantage in better understanding the dynamics of the crisis in question, as well as neighborhood history and culture, and may be (although this is by no means always the case) more acceptable peacemakers and peacekeepers than outsiders. They are likely to be cost effective, with peace operations in particular able to be deployed more cheaply and faster than from further abroad. They are likely to have a greater sense of "ownership" of the crisis, both because their members will be more affected by any spillover and because their performance will be closely scrutinized for effectiveness by the wider international community. And in a number of cases in recent years, these various factors have coalesced into a greater will to deploy in situations where more robust action is required than the UN has found itself able to deliver: the AU's short-term stabilization or peace enforcement operations in Burundi in 2003, Somalia in 2007, and Comoros in early 2008 are such cases, as were the earlier missions of its subregional partner, the Economic Community of West African States (ECOWAS), in Liberia and Sierra Leone.

The attractiveness in principle of UN delegation to or cooperation with regional organizations should not obscure the many difficulties that remain in practice, as the case of Darfur makes particularly clear.[24] Insufficient interest in playing a peace and security role, insufficient capability when there is, ad hoc arrangements, lack of a common vision of both the conflict dynamics and the objectives of particular peace operations, and sometimes questionable neutrality are among the key issues that require greater attention by policymakers.

EUROPEAN UNION

Of all the regional organizations capable of helping make R2P a reality, the twenty-seven-member EU brings by far the greatest potential strengths. Not only are its population size and wealth comparable to the United States, but it enjoys the status of being possibly the world's most successful conflict prevention model, making by its very existence another war among its member states effectively impossible, and it has the capacity to apply leverage at both the soft- and hard-power ends of the policy response spectrum.[25]

Europe has sought to exercise its soft power in three main ways: by simply holding out the promise of EU membership, which former commissioner for external relations Chris Patten described in 2003 as "undeniably . . . over the past decade, the Union's most successful foreign policy instrument"; by its development assistance; and by its diplomatic good offices.[26] Since the inception of the Common Foreign and Security Policy (CFSP) in the 1992 Maastricht Treaty, and more particularly since the emergence under that umbrella in 1999 of the European Security and Defense Policy (ESDP), the EU has been increasingly focused on developing an integrated set of strategies for conflict prevention and management, working both through the intergovernmental European Council, directly involving member states, and the notionally "communitarized" European Commission (EU terminology never wins prizes for elegance). The Göteborg Program of 2001 articulated a useful four-part conceptual framework for diplomatic and development-focused activity, built around setting political priorities for preventive action; improving early warning, action, and policy coherence; developing enhanced instruments for long- and short-term prevention; and creating partnerships with other international organizations—most of which themes have found expression in a now quite bewilderingly complex and ever-evolving set of institutional arrangements.[27] In practical and less elevated terms, what all this tends to come down to, as one senior official has described it, is "Speak softly, but carry a big carrot."[28]

The financial assistance carrot is certainly not small. Together, the European Commission's aid budget and those of all the member states provide more than 50 percent of all development assistance worldwide. The distribution of that aid has been very attentive to conflict root causes but very much in a soft-power context: there has been some willingness to apply aid conditionally, subject to reform benchmarks being satisfied (as with the European Neighborhood Policy since 2005) but much less enthusiasm for threatening withdrawal of financial support to improve behavior (for example, to concentrate Serbia's mind on cooperation with the Hague Tribunal and on Kosovo). The 2005 Consensus on Development lays out the objective to "promote democracy, human rights, good governance and respect for international law, with special attention given to transparency and anti-corruption," and resources have been applied in a variety of pre- and postconflict settings, for example, in support of better regional management of shared water resources, the Kimberley Process on conflict diamonds, security sector reform in the Democratic Republic of the Congo (DRC), and now the European Union Rule of Law Mission in Kosovo (EULEX Kosovo). Governance, usefully, has been put at the heart of the relations between the EU and seventy-seven partner countries in Africa, the Caribbean, and the Pacific, as laid out in the Cotonou Agreement in 2000, and the EU has also invested more than 300 million euros over the past five years in delivering capacity-building and technical and material support to electoral processes in more than forty countries.[29] And as to shorter-term demands, there is a recognition, through such mechanisms as the Instrument for Stability, of the need for fast responses to emerging crises in fragile countries: EU resources have been applied to good effect in, for example, supporting Martti Ahtisaari's Aceh peace negotiations and the subsequent highly effective post-agreement Aceh Monitoring Mission in 2005–06.

All this has been accompanied by increasing efforts to play a direct diplomatic role in conflict prevention and resolution, with the High Representative for the CFSP, Javier Solana, playing a quasi–foreign minister role—albeit with less authority than his national counterparts—and much of this occurring since 2003 within the "effective multilateralism" doctrinal framework of the European Security Strategy (ESS), designed to identify the kind of threats to which the EU needed to be able to respond effectively.[30] European representatives participate in a number of key "mini-lateral" forums like the Contact Group on the Balkans, the Middle East "Quartet," and the "E3 +3" on Iran (United Kingdom, France, Germany, plus the United States, China, and Russia, also known as the P5+1), and there are eleven permanent special representatives currently working on Afghanistan, the African Union, Great Lakes Region, Bosnia and Herzegovina, Central Asia, Kosovo, Macedonia, the Middle East peace process, Moldova, the South Caucasus, and Sudan.[31] Valuable as much of this activity has been, EU diplomacy has had to contend with a steady drumbeat of criticism—a good deal of it coming from my own International Crisis Group—that too often Europe has been punching well below its collective weight, not using effectively the leverage that its extraordinary financial commitment gives it, and often being simply too deferential to the policy enthusiasms or anxieties of the United States. That criticism has been particularly consistent, strong, and well-founded in the context of the Israeli-Palestinian conflict, where the disposition of the EU (and to be fair, the UN and Russia as well) to follow reflexively the U.S. lead on issues such as the recognition of the government of national unity in 2007 has led to the Quartet being described as the "Quartet *sans trois.*"[32]

The EU has had less taste for exercising coercive, or hard, power, though it has considerable capacity to do so through both sanctions and military intervention. Sanctions, involving a range of measures from arms embargoes to financial or economic restrictions and visa and travel bans, have been frequently imposed by the EU in recent years, either on an autonomous EU basis or implementing binding resolutions of the UN Security Council, with measures against nearly thirty countries currently in force. The EU prefers to impose narrowly targeted or "smart sanctions," designed to minimize their impact on the well-being of the general population, for example, the highly selective travel and financial restrictions on regime members, such as is the case with Zimbabwe (not that these restrictions inhibited Robert Mugabe from being invited to, and attending, the EU-Africa Summit in December 2007).[33] But here, as often elsewhere in EU policy, the consensual decisionmaking process combined with strong member state interests can often produce less than optimal policy outcomes. The most disappointing example of recent times—and on an issue squarely related to the commission of a mass atrocity crime— was the EU's suspension in late 2007, following a determined campaign by Germany, of the visa bans it had imposed on senior Uzbekistan officials believed responsible for the massacre of hundreds of demonstrators in May 2005, without the condition of an independent inquiry being satisfied or any significant improvement in the country's appalling human rights record being evident.[34]

The use of military power is the area in which the EU has found it hardest of all to reach and sustain internal consensus. Individual EU countries have been prepared to mount peace enforcement missions from time to time—notably the important interventions by the United Kingdom to rescue the floundering UNAMSIL mission in Sierra Leone in 2000, and by France to stabilize the rapidly deteriorating situation in Côte d'Ivoire in 2002.[35] But the EU collectively has, generally speaking, been more comfortable performing civilian-focused missions, often at a high level of competence in quite tough conditions, for example, the Aceh peace monitoring mission already referred to.[36] But a gradual mood shift has become apparent: while the Europeans have continued to insist, properly, that crisis management must be integrated, comprehensive, and not exclusively based on the use of force, there is an increased willingness to acknowledge that the use or threat of military force must sometimes be part of the equation, and the EU itself as a responsible global player—and not just European countries in their individual capacities or, in most cases, as members of NATO—could not avoid providing its share of what was needed. The establishment of the ESDP in 1999, on the initiative of the United Kingdom and France, was a watershed in the EU's development toward becoming a serious global security actor, with EU member states effectively committing themselves to an open-ended range of military, as well as civilian, tasks.[37] Moreover the ESS, as agreed to in 2003, talks in terms of bringing together military as well as civilian capabilities to deal with a variety of scenarios, including out-of-area regional conflicts and state failure. And the new Lisbon Treaty—designed to reshape basic EU institutions in the light of the rapid expansion of its membership and scheduled for implementation in 2009 (subject to member state ratification)—was more explicit both on the wide range of military tasks that the EU could perform, including "post-conflict stabilisation," and the need for member countries to supply appropriate capability. [38]

Against this background, in recent years the EU has mounted under the ESDP two small deterrent military deployments in Macedonia in 2003 and Bosnia in 2004, a significant civilian protection mission (Operation Artemis) in the eastern Congo in 2003, and a similarly focused stabilization and civilian protection mission in Chad and the Central African Republic in 2008. Moreover, the EU is now engaged in a serious effort to develop its rapid reaction capability, with agreement in 2004 to create a number of multinational battlegroups, each roughly 1,500 strong, with associated command and support services, self-sustaining and deployable within fifteen days, based essentially on the Artemis model. By January 2007 these groups were fully operational, in the sense that a sufficient number had been pledged to enable the EU on an ongoing basis to undertake two battlegroup-sized operations concurrently, or deploy them simultaneously into the same field, with rotation every six months.[39] Planning also continues for the projected "Helsinki Headline Goal Force," which is intended to involve up to 60,000 soldiers, deployable within one to two months from decision and for at least a year at a time.[40] And in addition to all this, there have been important moves to better integrate EU and NATO capability, with NATO agreeing in 2003, under the "Berlin Plus" arrangements, to allow NATO military assets and capabilities to be used for EU-led operations.[41]

For all their encouraging quality, none of these developments necessarily mean that the EU will be a fully responsive actor when the next major R2P situation arises, particularly if it is one that cries out for a full-scale military peace enforcement operation. Member states seem to "want to remain free to choose whether to act through the EU, NATO, the United Nations or other, looser formats on a case-by-case basis," and, as has become very visibly evident in the role of various European states in the NATO operation in Afghanistan, their readiness to resort to force at all in peace operations remains very uneven, to the extent this could create "a two-tier system which would raise sensitive questions about internal solidarity and burden-sharing."[42] So too with nonmilitary coercive options, as "differences persist regarding member states' willingness to resort to 'negative diplomacy' (sanctions and penalties) when these could be useful and necessary."[43] By June 2008 the EU had made no fewer than seventy formal statements of "concern" (sometimes "particular," or "deep" or even "utmost") on the situation in Darfur, but with very few substantive measures to back them up.[44] Uncertainty about the future effectiveness of the EU's institutional arrangements has been further compounded now by Ireland's rejection in June 2008 of the Lisbon Treaty, denying the unanimity needed for its coming into effect.

All of this will no doubt reinforce the skepticism of those minded to characterize Europe as a "geopolitical dwarf" or to play down its collective testosterone quotient by comparison with the Mars-like United States.[45] But it is important to recognize, when it comes to martial qualities, that the

Europeans have suffered more than most from the folly and horror of war and are properly extremely cautious about rushing into military solutions when nonmilitary ones may be as viable. When it comes to united fronts and fully developed institutional responses, what is most extraordinary is not the miles that remain to be traveled but the remarkable distance these twenty-seven very different states—all with their own history, culture, and pride—have come already in finding common ground. There will be many more frustrations ahead, but as a net contributor to global as well as European regional peace and security—and as a particularly significant potential player when it comes to responding to mass atrocity crimes—the EU is a good news story.

African Union

The fifty-three-member AU has emerged as an important player in general conflict prevention and resolution in Africa and in the implementation of R2P principles in particular. Its Constitutive Act of 2000 enshrines—as did the charter of its predecessor, the Organization of African Unity (OAU)—the principle of noninterference in the internal affairs of other member states but makes a major exception "in respect of grave circumstances, namely: war crimes, genocide and crimes against humanity."[46] Appropriate machinery was created, in the Peace and Security Council (PSC), to recommend and implement intervention, including by military force, in appropriate cases.[47] Other innovative structures, for example, a consultative Panel of the Wise and a Continental Early Warning System (CEWS), have been established or are in process of development. And in terms of military capability, an ambitious plan has been agreed upon to build an African Standby Force (ASF) by the year 2010, with five regional brigades of 3,000 to 4,000 troops each, providing the AU with a combined standby capacity of 15,000 to 20,000 peacekeepers and a wide range of identified potential missions, from advice and observation to full-scale intervention.[48]

Underlying all this is the self-reliant mind-set of "African solutions to African problems," with the engagement of other countries and organizations on the continent only on the basis of invitation and their willingness to cooperate within an AU framework.[49] This is an approach that has been broadly welcomed by an international community only too happy to relieve itself of some of the burden of responding to the region's problems; in 2007, not an untypical year, nearly 60 percent of the Security Council's agenda concerned either specific crises in Africa or thematic issues of concern to the continent. At the same time, the AU leadership has recognized that there is a long way to go if actual capability is to meet aspirations, and has both entered into a ten-year capacity building program with the UN to match its doctrine and planning to UN standards so as to enable seamless cooperation in a full range of diplomatic and peace operations, and accepted U.S., EU, and other bilateral support for programs to redress shortfalls in presently extremely limited training, equipment, and logistic capabilities.[50]

While its structures and processes are still evolving and very much works in progress, the AU has played an active role, diplomatically and in some cases militarily, around the continent in a variety of democracy restoration (including Togo and Mauritania) and peace and security (including in Darfur, Burundi, Somalia, Comoros, the DRC, Côte d'Ivoire, and Kenya) situations. For the most part these exercises have been carried out with a reasonable degree of effectiveness, but in some cases—most notably the deployment of the African Union Mission in Sudan (AMIS) and Mission to Somalia (AMISOM)—there has been a significant gap between the aspiration to prevent massive abuses and the reality of the protection supplied.

Both a strength and weakness of the AU has been its willingness to defer on peace and security issues to the main preexisting subregional organizations in their respective geographical areas, in particular the big three: the fifteen-member Economic Community of West African States (ECOWAS), the seven-member Intergovernmental Authority for Development (IGAD) in the Horn, and the fifteen-member Southern African Development Community (SADC). They have the familiar advantages of all regional organizations described above, in terms of understanding of local issues and a higher evident stake in resolving them, and have each mounted military operations on various scales—most significantly in the case of the ECOWAS missions in Liberia, Sierra Leone, Guinea-Bissau, and Côte d'Ivoire—which helped to relieve the burden on the AU or its predecessor and on others in the wider international community. All the subregional organizations, not just the major three, are also expected to provide, over time, the building blocks from which the African Standby Force will eventually be constructed.

But on the other hand, subregional military success stories have to date been patchy—with the ECOWAS deployments in Sierra Leone and Liberia in 1990, and the SADC missions to the DRC and Lesotho in 1998, being widely criticized for their ineffectiveness, heavy-handedness, or partiality—and in central and north Africa, outside the areas of the big three organizations, there is little evident ability to create effective military capability. IGAD has been comatose for some time, with nearly every one of its members currently in conflict with at least one other and some of the action taken under its auspices having a decidedly individual—rather than collective—interest character, for example, Ethiopia's intervention in Somalia to attack the Union of Islamic Courts after the latter had threatened jihad against it.[51] And diplomatic achievements at the subregional organization level have been for the most part minimal, as with SADC in Zimbabwe through the period of Robert Mugabe's worst excesses. Successful mediations, like Kenya's in Sudan producing the north-south peace agreement, have been more often the product of individual country than collective enterprise. The effort to improve the effectiveness of the subregional organizations, and to better integrate their roles with that of the pan-African AU, is eminently worthwhile but still has a considerable distance to go.

NATO

When it comes to capability at the hard-power end of the spectrum, the North Atlantic Treaty Organization has a great deal going for it. Its twenty-six countries together have a formidable war-fighting capacity, in terms not only of the raw numbers of both personnel (over 2.4 million in uniform) and equipment (over 5,000 helicopters for a start) but also their interoperability, highly professional and integrated military command structure, and ability draw on the contributions of non-EU countries like Turkey and Norway.[52] While never having had to fire a shot during the cold war, it has demonstrated in recent years considerable competence in the actual conduct of military operations, whether those missions have been highly controversial, as with Operation Allied Force in Kosovo from March to June 1999 (because of the absence of Security Council authority), or much more accepted, as in the cases of the Implementation Force (IFOR) and Stabilization Force (SFOR) in Bosnia from 1995 to 2004 (NATO'S first ever out-of-area deployments), the Kosovo Force (KFOR) from June 1999, and the International Security Assistance Force (ISAF) in Afghanistan since 2001.

In 1999 NATO updated its Strategic Concept to provide for members of the alliance to defend not just other members but to conduct a full range of "non-Article 5 Crisis Response Operations" to ensure peace and stability in its region and periphery; at its Prague conference in 2002, it agreed even more specifically that its forces could be sent "wherever they are needed," abandoning the restriction of acting in defense of the treaty area alone.[53] It has in recent years reorganized its military structure to meet evolving demands and has had fully operational since 2006 a NATO Response Force (NRF) of 25,000 troops—with land, air, and sea components that train together and become available for six months before being replaced—whose role is to act as a stand-alone military force available for rapid deployment as a collective defense, crisis management, or stabilization force. NATO doctrine is cautious and less than clear in its application to the protection of civilians under imminent threat, but that hardly makes it unique among either multilateral organizations or national governments in this respect and would not in itself be an inhibiting factor for this kind of deployment.[54] So on the face of it, although NRF members have so far performed only relatively minor and uncontroversial tasks, like providing humanitarian relief after Hurricane Katrina and the Pakistan earthquake in 2005, the NRF appears to be exactly the kind of "highly mobile, self-sustaining rapid reaction force . . . uniquely prepared to respond to a fast moving genocide, such as occurred in Rwanda in 1994."[55]

And yet. The operation in Afghanistan has exposed some of NATO's endemic institutional problems, in particular serious differences in the willingness of its member states to contribute troops and resources, to make them available for hard-end fighting tasks when they are contributed, and to agree on common rules of engagement when they are so deployed.[56] Moreover, given the other demands on NATO members in Afghanistan, Iraq, and elsewhere, it cannot accordingly be assumed—despite the explicit commitment of resources to the NRF—that the necessary troops will be readily available. Force configurations in most NATO countries are still very much those of the cold war, and the percentage of uniformed military personnel that are actually deployable on international peace operations at any given time is very small—most informed estimates suggest the figure is not much more than 3 percent.[57] It certainly cannot be assumed, given the requirement for consensus in any decisions of this kind by NATO's governing body, the North Atlantic Council, that agreement will be reached, quickly or at all, to send them. And it certainly cannot be assumed that any military enterprise by NATO, even if mandated or endorsed by the Security Council, will be greeted without suspicion or hostility elsewhere.

The more fundamental problem is that NATO has still not worked out, in the post–cold war world, what kind of organization it wants to be, and there is bound to remain a degree of both external hostility and internal division (with France in particular retaining its traditional preference for operating under European rather than NATO colors, although moderating its position under President Sarkozy) until it does. There seem to be four broad options. One is for it to retreat into cold war nostalgia and remain essentially the organization it was in the past, a transatlantic regional defense alliance concerned above all about threats from the east, willing to embrace as new members any Euro-Atlantic countries committed to democratic, market-oriented values but nervous about Russia and incapable of even conceptualizing it as a member of the organization itself, and prepared to deploy out-of-area only in situations, like Afghanistan after September 11, where the security interests of alliance members are seen as directly and immediately at risk. A second option would be for NATO to in effect reconfigure itself as the sharp end of a global league of democracies, accepting as members any country around the world fully embracing its values, and committed basically to their mutual defense: not a course advocated, it must be acknowledged, by even the most enthusiastic league of democracies proponents because this would not merely show nostalgia for the old cold war but precipitate a new one.

A third option, advanced by five retired NATO generals in 2007, is one certainly rooted in cold war nostalgia but with some nuanced and sophisticated additions: there would continue to be an inner ring of transatlantic members wholly committed to existing standards of democracy, human rights, and good governance, and to mutual defense (including by nuclear first strikes if that's what it took); a second circle of partners—including Russia, and possibly China and India—with whom the inner ring could work on conflict and crisis prevention; and an outer ring of more distant partners and allies who shared inner-ring values and convictions—presumably including countries like Japan and Australia—with whom the inner group could promote general stability and possibly join in coalition-of-the-willing interventions and stabilization operations, not necessarily feeling constrained by the need to seek prior approval from the UN Security Council for any use of coercive force.[58]

A fourth option would be for NATO to quite fundamentally recast its role and become a global military resource, potentially available to prevent and resolve security problems worldwide in partnership with others as circumstances required or allowed, but deploying anywhere only with UN authority. Such a NATO would not just defend its members against attack from within or without but above all be prepared to play the role of emergency force provider in response to conscience-shocking mass atrocity crimes.[59] *Gendarmes du monde*—"policemen of the world"—is a phrase that already causes much concern both for nervous NATO members themselves and for others concerned by the organization's perceived liking for throwing its weight around, and this badge would no doubt be applied to any enterprise of the kind described. But there is a large difference between an organization operating within constraints set by the UN Security Council and one working freelance, and it is not inconceivable that in this context the badge could become one of honor. That said, a fundamental reshaping of NATO's role in this way is not likely to be possible any time soon and certainly will not be achieved in a single leap.

Perhaps the best starting point for rethinking the kind of contribution NATO could most usefully make to global peace and security in the twenty-first century is the "three circles" approach in the third option described above but to put aside its cold war flavor once and for all and make it more universally attractive. This would involve being overtly willing to welcome Russia into the "inner ring" if it satisfies the kind of conditions being demanded of other former Soviet bloc countries; probably being prepared over time to relax the wholly Euro-Atlantic geographic character of that inner ring; and certainly being prepared, in a way the five generals were not, to accept the constraint of Security Council approval for any use of force not involving self-defense in response to actual or genuinely imminent attack.

OSCE

The Organization for Security and Cooperation in Europe (OSCE), established initially under the Helsinki Final Act in 1975, is the largest of the regional security organizations, with fifty-six member states stretching from Vancouver to Vladivostok. Its brief is not military but diplomatic and political, covering conflict prevention, crisis management, and postconflict rehabilitation, and addressing a wide range of security-related concerns, including arms control, confidence-building measures, human rights, national minorities, democratization, policing strategies, counterterrorism, and the environment.[60] Its best-known and highest-regarded work in conflict prevention has been that of the high commissioner on national minorities, mainly in the 1990s after the independence of Latvia, Lithuania, and Estonia in resolving the pent-up grievances that emerged, potentially explosively, between the Baltic peoples and their substantial ethnic Russian populations.[61] The OSCE's Conflict Prevention Center maintains an early warning situation room and focuses operationally on confidence-building measures (particularly involving military transparency), helping states with border security and small arms stockpile management, and supporting multiple field missions—nineteen currently, engaging over 2,800 staff members—working mainly on postconflict capacity building.[62] Its Office for Democratic Institutions and Human Rights (ODIHR) conducts projects in the field of elections, democratization, tolerance and nondiscrimination, and the protection of minorities such as Sinti and Roma.[63] OSCE election observer missions have, however, earned over the years as many brickbats as bouquets, most recently for the positive assessment of Armenian presidential elections in February 2008 that were fraught with problems and led to fatal clashes between police and demonstrators.[64] The diversity of the organization's membership and the requirement for consensus make more often than not for lowest common denominator decisionmaking and less than vibrant operational impact, but in the R2P-related areas in which it has performed well—above all, the protection of national minorities—it has performed very well indeed.

Other Intergovernmental Institutions, National Governments, and NGOs

There are three other groups of actors who are capable of playing significant roles across the spectrum of R2P responsibilities to prevent, react, and rebuild: intergovernmental organizations and institutions (other than the UN and the regional organizations already discussed), national governments, and nongovernmental organizations (NGOs). Most of them have made multiple appearances already in earlier chapters and are mentioned here essentially for the sake of completeness. To properly evaluate the contribution, actual and potential, that could be made, especially, by different governments and by the legion of NGOs that are actively engaged in peace, security, and human rights issues, both internationally and domestically, would take another volume.

OTHER INTERGOVERNMENTAL INSTITUTIONS

The key economic players are the Bretton Woods institutions, the *World Bank* and *International Monetary Fund* (IMF), which are sometimes characterized as being part of the broader UN system and sometimes as standing outside it. Either way, they have a major impact at both the prevention and rebuilding ends of the conflict response spectrum: the IMF particularly when it comes to currency stabilization, on which so much other societal stability depends, and the World Bank both as a major provider of development assistance and advice in its own right, both before and after conflict, and as a trustee in postconflict situations through which other donors can sensibly channel and coordinate their own support. Their economic role is supplemented by the major regional development banks in Asia, Africa, Europe, and Latin America.[65]

Legally the international institutions that matter most are the *International Court of Justice* (ICJ)—with an important advisory and norm-setting role, as shown for example in the Serbian genocide case, even if its capacity to engage in actual dispute resolution is limited by the unwillingness of so many states to accept its jurisdiction—and the *International Criminal Court* (ICC), still finding its feet, but an absolutely critical element in building over time a climate in which those who perpetrate mass atrocity crimes can feel no confidence at all that they will remain immune from prosecution and punishment. Ad hoc international or hybrid tribunals like those for the former Yugoslavia, Rwanda, Sierra Leone, and Cambodia are as important now as the ICC, but the future lies in building up a single global institution of formidable professional competence, supported to the maximum extent—not least in the execution of arrest warrants—by the whole international community.[66]

A diplomatic or political role in peace and security issues is played from time to time by several intergovernmental organizations, functionally equivalent in many ways to the regional organizations discussed above but more global in their membership. The most significant and active in this respect is the *Commonwealth of Nations*, with its fifty-three highly racially and culturally diverse members, amounting together to a third of the world's population and united essentially by their status as former British dependencies. As anachronistic and idiosyncratic as it may appear—and as its meetings certainly sometimes feel—the Commonwealth has a strong and honorable track record of opposition over many years to racism and authoritarianism, although its weapons are limited, being confined essentially to mobilization of international political and economic campaigns (as against South Africa during the apartheid years) or suspension or expulsion from the group (a power exercised over the years against Nigeria, Fiji, Pakistan, and Zimbabwe). *La Francophonie* brings together fifty-five wholly or partly French-speaking states: primarily focused on promoting French language, culture, and linguistic diversity, it would probably be fair to describe its contributions to peace, democracy, and human rights until now as more rhetorical than substantive. The *Organization of the Islamic Conference (OIC)*, comparably, draws its fifty-seven members from primarily Islamic states around the world and has tended to operate more in solidarity-expressing conference-resolution mode than in any hands-on way in relation to conflict prevention and resolution.[67]

NATIONAL GOVERNMENTS

The role played by individual states and their governments, for good or ill, across all the issues addressed in this volume is self-evidently central. It is the inability or unwillingness of national governments to exercise their sovereign responsibility to protect all their own people from catastrophic human rights violations that creates the problem in the first place. And it is the ability and willingness of national governments to act as good friends and neighbors, as generous donors, as persuasive diplomats, and—if the circumstances demand it—as appliers of coercive pressure and, in really extreme cases, military intervention, that is crucial to any solution. States remain, for better or worse, and will be for the foreseeable future, the primary actors in international affairs. Intergovernmental organizations can only decide if their member states agree and can only act if their member states deliver, and nongovernmental organizations can only be influential in their advice or effective in their program delivery if individual states listen and allow them to act. Some states will always be more inherently powerful, influential, and capable than others, but *every* state and government has a responsibility to protect its own people and to do what it can to help others.

For present purposes it is possible to do no more than offer a checklist of what that combination of responsibilities entails. In relation to its own people, the first responsibility of any government is to do no harm. Beyond that, it should work to the extent of its capacity to do good: to educate for tolerance; to fully embrace the rule of law; to put in place legal and constitutional protections for minorities; to ensure equal economic opportunity; to ensure a genuinely open, honest, and responsive political and governmental system; to embrace international norms and treaty regimes and cooperate actively in intergovernmental organizations; to be openminded and receptive about offers of external support; and to be prepared (on the basis of sound evidence and using proper lawful means) to strangle at birth any early manifestation of mass atrocity crimes in the making—whether it be hate speech, early-stage ethnic or sectarian violence, preparation of enemies' lists, or anything else.

For national governments' responsibilities to each other and to people at risk in countries other than their own, the checklist is just as long. The 2005 Summit Outcome Document emphasized the obligation to help states "build capacity to protect their populations from genocide, war crimes, ethnic cleansing, and crimes against humanity and to assisting those who are under stress before crises and conflicts break out."[68] And that must mean, if nothing else, generous financial and technical assistance from those capable of providing it, supplied bilaterally or through international institutions, across the whole spectrum of relevant economic, governance, legal, and security programs, both long and short term, of the kind discussed in chapter 4. Similar obligations are involved, as discussed in chapter 7, in the aftermath of conflict or crisis, when the responsibility to rebuild means, above all else, ensuring the nonrecurrence of whatever horrors that have occurred. But the kind of capability that needs to be built, to be an effective R2P contributor, is not just to provide aid. It means having, within the government system, appropriate focal points for analysis and early warning, and the mobilization and coordination of effective action at all stages of the conflict cycle. A number of governments are making major efforts in this respect, including the United Kingdom, United States, and Canada, but much more remains to be done.[69] And it means, within the constraints set by a state's size and wealth, developing and making available appropriate diplomatic, civilian, and military resources of the kind discussed below.

NONGOVERNMENTAL ORGANIZATIONS

Policymakers can no longer ignore civil society organizations, as much as they might often like to. Some 40,000 NGOs now operate internationally, and literally millions more operate within states' borders, most in the health and education sectors; but all together they engage in research, advocacy, or operational activity in every conceivable area of human endeavor. Although their size, capacity, and influence vary enormously—with a significant number existing more on paper than in flesh and blood, as I can personally testify—nearly all aspire to influence policy in some way or deliver some service or support, a great many command large public support, and together they make a surprisingly significant contribution to national economies.[70] In the peace and security area, NGOs and related nonprofit institutions play, generally speaking, four distinct kinds of roles: as think tanks, research institutions, or policy forums (such as the Brookings Institution, Council on Foreign Relations, various institutes of international affairs, and a number of foundations); campaign and advocacy organizations (like Human Rights Watch and Amnesty International); on-the-ground operational organizations promoting peace through mediation, capacity building, confidence building, and the like (such as the Carter Center, Centre for Humanitarian Dialogue, The Elders, Open Society Institute, Search for Common Ground, Seeds of Peace, and Initiative for Inclusive Security); and humanitarian relief organizations (like Oxfam, Médecins Sans Frontières, and CARE International). As has been made clear in earlier chapters, all these roles are relevant in various ways to the R2P task—at all three stages of prevention, reaction, and rebuilding—and it is important that all those organizations capable of making a difference, and there are many more of them than just those mentioned here, continue to be supported. They are not a substitute for governments and intergovernmental organizations but complementary to them, filling gaps that official organizations and institutions cannot or will not.

An example of the distinctive contribution that NGOs are now making, in an area thought traditionally to be the almost exclusive preserve of governments, is that of my own International Crisis Group. This fills an unusual niche, straddling—with its combined think tank, advocacy, and field-based role—three of the usually distinct categories identified above. Founded in 1995, essentially as a response to government inaction in the face of the catastrophes in Rwanda and Bosnia, Crisis Group is now generally regarded as one of the world's leading independent, nonpartisan sources of analysis and advice to governments and intergovernmental bodies on the prevention and resolution of deadly conflict—and mass atrocity crimes. It has a worldwide staff of some 140, from around 50 nationalities and speaking as many languages, working not only in major capitals, but on the ground from regional or field offices covering over 60 situations of actual or potential conflict. It has produced during its lifetime over 800 reports and briefings, as well as—since 2003—the monthly *CrisisWatch* bulletin. Crisis Group has played a major role in sounding early warning alarm bells (for example, in Darfur, Somalia, Ethiopia/Eritrea, and Pakistan), working behind the scenes on peace negotiations (for example, in Sudan, Aceh, Nepal, and Kenya), arguing for major new strategies on complex and intractable issues (for example, Israel-Palestine, Iran, and North Korea), analyzing some key cross-cutting thematic issues (for example, Islamism), and addressing innumerable specific problems arising at all stages of the conflict prevention-management-resolution-peacebuilding cycle in many different countries and regions. What has made Crisis Group distinctive among the many organizations working in this field is its unique focus on field-based analysis and policy recommendations, which flow bottom-up from that analysis rather than top-down from think tank computers. And what has made its work attractive to many governments and intergovernmental organizations is that, as an NGO, it has been able to work freely in many volatile environments where diplomatic officers, constrained by security rules, have found themselves locked up in compounds most of the time and unable to fully gauge local dynamics; it has called situations exactly as it has found them, unconstrained by received wisdom or policy orthodoxy; and it has felt free to make often adventurous policy recommendations of a kind that do not travel well up official institutional hierarchies.[71]

CHAPTER NINE

Building Diplomatic, Civilian, and Military Capability

Almost nine months after adoption of Resolution 1769 (2007), critical air assets [are] still missing, including three medium utility helicopter units [and] four additional light helicopters.
—Report to the Security Council on AU-UN operation in Darfur, May 2008[1]

Number of helicopters in the global military inventory: 11,842.
—International Institute for Strategic Studies, *The Military Balance 2008*[2]

What more needs to be done, in the crucial areas of diplomatic, civilian, and military capability, to improve the effectiveness of the response to R2P situations, across the spectrum from prevention to reaction to rebuilding? This chapter offers some answers, with the bottom line being that capability in all these areas is, like almost everything else in public policy, a function of political will. None of the resources needed to stop mass atrocity crimes once and for all are inherently beyond reach: if the political will is there, the relevant capability will be there. It is another question whether policymakers will ever actually be willing to *use* whatever capability they have: that problem is tackled in the final chapter.

Diplomatic Capability

UN DIPLOMACY

For some years now, the United Nations has been making ever more extensive use of special and personal representatives and envoys of the secretary-general (SRSGs) to direct and carry out its missions in preventive diplomacy, peacemaking, peacekeeping, and postconflict peacebuilding. They have been involved, with varying degrees of success, in peacemaking in such disparate places as Afghanistan, Angola, Bougainville, Colombia,

Cyprus, East Timor, El Salvador, the former Yugoslavia, Guatemala, Georgia, Haiti, Nicaragua, Tajikistan, and Western Sahara, among others. As well, SRSGs have headed many different types of peacekeeping missions ranging from maintaining the thin blue line in Cyprus, to being in charge of large multidimensional peacekeeping operations in Liberia, Sierra Leone, and the Democratic Republic of the Congo, to being given an executive mandate and becoming the virtual governing entity for a time in cases such as Cambodia, East Timor, and Kosovo. They have also been appointed to head postconflict peacebuilding missions, such as those in Tajikistan, Guinea-Bissau, Guatemala, and Burundi.[3] Until now, most of this effort has been focused downstream, on reaction and rebuilding, rather than upstream on prevention. To really adhere to the spirit of R2P, more attention needs to be given to creating the capacity for the UN and its SRSGs to work in prevention. And, given the centrality of the special representatives' role, more attention needs to be given to their selection, training, and support.

Selecting the right persons for these jobs is crucial. As the Brahimi Report succinctly put it, the "tenor of an entire mission can be heavily influenced by the character and ability of those who lead it."[4] The demands upon SRSGs, working almost invariably in fragile environments hanging in the balance between war and peace, with potential spoilers around every corner, are well summarized in the 600-page volume, based on in-depth interviews with many current and former representatives, prepared by Connie Peck of the UN Institute for Training and Research (UNITAR) for in-house UN use:

> From the time they arrive in the mission area, SRSGs must negotiate on a day-to-day, hour-to-hour basis with the parties themselves, as well as with civil society and the local population to keep the peace process on track, the population on side and to prevent problems from arising—or to address them when they do. They must harmonize different mission components, including all senior staff, into a well functioning team and, in large missions, keep diverse international and local staff, as well as the rotating national contingents of peacekeepers and police, working smoothly towards the same objectives. In even the smallest missions, SRSGs must use the same skills to create good working relationships with staff at Headquarters in

order to foster sufficient trust in their leadership so that they can avoid micro-management, while still taking advantage of useful guidance from their departments and, in return, providing them with the information they require to keep Member States informed and engaged. SRSGs also need to be able to negotiate solid working relationships with the specialized agencies, funds and programmes in order to overcome the usual barriers and institutional rivalries and create an atmosphere in which the United Nations can truly work as a family—with coordinated objectives and approaches.

Further, SRSGs must work closely with member states, developing the necessary relationships with diplomatic staff on the ground, in UN capitals, and within relevant ministries in key capitals to engender political support and leverage and to mobilize the resources needed to sustain the mission and make a significant impact on the mission area. In particular, they must be able to develop a supportive relationship with the Security Council in order to keep the Council actively engaged with the mission, as well as to ensure that the mission's mandate and resources remain appropriate to the evolving situation on the ground. Developing a close relationship with regional actors, including regional and subregional organizations and regional leaders, is necessary to foster a coordinated approach between the UN and the region. Among the many other actors that SRSGs have to work with are the multitude of non-governmental organizations, many of whom are pursuing their own objectives and funding, but whose energy and flexibility, if appropriately harnessed, can add synergy to particular mission goals. Finally, SRSGs have to develop effective relationships with the media in order to raise international awareness of the situation and to communicate with the local population about the mission's objectives and methods, while encouraging greater understanding of issues such as human rights and democracy.[5]

What this all means is that SRSGs need "excellent political, negotiation, leadership and management skills . . . [and] a superabundance of optimism, persistence and patience"—and there can be real problems when those are lacking, not least in fast-moving R2P situations.[6] The *Report of the Independent Inquiry into the Actions of the United Nations during the 1994*

Genocide in Rwanda pointed specifically to lack of political leadership on the part of the SRSG and the poor relationship between the SRSG and force commander as among the key factors contributing to the UN's lack of effectiveness.[7] The trouble is that although there has been much discussion of the need to select the best people to head such missions, the UN's selection process for SRSGs remains largely ad hoc, involving an informal consultation process between the departments and the Executive Office of the Secretary-General. One representative has confessed that he almost certainly found himself top of the list for a post for which he was, on the face of it, only marginally qualified (although in which, in fact, he performed excellently) because his surname began with "A."[8] Past attempts at preparing lists of qualified candidates have not been very successful, and a much more systematic search is required for the very best individuals for these most challenging of jobs. Doubling the size of the pool from which selections are normally made would help for a start. At the time of this writing, only seven women have ever been drafted as SRSGs, with only one currently appointed—despite the fact that Security Council Resolution 1325 (2000) on women, peace, and security "urges the Secretary-General to appoint more women as special representatives and envoys to pursue good offices on his behalf, and in this regard calls on Member States to provide candidates to the Secretary-General for inclusion in a regularly updated centralized roster."[9]

Good selection must be accompanied by carefully designed and implemented training. This is not something that has been readily acknowledged in the past, by either the UN system or appointees with, invariably, long careers already behind them in diplomacy, politics, or both; but things have recently changed for the better with the implementation in 2001 of a formal UNITAR program for briefing and debriefing SRSGs. This has involved the recording and passing on of lessons learned by current and former representatives and envoys, embodied in the above-mentioned book and accompanying DVDs; yearly seminars led by Dr. Peck in which all current SRSGs and senior headquarters staff (including now the secretary-general's special advisers on genocide prevention and on the implementation of R2P) share experiences and discuss in depth the obstacles and challenges confronting the various missions; and a variety of follow-up meetings. This has in fact been part of a broader culture shift in the UN in which on-the-job training in preventive diplomacy and peacemaking, involving the inculcation of mediation and negotiation skills, has now—no doubt to the astonishment of earlier generations of senior officials—become routine for midlevel diplomats and UN staff as well. This discomfiting innovation actually started when, as Australian foreign minister in the early 1990s, I secured funding for the indefatigable Dr. Peck to create such a UNITAR program: now in its sixteenth year, and supported by many more governments and foundations, it has provided intensive training to hundreds of UN staff and diplomats, many of whom have risen to positions of real responsibility in the UN system or within their ministries.

Practitioners in the field need to be not only well selected and trained but better supported in their initial briefing and with ongoing advice and assistance. Things are again improving in this respect, at least on paper, with the recent creation of a Mediation Support Unit within the Department of Political Affairs, following the 2005 World Summit's support for strengthened capacity in this area.[10] This is designed to be a center of expertise, best practice, and knowledge management on mediation-related activities worldwide, serving the UN as a whole as well as regional organizations and other peacemaking bodies, and it has made one of its first priorities the development of a "UN Peacemaker" website that includes a comprehensive collection of modern peace agreements, as well as mediation advice, and will include an online forum (for envoys and their staff to exchange questions with other conflict mediators inside and outside the UN system).[11] The unit has been working closely with Jan Egeland, special adviser to the secretary-general on matters relating to the prevention and resolution of conflict, and in March 2008 launched a full-time standby team of recognized experts to provide, at short notice, advice to mediators on many of the key issues that arise in peace talks: it remains to be seen, however, how extensively and effectively this capacity will be used in practice. Another useful capacity-building enterprise of recent years has been the development of structures within the Departments of Peacekeeping Operations and of Field Support to record and disseminate lessons learned and best practices, in order to further develop policy and provide better "toolbox" advice to missions.[12]

REGIONAL ORGANIZATION DIPLOMACY

As discussed in the last chapter, a number of regional and subregional organizations are increasingly, and usefully, involved in diplomatic efforts to prevent and resolve conflicts and crises in their own areas and sometimes beyond. They use, variously, the good offices of their secretaries-general and senior staff, including special representatives and envoys; delegations from their member states, such as heads of state or government, foreign ministers, or ambassadors; and specialized mechanisms, such as the OSCE's High Commissioner on National Minorities, ECOWAS's Panel of Elders, or the AU's Panel of the Wise. There remains, however, considerable scope for further development and capacity building in all of these institutions, particularly in relation to prevention—the single most important dimension of the responsibility to protect, as with conflict generally, and the weakest in terms of existing capacity.

This capacity can be developed in numerous ways. One is through training, an example which could be emulated on a significantly wider scale being the UNITAR regional training program to enhance conflict prevention and peacebuilding in Africa, which since 2000 has provided a two-week annual training program in conflict prevention and resolution to staff from regional and subregional organizations, as well as diplomats from foreign ministries, throughout the continent.[13] Another is through sharply focused conferences, of the kind organized by the Council for Security Cooperation in the Asian-Pacific Region (CSCAP), launched in 1993 to bring together a group of research institutes and think tanks to hold meetings and workshops generating policy analysis and recommendations for regional governments.[14] A third option is engaging the assistance of experts, perhaps through the Conflict Prevention and Peace Forum (CPPF)—established in 2000 to, among other things, recommend experts on or from conflict-affected countries and create networks of experts who can be on-call, including through the commission of targeted research— or through the excellent International Institute for Democracy and Electoral Assistance (IDEA).[15] Yet another is to develop specialized mechanisms to support the diplomacy needed, for example the Foundation on Inter-Ethnic Relations created by the OSCE's Max van der Stoel as high commissioner on national minorities in the early 1990s to conduct research, convene expert consultations, and prepare recommendations for adoption as standards on the protection of national minorities.[16] And another again is to support, at the regional and subregional level, the creation of training, best practices, and support units following the models recently developed by the UN itself, discussed above.

An important need in all of this is for the UN and regional and subregional organizations to work together more effectively. In the past, especially with regard to R2P issues, there has been a tendency for each to abdicate responsibility on the basis that the other—or some bilateral actor—would do something, with everyone then being mutually critical for their collective failure to act. Equally problematic have been bureaucratic jealousies and institutional rivalries, which too often plague efforts at coordination, exacerbate tensions, and waste time. One such problem that has sometimes impeded R2P efforts is a proliferation of mediators. As the then representative of the secretary-general for Burundi Ould-Abdallah has noted, it was rather too much of a good thing to have at one stage during the 1990s a total of twelve representatives from different organizations simultaneously in Bujumbura:

> Although most of these representatives were highly experienced and dedicated to their tasks and to peace, their sheer number and their lack of coordination were seen by the Burundians as an opportunity to press for all sorts of concessions and accommodations, material as well as political, from a divided international community. Whereas a cohesive international community could have helped to lessen tensions and to strengthen preventive efforts, the multiplicity of players served only to heighten tensions, fears and expectations.[17]

New efforts to work more collaboratively appear to be gradually bearing fruit, with a series of high-level meetings since 1994 between the UN secretary-general and heads of regional organizations, and the Security Council holding regular thematic debates on the issue. The recent (2008) report of the secretary-general on relations with regional organizations makes a number of further recommendations on how to strengthen the relationship, particularly with regard to the African Union, among them the establishment of regional offices under the Department of Political Affairs.[18] Two such offices have already been established. The first is the UN Office for West Africa (UNOWA), which has worked closely since 2002 with ECOWAS on both good offices missions and a range of thematic issues, and in establishing a trilateral relationship with the EU as well.[19] The second, since December 2007, is the UN Regional Center for Preventive Diplomacy for Central Asia (UNRCCA) in Turkmenistan, the product of several years of consultations with the governments of Central Asia and intended to work closely with the OSCE, the Commonwealth of Independent States (CIS), and the Shanghai Cooperation Organization (SCO).[20] In addition to these institutional developments, joint diplomatic efforts have become more common—albeit with mixed results—as, for example, between the UN and OAS in Haiti, and the UN and AU in the Great Lakes and Darfur.

BILATERAL DIPLOMACY

Of course it is not only in an intergovernmental context that diplomatic effectiveness is crucial in relation to conflict prevention and resolution generally, and to R2P situations in particular; traditional bilateral diplomacy remains hugely important, with some of the best-known examples of the post–cold war years being the enterprise of Norway in generating through the Oslo process the first serious moves toward Israeli-Palestinian peace, the United States in brokering the Dayton Agreement for Bosnia, and South Africa in holding together an extremely fragile Burundi. One of the advantages of bilateral action is that single actors do not become bogged down in collective decisionmaking, allowing at the very least decisions to be made more quickly. Bilateral actors also may have more leverage than multilateral actors, including the ability to offer aid or trade concessions, but on the other hand they tend to be more exposed to charges of acting in their own narrow self-interest.

One way or another, they will always be players, and it is important in the context of R2P capacity building that diplomatic academies and training programs are appropriately conscious of the relevant principles and methodology. It is also possible to hope—although probably in vain—that both graduate and undergraduate university international relations courses, the intellectual breeding ground for so many future diplomats around the world, will also pay some regard to the practical policy issues involved in preventing and responding to mass atrocity crimes. A helpful development has been the greater willingness of governments in recent years to fund independent research and training institutes or think tanks devoted, among other things, to building bilateral capacity for diplomatic efforts, such as Swisspeace (funded by the Federal Department of Foreign Affairs of Switzerland) and the United States Institute of Peace (funded by the U.S. Congress). The latter, for example, seeks to build capability through its extensive grant and fellowship, publication, and professional training programs; through targeted meetings and conferences around the world; and specifically focused task forces like that recently established on genocide prevention.[21] The main challenge for all these centers working at some remove from government is to translate their knowledge and ideas to those actually working in the field, and effort and resources should continue to be applied to bridging that gap.

Just as with regional organizations, it is important that bilateral diplomacy works as closely as possible with that of the UN. A comparatively recent innovation—first employed in El Salvador by Personal Representative for the Central American Peace Process, Alvaro de Soto, and now used widely in peacemaking efforts—is the mechanism of "Friends of the Secretary-General." In this process, a select number of member states are invited by the secretary-general to act as Friends on a bilateral basis to, variously, provide resources for the process, host peace talks, urge the parties to be creative and flexible, reinforce positive efforts and progress, provide ideas, offer technical expertise, and show international support for the process from its beginning until the signing of the peace agreement. [22] The enterprise has proved its worth in a variety of conflict resolution contexts already and is worth applying more broadly across the spectrum from prevention to rebuilding.

Civilian Response Capability

Some lessons take a long time to sink in. One it seems to have taken the international community forever to absorb is that when any international peace operation is mounted requiring the deployment of forces in the context of postconflict peacebuilding or nation building, the civilian components—covering everything from policing and human rights protection, to rehabilitation and repatriation, to election administration and specialist civil administration—are at least as important, if not more so, than the military. That was very obvious in the first major UN mission I had the opportunity to observe, the United Nations Transitional Authority in Cambodia (UNTAC), from 1992 to 1993, where although a number of these functional areas performed quite well, the police contingents that were initially deployed engaged in more rape, pillage, and general misbehavior than the criminal and other elements against whom they were supposed to be helping protect the population. And despite the centrality, in the peace plan as it had been negotiated, of the civil administration support and oversight function, specialist administrators were slower to deploy than anyone else and remained throughout the weakest reeds in the enterprise.[23]

In almost all of these postcrisis stabilization situations there will be, as discussed in chapter 7, a public security gap: a major breakdown in the rule of law and all the institutions needed to support it, and an immediate need as a result to restore not just effective policing but functioning courts and prisons, and in some cases a new and more acceptable body of basic substantive law. Civilians are at risk, and there is a responsibility to protect them. As always, that responsibility should be exercised by the local sovereign authority if one is in place and able to cope—but if there isn't, or it can't, the international community must be prepared to play its part. The tasks in question are not ones for military forces, even if they wanted to undertake them, which they practically never do. While some extreme order-restoration situations do call for a quasi-military gendarmerie, and the EU is developing some welcome rapid reaction capability in this respect, for the most part the restoration of basic law and order means a capacity to deal with lesser-scale violence, for which ordinary police are more suited.[24] Beyond that, it means a capacity to deal with economic and property crime, and an ability to disentangle and provide an appropriately differentiated response to breaches of criminal law, civil law, and, in some societies, religious law as well, for which the military is not inherently suited at all.[25] In most of these situations, the public security gap is likely to be part of a larger public administration problem, which again will require rapidly deployed international help to overcome. As Sierra Leone Foreign Minister Zainab Bangura put it to the Security Council in May 2008: "In the light of the capacity gap occasioned by massive flights of badly needed skilled human resources in the wake of crisis situations, the civilian components of peacekeeping operation personnel are as significantly essential as their military counterparts."[26]

Civilian components are indeed a regular part of UN and other peacekeeping missions: of the 88,000 international personnel currently deployed in UN peacekeeping missions in mid-2008, over 11,000 were civilian police, and another 5,000 were other civilian officials.[27] The mandates for UN missions have dramatically expanded, with greater attention to police and rule of law activities; the police component of UN missions has grown

from around 2 percent in 1995 to 12 percent now; and the policing mandates themselves have expanded, from an initial limited focus on monitoring and reporting on the activities of local police forces, to a much broader
role in reforming and restructuring those forces, to occasionally having
the internationals carry out full law enforcement duties themselves.[28]

Moreover, substantial notional standby capacity now exists internationally across the full range of needed civilian roles, not just police. This is particularly the case in the EU, where targets have been established, met, and
in some cases exceeded for five categories of civilian rapid reaction capacity. So there are now, accordingly, on the face of it, nearly 6,000 EU police
available, of whom 1,400 are deployable within thirty days; at least 600
rule of law experts (prosecutors, judges, and jailers), deployable within
thirty days; a pool of rapidly deployable general civil administrators (now
comprising nearly 600 personnel) able to take on assignments related to
customs and general local administration; three "civil protection" assessment teams of 10 experts each available on call at a few hours' notice to
assess emergency rescue situations and the like, together with another 4,500
personnel available for follow-up deployments; and over 500 civilians ready
to take part in "monitoring missions" of various kinds.[29] A number of individual EU countries have also announced their own national standby targets, for example the United Kingdom, which has promised to have 1,000
civilian personnel, including police, emergency service professionals,
judges, and trainers available to be deployed to the world's hotspots at
short notice.[30]

In the UN itself, where it has regularly taken months to get senior police
leadership teams selected and deployed into new operations, a twenty-
seven-person "Standing Police Capacity" has been established and deployed
for the first time in Chad in November 2007; this followed the call of the
High-Level Panel in 2004 for the creation of a "small corps of senior police
officers and managers (50–100 personnel) who could undertake mission
assessments and organize the start-up of police components of peace operations."[31] There is also the civilian dimension of the Standby Arrangements
System (UNSAS), discussed below in the context of military capability. In
other key multilateral organizations, the OSCE has had for some years a
pool of civilian experts for rapid deployment in crisis situations with its
Rapid Expert Assistance and Cooperation Teams (REACT), and in the
African Union the proposed new African Standby Force, the first subre-

gional elements of which may begin becoming operational by the end of 2008, includes provision for police and civilian expert standby rosters.

Elsewhere, the most interesting recent development is in the United States, where the proposed new Civilian Reserve Corps, designed to give civilian support to U.S. military stabilization operations, and which up until February 2008 had been little more than a pilot project, has seen President Bush requesting $248 million for the program for fiscal year 2009, as compared with the $7.2 million it received in 2007. Administered by the Coordinator for the Office of Reconstruction and Stabilization, the proposal involves an active response unit of some 250 specialists drawn from all relevant branches of government and deployable immediately, backed by a larger standby response group of some 2,000 similar government specialists deployable within two months, and a civilian response corps, again of around 2,000, which could be required to serve for up to a year.[32] There is a long history in Washington, however, of major budgetary requests generating very little actual return, and it remains to be seen whether any of these initiatives proves to be as good in practice as they look on paper.

All this attention to building standby capability is heartening, but there is less occasion for self-congratulation than it might imply. Hard experience has shown over and again that formal standby commitments by government are one thing, and the timely honoring of those commitments is something else. Months of delay remain the norm, and many missions never get the total numbers their planning demands. Despite the fact that the twenty-seven countries of the EU have more than 2 million police officers among them, they have still only managed to muster together 150 to send to Afghanistan to train a new Afghan police force of 16,000.[33] Moreover, the EU's first police chief, Friedrich Eichele, resigned in September 2007 after only three months in the job; it is said that he had no furniture, computers, or cars and that his own bureaucracy delayed the delivery of some seventy armor-plated vehicles, thereby preventing his initial staff of 85—well below the number he was meant to have—leaving Kabul to assist with training in the provinces.[34] In the UN system in 2007, average civilian vacancy rates in UN missions were about 30 percent, the bulk of which were for critical areas such as judicial reform.[35]

There are in fact many well-documented problems with the global civilian standby system as it presently operates.[36] States invariably retain the right to refuse to commit to specific operations, and often do, with additional policing requirements at home being a favored explanation following September 11 and subsequent terrorist alarms in a number of European capitals. It will often be the case that overlapping commitments are made, for example, by individual European states to the EU and the UN (and likely the OSCE as well), so that personnel registered in a database may actually be engaged in an operation elsewhere. And even when identified resources are notionally available and there is a willingness by governments to supply them, the individuals involved—many of whom (including retired police officers and other professionals) will not be in government employment—may well, when it comes to the point, find themselves with better things to do. Recruiting large enough numbers to cope with these contingencies is difficult when complex questions of conditions of service overseas, insurance and the like, are necessarily involved: this is not a problem with military personnel, where potential service overseas comes with the job, but it constitutes a major set of obstacles for civilians, including police, whose day jobs are essentially domestic. Generally speaking, it is almost as difficult and time-consuming a business to find and register standby personnel as it has always been for the UN and others, unable as they are to offer career continuity, to directly recruit contract staff for particular missions. And there is always a financial bottom line: current funding instruments and appeal mechanisms do not usually provide rapid, upfront support for the range of civilian requirements needed in the immediate aftermath of a crisis, and while individual governments have often self-funded these deployments, it cannot be assumed that the capacity and willingness to do so on the necessary scale required will always be there.

Even if all these obstacles are overcome and civilian resources are deployed, there is something else that cannot be assumed: that they will be of the requisite quality, either at the leadership or rank-and-file level. Even if basic criteria of professional competence and character are satisfied, which screening arrangements currently in place have not always been able to guarantee, as often as not there will be, at the very least, an absence of local language skills, with all the limitations of effectiveness that implies in almost every area of civilian support. There has also been a significant gender imbalance, with many fewer women in UN police missions than in home forces, a particularly important consideration when sexual violence issues arise as often as they do in these fragile and chaotic situations. A further problem that arises repeatedly on the ground with civilian deployments is welding together individuals of very disparate backgrounds into effectively functioning teams capable of collectively performing the tasks required. In the context of policing, particularly in highly volatile situations, the UN has a strong preference for "formed police units," preexisting operational entities that have trained and worked together, and these are gradually becoming the norm, although—as everywhere else—there is some distance to go in moving from conception and commitment to reality.[37]

Because civilian commitments are generally much less domestically politically sensitive than military ones, and because it has been far easier to announce, and notionally meet, standby targets for these resources, there is some perception that this is a relatively problem-free area when it comes to rapidly deployable capability. But any such impression would be quite misleading, as was evident, for example, in the Security Council open debate in May 2008, initiated by U.K. Prime Minister Gordon Brown, on what more remained to be done, when the full range of problems described above were fully aired. Secretary-General Ban Ki-moon was explicit in noting the importance of clarity of leadership, sufficient on-the-ground capacity, and scaled-up expertise, emphasizing that "we remain desperately short of judges, prison wardens, state administrators and managers," and adding, pertinently, that "ultimately, all this requires early and flexible funding."[38] The session resulted in Secretary-General Ban being invited by the Council to provide advice within twelve months to the relevant UN organs on how to move forward on these issues. [39] He was specifically asked also to take into account the views of the Peacebuilding Commission—which hopefully, as it continues to find its feet, will play a larger role in the overall mobilization and coordination of these efforts.

Military Response Capability

The responsibility to protect, as has been made clear over and again through the course of this volume, should only involve the use of coercive military force as a last resort: when no other options are available, it is the right thing to do morally and practically, and this is lawful under the UN Charter. If such force from outside has to be used, as the only way to protect people from genocide and mass atrocity crimes, then it is far better for this to happen with the consent of the government in question. But if that consent is not forthcoming, perhaps because the government itself is part of the problem, then—in extreme cases—outside forces will have to take action without it.

Exercising this responsibility poses a number of very difficult problems for military planners because it is not the kind of role in which militaries have been traditionally engaged, where they have well-developed doctrine and for which they can draw on a large body of experience. What is involved here is neither traditional war fighting (where the object is to defeat an enemy, not just to stop particular kinds of violence and intimidation), nor, at the other extreme, traditional peacekeeping (which assumes that there is a peace to keep and is concerned essentially with monitoring, supervision, and verification). The new task is partly what is now described (as discussed in chapter 5) as "peacekeeping plus" or "complex peacekeeping," where it is assumed from the outset that the mission, while primarily designed to hold together a cease-fire or peace settlement, is likely to run into trouble from spoilers of one kind or another; that military force is quite likely to have to be used at some stage, for civilian protection purposes as well as in self-defense; and where, accordingly, a Chapter VII rather than just a Chapter VI mandate is required. New peacekeeping missions in recent years have been constructed almost routinely on this basis, as noted earlier, but that does not mean that military planners and commanders are yet comfortable with running them. And that is not the end of the R2P story: the other part of the task is that which may arise in a Rwanda-type case, where there is the sudden eruption of conscience-shocking crimes against humanity, beyond the capacity of any existing peacekeeping mission to deal with, demanding a rapid and forceful "fire brigade" response from a new or extended mission to quash the violence and protect those caught up in it. This is more than just "peacekeeping plus"—dealing with spoilers—but, again, it is not traditional war fighting either.

Together, these "peacekeeping plus" and "fire brigade" operations have been described as "coercive protection missions," which is as useful terminology as any to use in addressing what is needed to create the capability—essentially the same in both cases—to operate them effectively.[40] But getting reasonably clear the overall concept of operations, as this language does, is only the beginning of the story. Operational effectiveness in practice depends on getting a number of other things right: *force configuration* (what kind of force structure, and quantities of personnel and equipment, do militaries have to have to be able to mount these kinds of operations, individually or collectively); *deployability* (how rapidly can the necessary forces get to whatever theater is involved); *preparation* (ensuring that doctrine and training are matched to these operations); *mandates and rules of engagement* (ensuring that they are appropriate for the particular mission proposed); and *military-civilian cooperation* (ensuring that structures and processes are in place to maximize the effectiveness of each). As discussed below, systematic attention is being paid now to all these issues by a number of national forces, and increasingly by those multilateral actors capable of mounting military operations, but still not enough.

A Standing UN Rapid Reaction Force?

A perennial question that arises at the outset is why is it not possible for the UN to create a standing rapid reaction capability of its own, formed either from troops contributed by member states or by volunteers? The first secretary-general, Trygve Lie, had floated the idea of a "UN Legion" in 1948, but the main proponent of such a force in recent years has been the enormously respected and long-serving former UN under-secretary-general Sir Brian Urquhart. In a widely debated and still resonating 1993 article, Urquhart argued for a 5,000-strong light infantry volunteer force, under the direction of the Security Council, that would be able and willing to forcibly intervene to "break the cycle of violence at an early stage in low-level but dangerous conflicts."[41] This, uncannily, anticipated by a year the assessment of General Romeo Dallaire, discussed in chapter 1, that having a capable force of just this size rapidly available to him could have stopped the Rwandan genocide in its tracks, a view supported by other military professionals.[42] Subsequent variations on Urquhart's theme have been developed by the government of the Netherlands and promoted by a number of commentators, and the idea has had many high-level supporters, with Gerald Ford, Helmut Schmidt, and Mikhail Gorbachev, for example, recommending in mid-1994 "the creation of a modest size standing force of volunteers under UN auspices . . . backed up by regional or subregional peace-keeping forces."[43] And whenever tested, the idea has always enjoyed a considerable measure of popular support. For example, a 2007 global survey conducted in association with the Chicago Council on Global Affairs, covering 56 percent of the world's population, found in twelve out of the fourteen countries surveyed strong majorities in favor of "having a standing UN peacekeeping force selected, trained and commanded by the United Nations": Peru was the most enthusiastic (77 percent), with France (74 percent), Thailand (73 percent), and the United States (72 percent) not far behind.[44]

But within the UN system the idea has never taken hold, killed basically by the endemic suspicion that prevails against military activity generally, and the more particular suspicion that prevails among the membership about any military capability controlled directly by the Security Council; even more alarming to some members, including the Permanent Five and Washington in particular, is the thought that a standing force might possibly be influenced in its role by the secretary-general and his staff. For all practical purposes, unfortunately, the proposal seems as politically dead as the Military Staff Committee (MSC), the institution within the UN that might have been the vehicle for bringing it to life.[45] The MSC is, or was, the body of permanent-member chiefs of staff created under the UN Charter itself to be "responsible under the Security Council for the strategic direction of any armed forces placed at the disposal of the Security Council," which was rendered immediately moribund by the antagonisms of the early cold war and has remained so since—although an empty office in the Secretariat, not much bigger than a broom cupboard, is still labeled wistfully in its memory. There are other practical arguments against a standing force, for example, that to have 5,000 troops always operational at the sharp end means having another 10,000 to 15,000 personnel in support, adding up to a total establishment that it would be extremely expensive to recruit, train, equip, and house on a continuing basis, as well as deploy, and that would in practice, given the demands likely to be placed on the standing force, need to be supplemented anyway by major additional contributions from member states, which would bring us straight back to the original problem of dilatory response.[46] But as Urqhart has responded, "There are plenty of arguments against such a force. There is one overwhelming argument for it. It is desperately needed."[47]

What can be said is that in recent years the UN system has at least been shamed enough by the obviousness of this need—and the larger problem of generating in a timely manner forces for the whole range of peace operations it administers, not just "fire brigade deployments"—to put in place a number of interrelated *standby* arrangements that have done at least something to make the process a little less ad hoc, although they are still for the most part applicable only to Chapter VI operations, not the more robust ones under discussion here.[48] On the initiative of Secretary-General Boutros-Ghali in the mid-1990s, a basic United Nations Standby Arrangements System (UNSAS) was created as a database of military and civilian personnel, as well as matériel and equipment, that member states say they are willing to commit to future Chapter VI peacekeeping operations at the request of the secretary-general. In 1994 there was established in Brindisi, Italy, a permanent United Nations Logistics Base (UNLB), which stores and makes shipments of supplies to and from UN peace operations worldwide and operates as the UN relay center for telecommunications networks connecting all UN peacekeeping missions, as well as several UN agencies and headquarters. And—at least initially for less demanding traditional peacekeeping operations, mandated under Chapter VI of the Charter—there has been operating since 2000, Danish-led and with some sixteen states now participating, the Multinational Standby High Readiness Brigade (SHIRBRIG), which aims to provide the UN with a well-trained multinational force of 4,000 to 5,000 troops with a reaction time of fifteen to thirty days, and with units self-sufficient for up to sixty days and deployable for a maximum of six months. As with all such standby arrangements, participating member states maintain sovereignty over troops and decide whether to participate in an operation on a case-by-case basis. The Brigade formed the initial core of the the UN Mission in Ethiopia and Eritrea and has deployed several times since, mainly in relatively small headquarters formations.[49]

Standby arrangements—and there are comparable developments evolving in the EU, AU, and NATO, as discussed in the last chapter—can never be as efficient as an immediately available standing force, but for the foreseeable future they are all we are likely to have to supplement the otherwise totally ad hoc process of compiling a multilateral expeditionary force. On the assumption, then, that coercive protection missions will have to be put together in this laborious way, what has to be done—in relation to the issues of force configuration, deployability, and the like, foreshadowed above—to ensure that they will in fact be available and operationally effective?

FORCE CONFIGURATION

While with appropriate support and preparation a number of countries in the global South could mount very capable coercive protection missions, there are a relatively small number of countries which on the face of it are well enough equipped now to provide the necessary resources, and not excessively distracted (as is the United States) by very large-scale commitments elsewhere—namely, the NATO European allies. But the trouble is that these countries for the most part have force structures that are largely relics of the cold war years, very focused on static territorial defense, with large and relatively immobile troop concentrations and equipment to match. The usual estimate, as noted in the last chapter, is that not many more than 3 percent of all men and women in uniform are internationally deployable at any given time—around 10,000 in every 250,000. And there is a serious shortfall in the kind of expeditionary assets that are critical to the management of quick, flexible, mobile operations in far-flung environments: strategic lift; aerial refueling; sustainability and logistics; deployable command, control, communications, computers, intelligence, surveillance, target acquisition, and reconnaissance; and precision strike weapons. The countries in question are gradually trying to modernize their capability, with, for example, the French Defense Ministry White Paper (June 2008) acknowledging, among many other changes, the need for its forces to be able to make an effective contribution to "la responsibilité de protegér."[50] But there is still a long way to go.

All that said, with some 23 million men and women in uniform worldwide (and another 54 million reservists and 9 million paramilitaries) and with less than 100,000 of them currently deployed in UN missions, it hardly seems beyond the wit of man to work out a way of making some of that national human capacity available when and where it is needed to prevent and react to man-made catastrophes.[51] Similarly with equipment: one of the hardest things to explain is why there has been so little will evident to supply helicopters to current missions where they are hugely needed, above all the hybrid AU-UN mission in Darfur. From the roughly 12,000 available in the global military inventory, it has not been possible to find just twenty-two to support this critical civilian protection mission (see the lead to this chapter). There are issues about the suitability of many of these aircraft for the particular conditions and operational needs of that mission; moreover, these machines, with the flight and maintenance crews that need to with them, are not at all cheap to supply. But as so often is the case, lack of resources ultimately comes down to a simple lack of political will.

DEPLOYABILITY

Having troops and equipment potentially available in the necessary numbers and volume does not mean very much if they cannot get to where they are needed when they are needed. Resolving this problem is partly a matter of national forces having the right configuration, as just discussed, with enough personnel in the right formations having the right skills to *be* deployed, and enough of the right strategic lift capability to get them there. It is also a matter, however, of the relevant multilateral actors having their own act together and being able to effectively utilize such assets as they have. As former U.S. secretary of defense Donald Rumsfeld has put it—and he did get some things right—"If NATO does not have a force that is quick and agile, which can deploy in days or weeks instead of months or years, then it will not have much to offer the world in the 21st century."[52]

If the proper standard of comparison is the U.S. 82nd Airborne Division, which can be anywhere in the world in three days, there is obviously some distance to go if there is to be any confidence that the capability exists elsewhere to halt a quickly spreading, large-scale genocide. The EU's 1,500-strong battlegroups are targeted to be deployed to crisis regions outside Europe, as needed, within fifteen days from decision, and the goals of the other organizations are either inexplicit (as with the new NATO Response Force) or even more modest. The UN's target of deployment within thirty to ninety days is clearly too slow in these situations; the AU and ECOWAS would like to be more ambitious but usually have to rely on outside partners for lift and logistics support.[53]

PREPARATION

The distinctiveness of coercive protection operations from more familiar military tasks—and the need to tread a line that involves something short of a full-scale war-fighting mind-set but more than an observing and monitoring one—makes it crucial that forces be properly prepared for them. That in turn means much attention to training but also, to ensure that the training is properly focused, the principles or doctrine on which it is based. "Doctrine," in military parlance, is essentially the formal written guidance that translates broad concepts—for example, the umbrella concept of "coercive protection operations" being used here—into the kind of actual action required at the strategic, operational, and tactical levels. The ICISS commissioners spelled out their own view of the principles on which the doctrine required for UN-mandated human protection operations should be based:

- the operation must be based on a precisely defined political objective expressed in a clear and unambiguous mandate, with matching resources and rules of engagement;
- the intervention must be politically controlled, but be conducted by a military commander with authority to command to the fullest extent possible, who disposes of adequate resources to execute his mission, and with a single chain of command which reflects unity of command and purpose;
- the aim of the human protection operation is to enforce compliance with human rights and the rule of law as quickly and as comprehensively as possible, but it is not the defeat of a state; this must properly be reflected in the application of force, with limitations on the application of force having to be accepted, together with some incrementalism and gradualism tailored to the objective to protect;
- the conduct of the operation must guarantee maximum protection of all elements of the civilian population;
- strict adherence to international humanitarian law must be ensured;
- force protection for the intervening force must never have priority over the resolve to accomplish the mission; and
- there must be maximum coordination between military and civilian authorities and organizations.[54]

For the most part national militaries have developed doctrine for different kinds of peace support operations, although of varying degrees of sophistication and detail. Of the key nations surveyed in this respect by Holt and Berkman, Canada and the United Kingdom appear to provide the clearest guidance to their armed forces on coercive protection, closely reflecting R2P language. By contrast, none of the relevant multilateral organizations—the UN, EU, AU, ECOWAS, or even NATO—have doctrine designed specifically for operations involving the protection of civilians under imminent threat. NATO has a good deal of fully developed doctrine on various kinds of missions and recognizes many individual military tasks required to protect civilians, but it has no specific civilian protection section as such.[55] These are gaps that need to be filled, and so far as possible with common concepts and terminology among the different governments and organizations.

Training, similarly, leaves much to be desired, to the extent that practically nowhere is it very well geared—either in general or in the case of specific pre-deployment training—to missions where civilian protection is the central task, or at least a very explicit goal, of the mission, and coercive force is a permissible element in the response. Changes are gradually being made to reflect the nature of these contemporary missions and the stronger mandates that are going with them, but in both national and multilateral contexts, current modules are often strong in areas like managing evacuations, crowd control, securing facilities, and conducting patrols—but not, for example, on how to stop a belligerent from committing gross human rights abuses. It is better understood now than it was at the time of Srebrenica that UN peacekeeping principles of minimum use of force, impartiality, and consent do not justify inaction in the face of atrocities, but what actual action is required and permitted, and how to carry it out, needs more attention, with many more well-developed exercises and simulations.[56]

MANDATES AND RULES OF ENGAGEMENT

These are the legally binding instructions for particular missions, describing at different levels of generality not only what are their basic tasks but when, where, and to what extent their members may use force. For example, in the case of the UN Mission in the Democratic Republic of the Congo (MONUC), the mandate spelled out in Security Council Resolution 1565 of 2004 included paragraphs making clear that the Security Council was *acting* "under Chapter VII of the Charter of the United Nations"; that it was *mandating* (that is, instructing) MONUC, among a number of other tasks, "to ensure the protection of civilians, including humanitarian personnel, under imminent threat of physical violence"; and that it was *authorizing* the mission, in carrying out this among other tasks "to use all necessary means, within its capacity and in the areas where its armed units are deployed." The rules of engagement (ROEs) for this mission made clear, in turn, exactly what "all necessary means" meant, with ROE 1.7 reading, "Forces may use up to deadly force to protect civilians when competent local authorities are not in a position to do so."[57] The "up to" language used here of course indicates that any such use of force should be proportional to the situation faced.

There is a crucial need that in every coercive protection mission—and indeed every military mission of any kind—mandates and rules of engagement be, first, completely appropriate to the task required, with Chapter VII powers being given where they are needed, and second, articulated with absolute clarity, with no ambiguity or room for any other misunderstanding as to what is intended.[58] The operational effectiveness of a mission is as dependent on these instructions being right as on anything else. That these propositions are self-evident, however, is no reason to assume they have been observed in the past or will be in the future.

Military-Civilian Cooperation

Civil-military cooperation (CIMIC) simply means coordination and cooperation, in support of the mission, between the commander and civil actors, including national populations and local authorities, as well as international, national, and nongovernmental organizations and agencies.[59] The need to get this right can scarcely be overestimated, above all in coercive protection missions where very sensitive issues are likely to arise in juggling the respective roles of a military force trying to protect people from violence and intimidation, humanitarian relief agencies trying to bring their own assistance and protection to populations at risk, and civil authorities trying to govern and reconstruct the country or assist others to do so. As the ICISS report rather drily commented,

> Coordination is a topic that is of perpetual concern but which is extremely difficult to achieve satisfactorily, since coordination implies independent authorities attempting to cooperate with each other. Often, coordination does not translate into integrated decision making on a regular basis, nor to genuine unity of effort. While coordination efforts have markedly improved effectiveness in some cases, in others they have amounted to little more than trying to minimize turf wars.[60]

While there are innumerable textbook examples of this coordination not working as it should—with Afghanistan a prime current example—this is an area where operational effectiveness depends crucially on institutional and personal egos being submerged to the maximum possible extent and on the effort being intensely sustained.[61]

CHAPTER TEN

Mobilizing Political Will

If we believe that all human beings are equally entitled to be protected from acts that shock the conscience of us all, then we must match rhetoric with reality, principle with practice. We cannot be content with reports and declarations. We must be prepared to act. We won't be able to live with ourselves if we do not.

—ICISS, *The Responsibility to Protect*, 2001[1]

Don't mourn, organize!

—Joe Hill, 1915

Without the exercise of political will, by the relevant policymakers at the relevant time, almost none of the things for which this book has argued will actually happen. The institutional capability to deliver the right kind of response at the right time—by way of prevention, reaction, or rebuilding as the case demands—simply will not be there. And even if the capability is there, it will not be used. For almost any spread of options, inertia will have the numbers. The loudest and most oft-repeated lamentation of them all is that there is a "lack of political will" to do what needs to be done.

I have been familiar with that lamentation, and wailed it often enough myself, through a lifetime of trying to influence public policy. First as a young civil society activist trying to get local, state, and national politicians engaged and energized on issues like indigenous land rights, law reform, and apartheid. Then as a politician and cabinet minister myself, trying to mobilize my peers within the national government to see issues the way I did and give me the budgetary resources to tackle them. Then also as foreign minister for a number of years, trying to energize my peers in the international community to initiate and follow through collective responses to various problems we faced. And now again as a rather older civil society activist with the International Crisis Group, in the somewhat unusual position of playing the traditional NGO bottom-up advocacy role but being able as well to work the high-level peer group access track. Whether one is inside or outside the decisionmaking tent, or somewhere in between, the frustrations— I can testify better than most—are just as acute.

But what I have learned very clearly from four decades of trying to make things happen, nationally and internationally, is that there is no point in simply mourning the absence of political will: this should be the occasion not for lamentation, but mobilization. To explain a failure as the result of lack of political will is simply to restate the problem, not provide an explanation or any kind of strategy for change. The need to generate the necessary will to do anything hard, or expensive, or politically sensitive, or seen for better or worse as not directly relevant to the national interest, is just a fact of public policy life. Political will is capable of creation and subject to change: its presence or absence is not a given. It is not a missing ingredient, waiting in each case to be found if we only had the key to the right cupboard or lifted the right stone. It has to be painfully and laboriously constructed, case by case, context by context. And all of us have a role in this respect. It is a matter of key officials in key governments, and those who can influence them directly, making the effort to persuade and mobilize their peers in the international community to take the necessary action in the UN Security Council and everywhere else that matters. It is also a matter of bottom-up mobilization: making the voices of ordinary concerned citizens heard in the corridors of power, using all the resources and physical and moral energy of civil society organizations all round the world to force the attention of policymakers on what needs to be done, by whom, and when.

Those who want to mobilize political will have to understand and be responsive to all the different elements that go into making it up. The key elements, discussed in turn in what follows, are knowledge of the problem; concern to do something about it; confidence that doing something will make a difference; institutional processes capable of translating that knowledge, concern, and confident belief into relevant action; and leadership—without which the ticking of all four other boxes will not matter: inertia will win, every time. The discouraging news is that achieving all these things, in both national and international decisionmaking, is very hard work indeed: it needs good arguments, sustained energy and creativity in advancing them, and, especially in the case of leadership, a measure of luck. The better news is that at least the arguments and strategies are there, and that there are plenty of civil society and governmental actors around with the competence, commitment, and organizational capacity to advance them.

It should hardly need to be added that what is at issue here is not just political will as such, but the right *kind* of political will. Getting what one asks for in life can be a risky business, and here as elsewhere it is important to stay clearheaded. There was no shortage of will involved in the coalition invasion of Iraq in 2003 or some Washington alarums and excursions of recent memory. The problem of political will can on occasion be not so much its absence as its overexuberant presence.

Ensuring Knowledge

Knowing about the occurrence or imminence of mass atrocity crimes is rarely the problem it is sometimes thought to be. Leaders trying to explain their inaction in the face of catastrophes such as Rwanda like to be able to say, "We didn't know what was happening," or, more subtly, "We didn't fully appreciate how serious the problem was." But over and again, when these claims are evaluated after the event—sometimes by conscience-ridden officials, more often by historians like Samantha Power—they turn out to be quite false.[2] There was always someone within the system in question who had a clear sense of the nature and scale of the catastrophe that was unfolding, and in most of the worst cases, there was at least some kind of memorandum conveying that information finding its way to the most senior decisionmaking level. That nothing, or not enough, then happened was a function of there going missing one or more of the other elements that make up political will—insufficient concern, insufficient belief that external action would make a difference, poor institutional process in shaping deliverable options and acting on them, or simply failed leadership.

One of the clearest examples remains the United States reaction to Rwanda in 1994. When President Clinton visited Kigali in 1998, he said, in the course of a moving speech to the crowd at the airport, "All over the world there were people like me sitting in offices, day after day, who did not fully appreciate the depth and the speed with which you were being engulfed in this unimaginable terror." But a subsequent report in 2004 by the National Security Archive, an independent nongovernmental research institute based in Washington, D.C., which went to court to obtain the material, disclosed that the CIA's national intelligence daily, a secret briefing distributed directly to the president, vice president, and hundreds of senior officials, included at the relevant time almost daily reports on Rwanda, with considerable detail about what was happening.[3]

There are few excuses these days for any decisionmaking system, national or intergovernmental, not to know about what have been described in this book as "R2P situations," those where mass atrocity crimes are actually occurring or imminently about to occur, or where the situation could deteriorate to this extent in the medium or longer term unless appropriate preventive measures are taken. Officials on the ground report back up through their communication lines, there are sometimes graphic descriptions in the print and electronic media, and above all there are now nongovernmental organizations pumping out the necessary information through all the real-time forms of electronic communication that earlier generations of advocates and activists could only dream about.

That said, there is always more that could be done, in all three of these areas, to make necessary information more salient, or unmistakably prominent, in the minds of relevant decisionmakers. Those who have never been involved in decisionmaking at the highest levels can scarcely begin to imagine how many problems and issues are simultaneously clamoring for attention at any given time, how hard it is to get anyone to focus on anything but the most immediate and urgent, and how tempting it is to deny, diminish, or defer a problem in the hope that it will disappear entirely or be seen as someone else's. Governments and large intergovernmental organizations need (as will be discussed further below) focal points within their systems staffed by officials whose full-time day job it is to keep track of this information, evaluate it, ensure that it gets onto the relevant desks, identify response options, and follow them through.

For NGOs the need (again discussed further below) is to supplement the kind of sharply focused reports and briefings and alert bulletins being regularly distributed by organizations like the International Crisis Group and Human Rights Watch with more broadly based, coordinated, and sustained public advocacy on such a scale and of such an intensity that it simply cannot be ignored by senior decisionmakers. The Darfur campaign in the United States—well described by, among others, Don Cheadle and John Prendergast in their *Not on Our Watch: The Mission to End Genocide in Darfur and Beyond*—is an all too rare example of what is possible in this respect.[4]

In the case of the media, there is no question but that good reporting, well-argued opinion pieces, and, in particular, real-time transmission of images of suffering do generate both domestic and international pressure to act. The "CNN effect" can be almost irresistible. But it has to be acknowledged that, with very occasional exceptions—Darfur being one—there is rather less to this than first meets the eye. Part of the problem is that many atrocity crimes occur in security environments too hair-raising to expect television crews to stick around, or in areas where they have been refused access by the authorities, and conscience-shocking and action-motivating images just do not get into circulation. But beyond that inevitable limitation, there is in most countries, not least the United States, much less attention paid to international issues in the mainstream media than ideally would be the case: at home the CNN effect is rather diminished by the reality that on the company's national channels (as distinct from CNN International that the rest of the world sees), it is deeply unusual to find any serious field-based international reporting at all. The mainstream domestic channels—apart from an occasional late-night ABC Nightline-type story—do not do much better. And the print media almost invariably deals with such international stories briefly, selectively, and without sustained follow-up: in an "infotainment"-oriented media universe, the *New York Times*, it hardly needs saying, is not the norm.

It may be that the traditional role of the mainstream media as the basic information source for policymakers, as well as publics at large, is now being superseded, particularly for generations younger than mine, by all the new forms of electronic communication—broadcast, narrowcast, and direct personal messaging. But the lesson is that if civil society organizations and activists do want to ensure that decisionmakers continue to have no excuses when it comes to knowledge of R2P situations, they will have to continue to work hard to communicate the relevant information by every means that modern technology has to offer.

Encouraging Concern

Knowing about an actual or emerging mass atrocity crime is one thing; being concerned enough to want to take some action in response is something else. What can be done to encourage in decisionmakers in national governments, and relevant intergovernmental organizations, the sense that they do in fact have a responsibility to take appropriate action that is within their physical and financial capacity? The key is to have the right arguments being directed to the right people—by individuals or organizations who themselves have credibility with the decisionmakers in question. From my own experience, both in government and beating on the doors of government, one has to recognize that there are certain individuals, at or near the top of the food chains, whose attitudes are going to be decisive, and good arguments have to be found that will both appeal to them and be useful to them in explaining and defending their decisions. There are four different kinds of argument that matter in this respect: moral, national interest, financial, and political.

It cannot be assumed that *moral* imperatives, important as they are in every culture, will have sufficient momentum on their own to carry the day. Part of the problem stems from basic characteristics of the human psyche. There is emerging experimental evidence that Stalin was not far off the mark when he reputedly said that "One man's death is a tragedy; a million is a statistic." The capacity to experience "affect"—the emotional rather than rational component of decisionmaking, that which enables us to *feel* an issue and want to do something about it—appears to be dulled rather than enhanced by large numbers. One recent U.S. study went so far as to demonstrate that donations to aid a particular starving seven-year-old girl in Africa actually declined sharply when her image was accompanied by a statistical summary of millions like her elsewhere on the continent. If we are looking for spontaneous compassion to light the policymakers' flame when it comes to mass atrocities, this may not be as easy as we sometimes assume.[5]

Another issue is that moral imperatives do tend to be viewed a little differently in different cultural environments. The point has often been made that in a number of Asian societies the notion of universal values, or universal responsibility towards one's fellow human beings in the world at large, tends to have less resonance than the notion of obligation to family, friends, and, at its widest, fellow countrymen: because the bestowing of favors creates a very specific sense of reciprocal obligation, it is not difficult to characterize what others might think of as morally driven charity as, rather, unwelcome interference.[6] But against that, it is strongly arguable that the course of history has shown human society steadily expanding its "circle of empathy," from an initial kernel of relations and friends, to the clan, the tribe, the nation, and wider and wider groups including other races, with this phenomenon much reinforced in recent times by ever growing international movement and communication, and the cosmopolitanism associated with that.[7] From this perspective, the basic case for R2P, and for responding in some productive way when one becomes aware of an actual or imminent mass atrocity crime, rests simply on our common humanity: the impossibility of ignoring the cries of pain and distress of our fellow human beings. To yet again do so, and once again make "never again" a cry that rings totally emptily, is to diminish that common humanity to the point of despair.

At the end of the day, these kinds of straightforward moral arguments will have some resonance in every multilateral forum and every national political system. Politicians and public officials, after all, always rather like to be seen as acting from higher motives, however base their real ones may be. But it remains important to be able to make a case for action on other grounds as well—national interest, political, and financial—with good arguments, intelligently and energetically advanced.[8]

National interest arguments, as noted already in chapter 6, are much easier to make now in relation to the kind of "quarrel in a faraway country between people of whom we know nothing" about which the British Prime Minister Neville Chamberlain was so famously dismissive in the lead-up to Munich.[9] This is because of what we know now about the capacity of failed, failing, rogue, and phantom states, in this ever more globalized and interdependent world, to be a source of havoc for others. Put simply, states that cannot or will not stop internal atrocity crimes are the kind of states that cannot or will not stop terrorism, weapons proliferation, drug and people trafficking, the spread of health pandemics, and other global risks.

There is, moreover, another dimension to national interest these days, quite distinct from the familiar duo of security and economic interests, and protecting oneself from the essentially physical threats just mentioned. Every country has an interest in being, and being seen to be, a good international citizen. The interest in question here is more than just the pleasure of basking in approbation. There are many direct reciprocal benefits to be gained in a world where no country can solve all its own problems: my assistance for you today in solving your drugs and terrorism problem might reasonably lead you to be more willing to help solve my environmental problem tomorrow. But the reputational benefit does also count. The perception of being a country willing to take principled stands for other than immediately self-interested reasons does no harm at all—as the Scandinavians in particular seem to have well understood—when it comes to advancing one's own commercial or political agendas.[10]

Financial arguments can also be compelling in many contexts. Preventive action is likely to be cheaper, by many orders of magnitude, than responding after the event—whether through military action, humanitarian relief assistance, postconflict reconstruction, or all three. This is not a hard argument to establish. For example, when I was Australian Foreign Minister, I tasked my department after the first Gulf War in 1991 to assess the cost to the allies of waging it, as compared with what the cost would have been in setting up a credible worldwide system of preventive diplomacy centers, staffed by professionals, which might conceivably have averted Iraq's invasion of Kuwait—still generally acknowledged to be one of history's better examples of missed opportunities for such diplomacy. The result: cost of establishing the centers, in 1991 dollars, $21 million; material cost to the allies of fighting the war—not to Iraq and leaving aside any calculation of human cost—$70 *billion*.

The U.K. Foreign Secretary, then Jack Straw, made the same point in a speech in 2002 with some revealing figures about the Balkans: "Early treatment of some ugly symptoms in Macedonia was highly effective last year in stopping a slide into failure and preventing the re-emergence of chaos in the Balkans. Sorting out Bosnia cost the British taxpayer at least £1.5 billion. Kosovo cost £200 million. Macedonia cost just £14 million."[11] In the case of the invasion of Iraq in 2003, which at the time of this writing in mid-2008 had cost the United States alone an extraordinary $444 billion—with the meter still now ticking at over $134 billion a year—it may not be impolite to suggest that effective diplomacy through the Security Council, backed by a continued strong weapons inspection regime, and sanctions disciplines to compel greater respect for human rights could have achieved a much better result at a tiny fraction of that expense.[12]

Political arguments are the stock-in-trade of national decisionmaking and, although not always as overt, invariably part of the subtext in multilateral institutions as well. Political risk and reward calculations come very much in play when the expenditure of blood or treasure is on the line, not only in high-visibility emergency response situations but more prosaic ones as well. One of the perennial problems about mobilizing support for *preventive* action at all levels is that the political returns tend to be so slight. Because prevention succeeds most when nothing happens and nobody notices, there are few immediately visible returns for those who make the right decisions—and for most people in public office, performing good works without anyone noticing is like having one's teeth pulled. A continuing challenge for peace advocates the world over is to find ways of overtly recognizing and rewarding not just successful conflict and crisis resolution efforts, but successful prevention.

Mounting arguments that will address domestic political concerns is, however, a subtler business than just calculating what majority reactions will be. Governments—even those directly dependent for their support on the ballot box—often do things without knowing what the majority view is and even when they know that majority sentiment may well be against the proposed action. What matters more is that they have arguments that will appeal to, or at least not alienate, their own political support base, and arguments that they can use to deflate, or at least defend against, the attacks of their political opponents. The United States in recent years has offered good examples of very partisan considerations being hitched simultaneously to both good and bad conflict management practice. The Christian right, if not in the mainstream of national opinion, has certainly been a strong influence on the George W. Bush administration. In Sudan that influence has been exercised positively insofar as, motivated by concerns about religious freedom and slavery, it led the United States to play a very active and positive role in the north-south peace process. But in the case of the Israeli-Palestinian conflict, the influence of the Christian right has been rather less positive to the extent that—whether motivated by the notion of a Judeo-Christian bulwark against heathen Muslims, or bizarre apocalyptic beliefs premising the second coming of Jesus on the creation of Israel—it has, for most of the administration's term, encouraged an extremely one-sided approach.

Of course democracy requires that opportunism be tempered by appropriate caution, and most political leaders are risk-averse most of the time. That has certainly played an important part in some of the limp responses to mass atrocity crimes in the past, no more notoriously so than in the Clinton administration's ignoring of the situation in Rwanda in 1994, stung as it still was by the fallout from the debacle in Somalia not long before, involving the killing and parading of its troops in the Mogadishu "Black Hawk Down" incident. Probably the most extreme example of rationalizing unwillingness to act was the U.S. Defense Department's position during the first weeks of the genocide that C-130 aircraft could not be devoted to ferrying armored personnel carriers to General Dallaire because that would sacrifice readiness to respond to some higher-priority crisis should one arise.[13]

But decisionmakers in many countries, democracies and non-democracies alike, may be surprised to find that domestic public opinion is well ahead of them on R2P-related issues, much more willing than they may be to take appropriate action in the face of mass atrocity crimes. In the case of democratic states, it may be that the political cost of inaction in the face of mass atrocities may be higher, in terms of lost votes and financial contributions, than the potential political risks of action. An intriguing survey was conducted in this respect in 2007 by the Chicago Council on Global Affairs and WorldPublicOpinion.org in cooperation with polling organizations around the world, in which respondents were interviewed in more than a dozen countries representing between them more than half the world's population. It is worth quoting in full the summary of its findings on the subject of intervention in response to genocide:

> Publics show very strong support for allowing the UN Security Council to use military force to "prevent severe human rights violations such as genocide." Very large majorities in all twelve countries polled on this issue agree that the Security Council should have the right to use force in such cases. The lowest levels of support are in Thailand (62 percent) and India (63 percent), and the highest are in France (85 percent), Israel (83 percent) and the United States (83 percent). Average support across the publics polled is 74 percent.
>
> This poll probed further about whether the Security Council has not just the right but the responsibility to intervene militarily to protect people from severe human rights abuses. "Some people say that the Security Council has the responsibility to authorize the use of military force to protect people from severe human rights violations such as genocide, even against the will of their own government," respondents were told. "Others say that the Security Council does not have such a responsibility."

The idea that the Security Council has this responsibility is the most common view in all twelve of the publics polled and the majority view in eight of them. Interestingly the Chinese (76 percent) show the strongest support for this idea, followed by Americans (74 percent) and Palestinians (69 percent). In four countries, only pluralities agree: Ukrainians (40 percent), Thais (44 percent), Russians (48 percent), and Argentines (48 percent). In no country, do more than four in ten say that the UN does not have a responsibility to act against genocide. On average 57 percent said the UN has this responsibility.[14]

International political will is more than just the sum of attitudes and policies of individual countries. What happens between states and their representatives in bilateral and multilateral contacts, and within intergovernmental organizations, is obviously also crucial. To get the right words uttered, and to turn them into deeds, requires—at international as at domestic level—the same kind of commitment and leadership, and the same kind of constant campaigning. The biggest constituency is always for inaction. It is just as important in the international arena as it is in the domestic to be able to produce arguments appealing to morality, resource concerns, institutional interests, and political interests.

Building Confidence

If knowledge of a problem and concern to do something about it are to be translated into action, it is extremely helpful if decisionmakers can be confident that the action they endorse will actually make a difference. This is not a universal imperative, in that sometimes honor will be thought to be satisfied simply by the authority in question being seen to be doing something, whether that something is of any practical utility or not. And it has to be acknowledged that decisions to impose sanctions have been rather too often of this kind. But it makes for a much better story if doing something does in fact matter.

Very good evidence is now to hand, mentioned several times earlier in the course of this book and which deserves to be much better known in international policy circles, that serious efforts to stop conflicts and mass atrocity crimes, and to prevent new ones recurring, make a very great difference indeed. It comes in the form of some compelling statistics assembled over the last few years in successive reports of the Human Security Report Project in Canada, led by Andrew Mack, a previous head of UN Secretary-General Kofi Annan's Strategic Planning Unit.[15] Contrary to conventional wisdom, and perhaps all our intuitions, there has been a very significant trend decline—after a high point in the late 1980s and very early 1990s—in the number of wars taking place, both between and within states, in the number of genocidal and other mass atrocities, and the number of people dying violent deaths as a result of them.

In the case of serious conflicts (defined as those with 1,000 or more battle deaths in a year) and political mass murders (of the kind we associate with Cambodia and Rwanda), there has been an extraordinary 80 percent decline since the early 1990s. And overall there are now 40 percent fewer conflicts taking place than there were in 1992: in simple terms because many more old conflicts have stopped than new ones started. There has been an even more striking decrease in the number of battle deaths. Whereas most years from the 1940s through to the 1990s had over 100,000 such reported deaths—and sometimes as many as 500,000—the average for the first years of this new century has been more like 20,000. Of course violent battle deaths are only a small part of the whole story of the misery of war: 90 percent or more of war-related deaths are due to disease and malnutrition rather than direct violence, as we have seen, for example, in the Congo and Darfur. But the trend decline in battle deaths is significant and highly encouraging.

The most dramatic single area of improvement, counterintuitive again as this may seem, is in the security landscape of sub-Saharan Africa, fully documented in the *Human Security Brief 2007*. In the late 1990s, this region was the world's most war torn, but between 1999 and 2006, the number of "state-based" conflicts (those in which a government is one of the warring parties) had dropped by more than half, and the number of battle deaths had shrunk to just 2 percent of the 1999 toll—an extraordinary decline. New figures, not previously compiled, for "non-state" conflicts (intercommunal and other conflicts in which a government is not one of the warring parties) and "one-sided violence" (the killing of defenseless civilians by governments or rebel groups) also showed dramatic declines, of two-thirds or more, between 2002 and 2006.

A number of reasons contributed to the turnarounds on conflicts, including the end of the era of colonialism, which generated two-thirds or more of all wars from the 1950s to the 1980s, and of course the end of the cold war, which meant no more proxy wars being fueled by Washington or Moscow, and the end of the road for a number of authoritarian governments, propped up by each side, who had been provoking internal resistance. But, as argued by Andrew Mack and his team—and already noted in chapter 8—the best explanation is the one that stares us in the face, even if a great many don't want to acknowledge it. And that is the huge upsurge in activity in conflict prevention, conflict management, negotiated peacemaking, and postconflict peacebuilding activity that has occurred over the last decade and a half, with most of this being spearheaded by the much maligned UN, albeit with a great deal of additional input from regional organizations, governments, and NGOs.

We are doing better at diplomatic peacemaking, with successes from Cambodia to the Balkans to Northern Ireland to West Africa to Nepal and Aceh well outnumbering in recent years what remain so far the failures, for example, in Sri Lanka and Darfur. In the cold war years, by contrast, more wars were decided on the battlefield than ended in negotiation. We are becoming ever more professional at peacekeeping. And we are certainly now doing much better at postconflict peacebuilding, having finally learned—after the horrendous experiences of Angola, Rwanda, Afghanistan, and Haiti—that the best single predictor of future conflict is past conflict in the same place, and that there is an absolutely critical need to put in sustained resources and commitment during the years that follow peace agreements to stop the whole horrible cycle of violence starting again. If all these realities were better known and appreciated by decisionmakers, it might well prove markedly easier to persuade them to invest the resources and political capital that effective R2P response requires.

Establishing Process

A further critical ingredient in the fashioning of political will is the existence of institutional processes capable of translating knowledge, concern, and confident belief in the utility of action into actual action. As foreshadowed above in discussing the issue of knowledge, focal points are necessary within governments and relevant intergovernmental organizations for the collection, analysis, and dissemination of information, the thinking through and "pre-positioning" of response options, the focusing and energizing of decisions when responses are required, and the overseeing of the implementation of decisions once made. The greater the number of actors within the system in question with relevant authority—for example, ministers, departments, agencies, or member states—and the longer and more entrenched the tradition of protracted internecine squabbling before any decision is made about anything, the greater the need for focal points of this kind, with real stature of their own.

There would also be such a need for such a central player in even the most congenitally harmonious decisionmaking system, because of the difficulty—in the sheer, relentless, day-to-day grind of top-level governance—of winning attention for any but the most urgent and dramatic matter. In designing decisionmaking systems, progress is sometimes made by "mainstreaming" particular kinds of concerns (gender sensitivity and conflict prevention being familiar examples): ensuring that every relevant unit in the system is required to take them into account in the performance of its own functions. But for something as specific, and important, as ensuring that there is a proper response to emerging mass atrocity crimes, there is no substitute for having centrally located and authoritative people whose day jobs are the functions described above. Generally, the more institutional effort and resources that go into creating this kind of capacity—with appropriate mechanisms, skilled personnel, good analytical capacity, well-developed and tested options, and attention to best practice in the past and elsewhere—the greater the likelihood of a sharply focused, quick, and useful response to the next crisis that comes along.

There is something of a chicken-and-egg issue here because to establish in the first place this kind of capability—which, it is being suggested, is a key ingredient in the mobilizing of political will in response to R2P situations—will, particularly to the extent that significant resources are required, itself require some serious political will! Happily, there is growing evidence that key governments and intergovernmental organizations are not feeling so paralyzed by this philosophical conundrum that they are unable to make the moves necessary to put at least rudimentary capability of this kind in place. There has already been mentioned in chapter 8 the gradual evolution in national governments, like those of the United Kingdom, United States, and Canada, of "joined up" arrangements, bringing together defense, foreign affairs, aid, and central executive assets to focus

on conflict prevention and crisis management, and it is extremely important that this trend consolidate and continue elsewhere.

A similar momentum is developing in intergovernmental
organizations—both global and regional—as described again in chapter
8—with interest being shown, particularly in the EU, in developing
regional intergovernmental centers devoted to the prevention of genocide
and crimes against humanity.[16] The most advanced such enterprise—
although it has by no means yet fully realized its potential—is the UN's
Office of the Special Adviser on the Prevention of Genocide (OSAPG),
headed full-time since August 2007 by Francis Deng at Under-Secretary-
General level, located in New York with an authorized staff of around ten
(funded by both regular and voluntary UN budgets), and given external
support and guidance by an Advisory Committee on Genocide Prevention, appointed by Secretary-General Kofi Annan in 2006, chaired by Dr.
David Hamburg, and including Romeo Dallaire, Desmond Tutu, and
Sadako Ogata among its members.[17]

The Special Adviser's mandate, given in 2004 to Deng's part-time predecessor, Juan Méndez, is an ambitious one: "to collect existing information, in particular from within the United Nations system, on massive and
serious violations of human rights and international humanitarian law of
ethnic and racial origin that, if not prevented or halted, might lead to genocide; to act as a mechanism of early warning to the Secretary-General, and
through him to the Security Council, by bringing to their attention situations that could potentially result in genocide; to make recommendations
to the Security Council, through the Secretary-General, on actions to prevent or halt genocide; and to liaise with the United Nations system on
activities for the prevention of genocide and work to enhance the United
Nations' capacity to analyze and manage information regarding genocide
or related crimes."[18]

Although Deng and his predecessor have been keen to raise the profile
and influence of the office, as of this writing in mid-2008, it remained
understaffed, even against its very modest authorized level, and still has
some distance to go in making its presence seriously felt. There will always
be a New York UN–member state constituency very content with the Special Adviser operating in quiet engagement mode in perpetuity, and it is
important that he and his staff not succumb to the understandable temptation to do so if circumstances demand otherwise. The Advisory Commit-

tee, if it continues as it should as a standing rather than ad hoc body, may be able to play a useful political supporting role in this respect, making waves as occasion demands and ensuring that never again do early warnings fall into the black hole of UN indifference that confronted General Dallaire in 1994.

Just as decisionmaking systems need people for whom the prevention of and response to mass atrocity crimes is their day job, so too is this the case for those in the mobilizing, energizing, and proselytizing community. An important step forward in this respect has been the launching early in 2008 in New York of the Global Centre for the Responsibility to Protect (GCR2P), still in its organizational infancy at the time of this writing but aimed at becoming the worldwide focal point for the efforts now needed to consolidate and operationalize the R2P norm in all the ways described in this book. Initiated by a coalition of major global nongovernmental organizations (including the International Crisis Group, Human Rights Watch, and Oxfam International), supported by a number of governments and foundations, with an International Advisory Board cochaired by the ICISS cochairs, and a very distinguished cast of patrons, the GCR2P intends to operate as a research and advocacy center and an information clearinghouse working to promote better understanding of R2P, building worldwide support for it, and recommending strategy to both the broader civil society community and like-minded governments. To be successful it will need from the outset to be determinedly North-South in character—having effective outreach to associated centers in Africa, Asia, Latin America, and the Middle East as well as in the global North—and to develop very close working relationships with governments, international institutions (including especially the Office of the UN's Special Adviser), and nongovernmental organizations.[19]

A preoccupation with process at the expense of substance can lead in many contexts to mind-numbing irrelevance, but there is not much doubt that when it comes to mobilizing support for R2P worldwide, a little more systematic institutional process than has been the case so far will be very helpful indeed. On the civil society side, it is intended that the GCR2P liaise closely with a global coalition of like-minded NGOs being put together under the leadership of the WFM–Institute of Global Policy, which has had for several years a program for engaging civil society worldwide (Responsibility to Protect–Engaging Civil Society [R2PCS]) that has involved, among other things, creating a useful website resource and convening a series of regional meetings to raise awareness of the R2P norm and the need for its effective operationalization. There are a legion of individual NGOs working on these issues in many countries, but there remains a real need to coordinate and focus their efforts.

The same is true on the government side. There are many like-minded governments in both North and South who are keen to work in a more systematic way on consolidating the norm internationally and halting any backsliding in the General Assembly or elsewhere; building the appropriate diplomatic, civilian, military, and general organizational capability that is needed; gaining acceptance for detailed criteria governing the use of force; and above all, ensuring that no new R2P situation goes unnoticed or, until it is too late, unredressed. An informal "Friends of R2P" group already exists for this purpose at the UN in New York, now cochaired by Canada and Rwanda, and it is to be hoped that its efforts will be assisted by close working cooperation with the new Global Centre: proactive leadership (of the right kind) serves as a model for others, and like-minded coalitions can certainly generate a great deal of necessary momentum in R2P situations crying out for rapid response.

Demanding Leadership

Mobilizing the political will to respond effectively to mass atrocity crimes ultimately demands—as does just about every other form of effective decisionmaking—someone, somewhere in the system, able and willing to make things happen. Unless the relevant decisionmakers, at the national or international level, want action, there won't be any. All the knowledge, concern, confidence, and process in the world will not count for much if there is inertia, indecisiveness, or hostility at the top.

Of course it is not just *any* leadership that is required. It is not easy to overestimate the capacity of individual leaders to choose cynicism over statesmanship, miss crucial opportunities, or simply, with the best of intentions, create havoc. And it is important to remind ourselves of just how monstrously, horribly astray a country can go when it succumbs to the collective belief that the only thing that matters in a chaotic environment is leadership strength: a visit to Nuremberg, spending some quiet time at the trial courtroom, Zeppelin Field party rally ground, and Nazi Congress

Hall, with its stunning new documentation center, is an intensely sobering experience in this respect.

The kind of leadership needed is what we can all recognize when we see it, and lament when it goes missing. It recognizes the big turning points in national or global history, makes the right calls, and delivers the right responses—as Roosevelt did in the 1930s; or Truman and Marshall did after the Second World War; or as Dag Hammarskjold did in inventing peacekeeping and keeping the UN flame at least partially burning during the worst of the cold war years; or as Gorbachev did in the Soviet Union, seeing the impossibility of sustaining the cold war; or—more controversially—as Deng Xiaoping did in China, at least in setting a wholly new economic course for the country in the chaotic and desolate aftermath of Mao; or as George Bush senior did in leading, through the UN, the unequivocal response to Iraq's invasion of Kuwait in 1991, the first big post–cold war test of the system of international order.

It is the kind of towering moral and political leadership showed, above all, by Nelson Mandela in South Africa's transition, completely avoiding—with crucial support, it should be acknowledged, from another leader, F. W. de Klerk, who came to understand, late but not *too* late, what the moment demanded—what just about everyone feared would be an unavoidable racial bloodbath. It is the kind of leadership shown by Kofi Annan over many difficult years confronting head-on the notion, so strongly entrenched among his colleagues from the global South, that state sovereignty entails inviolability. And it is the kind of leadership which Dr. Mo Ibrahim is trying to create in Africa with his spectacularly generous and creative Prize for Achievement in African Leadership, given first to former Mozambique president Joaquim Chissano, not only for his outstanding contribution in leading his country from peace to democracy but also for his decision to step down without seeking the third term its constitution allowed.[20]

The leadership required if the world is to respond as it should to genocide, war crimes, ethnic cleansing, and crimes against humanity does not always have to be delivered in a spectacular way to be effective, nor by the biggest figures or the greatest powers. It is the kind of leadership shown by Sadako Ogata as UN High Commissioner for Refugees and Jan Egeland as the UN's humanitarian relief coordinator, in speaking out strongly and consistently and relentlessly about the horrors they saw unfolding around them and demanding an international response. Or perhaps the kind of leadership that was shown by Indonesia and Australia, in crafting together the UN peace plan that brought a final end, at the beginning of the 1990s, to Cambodia's protracted nightmare. And the kind of leadership—without which I would not have had much to write about in this book—that was shown by Canada and its Prime Minister Paul Martin, who worked away diligently behind the scenes for months in the run-up to the 2005 World Summit to ensure, despite all the forces arrayed against it, that the responsibility to protect norm would be embraced.

We know all too well that when it comes to this crucial ingredient of leadership, there is a huge amount of pure chance in play. So much does seem to depend just on the luck of the draw: whether at a time of fragility and transition a country finds itself with a Mandela, or a Milosevic or Mugabe; an Atatürk or an Arafat; a Rabin who can see and seize the moment, and change course, or someone who never will. Despite all our best efforts, that has always been so and probably always will be. Looking around the world at those individuals who currently matter most, we just have to express the fervent hope that even if leaders are not always born, and only on very rare occasions are elected, they can at least on occasion be made.

* * *

It has been said that the world is divided among those who make things happen, those who watch things happen, and those who wonder what happened. Too often, when it comes to mass atrocity crimes, too many of us have been left wondering—how could this horror possibly have happened yet again when there were so many reasons and so much international capability to make it avoidable. The emergence of the responsibility to protect norm in 2001, and its embrace by the World Summit in 2005, brings us much closer to ending such crimes once and for all. But if we are to realize that dream, it is going to require continuing determined action from all those passionately committed to making it happen—not just from national and international leaders but from everyone, ordinary citizens in every country across every corner of the globe included, who are capable of influencing them. You don't get to change the world simply by observing it.

Definitions of Genocide, Crimes against Humanity, and War Crimes

Convention on the Prevention and Punishment of the Crime of Genocide

Approved and proposed for signature and ratification or accession by the UN General Assembly Resolution 260 A (III), December 9, 1948, and entered into force January 12, 1951. As of January 2008, 137 states ratified the convention.

ARTICLE 1

The Contracting Parties confirm that genocide, whether committed in time of peace or in time of war, is a crime under international law which they undertake to prevent and to punish.

ARTICLE 2

In the present Convention, genocide means any of the following acts committed with intent to destroy, in whole or in part, a national, ethnical, racial or religious group, as such:

(a) Killing members of the group;
(b) Causing serious bodily or mental harm to members of the group;
(c) Deliberately inflicting on the group conditions of life calculated to bring about its physical destruction in whole or in part;
(d) Imposing measures intended to prevent births within the group;
(e) Forcibly transferring children of the group to another group.

ARTICLE 3

The following acts shall be punishable:
- (a) Genocide;
- (b) Conspiracy to commit genocide;
- (c) Direct and public incitement to commit genocide;
- (d) Attempt to commit genocide;
- (e) Complicity in genocide.

Rome Statute of the International Criminal Court

Treaty establishing the International Criminal Court, adopted in Rome July 17, 1998, and entered into force July 1, 2002. As of January 2008, 105 states are party to this statute defining genocide, crimes against humanity, and war crimes.

ARTICLE 6: GENOCIDE

For the purpose of this Statute, "genocide" means any of the following acts committed with intent to destroy, in whole or in part, a national, ethnical, racial or religious group, as such:
- (a) Killing members of the group;
- (b) Causing serious bodily or mental harm to members of the group;
- (c) Deliberately inflicting on the group conditions of life calculated to bring about its physical destruction in whole or in part;
- (d) Imposing measures intended to prevent births within the group;
- (e) Forcibly transferring children of the group to another group.

ARTICLE 7: CRIMES AGAINST HUMANITY

1. For the purpose of this Statute, "crime against humanity" means any of the following acts when committed as part of a widespread or systematic attack directed against any civilian population, with knowledge of the attack:
- (a) Murder;
- (b) Extermination;
- (c) Enslavement;
- (d) Deportation or forcible transfer of population;

(e) Imprisonment or other severe deprivation of physical liberty in violation of fundamental rules of international law;

(f) Torture;

(g) Rape, sexual slavery, enforced prostitution, forced pregnancy, enforced sterilization, or any other form of sexual violence of comparable gravity;

(h) Persecution against any identifiable group or collectivity on political, racial, national, ethnic, cultural, religious, gender as defined in paragraph 3, or other grounds that are universally recognized as impermissible under international law, in connection with any act referred to in this paragraph or any crime within the jurisdiction of the Court;

(i) Enforced disappearance of persons;

(j) The crime of apartheid;

(k) Other inhumane acts of a similar character intentionally causing great suffering, or serious injury to body or to mental or physical health.

2. For the purpose of paragraph 1:

(a) "Attack directed against any civilian population" means a course of conduct involving the multiple commission of acts referred to in paragraph 1 against any civilian population, pursuant to or in furtherance of a State or organizational policy to commit such attack;

(b) "Extermination" includes the intentional infliction of conditions of life, inter alia the deprivation of access to food and medicine, calculated to bring about the destruction of part of a population;

(c) "Enslavement" means the exercise of any or all of the powers attaching to the right of ownership over a person and includes the exercise of such power in the course of trafficking in persons, in particular women and children;

(d) "Deportation or forcible transfer of population" means forced displacement of the persons concerned by expulsion or other coercive acts from the area in which they are lawfully present, without grounds permitted under international law;

(e) "Torture" means the intentional infliction of severe pain or suffering, whether physical or mental, upon a person in the custody or under the control of the accused; except that torture shall not include pain or suffering arising only from, inherent in or incidental to, lawful sanctions;

(f) "Forced pregnancy" means the unlawful confinement of a woman forcibly made pregnant, with the intent of affecting the ethnic composition of any population or carrying out other grave violations of international law. This definition shall not in any way be interpreted as affecting national laws relating to pregnancy;

(g) "Persecution" means the intentional and severe deprivation of fundamental rights contrary to international law by reason of the identity of the group or collectivity;

(h) "The crime of apartheid" means inhumane acts of a character similar to those referred to in paragraph 1, committed in the context of an institutionalized regime of systematic oppression and domination by one racial group over any other racial group or groups and committed with the intention of maintaining that regime;

(i) "Enforced disappearance of persons" means the arrest, detention or abduction of persons by, or with the authorization, support or acquiescence of, a State or a political organization, followed by a refusal to acknowledge that deprivation of freedom or to give information on the fate or whereabouts of those persons, with the intention of removing them from the protection of the law for a prolonged period of time.

3. For the purpose of this Statute, it is understood that the term "gender" refers to the two sexes, male and female, within the context of society. The term "gender" does not indicate any meaning different from the above.

Article 8: War crimes

1. The Court shall have jurisdiction in respect of war crimes in particular when committed as part of a plan or policy or as part of a large-scale commission of such crimes.

2. For the purpose of this Statute, "war crimes" means:

(a) Grave breaches of the Geneva Conventions of 12 August 1949, namely, any of the following acts against persons or property protected under the provisions of the relevant Geneva Convention:

(i) Wilful killing;

(ii) Torture or inhuman treatment, including biological experiments;

(iii) Wilfully causing great suffering, or serious injury to body or health;

(iv) Extensive destruction and appropriation of property, not justified by military necessity and carried out unlawfully and wantonly;

(v) Compelling a prisoner of war or other protected person to serve in the forces of a hostile Power;

(vi) Wilfully depriving a prisoner of war or other protected person of the rights of fair and regular trial;

(vii) Unlawful deportation or transfer or unlawful confinement;

(viii) Taking of hostages.

(b) Other serious violations of the laws and customs applicable in international armed conflict, within the established framework of international law, namely, any of the following acts:

(i) Intentionally directing attacks against the civilian population as such or against individual civilians not taking direct part in hostilities;

(ii) Intentionally directing attacks against civilian objects, that is, objects which are not military objectives;

(iii) Intentionally directing attacks against personnel, installations, material, units or vehicles involved in a humanitarian assistance or peacekeeping mission in accordance with the Charter of the United Nations, as long as they are entitled to the protection given to civilians or civilian objects under the international law of armed conflict;

(iv) Intentionally launching an attack in the knowledge that such attack will cause incidental loss of life or injury to civilians or damage to civilian objects or widespread, long-term and severe damage to the natural environment which would be clearly excessive in relation to the concrete and direct overall military advantage anticipated;

(v) Attacking or bombarding, by whatever means, towns, villages, dwellings or buildings which are undefended and which are not military objectives;

(vi) Killing or wounding a combatant who, having laid down his arms or having no longer means of defence, has surrendered at discretion;

(vii) Making improper use of a flag of truce, of the flag or of the military insignia and uniform of the enemy or of the United Nations, as well as of the distinctive emblems of the Geneva Conventions, resulting in death or serious personal injury;

(viii) The transfer, directly or indirectly, by the Occupying Power of parts of its own civilian population into the territory it occupies, or the deportation or transfer of all or parts of the population of the occupied territory within or outside this territory;

(ix) Intentionally directing attacks against buildings dedicated to religion, education, art, science or charitable purposes, historic monuments, hospitals and places where the sick and wounded are collected, provided they are not military objectives;

(x) Subjecting persons who are in the power of an adverse party to physical mutilation or to medical or scientific experiments of any kind which are neither justified by the medical, dental or hospital treatment of the person concerned nor carried out in his or her interest, and which cause death to or seriously endanger the health of such person or persons;

(xi) Killing or wounding treacherously individuals belonging to the hostile nation or army;

(xii) Declaring that no quarter will be given;

(xiii) Destroying or seizing the enemy's property unless such destruction or seizure be imperatively demanded by the necessities of war;

(xiv) Declaring abolished, suspended or inadmissible in a court of law the rights and actions of the nationals of the hostile party;

(xv) Compelling the nationals of the hostile party to take part in the operations of war directed against their own country, even if they were in the belligerent's service before the commencement of the war;

(xvi) Pillaging a town or place, even when taken by assault;

(xvii) Employing poison or poisoned weapons;

(xviii) Employing asphyxiating, poisonous or other gases, and all analogous liquids, materials or devices;

(xix) Employing bullets which expand or flatten easily in the human body, such as bullets with a hard envelope which does not entirely cover the core or is pierced with incisions;

(xx) Employing weapons, projectiles and material and methods of warfare which are of a nature to cause superfluous injury or unnecessary suffering or which are inherently indiscriminate in violation of the international law of armed conflict, provided that such weapons, projectiles and material and methods of warfare are the subject of a comprehensive prohibition and are included in an annex to this

Statute, by an amendment in accordance with the relevant provisions set forth in articles 121 and 123;

(xxi) Committing outrages upon personal dignity, in particular humiliating and degrading treatment;

(xxii) Committing rape, sexual slavery, enforced prostitution, forced pregnancy, as defined in article 7, paragraph 2 (f), enforced sterilization, or any other form of sexual violence also constituting a grave breach of the Geneva Conventions;

(xxiii) Utilizing the presence of a civilian or other protected person to render certain points, areas or military forces immune from military operations;

(xxiv) Intentionally directing attacks against buildings, material, medical units and transport, and personnel using the distinctive emblems of the Geneva Conventions in conformity with international law;

(xxv) Intentionally using starvation of civilians as a method of warfare by depriving them of objects indispensable to their survival, including wilfully impeding relief supplies as provided for under the Geneva Conventions;

(xxvi) Conscripting or enlisting children under the age of fifteen years into the national armed forces or using them to participate actively in hostilities.

(c) In the case of an armed conflict not of an international character, serious violations of article 3 common to the four Geneva Conventions of 12 August 1949, namely, any of the following acts committed against persons taking no active part in the hostilities, including members of armed forces who have laid down their arms and those placed hors de combat by sickness, wounds, detention or any other cause:

(i) Violence to life and person, in particular murder of all kinds, mutilation, cruel treatment and torture;

(ii) Committing outrages upon personal dignity, in particular humiliating and degrading treatment;

(iii) Taking of hostages;

(iv) The passing of sentences and the carrying out of executions without previous judgement pronounced by a regularly constituted court, affording all judicial guarantees which are generally recognized as indispensable.

(d) Paragraph 2 (c) applies to armed conflicts not of an international character and thus does not apply to situations of internal disturbances and tensions, such as riots, isolated and sporadic acts of violence or other acts of a similar nature.

(e) Other serious violations of the laws and customs applicable in armed conflicts not of an international character, within the established framework of international law, namely, any of the following acts:

(i) Intentionally directing attacks against the civilian population as such or against individual civilians not taking direct part in hostilities;

(ii) Intentionally directing attacks against buildings, material, medical units and transport, and personnel using the distinctive emblems of the Geneva Conventions in conformity with international law;

(iii) Intentionally directing attacks against personnel, installations, material, units or vehicles involved in a humanitarian assistance or peacekeeping mission in accordance with the Charter of the United Nations, as long as they are entitled to the protection given to civilians or civilian objects under the international law of armed conflict;

(iv) Intentionally directing attacks against buildings dedicated to religion, education, art, science or charitable purposes, historic monuments, hospitals and places where the sick and wounded are collected, provided they are not military objectives;

(v) Pillaging a town or place, even when taken by assault;

(vi) Committing rape, sexual slavery, enforced prostitution, forced pregnancy, as defined in article 7, paragraph 2 (f), enforced sterilization, and any other form of sexual violence also constituting a serious violation of article 3 common to the four Geneva Conventions;

(vii) Conscripting or enlisting children under the age of fifteen years into armed forces or groups or using them to participate actively in hostilities;

(viii) Ordering the displacement of the civilian population for reasons related to the conflict, unless the security of the civilians involved or imperative military reasons so demand;

(ix) Killing or wounding treacherously a combatant adversary;

(x) Declaring that no quarter will be given;

(xi) Subjecting persons who are in the power of another party to the conflict to physical mutilation or to medical or scientific experiments of any kind which are neither justified by the medical, dental or hospital treatment of the person concerned nor carried out in his or her interest, and which cause death to or seriously endanger the health of such person or persons;

(xii) Destroying or seizing the property of an adversary unless such destruction or seizure be imperatively demanded by the necessities of the conflict;

(f) Paragraph 2 (e) applies to armed conflicts not of an international character and thus does not apply to situations of internal disturbances and tensions, such as riots, isolated and sporadic acts of violence or other acts of a similar nature. It applies to armed conflicts that take place in the territory of a State when there is protracted armed conflict between governmental authorities and organized armed groups or between such groups.

3. Nothing in paragraph 2 (c) and (e) shall affect the responsibility of a Government to maintain or re-establish law and order in the State or to defend the unity and territorial integrity of the State, by all legitimate means.

The Mass Atrocity Toolboxes: Prevention, Reaction, and Rebuilding

		PREVENTION	REACTION	REBUILDING
		Political and Diplomatic		
Direct / Structural	Structural	Promote good governance Promote membership in international organizations		Rebuilding governance institutions Maximizing local ownership
	Direct	Preventive diplomacy Threat of political sanctions	Diplomatic peacemaking Political sanctions and incentives	
		Economic and Social		
Direct / Structural	Structural	Support economic development Support education for tolerance Community peacebuilding		Support economic development Social programs for sustainable peace
	Direct	Aid conditionality Threat of economic sanctions Economic incentives	Application of economic sanctions Economic incentives	

	PREVENTION	**REACTION**	**REBUILDING**
	Constitutional and Legal		
Structural	Promote fair constitutional structures Promote human rights Promote rule of law Fight corruption		Rebuilding criminal justice Managing transitional justice Supporting traditional justice Managing refugee returns
Direct	Legal dispute resolution Threat of international criminal prosecution	Criminal prosecution	
	Security Sector		
Structural	Security sector reform Military to civilian governance Confidence-building measures Small arms and light weapons control		Peacekeeping in support of nation building Disarmament, demobilization, and reintegration Security sector reform
Direct	Preventive deployment Nonterritorial show of force Threat of arms embargo or end of military cooperation programs	Peacekeeping for civilian protection Safe havens and no-fly zones Arms embargoes Jamming of radio frequencies Threat or use of military force	

APPENDIX C

Further Reading

The following is not a complete bibliography of the books, articles, and reports cited in this book, and is only a fraction of the huge literature on this subject, which is more comprehensively assembled in the ICISS supplementary volume, The Responsibility to Protect: Research, Bibliography, Background, as updated at www.globalr2p.org/biblio.html. It is simply a selection of some works found useful in writing this volume and which would repay closer reading.

The Problem: Mass Atrocities

Dallaire, Romeo. 1999. *Shake Hands with the Devil: The Failure of Humanity in Rwanda.* Toronto: Knopf Canada.

Gourevitch, Philip. 1999. *We Wish to Inform You That Tomorrow We Will Be Killed with Our Families: Stories from Rwanda.* New York: Picador.

Hiltermann, Joost. 2007. *A Poisonous Affair: America, Iraq and the Gassing of Halabja.* Cambridge University Press.

Kiernan, Ben. 2007. *Blood and Soil: A World History of Genocide and Extermination from Sparta to Darfur.* Yale University Press.

Power, Samantha. 2002. *"A Problem from Hell": America and the Age of Genocide.* London: Flamingo.

Robertson, Geoffrey. 2000. *Crimes against Humanity: The Struggle for Global Justice.* London: Penguin.

Slim, Hugo. 2007. *Killing Civilians: Method, Madness and Morality in War.* London: Hurst.

Totten, Samuel. 2004. *Century of Genocide.* New York: Routledge.

United Nations. 1999. *Report of the Independent Inquiry into the Actions of the United Nations during the 1994 Genocide in Rwanda.* S/1999/1257. New York.

The Solution: From The Right to Intervene to The Responsibility to Protect

Annan, Kofi. 2005. *In Larger Freedom: Toward Development, Security and Human Rights for All,* A/59/2005. United Nations; available at www.un.org/largerfreedom.

Chesterman, Simon. 2001. *Just War or Just Peace: Humanitarian Intervention and International Law.* Oxford University Press.

Cooper, Richard, and Juliette Voinov Kohler, eds. Forthcoming. *The Responsibility to Protect: The Global Moral Compact for the XXIst Century.* Basingstoke, England: Palgrave Macmillan.

High-Level Panel on Threats, Challenges, and Change. 2004. *A More Secure World: Our Shared Responsibility.* United Nations; available at www.un.org/secure-world.

Holzgrefe, J. L., and Robert O. Keohane, eds. 2003. *Humanitarian Intervention: Ethical Legal and Political Dilemmas.* Cambridge University Press.

International Commission on Intervention and State Sovereignty (ICISS). 2001. *The Responsibility to Protect;* and *Supplementary Volume: Research, Bibliography, Background.* Ottawa: International Development Research Center; available at www.iciss-ciise.gc.ca.

MacFarlane, Neil, and Yuen Foon Khong. 2006. *Human Security and the UN: A Critical History.* Indiana University Press.

Thakur, Ramesh. 2006. *The United Nations, Peace and Security: From Collective Security to the Responsibility to Protect.* Cambridge University Press.

Weiss, Thomas G. 2007. *Humanitarian Intervention.* Cambridge, U.K.: Polity.

Wheeler, Nicholas. 2000. *Saving Strangers: Humanitarian Intervention in International Society*. Oxford University Press.

Prevention

Ballentine, Karen, and Jake Sherman, eds. 2003. *The Political Economy of Armed Conflict: Beyond Greed and Grievance*. Boulder, Colo.: Lynne Rienner.

Barton, Frederick, and Karen von Hippel. 2008. "Early Warning? A Review of Conflict Prediction Models and Systems." PCR Special Project Briefing. Washington, D.C.: Center for Strategic and International Studies (February).

Berdal, Mats, and David M. Malone, eds. 2000. *Greed and Grievance: Economic Agendas in Civil Wars*. Boulder, Colo.: Lynn Rienner.

Collier, Paul. 2007. *The Bottom Billion: Why the Poorest Countries Are Failing and What Can Be Done about It*. Oxford University Press.

Hamburg, David. 2008. *Preventing Genocide: Practical Steps toward Early Detection and Effective Action*. Boulder, Colo.: Paradigm.

Hamburg, David A., and Beatrix A. Hamburg. 2004. *Learning to Live Together: Preventing Hatred and Violence in Child and Adolescent Development*. Oxford University Press.

Lund, Michael S. 1996. *Preventing Violent Conflicts: A Strategy for Preventive Diplomacy*. Washington, D.C.: U.S. Institute of Peace Press.

Sokalski, Henryk J. 2003. *An Ounce of Prevention: Macedonia and the UN Experience in Preventive Diplomacy*. Washington, D.C.: U.S. Institute of Peace Press.

Reaction

Bellamy, Alex J., Paul Williams, and Stuart Griffin. 2004. *Understanding Peacekeeping*. Cambridge, England: Polity.

Brekke, Torkel, ed. 2005. *The Ethics of War in Asian Civilizations: A Comparative Perspective*. London: Routledge.

Cortright, David, ed. 1997. *The Price of Peace: Incentives and International Conflict*. Lanham, Md.: Rowman and Littlefield.

Cortright, David, and George A. Lopez. 2000. *The Sanctions Decade: Assessing UN Strategies in the 1990s*. Boulder, Colo.: Lynne Rienner.

Crocker, Chester A., and Fen Osler Hampson, eds. 1996. *Managing Global Chaos*. Washington, D.C.: U.S. Institute of Peace Press.

Gazzini, Tarcisio. 2005. *The Changing Rules on the Use of Force in International Law*. Manchester University Press.

Guthrie, Charles, and Michael Quinlan. 2007. *Just War: The Just War Tradition: Ethics in Modern Warfare*. London: Bloomsbury.

Robinson, Paul, ed. 2003. *Just War in Comparative Perspective*. Burlington, Vt.: Ashgate.

Waddell, Nicholas, and Phil Clark, eds. 2008. *Justice, Peace and the ICC in Africa*. London: Royal African Society.

Wallensteen, Peter, Carina Staibano, and Mikael Eriksson, eds. 2003. *Making Targeted Sanctions Effective: Guidelines for the Implementation of UN Policy Options*. Uppsala University.

Rebuilding

Dobbins, James, and others. 2003. *America's Role in Nation-Building: From Germany to Iraq*. Santa Monica, Calif.: Rand Corporation.

———. 2005. *The UN's Role in Nation-Building: From the Congo to Iraq*. Santa Monica, Calif.: Rand Corporation.

———. 2007. The *Beginner's Guide to Nation-Building*. Santa Monica, Calif.: Rand Corporation.

Hughes, Edel, William A. Schabas, and Ramesh Thakur, eds. 2007. *Atrocities and International Accountability: Beyond Transitional Justice*. Tokyo: United Nations University Press.

International Institute for Democracy and Electoral Assistance (IDEA). 2005. *Electoral System Design: The New International IDEA Handbook*; available at www.idea.int.

Institutional Capability and Mobilization

Abass, Ademola. 2004. *Regional Organizations and the Development of Collective Security: Beyond Chapter VIII of the UN Charter.* Portland, Ore.: Hart Publishing.

Cheadle, Don, and John Prendergast. 2007. *Not on Our Watch: The Mission to End Genocide in Darfur and Beyond.* New York: Hyperion.

Durch, William J., and others. 2003. *The Brahimi Report and the Future of UN Peace Operations.* Washington, D.C.: Henry L. Stimson Center.

Hannay, David. 2008. *New World Disorder: The UN after the Cold War—An Insider's View.* London: I.B. Tauris.

Holt, Victoria K., and Tobias C. Berkman. 2006. *The Impossible Mandate: Military Preparedness, the Responsibility to Protect and Modern Peace Operations.* Washington, D.C.: Henry L. Stimson Center.

Human Security Center. 2005. *Human Security Report 2005: War and Peace in the 21st Century.* Oxford University Press; this and the 2006, 2007, and 2008 *Security Brief* are all available at www.hsrgroup.org.

———. 2006. *Human Security Brief 2006.* University of British Columbia.

Human Security Report Project. 2007. *Human Security Brief 2007.* Simon Fraser University.

Malone, David, ed. 2004. *The UN Security Council: From the Cold War to the 21st Century.* Boulder, Colo.: Lynne Rienner.

Peck, Connie. 2006. *On Being a Special Representative of the Secretary-General.* Geneva: United Nations Institute for Training and Research (UNITAR).

United Nations. 2000. *Report of the Panel on United Nations Peace Operations* (Brahimi Report). A/55/305-S/2000/809. New York.

Weiss, Thomas G., and Sam Daws, eds. 2007. *Oxford Handbook on the United Nations.* Oxford University Press.

Whitfield, Teresa. 2007. *Friends Indeed: The United Nations, Groups of Friends and the Resolution of Conflict.* Washington, D.C.: U.S. Institute of Peace Press.

Further Action

The following lists, which do not purport to be in any way comprehensive, identify some of the advocacy organizations most active in working to prevent mass atrocity crimes, and the intergovernmental organizations and governments who are most influential in decisionmaking in this area and to whom it is appropriate, accordingly, to make R2P-related representations. Brief information is given on how each of them may be contacted, or at least further information about their activities obtained.

Advocacy Organizations

Primarily R2P-Focused

Global Centre for the Responsibility to Protect (GCR2P)
The New York–based Global Centre for the Responsibility to Protect was launched in 2008 as a research and advocacy catalyst for the worldwide consolidation and implementation of the R2P norm. It will work closely with designated "associated centers" in Africa, Asia, and elsewhere, and with like-minded nongovernmental organizations and governments through new and existing coordinating mechanisms.
Website: www.globalr2p.org
E-mail: info@globalr2p.org

Responsibility to Protect–Engaging Civil Society (R2PCS)
This project of the New York-based WFM–Institute for Global Policy works to coordinate and mobilize nongovernmental organizations worldwide to

advance R2P and to promote concrete policies to better enable governments, regional organizations, and the United Nations to protect vulnerable populations. It is a founding sponsor of the GCR2P.
Website: www.responsibilitytoprotect.org
E-mail: info@responsibilitytoprotect.org

R2P Coalition

This new Chicago-based organization aims to convince U.S. publics and decisionmakers to embrace the R2P norm and to support the empowerment of the United Nations and the International Criminal Court with a more effective enforcement mechanism.
Website: www.r2pcoalition.org
E-mail: info@R2Pcoalition.org

Genocide Watch

Based in Washington, D.C., Genocide Watch aims to mobilize support to predict, prevent, stop, and punish genocide and other forms of mass murder, and coordinates the International Campaign to End Genocide, founded in 1999.
Website: www.genocidewatch.org
E-mail: genocidewatch@aol.com

Primarily Conflict-Focused

International Crisis Group

Based in Brussels but with an advocacy presence in New York, Washington, London, Moscow, and Beijing, and field staff covering some sixty conflict or high-risk areas across four continents, Crisis Group works through field-based analysis and high-level advocacy to prevent and halt deadly conflict and mass atrocity crimes. It publishes up to 100 reports and briefings every year, and the monthly *CrisisWatch* bulletin, and is a founding sponsor of GCR2P.
Website: www.crisisgroup.org
E-mail: brussels@crisisgroup.org

ENOUGH! The Project to End Genocide and Crimes against Humanity

Beginning life as the campaign arm of the International Crisis Group, ENOUGH is now a project of the Washington-based Center for American

Progress, focusing on analyzing and mobilizing support for effective action on the situations in Congo, northern Uganda, Darfur, southern Sudan, and Chad. It works closely with organizations like Genocide Intervention (www.genocideintervention.net).
Website: www.enoughproject.org
E-mail: via www.enoughproject.org/feedback

Crisis Action
Based in London, with offices in Berlin, Brussels, and Paris, Crisis Action is an international, nonprofit organization that aims to help avert conflicts, prevent human rights abuses, and ensure that governments fulfill their obligations to protect civilians.
Website: www.crisisaction.org
E-mail: mail@crisisaction.org.

PRIMARILY HUMAN RIGHTS–FOCUSED

Human Rights Watch
Based in New York but with worldwide reach, Human Rights Watch conducts fact-finding investigations into human rights abuses in all regions, and presses for the withdrawal of military and economic support from governments that egregiously violate the rights of their people. It is a founding sponsor of the GCR2P.
Website: www.hrw.org
E-mail: hrwnyc@hrw.org

Amnesty International
Amnesty International, based in London but with a worldwide organizational structure, campaigns for internationally recognized human rights across the spectrum.
Website: www.amnesty.org
E-mail: via website www.amnesty.org/en/contact

PRIMARILY HUMANITARIAN AID–FOCUSED

Oxfam
Oxfam International, based in the United Kingdom but with worldwide reach, is a confederation of thirteen like-minded organizations focused on

ending poverty and injustice through strategic campaigns and emergency relief operations. It is a founding sponsor of the GCR2P.
Website: www.oxfam.org
E-mail: via www.oxfam.org.uk/contact

Médecins Sans Frontières
MSF, with its international office in Switzerland but worldwide organizational reach, provides emergency medical assistance to populations in danger in more than seventy countries.
Website: www.msf.org
E-mail: office-gva@geneva.msf.org

Refugees International
Washington, D.C.–based RI generates lifesaving humanitarian assistance and protection for refugees and internally displaced people around the world and works to end the conditions that create displacement. It is a founding sponsor of the GCR2P.
Website: www.refugeesinternational.org
E-mail: ri@refintl.org

Decisionmakers

United Nations

Special Adviser for the Prevention of Genocide
Website: www.un.org/Depts/dpa/prev_genocide/index.htm

Department of Peacekeeping Operations (DPKO)
Website: www.un.org/Depts/dpko/dpko/

Peacebuilding Commission
Website: www.un.org/peace/peacebuilding/

UN Development Program Bureau for Conflict Prevention and Recovery
Website: www.undp.org/bcpr/

OTHER INTERGOVERNMENTAL ORGANIZATIONS

Association of Southeast Asian Nations (ASEAN)
General: www.aseansec.org
ASEAN Regional Forum: www.aseanregionalforum.org

African Union (AU)
General: www.africa-union.org
Peace and Security Council: www.africa-union.org/organs/The_Peace_ %20and_Security_Council.htm

European Union (EU)
Commission: Conflict Prevention and Civilian Crisis Management
Website: ec.europa.eu/comm/external_relations/cfsp/cpcm/cm.htm

Secretary-General and High Representative for Common Security and Foreign Policy (CFSP)
Website: www.consilium.europa.eu
E-mail: public.info@consilium.europa.eu

NATO
Crisis Management
Website: www.nato.int/issues/crisis_management/index.html

Organization of American States (OAS)
General: www.oas.org

Organization for Security and Cooperation in Europe (OSCE)
High Commissioner for National Minorities
Website: www.osce.org/hcnm/

Conflict Prevention Center
Website: www.osce.org/cpc/

Permanent Five National Governments

China
Permanent Mission of China to the UN
Website: www.china-un.org
E-mail: chinamission_un@fmprc.gov.cn

France
Foreign Ministry
E-mail: https://pastel.diplomatie.gouv.fr/bacou/default.asp?lang=gb

Permanent Mission of France to the UN
E-mail: france@un.int

Russia
Permanent Mission of the Russian Federation to the UN
E-mail: rusun@un.int

United Kingdom
Foreign and Commonwealth Office (FCO), Conflict Issues Unit
Website: www.fco.gov.uk/en/fco-in-action/conflict/

Stabilisation Unit (jointly operated by the Department for International Development [DFID], FCO, and Ministry of Defence [MOD])
Website: www.stabilisationunit.gov.uk/
E-mail: info@stabilisationunit.gov.uk

Permanent Mission of the United Kingdom to the UN
Website: www.ukun.org
E-mail: uk@un.int

United States
State Department, Office of the Coordinator for Reconstruction and Stabilization
Website: www.state.gov/s/crs
E-mail: scrs_info@state.gov

U.S. Agency for International Development (USAID), Office of Conflict Management and Mitigation
Website: www.usaid.gov/our_work/cross-cutting_programs/conflict/
E-mail: conflict@usaid.gov

Permanent Mission of the United States to the UN
Website: www.usunnewyork.usmission.gov
E-mail: usa@un.int

Notes

Introduction

1. C. Wijeyawickrema, "Professor Rajan Hoole's Human Rights Award," October 17, 2007 (www.lankaweb.com/news/items07/171007-5.html).

Chapter One

1. See UN General Assembly, "2005 World Summit Outcome," A/RES/60/1, October 24, 2005 (http://unpan1.un.org/intradoc/groups/public/documents/UN/UNPAN021752.pdf); see also chapter 2 in this volume, box 2-2.

2. For the full text of the relevant provisions see appendix A.

3. UN, *Report of the International Commission of Inquiry on Darfur to the United Nations Secretary-General* (Geneva: January 25, 2005), p. 131; available at www.un.org/news/dh/sudan/com_inq_darfur.pdf.

4. David Scheffer, "Genocide and Atrocity Crimes," *Genocide Studies and Prevention* 1, no. 3 (2006): 238. See also William A. Schabas, "Preventing the 'Odious Scourge': The United Nations and the Prevention of Genocide," *International Journal on Minority and Group Rights* 14, no. 2-3 (2007): 379–97 (in particular pp. 395–97).

5. Steven Pinker, "The Decline of Violence," *New Republic,* February 21, 2007, p. 20, citing the work of Lawrence Keeley, Stephen Leblanc, Phillip Walker, Richard Wrangham, and Bruce Knauft. He explains, "It is true that individual raids and battles kill a tiny fraction of the numbers that are mown down in modern warfare. But in tribal violence, the battles are more frequent, the mobilization is more complete, the prisoners are fewer, and the death rates are higher." Pinker's figure of 100 million for the twentieth century may be an underestimate; Rummel gives a final figure for all its wars, pogroms, and genocides of around 217 million. See Rudolph J. Rummel, *Death by Government* (New Brunswick, N.J.: Transaction Publishers, 1994), chap. 1.

6. Pinker, *Decline of Violence*. See for example Deuteronomy, chapters 7 and 20.

7. See Neil MacFarlane and Yuen Foon Khong, *Human Security and the UN: A Critical History* (Indiana University Press, 2006), p. 28.

8. Ibid., p. 34.

9. For example, see Hugo Slim, *Killing Civilians: Method, Madness and Morality in War* (London: Hurst, 2007), p. 49.

10. Christopher Tyerman, *God's War: A New History of the Crusades* (London: Penguin, 2006), pp. 157–58, quoted in Slim, *Killing Civilians*, pp. 47–48.

11. Slim, *Killing Civilians*, p. 48.

12. MacFarlane and Khong, *Human Security and the UN*, pp. 29-31.

13. The Thirty Years' War, from 1618–48, was the bloodiest on record in Europe (7 million deaths) until the First World War. See Norman Davies, *Europe: A History* (London: Pimlico, 1997).

14. For short accounts of sovereignty and its Westphalian origins, see Nico Schrijver, "The Changing Nature of State Sovereignty," in *British Year Book of International Law 1999*, vol. 70, edited by James Crawford and Vaughan Lowe (Oxford University Press, 2000), pp. 69–70; Stephen D. Krasner, "Compromising Westphalia," *International Security* 20 (Winter 1995–1996): 115; International Commission on Intervention and State Sovereignty (ICISS), *The Responsibility to Protect, Supplementary Volume: Research, Bibliography, Background* (Ottawa: International Development Research Center, 2001), pp. 5–13. The key criteria for recognition as a sovereign state— a permanent population, defined territory, and functioning government—were codified in the 1933 Montevideo Convention on the Rights and Duties of States.

15. See R. John Vincent, *Nonintervention and International Order* (Princeton University Press, 1974), pointing to the importance of the principle of nonintervention as the basis for order in the society of states.

16. These examples and most of the figures are taken from Slim, *Killing Civilians*, pp. 42–44, 46, 51–52, 54, 56–58, 78. See also Samuel Totten, *Century of Genocide* (New York: Routledge, 2004); Ben Kiernan, *Blood and Soil: A World History of Genocide and Extermination from Sparta to Darfur* (Yale University Press, 2007).

17. If the Holocaust is taken, as some would prefer, to encompass all those the Nazis specifically persecuted, imprisoned, executed, or worked to death—including Poles and other specifically targeted Slavic groups, Soviet prisoners of war and civilians, Roma, political opponents, gays and transsexuals, and those with disabilities— the figure rises to as high as 17 million. See Donald L Niewyk and Francis R. Nicosia, *The Columbia Guide to the Holocaust* (Columbia University Press, 2000), p. 45.

18. Some of these stories are movingly told in Samantha Power, *"A Problem from Hell": America and the Age of Genocide* (London: Flamingo, 2002), chap. 3.

19. Hedley Bull, *Justice in International Relations* (University of Waterloo Press, 1993), p. 13.

20. "In a strict system of state sovereignty there was no obvious justification for such interference with trade and the domestic affairs of other recognized states and no obvious power-political reason to do so. The only basis for the action was a belief

that basic human rights were universal and that states had the right, if not the obligation, to act internationally to promote the rights of noncitizens living in other jurisdictions." MacFarlane and Khong, *Human Security and the UN*, p. 47.

21. See "General Act of the Berlin Conference on West Africa, 26 February 1885" (http://africanhistory.about.com/od/eracolonialism/l/bl-BerlinAct1885.htm), article 6. King Leopold of Belgium secured recognition from the congress for his sovereignty over most of the area he claimed, and ruled over the "Congo Free State" as his personal domain from 1885 to 1908, exploiting that population with an almost indescribable brutality that resulted in up to 10 million deaths. See Adam Hochschild, *King Leopold's Ghost, A Story of Greed, Terror, and Heroism* (New York: Mariner, 1999).

22. MacFarlane and Khong, *Human Security and the UN*, pp. 48, 50.

23. For the language of the proposed mandate, see "Covenant of the League of Nations," December 1924 (www.yale.edu/lawweb/avalon/leagcov.htm), article 22.

24. See MacFarlane and Khong, *Human Security and the UN*, pp. 52–55.

25. Power, *"Problem from Hell,"* p. 14 (italics added). See also Geoffrey Robertson, *Crimes against Humanity: The Struggle for Global Justice* (London: Penguin, 2000), p. 210.

26. See, for example, Nicholas Wheeler, *Saving Strangers: Humanitarian Intervention in International Society* (Oxford University Press, 2000), p. 41; Ramesh Thakur, "Humanitarian Intervention," in *The Oxford Handbook on the United Nations*, edited by Thomas G. Weiss and Sam Daws (Oxford University Press, 2007), pp. 387–403; MacFarlane and Khong, *Human Security and the UN*, p. 48.

27. The Preamble of the Charter of the United Nations reaffirms the "faith in fundamental human rights, in the dignity and worth of the human person, in the equal rights of men and women." Article 55 commits the UN to the "universal respect for, and observance of, human rights and fundamental freedoms for all without distinction as to race, sex, language, or religion." See UN, *Charter of the United Nations* (www.un.org/aboutun/charter).

28. As did the later Geneva Optional Protocols of 1977 on the protection of victims in conflicts, and the Convention against Torture of 1984. Long a highly charged and much debated subject in international law, universal jurisdiction in respect to an alleged crime means that a state, if it legislates accordingly, can try a person irrespective of nationality, residence, or where the crime was committed. Such jurisdiction is also notionally available under customary international law for crimes against humanity and genocide. See Robertson, *Crimes against Humanity*, p. 237; Kenneth Roth, "The Case for Universal Jurisdiction," *Foreign Affairs*, vol. 80 (September–October 2001): 150–54.

29. See Power, *"Problem from Hell,"* p. 43. For the definition articles of the Genocide Convention, see appendix A.

30. Application of the Convention on the Prevention and Punishment of the Crime of Genocide (*Bosnia and Herzegovina v. Serbia and Montenegro*), Judgment, ICJ, February 26, 2007. For discussions of the ruling, see Diego E. Arria, "Srebrenica the Perfect Crime," paper presented at World Federalist Movement, New York, May 22, 2007;

Orna Ben Naftali and Miri Sharon, "What the ICJ Did Not Say about the Duty to Punish Genocide," *Journal of International Criminal Justice* 5, no. 4 (2007): 859–74.

31. UN, *Charter of the United Nations* (www.un.org/aboutun/charter/chapter1.htm).

32. Variously attributed but most plausibly to President Franklin D. Roosevelt in 1939, describing Nicaraguan president Anastasio Somoza.

33. See Totten, *Century of Genocide*, p. 239; Robert Cribb, ed., *The Indonesian Killings of 1965–1966: Studies from Java and Bali* (Monash University Center of Southeast Asian Studies, 1990).

34. Power, *"Problem from Hell,"* pp. 82–84.

35. See Iain Guest, *Behind the Disappearances: Argentina's Dirty War against Human Rights and the United Nations* (University of Pennsylvania Press, 1990); Patrice McSherry, *Predatory States: Operation Condor and Covert War in Latin America* (Lanham: Rowan and Littlefield, 2005). The Carter administration broke new ground in the scale of its efforts to make domestic human rights violations an international issue, with President Carter saying in his speech to the General Assembly in 1977 that "no member of the United Nations can claim that mistreatment of its citizens is solely its own business." The United States did make a major effort between 1977 and 1980 to put pressure on the Argentine government, denouncing the abuses, cutting military aid, opposing international financial institution loans, and supporting Argentine civil rights groups; however, that policy did not survive the advent of the Reagan administration. See Human Rights Watch, "Reluctant Partner: The Argentine Government's Failure to Back Trials of Human Rights Violators," report, December 2001 (www.hrw.org/reports/2001/argentina).

36. Ricardo Falla, *Massacres in the Jungle: Ixcán, Guatemala 1975–82* (Boulder, Colo.: Westview Press, 1994), p. 8.

37. Geoff Hill, *The Battle for Zimbabwe: The Final Countdown* (Cape Town: Zebra Press, 2003), pp. 76–80.

38. Joost Hiltermann, *A Poisonous Affair: America, Iraq and the Gassing of Halabja* (Cambridge University Press, 2007).

39. Truda Gray and Brian Martin, "My Lai: The Struggle over Outrage," *Peace and Change* 133, no. 1 (January 2008): 90.

40. Human Rights Watch estimates 3,000 protesters were killed in Burma; see "Burma (Myanmar)," *World Report 1989* (New York, 1989); available at www.hrw.org/reports/1989/WR89/Burma.htm#TopOfPage. For figures on the Chinese repression, see Amnesty International, *Preliminary Findings on Killings of Unarmed Civilians, Arbitrary Arrests and Summary Executions since 3 June 1989* (New York: August 30, 1989), p.19.

41. These cases are all discussed in detail, and analyzed in these terms, in ICISS, *Responsibility to Protect, Supplementary Volume*, chap. 4. The footnotes to this chapter and the detailed bibliography in this volume fully cite supporting reference material.

42. For an overview, see Richard Sisson and Leo E. Rose, *War and Secession: Pakistan, India and the Creation of Bangladesh* (Oxford University Press, 1992). On the role

of the UN, see John Salzberg, "UN Prevention of Human Rights Violations: The Bangladesh Case," *International Organization* 27 (Winter 1973): 115–27.

43. For background, see Wheeler, *Saving Strangers*, pp. 78–110; for an international law perspective, see Gary Klintworth, *Vietnam's Intervention in Cambodia in International Law* (Canberra: Australian Government Publishing Service, 1989).

44. See Farooq Hassan, "Realpolitik in International Law: After the Tanzanian-Ugandan Conflict—Humanitarian Intervention Reexamined," *Willamette Law Review* 17, no. 4 (1981): 893, citing Amnesty International's January 1997 submission to the UN Commission on Human Rights.

45. Again these cases are all discussed in ICISS, *Responsibility to Protect, Supplementary Volume*, chap. 4, and in the reference material cited there.

46. Walter Clarke and Jeffrey Herbst, "Somalia and the Future of Humanitarian Intervention," *Foreign Affairs* 75 (March-April 1996): 70–85.

47. Arthur Jay Klinghoffer, *The International Dimension of Genocide in Rwanda* (New York University Press, 1998).

48. See the report he later commissioned detailing with great frankness the failings of the UN system: *Report of the Independent Inquiry into the Actions of the United Nations during the 1994 Genocide in Rwanda*, S/1999/1257 (United Nations, 1999). The UN's failures are also mentioned in the Brahimi report: *Report of the Panel on United Nations Peace Operations*, A/55/305-S/2000/809 (United Nations, August 17, 2000), paragraph 50. See also William Shawcross, *Deliver Us from Evil: Warlords and Peacekeepers in a World of Endless Conflict* (London: Bloomsbury Publishing, 2000), pp. 124–54.

49. See Romeo Dallaire, *Shake Hands with the Devil: The Failure of Humanity in Rwanda* (Knopf Canada, 2003).

50. Philip Gourevitch, *We Wish to Inform You That Tomorrow We Will Be Killed with Our Families: Stories from Rwanda* (New York: Picador, 1999).

51. *Report of the Panel on United Nations Peace Operations*, paragraph 50.

52. Sumantra Bose, "The Bosnian State a Decade after Dayton," *International Peacekeeping* 12 (Autumn 2005): 322–35.

53. The exact number of people killed and expelled remains unclear, also due to the deliberate destruction of evidence by the Serb army. The International Criminal Tribunal for the Former Yugoslavia exhumed 4,300 bodies but reported another 3,500 missing. The number of internally displaced people is estimated at 800,000. See International Crisis Group, *Reality Demands: Documenting Violations of International Humanitarian Law in Kosovo 1999* (Brussels, 2000); Human Rights Watch, *Under Orders: War Crimes in Kosovo* (New York, 2001), pp. 119–25, 134–40; Crisis Group, "Return to Uncertainty: Kosovo's Internally Displaced and the Return Process," *Europe Report* 139 (December 13, 2002), p. 1.

Chapter Two

1. For other treatments of the evolution of R2P by authors who played a central role in ICISS, see Thomas G. Weiss, *Humanitarian Intervention* (Cambridge: Polity, 2007), and Ramesh Thakur, *The United Nations, Peace and Security: From Collective Security to the Responsibility to Protect* (Cambridge University Press, 2006). For a recent independent assessment of the state of the international debate, see Adele Brown, "Reinventing Humanitarian Intervention: Two Cheers for the Responsibility to Protect?" House of Commons Research Paper 08/55, June 17, 2008, available at www.parliament.uk/commons/lib/research/rp2008/rp08-055.pdf.

2. The phrase was used in reference to the interventions in Greece and Syria in the nineteenth century, as described in chapter 1 of this volume. See also ICISS, *The Responsibility to Protect, Supplementary Volume: Research, Bibliography, Background* (Ottawa: International Development Research Center, 2001), p. 16, footnote 4.

3. See, for example, Malbone W. Graham, "Humanitarian Intervention in International Law as Related to the Practice of the United States," *Michigan Law Review* 22 (February 1924): 312–28; Nicholas Onuf, "Humanitarian Intervention: The Early Years," *Florida Journal of International Law* 16 (December 2004): 753.

4. See Mario Bettati and Bernard Kouchner (eds.) *Le devoir d'ingérence* (Paris: Denoël, 1987), p. 300. While the term *devoir* in their title means duty rather than right (*droit*), the book's text makes clear that the key concept for Kouchner was "droit": he took the moral duty or obligation as a given, and was arguing for something stronger—a right, and one that should be recognized in international law. See Tim Allen and David Styan, "A Right to Interfere? Bernard Kouchner and the New Humanitarianism," *Journal of International Development* 12, no. 6, (2000): 825–42, at p. 828. Also on Kouchner's role, including the 1987 conference, see James Traub, "A Statesman without Borders," *New York Times Magazine*, February 3, 2008, p. 44.

5. Tony Blair, "Doctrine of the International Community," speech delivered at the Chicago Economic Club, April 24, 1999; available at www.number-10.gov.uk/output/Page1297.asp.

6. See also Chris Abbott, "Rights and Responsibilities: Resolving the Dilemma of Humanitarian Intervention," briefing paper (London: Oxford Research Group, September 2005).

7. UNDP, *Human Development Report 1994: New Dimensions of Human Security* (Oxford University Press, 1994), p. iii. For an excellent discussion of not only this seminal report but the intellectual antecedents of the concept and its subsequent application, see Neil MacFarlane and Yuen Foon Khong, *Human Security and the UN: A Critical History* (Indiana University Press, 2006).

8. See, for example, Commission on Human Security (cochairs Sadako Ogata and Amartya Sen), *Human Security Now* (New York, 2003); available at www.humansecurity-chs.org. See also the publications of the Human Security Center, University of British Columbia, including the seminal *Human Security Report 2005: War and Peace in the 21st Century* (Oxford University Press, 2005), and those of its succes-

sor, the Human Security Report Project at Simon Fraser University (see www.hsr-group.org).

9. For criticism, see Roland Paris, "Human Security–Paradigm Shift or Hot Air?" *International Security* 26 (Fall 2001): 87–102; for the reply, see Don Hubert, "An Idea that Works in Practice," *Security Dialogue* 35 (September 2005): 351–52.

10. Personal communication from Francis Deng, 2007–08. Other publications by Deng in collaboration with the Brookings team included Francis M. Deng, *Protecting the Dispossessed: A Challenge for the International Community* (Brookings, 1993); Roberta Cohen and Francis M. Deng, *Masses in Flight: The Global Crisis of Internal Displacement* (Brookings, 1998); Francis M. Deng and Roberta Cohen, *The Forsaken People: Case Studies of the Internally Dispossessed* (Brookings, 1998). Deng subsequently drew on the sovereignty-as-responsibility approach in his role as the Secretary-General's Special Adviser on the Prevention of Genocide, a position to which he was appointed in May 2007. See also Thomas G. Weiss and David A. Korn, *Internal Displacement: Conceptualization and Its Consequences* (London: Routledge, 2005).

11. Roberta Cohen, *Human Rights Protection for Internally Displaced Persons* (Washington: Refugee Policy Group, 1991).

12. "States that refuse access to populations at risk could expect calibrated actions ranging from diplomacy to political pressure, sanctions and as a last resort, military intervention." See Roberta Cohen and Francis M. Deng, "Exodus within Borders: The Uprooted Who Never Left Home," *Foreign Affairs* 77, no. 4 (1998): 12–16.

13. Sadako Ogata, *The Turbulent Decade: Confronting the Refugee Crises of the 1990s* (Scranton, Pa.: W. W. Norton, 2005).

14. Kofi Annan, "Two Concepts of Sovereignty," *The Economist*, September 18, 1999, pp. 49–50.

15. Private conversations with the author, 2005.

16. Kofi Annan, *"We, the Peoples": The Role of the United Nations in the 21st Century*, UN Millennium Report (United Nations, 2000), p. 48; available at www.un.org/millennium/sg/report/full.htm.

17. See ICISS, *The Responsibility to Protect* (Ottawa: International Development Research Center, 2001). The quote is from the Foreword of cochairs Gareth Evans and Mohamed Sahnoun, p. vii. The major funding for the project came from Canada, but it was also generously supported by Switzerland and the United Kingdom, and by international foundations including the Carnegie Corporation of New York, the William and Flora Hewlett Foundation, the John D. and Catherine T. MacArthur Foundation, the Rockefeller Foundation, and the Simons Foundation. The Canadian government's experience in drafting and leading the negotiations to adopt UN Security Council Resolution 1265 (1999) on the protection of civilians in armed conflict, which opened up the problem without fully substantively addressing it, has been described.

18. E-mail communication to cochairs and commission staff, January 24, 2001. The process followed is described in detail in ICISS, "How the Commission Worked," *The Responsibility to Protect*, appendix B, pp. 81–85, and in "Part III: Background," *The Responsibility to Protect, Supplementary Volume*, pp. 339–98, with the latter containing

a detailed summary of the consultative meetings. The commission was served by a superb secretariat, under the leadership of Canadian Department of Foreign Affairs and International Trade (DFAIT) officials Jill Sinclair and Heidi Hulan, and research team, under the joint leadership of Thomas G. Weiss, professor and codirector of the UN Intellectual History Project at the City University of New York, and Zimbabwean lawyer and former UN official Stanlake Samkange. The research essays in the *Supplementary Volume*, an extraordinary 220-page repository of just about all previous wisdom and much current analysis on the subject, were primarily authored by Tom Weiss and Canadian DFAIT policy adviser Don Hubert, assisted by the input of over fifty other international scholars, in many cases in the form of papers presented at the consultative meeting. The equally pathbreaking, and subsequently applauded, 110-page bibliography was compiled under the direction of Oxford's Professor S. Neil MacFarlane. The ICISS publications are accessible online at www.iciss-ciise.gc.ca. A subsequently updated bibliography can be found at www.globalcentrer2p.org/biblio.html.

19. ICISS, *The Responsibility to Protect*, p. xi. The report included a further two-page synopsis of our proposed "Principles of Military Intervention"; see pp. xii–xiii.

20. World Commission on Environment and Development (chair Gro Harlem Brundtland), *Our Common Future* (Oxford University Press, 1987).

21. In the 2002 Constitutive Act of the African Union, although article 4(g) guarantees in familiar terms "noninterference by any Member State in the internal affairs of another," article 4(h) lays out "the right of the Union to intervene in a Member State pursuant to a decision of the Assembly in respect of grave circumstances, namely war crimes, genocide and crimes against humanity." For discussion, see, for example, Ben Kioko, "The Right of Interference under the African Union's Constitutive Act: From Non-Interference to Non-Intervention," *International Review of the Red Cross* 85 (December 2003): 807–25. A good short account of the contribution to the debate by Africa's "new interventionists" may be found in Michael Byers and Simon Chesterman, "Changing the Rules about Rules? Unilateral Humanitarian Intervention and the Future of International Law," in *Humanitarian Intervention: Ethical Legal and Political Dilemmas*, edited by J. L. Holzgrefe and Robert O. Keohane (Cambridge University Press, 2003), pp. 190–91.

22. See, for example, Roderic Alley, *Internal Conflicts and the International Community: Wars without End?* (Aldershot, England: Ashgate, 2004), pp. 138–64; David Chandler, "The Responsibility to Protect? Imposing the 'Liberal Peace,'" *International Peacekeeping* 11 (April 2004): 59–81.

23. High-Level Panel on Threats, Challenges, and Change, *A More Secure World: Our Shared Responsibility* (United Nations, 2004); available at www.un.org/secureworld. The members of the panel were Anand Panyarachun (chair, Thailand), Robert Badinter (France), João Baena Soares (Brazil), Gro Harlem Brundtland (Norway), Mary Chinery Hesse (Ghana), Gareth Evans (Australia), David Hannay (United Kingdom), Enrique Iglesias (Uruguay), Amre Moussa (Egypt), Satish Nambiar (India), Sadako Ogata (Japan), Yevgeny Primakov (Russian Federation), Qian Qichen (China), Salim Salim (Tanzania), Nafis Sadik (Pakistan), and Brent Scowcroft (United States).

Its terms of reference are described in annex 2, and its intense program of meetings (in the United States, Europe, and Africa) and consultations (in fifteen countries in all continents—except, as usual, Australia) is detailed in annex 3. The panel was served by an outstanding secretariat, led by research director Stephen Stedman and his deputy Bruce Jones, who, with some help from a small core of very actively engaged panel members, gave its report such quality and impact as it had, and played crucial roles in the subsequent follow-up, including the drafting of the secretary-general's own report to the 2005 World Summit. On the work of the panel on R2P (p. 245), and much else, see David Hannay, *New World Disorder: The UN after the Cold War—An Insider's View*, (London: I. B. Tauris, 2008).

24. High-Level Panel on Threats, Challenges, and Change, *A More Secure World*, annex 1, recommendation 55, p. 106.

25. Ibid., annex 1, pp. 106–07. The full text of the set of recommendations on "Using force: rules and guidelines" is as follows:

53. Article 51 of the Charter of the United Nations should be neither rewritten nor reinterpreted, either to extend its long-established scope (so as to allow preventive measures to non-imminent threats) or to restrict it (so as to allow its application only to actual attacks).

54. The Security Council is fully empowered under Chapter VII of the Charter of the United Nations to address the full range of security threats with which States are concerned. The task is not to find alternatives to the Security Council as a source of authority but to make the Council work better than it has.

55. The Panel endorses the emerging norm that there is a collective international responsibility to protect, exercisable by the Security Council authorizing military intervention as a last resort, in the event of genocide and other large-scale killing, ethnic cleansing or serious violations of humanitarian law which sovereign Governments have proved powerless or unwilling to prevent.

56. In considering whether to authorize or endorse the use of military force, the Security Council should always address—whatever other considerations it may take into account—at least the following five basic criteria of legitimacy:

(a) *Seriousness of threat.* Is the threatened harm to State or human security of a kind, and sufficiently clear and serious, to justify prima facie the use of military force? In the case of internal threats, does it involve genocide and other large-scale killing, ethnic cleansing or serious violations of international humanitarian law, actual or imminently apprehended?

(b) *Proper purpose.* Is it clear that the primary purpose of the proposed military action is to halt or avert the threat in question, whatever other purposes or motives may be involved?

(c) *Last resort.* Has every non-military option for meeting the threat in question been explored, with reasonable grounds for believing that other measures will not succeed?

(d) *Proportional means.* Are the scale, duration and intensity of the proposed military action the minimum necessary to meet the threat in question?

(e) *Balance of consequences.* Is there a reasonable chance of the military action being successful in meeting the threat in question, with the consequences of action not likely to be worse than the consequences of inaction?

57. The above guidelines for authorizing the use of force should be embodied in declaratory resolutions of the Security Council and General Assembly.

26. While insisting, as did many other states, that no intervention action should be taken without Security Council approval, in its June 2005 position paper on UN reform, China accepted that "massive humanitarian" crises were "the legitimate concern of the international community." See Alex J. Bellamy, "Whither the Responsibility to Protect? Humanitarian Intervention and the 2005 World Summit," *Ethics and International Affairs* 20 (June 2006): 151.

27. UN Millennium Project, *Investing in Development: A Practical Plan to Achieve the Millennium Development Goals* (London: Earthscan, 2005).

28. Kofi Annan, *In Larger Freedom: Toward Development, Security and Human Rights for All*, A/59/2005 (United Nations, 2005), paragraph 135; available at www.un.org/largerfreedom.

29. Ibid., annex, recommendation 7(b).

30. Recommendation 6(h) of Annan's report calls on the member states to "request the Security Council to adopt a resolution on the use of force that sets out principles for the use of force and expresses its intention to be guided by them when deciding whether to authorize or mandate the use of force; such principles should include: a reaffirmation of the provisions of the Charter of the United Nations with respect to the use of force, including those of Article 51; a reaffirmation of the central role of the Security Council in the area of peace and security; a reaffirmation of the right of the Security Council to use military force, including preventively, to preserve international peace and security, including in cases of genocide, ethnic cleansing and other such crimes against humanity; and the need to consider—when contemplating whether to authorize or endorse the use of force—the seriousness of the threat, the proper purpose of the proposed military action, whether means short of the use of force might reasonably succeed in stopping the threat, whether the military option is proportional to the threat at hand and whether there is a reasonable chance of success."

31. See Brian Urquhart, "One Angry Man," *New York Review of Books*, March 6, 2008, p. 14.

32. See, for example, Bellamy, "Whither the Responsibility to Protect?" pp. 167–69; Nicholas Wheeler, "A Victory for Common Humanity? The Responsibility to Protect after the 2005 World Summit," paper presented at the conference on "The UN at Sixty: Celebration or Wake?" University of Toronto, October 6–7, 2005.

33. Quoted in Urquhart, "One Angry Man," reviewing Bolton's *Surrender Is Not an Option: Defending America at the United Nations and Abroad* (New York: Simon and Schuster, 2007). The strongest U.S. support for the basic R2P concept came from the report of a congressionally mandated, bipartisan task force, cochaired by Newt Gingrich, former speaker of the House of Representatives, and George Mitchell, former

majority leader of the Senate. See Task Force on the United Nations, *American Interests and UN Reform* (Washington: U.S. Institute of Peace, 2005).

34. For one description of the general political dynamics of the World Summit, see Bellamy, "Whither the Responsibility to Protect?" Anecdotal accounts of the process from some of those immediately involved indicate a fairly hair-raising ride for R2P, with its being at risk a number of times of being dropped as "too controversial" by secretariat negotiators anxious to advance other institutional reforms: the full story remains to be written of its survival to become—almost through the back door—one of the major acknowledged achievements of the summit.

35. Resolution 1674 of April 28, 2006, operative paragraph 4, which reads: "*Reaffirms* the provisions of paragraphs 138 and 139 of the 2005 World Summit Outcome Document regarding the responsibility to protect populations from genocide, war crimes, ethnic cleansing and crimes against humanity"; available at www.un.org/News/Press/docs/2006/sc8710.doc.htm.

36. Resolution 1706 of August 31, 2006, the second preambular paragraph of which reads: "*Recalling also* its previous resolutions . . . and 1674 (2006) on the prohibition of civilians in armed conflict which reaffirms inter alia the provisions of paragraphs 138 and 139 of the 2005 United Nations World Summit outcome document"; available at www.un.org/News/Press/docs/2006/sc8821.doc.htm.

37. Ban Ki-moon, "Address to the Summit of the African Union," Addis Ababa, January 31, 2008 (www.un.org/apps/news/infocus/sgspeeches/search_full.asp?statID=180). Secretary-General Ban further made clear his commitment to R2P in a major speech delivered in Berlin on July 15, 2008, as this book was going to press: "Responsible Sovereignty: International Cooperation for a Changed World," available at www.un.org/apps/sg/sgstats.asp?nid=3297.

38. International Crisis Group, "Kenya in Crisis," Africa Report 137 (February 21, 2008), p. 1; available at www.crisisgroup.org.

39. In a statement made through his spokesperson on January 2, 2008, Ban reminded "the Government, as well as the political and religious leaders of Kenya of their legal and moral responsibility to protect the lives of innocent people, regardless of their racial, religious or ethnic origin." Available at www.un.org/apps/sg/sgstats.asp?nid=2937. For Deng's statement, see Office of the Spokesperson for the Secretary-General, daily press briefing, January 28, 2008; available at www.un.org/News/briefings.

40. Desmond Tutu, "Responsibility to Protect," *International Herald Tribune*, February 19, 2008.

41. UN General Assembly, Fifth Committee, 28th meeting, GA/AB/3837 (United Nations, March 4, 2008).

42. Nalin de Silva, "White Man's Burden in Black and White or R2P the LTTE?" *The Island*, August 8, 2007; available at www.kalaya.org/i070808.html. In a similar vein, see also the "Vasco da Gama" quote from fellow Sri Lankan C. Wijeyawickrema in the Introduction to this volume.

Chapter Three

1. The United Nations Preventive Deployment Force (UNPREDEP) to the Former Yugoslav Republic of Macedonia was established in March 1995 by the UN Security Council (S/RES/983, 1995) and ended in February 1999. For background on the mission, see, for example, Henryk J. Sokalski, *An Ounce of Prevention: Macedonia and the UN Experience in Preventive Diplomacy* (United States Institute of Peace, 2003). Preventive deployment is discussed further in chapter 4 of this volume.

2. See synopsis of Core Principles in box 2-1.

3. See full text in box 2-2.

4. See Core Principles, box 2-1.

5. See Alex de Waal, "No Such Thing as Humanitarian Intervention: Why We Need to Rethink How to Realize the 'Responsibility to Protect' in Wartime," web exclusive, *Harvard International Review*, March 21, 2007 (www.harvardir.org/articles/1482/), and also his comment, "Why Darfur Intervention Is a Mistake," Viewpoint, BBC News, May 21, 2008 (http://news.bbc.co.uk/1/hi/world/africa/7411087.stm), in which he continues to assert that R2P is only about coercive military intervention; Mahmood Mamdani, "The Politics of Naming: Genocide, Civil War, Insurgency," *London Review of Books*, March 29, 2007.

6. The International Crisis Group has continuously covered the Burundi peace process with twenty-two published reports since the first in 1998, "Burundi's Peace Process: The Road from Arusha," Africa Report 2; all are available at www.crisisgroup.org.

7. "Military intervention for human protection purposes is an exceptional and extraordinary measure. To be warranted, there must be serious and irreparable harm occurring to human beings, or imminently likely to occur, of the following kind: A. *large scale loss of life*, actual or apprehended, with genocidal intent or not, which is the product of either deliberate state action, or state neglect or inability to act, or a failed state situation; or B. *large scale ethnic cleansing*, actual or apprehended, whether carried out by killing, forced expulsion, acts of terror or rape." International Commission on Intervention and State Sovereignty, "Principles for Military Intervention," in *The Responsibility to Protect* (Ottawa: International Development Research Center, 2001), p. xii.

8. The full criterion reads, "*Seriousness of threat.* Is the threatened harm to State or human security of a kind, and sufficiently clear and serious, to justify *prima facie* the use of military force? In the case of internal threats, does it involve genocide and other large-scale killing, ethnic cleansing or serious violations of international humanitarian law, actual or imminently apprehended?" High-Level Panel on Threats, Challenges, and Change, *A More Secure World, Our Shared Responsibility* (United Nations, 2004), pp. 67, 106.

9. See ICISS, *The Responsibility to Protect*, "Synopsis," p. xii, and text pp. 35–37; High-Level Panel, *A More Secure World*, pp. 66–67, 106–07; Kofi Annan, *In Larger*

Freedom: Toward Development, Security and Human Rights for All, A/59/2005 (United Nations, 2005), pp. 43, 83. These criteria are discussed in full in chapter 6 in this volume.

10. Lee Feinstein, *Darfur and Beyond: What Is Needed to Prevent Mass Atrocities* (New York: Council on Foreign Relations, 2007), p. 48.

11. See, for example, the following reports from the International Crisis Group: "Darfur: Revitalising the Peace Process," Africa Report 125 (April 30, 2007); "Getting the UN into Darfur," Africa Briefing 43 (October 12, 2006); "To Save Darfur," Africa Report 105 (March 17, 2006), all available at www.crisisgroup.org.

12. ICISS, *The Responsibility to Protect*, p. 37 (discussing the "Reasonable Prospects" precautionary criterion).

13. See Stephanie Kleine-Ahlbrandt and Andrew Small, "China's New Dictatorship Diplomacy: Is Beijing Parting with Pariahs?" *Foreign Affairs* 87, no. 3 (January-February 2008): 23–37.

14. For Kouchner's widely reported statement, see, for example, Darren Schuettler, "Myanmar Must Act Now to Clear Aid Red Tape," Reuters, May 7, 2008, available at www.reuters.com/article/featuredCrisis/idUSBKK328448. For some of the reaction it engendered, see Seth Mydans, "Myanmar Faces Pressure to Allow Major Aid Effort," *New York Times*, May 8, 2008; Louis Charbonneau, "China, Indonesia Reject France's Myanmar Push," Reuters, May 8, 2008; James Blitz, "Western Diplomats Assess Risks of Unilateral Intervention," *Financial Times*, May 10, 2008; and Maggie Farley, "U.N. Struggles over How to Help Nations That Reject Aid," *Los Angeles Times*, May 14, 2008.

15. See further my response to Bernard Kouchner's initial statement, circulated widely in the UN and subsequently published as Gareth Evans, "Facing Up to Our Responsibilities," *The Guardian*, May 12, 2008, which appeared to have some influence in steering the R2P debate back along these lines.

16. See, for example, "To Protect Sovereignty, or Protect Lives?" *The Economist*, May 15, 2008; Timothy Garton Ash, "We Have a Responsibility to Protect the People of Burma. But How?" *The Guardian*, May 22, 2008; Ramesh Thakur, "Getting Real with R2P," *Daily Times* (Lahore), May 28, 2008; David Rieff, "Humanitarian Vanities," *New York Times Magazine*, June 1, 2008, p. 13. For some other commentary, see the materials collected at the Responsibility to Protect—Engaging Civil Society (R2PCS) website (www.responsibilitytoprotect.org/index.php/latest_news/1686).

17. That, for what it is worth, was certainly the view of senior officials of those two countries, as personally communicated to the author, May 2008. It was also the view of a former senior Burmese international official who traveled extensively in the country after the cyclone, personally communicated to the author, June 2008.

18. See Gareth Evans, "Humanity Did Not Justify This War," *Financial Times*, May 15, 2003, p. 15; Ken Roth, "War in Iraq: Not a Humanitarian Intervention," in *World Report 2004: Human Rights and Armed Conflict* (New York: Human Rights Watch, 2004).

19. *CrisisWatch*, the International Crisis Group's monthly bulletin on worldwide conflicts, is available at www.crisisgroup.org. The Human Rights Watch *World Report 2007* addresses human rights problems in over 70 countries; available at www.hrw.org/wr2k7/#nolink. Freedom House ranks 103 countries (of the 193 it analyzes) as Not Free or Partly Free; see "Combined Average Ratings—Independent Countries, 2007" (www.freedomhouse.org/template.cfm?page=366&year=2007).

20. See the statement of the UN secretary-general's then special adviser on genocide, Juan Méndez, on November 15, 2004, available at www.un.org/News/dh/infocus/westafrica/mendez-15nov2004.htm, drawing attention to the issue and indicating the possibility of prosecution under international law. The offensive behavior stopped shortly thereafter.

21. For documentation, see Human Rights Watch, *Russia/Chechnya—February 5: A Day of Slaughter in Novye Aldi* (Brussels, June 1, 2000); *Worse than a War: Disappearances in Chechnya—A Crime against Humanity* (March 2005). The Chechnyan conflict has been characterized throughout by atrocity crimes committed on all sides—by Chechen fighters, Russian federal forces, and pro-Moscow Chechen forces.

22. See Frederick Barton and Karen von Hippel, *Early Warning? A Review of Conflict Prediction Models and Systems* (Center for Strategic and International Studies, February 2008), which has a full bibliography and is available at http://forums.csis.org/pcrproject/?page_id=267.

23. See Paul Collier, *The Bottom Billion: Why the Poorest Countries Are Failing and What Can Be Done about It* (Oxford University Press, 2007).

Chapter Four

1. For Rwanda, for example, see Samuel Totten, "The Intervention and Prevention of Genocide: Sisyphean or Doable?" *Journal of Genocide Research* 6, no. 2 (2004): 229–47, citing inter alia Linda Melvern, *A People Betrayed: The Role of the West in Rwanda's Genocide* (London: Zed Books, 2000), pp. 55–56, and Alan J. Kuperman, *The Limits of Humanitarian Intervention: Genocide in Rwanda* (Brookings, 2001), p. 102. See also Daniela Kroslak, *France's Role in the Rwandan Genocide* (London: Hurst Publishers, 2007).

2. This theme is very well developed in David Hamburg, *Preventing Genocide: Practical Steps toward Early Detection and Effective Action* (Boulder, Colo.: Paradigm, 2008).

3. UN General Assembly, "World Summit Outcome 2005," Resolution A/RES/60/1 (October 24, 2005); available at www.un.org/summit2005/documents.html.

4. Charter of the United Nations, Chapter VI, Article 33; Chapter VIII, Articles 52–54.

5. Boutros Boutros-Ghali, *An Agenda for Peace* (United Nations, 1992), paragraphs 15 and 23; available at www.un.org/docs/SG/agpeace.

6. Carnegie Commission on Preventing Deadly Conflict, *Preventing Deadly Conflict: Final Report* (New York, 1997); available at http://wwics.si.edu/subsites/ccpdc/pubs/rept97/finfr.htm.

7. Kofi A. Annan, *Prevention of Armed Conflict* (United Nations, 2001); available at http://secint24.un.org/Depts/dpa/2001cpreport.pdf. The report was endorsed by the General Assembly and, in much more specific terms, by the Security Council in Resolution 1366 of 2001.

8. "Prevention" language can reasonably be applied at *all* stages of the conflict cycle: it is often quite useful in policy discussions to talk not only of preventing the initial outbreak of violence but also of preventing its continuance or escalation, and preventing its recurrence as well. This chapter will focus essentially on the first of these applications, the prevention of initial outbreak, but some of the measures here discussed—particularly those of a longer-term "root cause prevention" character—are also treated later in chapter 7. See appendix B for a tabular summary of the major measures applicable at all three stages of the conflict cycle.

9. Hamburg, *Preventing Genocide*, p. 34, citing Robert Gellately and Ben Kiernan, *The Specter of Genocide: Mass Murder in Historical Perspective* (Cambridge University Press, 2003), pp. 374–75.

10. "The Young Turks, Nazis and Khmer Rouge all thrived in wartime conditions that allowed them to seize power, recruit followers, demand unquestioning support, inculcate fear and suspicion against groups they identified as dangers to the common welfare, censor reports of their own atrocities while they fabricated reports of their victims' crimes, and finally, to carry out mass deportations and slaughter. The social context of war and/or revolution erodes norms of restraint and codes of ethical behaviour. Modern, technologically advanced methods of warfare have accelerated the slide to mass murder even as they conceal it. A related concern is the contemporary tendency of poor, developing countries worldwide to be sucked into unregulated civil conflict that traps and then trains teens—and even pre-teens—to be obedient and callous murderers." Hamburg, *Preventing Genocide*, p. 34.

11. See, for example, Michael E. Brown, ed., *The International Dimensions of Internal Conflict* (MIT Press, 1996); Mark Katz, "Collapsed Empires," in *Managing Global Chaos*, edited by Chester A. Crocker and Fen Osler Hampson (Washington: U.S. Institute of Peace Press, 1996), pp. 25–35.

12. A sophisticated example of this approach is found in Frances Stewart, "Horizontal Inequalities as a Source of Conflict," in *From Reaction to Prevention: Opportunities for the UN System*, edited by Fen Osler Hampson and David M. Malone (Boulder, Colo.: Lynne Rienner, 2002), pp. 105–36.

13. Paul Collier, *The Bottom Billion: Why the Poorest Countries Are Failing and What Can Be Done about It* (Oxford University Press, 2007), p. 18.

14. See, for example, Paul Collier, "Doing Well Out of War," in *Greed and Grievance: Economic Agendas in Civil Wars*, edited by Mats Berdal and David M. Malone (Boulder, Colo.: Lynn Rienner, 2000), pp. 91–111.

15. For example, Paul Collier and Anke Hoeffler, "Greed and Grievance in Civil War," Policy Research Working Paper 2355 (World Bank, 2001). The whole body of research of Collier and his team on this subject is succinctly and lucidly described in his *The Bottom Billion*, chap. 2. For an excellent short discussion of Collier's positions

and the whole greed versus grievance debate, see Karen Ballentine and Jake Sherman, eds., *The Political Economy of Armed Conflict: Beyond Greed and Grievance* (Boulder, Colo.: Lynne Rienner, 2003), pp. 3–6.

16. Karen Ballentine, "Beyond Greed and Grievance," in Ballentine and Sherman, *The Political Economy of Armed Conflict*, p. 280.

17. Example given by Charles Cater, "The Political Economy of Conflict and UN Intervention: Rethinking the Critical Cases of Africa," in *The Political Economy of Armed Conflict*, edited by Ballentine and Sherman, p. 23.

18. Collier, *The Bottom Billion*, p. 19.

19. This alphabet soup is explained, another twenty-two models are listed, and all of them are analyzed, in Frederick Barton and Karen von Hippel, "Early Warning? A Review of Conflict Prediction Models and Systems," PCR Special Project Briefing (Washington: Center for Strategic and International Studies, February 2008); available at http://forums.csis.org/pcrproject/pdf/earlywarning.pdf.

20. Ibid., pp. 11–12.

21. U.S. Ambassador Richard Holbrooke has kindly said of our monthly *CrisisWatch* bulletin, which describes the current state of play and immediately foreseeable conflict risks or peace opportunities in some seventy conflict situations, that "nothing I saw in government was as good as this." Personal communication, August 2005, much reprinted by permission in Crisis Group publications since. For full information about the International Crisis Group, which is further described in chapter 8, and access to all its publications, see www.crisisgroup.org.

22. For a good discussion of these and related dilemmas, see Ballentine, "Beyond Greed and Grievance," pp. 273–80.

23. Hamburg, *Preventing Genocide*, pp. 56, 71. See also Totten, "The Intervention and Prevention of Genocide."

24. Méndez's statement is available at www.un.org/News/dh/infocus/westafrica/mendez-15nov2004. As noted in chapter 3, it cannot be assumed that without this intervention the situation would in fact have exploded. But unprovables of this kind come with the territory with any preventive action.

25. See, for example, Michael S. Lund, *Preventing Violent Conflicts: A Strategy for Preventive Diplomacy* (Washington: U.S. Institute of Peace Press, 1996); David A. Hamburg, *No More Killing Fields: Preventing Deadly Conflict* (Lanham, Md.: Rowman and Littlefield, 2002).

26. See Ballentine, "Beyond Greed and Grievance," pp. 261–62, 280, citing Cater, "Rethinking the Critical Cases of Africa," both in Ballentine and Sherman, *The Political Economy of Armed Conflict*.

27. See, for example, International Crisis Group, "Burundi: The Issues at Stake. Political Parties, Freedom of the Press and Political Prisoners," Africa Report 23 (July 12, 2000); "Burundi: Democracy and Peace at Risk," Africa Report 120 (November 30, 2006); Juana Brachet and Howard Wolpe, "Conflict-Sensitive Development Assistance: The Case of Burundi," Conflict Prevention and Reconstruction Working Paper 27 (World Bank, June 2005). For examples of support for governance and institution

building, see, for example, Crisis Group, "Restoring Democracy in Bangladesh," Asia Report 151 (April 28, 2008); "Afghanistan's New Legislature: Making Democracy Work," Asia Report 116 (May 15, 2006).

28. In this and subsequent sections I have drawn on analysis and language in my earlier book, Gareth Evans, *Cooperating for Peace: The Global Agenda for the 1990s and Beyond* (Sydney: Allen and Unwin, 1993).

29. International Crisis Group, "Myanmar: Sanctions, Engagement or Another Way Forward?" Asia Report 78 (April 26, 2004).

30. There are endless varieties of mediation, which can take different forms depending on, inter alia, the phase of the conflict, the degree to which there is actual room to change positions through negotiation, and whether the mediation has been invited or forced upon one or more of the parties. For an overview of mediation in theory and practice, see I. William Zartman and J. Lews Rasmussen, eds., *Peacemaking in International Conflict: Methods and Techniques* (Washington: U.S. Institute of Peace Press, 1997); Saadia Touval and I. William Zartman, eds., *International Mediation in Theory and Practice* (Boulder, Colo.: Westview Press, 1985); Louis Kriesberg, "Varieties of Mediating Activities and Mediators in International Relations," in *Resolving International Conflict: The Theory and Practice of Mediation*, edited by Jacob Bercovitch (Boulder, Colo.: Lynne Reiner Publishers, 1996). See also Chester A. Crocker, Fen Osler Hampson, and Pamela Aall, eds., *Herding Cats: Multiparty Mediation in a Complex World* (Washington: U.S. Institute of Peace Press, 1999); Dennis Ross, *Statecraft: And How to Restore America's Standing in the World* (New York: Farrar, Straus and Giroux, 2007).

"Track one" diplomacy refers to negotiation by official representatives of governments or intergovernmental organizations, and "track two" denotes intervention by nonofficial negotiators—often eminent individuals or lower-profile but trusted go-betweens. See, for example, Zartman and Rasmussen, *Peacemaking in International Conflict*. Some analysts define the tracks differently; for example, Lutz, Babbitt, and Hannum add a track 1.5, in which nonofficial mediators interact with official representatives of the disputing parties. Under this formulation, track two then becomes engagement by nonofficial mediators with nonofficial representatives of the parties, for instance, influential community members. See Ellen Lutz, Eileen F. Babbitt, and Hurst Hannum, "Human Rights and Conflict Resolution from the Practitioners' Perspective," *Fletcher Forum of World Affairs* 27, no. 1 (2003): 173–93.

31. Human Security Center, *Human Security Report 2005* (Oxford University Press, 2005), p. 153; available at www.humansecurityreport.info.

32. For the case of Ethiopia and Eritrea, see International Crisis Group, "Ethiopia and Eritrea: Stopping the Slide to War," Africa Briefing 48 (November 5, 2007). The role of the OSCE high commissioner is discussed in Walter Kemp, *Quiet Diplomacy in Action: The OSCE High Commissioner on National Minorities* (The Hague: Kluwer Law International, 2001); Wolfgang Zellner, "The High Commissioner on National Minorities: His Work, Effectiveness, and Recommendations to Strengthen the HCNM as an Institution," in *Europe's New Security Challenges*, edited by Heinz Gartner, Adrian

Hyde-Price, and Erich Reiter (Boulder, Colo.: Lynne Rienner, 2001), pp. 265–95, and by van der Stoel's successor, Rolf Ekeus, in "Overcoming the Reluctance to Conflict Prevention," address to Seminar on Operational Conflict Prevention, New York, September 8 , 2006; available at www.osce.org/documents/hcnm/2006/09/20466_en.pdf.

33. For a discussion of the Commonwealth's instruments, see, for example, James Mayall, "Democratizing the Commonwealth," *International Affairs* 74, no. 2 (1998): 379–92; for Nigeria, see, for example, Abdulsalami Alhaji Abubakar, "Nigeria and the Commonwealth: A Record of Mutual Services," *Round Table* 93, no. 373 (2004): 43–49; the case of Zimbabwe is discussed by Ian Taylor, "'The Devilish Thing': The Commonwealth and Zimbabwe's Dénouement," *Round Table* 94, no. 380 (2005): 367–80.

34. South Africa's *Business Day* noted that "Bashir's 'consensual' dumping . . . indicates clearly that more African leaders have awoken to the reality of the atrocities afflicting millions in Darfur and are ready to put their weight behind finding a peaceful resolution to the conflict in that region." See "The Right Message," *Business Day*, January 31, 2007. *The Guardian* noted further that the African Union's decision to give the chairmanship to Ghana's John Kufuor instead is growing evidence of the merits of the African Peer Review Mechanism—a scheme under the New African Partnership for African Development (NEPAD) program in which African states voluntarily assess each other's political and economic management—from which Ghana has emerged well. See "Good Intentions, Sad Results," *The Guardian*, January 31, 2007.

35. On the continuing relevance of the "dollar a day" benchmark—best now applied as $1 in 2005 PPP terms—see "Has 'a Dollar a Day' Had Its Day?" *The Economist*, May 24, 2008, p. 92.

36. See Ballentine, "Beyond Greed and Grievance," pp. 261–62, 280, citing Cater, "Rethinking the Critical Cases of Africa," both in Ballentine and Sherman, *The Political Economy of Armed Conflict*.

37. Collier, *The Bottom Billion*, p. 20.

38. UN General Assembly, "World Summit Outcome 2005," paragraph 9.

39. The eight Millennium Development Goals are to eradicate extreme poverty and hunger; achieve universal primary education; promote gender equality and empower women; reduce child mortality; improve maternal health; combat HIV/AIDS, malaria, and other diseases; ensure environmental sustainability; and develop a global partnership for development. Further information is available at www.un.org/millennium-goals.

40. See Jeffrey Sachs, *The End of Poverty: Economic Possibilities for Our Time* (New York: Penguin, 2006); William Easterly, *The White Man's Burden: Why the West's Efforts to Aid the Rest Have Done So Much Ill and So Little Good* (New York: Penguin, 2007). The flavor of the sometimes less than temperate debate between them is well captured in an exchange recorded in *El Mundo*, May 26, 2007.

41. See Hamburg, *Preventing Genocide*, pp. 159–77; David A. Hamburg and Beatrix A. Hamburg, *Learning to Live Together: Preventing Hatred and Violence in Child and Adolescent Development* (Oxford University Press, 2004).

42. International Crisis Group, "Pakistan: Karachi's Madrasas and Violent Extremism," Asia Report 130 (March 29, 2007); "Pakistan: Reforming the Education Sector," Asia Report 84 (October 7, 2004). On comparable schools in Indonesia, see Crisis Group, "Indonesia Backgrounder: How the Jemaah Islamiyah Terrorist Network Operates," Asia Report 43 (December 11, 2002).

43. See Stuart J. Kaufman, "Peace-Building and Conflict Resolution," paper prepared for the conference "Living Together after Ethnic Killing: Debating the Kaufmann Hypothesis," Rutgers University, October 14, 2000; Amanda Paulson, "The Bonds of Friendship in a Bitter War," *Christian Science Monitor*, August 15, 2002.

44. For more information, see www.seedsofpeace.org.

45. This is what the European Commission calls "structural stability." See European Commission, "Communication from the Commission on Conflict Prevention," COM(2001) 211 final (April 11, 2001), p. 10; available at http://europa.eu.int/comm/external_relations/cfsp/news/com2001_211_en.pdf.

46. See Search for Common Ground, "Sierra Leone" (www.sfcg.org/programmes/sierra/programmes_sierra.html). On the work of Search and other NGOs in Burundi, see also Lennart Wohlgemuth, "NGOs and Conflict Prevention in Burundi: A Case Study," *Africa Development* 30, nos. 1 and 2 (2005): 183–209.

47. See Hunt Alternatives Fund, "Initiative for Inclusive Security" (www.huntalternatives.org/pages/7_the_initiative_for_inclusive_security.cfm).

48. For example, the U.S. threat to cut off development aid for Armenia after post-election violence in early 2008. See "Armenia: U.S. Officials Say Yerevan Risks Losing Development Funds," Radio Free Europe/Radio Liberty, April 18, 2008.

49. International Crisis Group, "Myanmar: Aid to the Border Areas," Asia Report 82 (September 9, 2004); "Myanmar: Sanctions, Engagement or Another Way Forward?" On the 2008 cyclone issue, chapter 3.

50. Lord Robert Skidelsky and Edward Mortimer, "Economic Sanctions as a Means to International Health," in *Preventive Diplomacy: Stopping Wars before They Start*, edited by Kevin M. Cahill (New York: Basic Books, 1996), p. 143.

51. For a full discussion of these and other examples, and all the relevant policy issues, see David Cortright, "Positive Inducements in International Statecraft," paper presented at Fraser Institute Conference on Promoting Human Rights: Isolation or Investment, Calgary, May 2, 2000; available at www.fourthfreedom.org/Applications/cms.php?page_id=39. See also David Cortright, ed., *The Price of Peace: Incentives and International Conflict* (Lanham, Md.: Rowman and Littlefield, 1997).

52. A course that the International Crisis Group has been recommending in relation to the Iran nuclear issue; see Crisis Group, "Iran: Is There a Way Out of the Nuclear Impasse?" Middle East Report 51 (February 23, 2006). See also Gareth Evans, "The Right Nuclear Red Line," *Washington Post*, December 5, 2007; "The Iran Nuclear Problem: The Way Forward," seminar presentation, School of International Relations, Ministry of Foreign Affairs, Tehran, November 22, 2007; available at www.crisisgroup.org/home/index.cfm?id=5187.

53. Cortright, "Positive Inducements," p. 8, citing an earlier study drawing on the insights of behavioral psychology by David A. Baldwin, "The Power of Positive Sanctions," *World Politics* 24, no. 1 (1971): 19–38.

54. See International Crisis Group, "A Strategy for Comprehensive Peace in Sudan," Africa Report 130 (July 26, 2007).

55. International Crisis Group, "Somaliland: Time for African Union Leadership," Africa Report 110 (May 23, 2006).

56. International Crisis Group, "Sri Lanka: Sinhala Nationalism and the Elusive Southern Consensus," Asia Report 141 (November 7, 2007); "Sri Lanka: The Failure of the Peace Process," Asia Report 124 (November 28, 2006).

57. For some examples of how pressure for human rights reform intersects with conflict prevention, see International Crisis Group, "Sri Lanka's Human Rights Crisis," Asia Report 135 (June 14, 2007); "Uzbekistan: The Andijon Uprising," Asia Briefing 38 (May 25, 2005); "Central Asia: What Role for the European Union?" Asia Report 113 (April 10, 2006); "Nepal: Dealing with a Human Rights Crisis," Asia Report 94 (March 24, 2005).

58. See International Crisis Group, "Central Asia: Islam and the State," Asia Report 59 (July 10, 2003); "Azerbaijan: Independent Islam and the State," Europe Report 191 (March 25, 2008).

59. See Simon Chesterman, "An International Rule of Law?" *American Journal of Comparative Law* 56, no. 2 (2008): 1–39.

60. For stark illustrations of the necessity for, and difficulties in achieving, legal reform, see, for example, International Crisis Group, "Kyrgyzstan: The Challenge of Judicial Reform," Asia Report 150 (April 10, 2008); "Afghanistan: Judicial Reform and Transitional Justice," Asia Report 45 (January 28, 2003).

61. See Anne-Marie Slaughter, "Pakistan's Black Revolution," *The Guardian,* April 25, 2008; and on the overall struggle for the restoration of democracy, International Crisis Group, "Winding Back Martial Law in Pakistan," Asia Briefing 70 (November 12, 2007).

62. International Crisis Group, "Macedonia's Public Secret: How Corruption Drags the Country Down," Europe Report 133 (August 14, 2002).

63. For further information check the respective websites of Transparency International (www.transparency.org), Revenue Watch (www.revenuewatch.org), Publish What You Pay (www.publishwhatyoupay.org), and Extractive Industries Transparency Initiative (www.eitransparency.org).

64. For the list of countries, see International Court of Justice (ICJ), "Declarations Recognizing the Jurisdiction of the Court as Compulsory" (www.icj-cij.org/jurisdiction/index.php?p1=5&p2=1&p3=3).

65. See *Land and Maritime Boundary between Cameroon and Nigeria* (Cameroon *v.* Nigeria), *Judgement, ICJ, June 11, 1998; Application of the Convention on the Prevention and Punishment of the Crime of Genocide* (Bosnia and Herzegovina *v.* Serbia and Montenegro), *Judgement, ICJ, February 26, 2007* (discussed in chapter 1).

66. Details of the case of *The Prosecutor v. Thomas Lubanga Dyilo* and other DRC cases are available at www.icc-cpi.int/cases/RDC.html. At the time of this writing the Lubanga case had run into procedural difficulties, with the trial chamber issuing a stay, and ordering Lubanga's release, on the ground that the prosecution had not disclosed to the defense certain exculpatory material, but with these decisions in turn on hold pending the prosecution's appeal. See also International Crisis Group, "Congo: Four Priorities for Sustainable Peace in Ituri," Africa Report 140 (May 13, 2008).

67. See Human Rights Watch, *Universal Jurisdiction in Europe: The State of the Art* (New York: 2006); available at www.hrw.org/reports/2006/ij0606. As to sitting officials, it is still the case that, as the ICJ ruled in the *Congo v. Belgium* case, "Under customary international law a foreign minister (and by extension a head of state) enjoys absolute immunity from 'any act of authority of another State' regardless of the gravity of the charges involved, for as long as he or she remains in office. A number of other national courts have reached similar conclusions, dismissing human rights charges against serving heads of state cases on immunity grounds." See Sarah Andrews, "U.S. Courts Rule on Absolute Immunity and Inviolability of Foreign Heads of State: The Cases against Robert Mugabe and Jiang Zemin," *ASIL Insights*, November 2004 (www.asil.org/insights/2004/11/insight041122.html).

68. For details see Human Rights Watch, "The Case against Hissène Habré, an African 'Pinochet'" (www.hrw.org/justice/habre).

69. See International Crisis Group, "Security Sector Reform in the Congo," Africa Report 104 (February 13, 2006); "Timor-Leste: Security Sector Reform," Asia Report 143 (January 17, 2008).

70. International Crisis Group, "Indonesia: Next Steps in Military Reform," Asia Report 24 (October 11, 2001), p. ii.

71. International Crisis Group, "Aceh: So Far, So Good," Asia Briefing 44 (December 13, 2005).

72. International Crisis Group, "Burma/Myanmar: After the Crackdown," Asia Report 144 (January 31, 2008); "Myanmar: The Future of the Armed Forces," Asia Briefing 21 (September 27, 2002).

73. See, for example, Public International Law and Policy Group, "Confidence-Building Measures: A Quick Guide," September 2007 (www.publicinternational law.org/areas/peacebuilding/PILPG_Confidence-Building-Measures_Sept-07.doc); Sarah Meek, "Confidence-Building Measures: A Tool for Disarmament and Development," DDA Occasional Paper 9 (UN Department for Disarmament Affairs, November 2004), pp. 12–21, available at http://disarmament.un.org/ddapublications/op9art02.

74. See Security Council, "Small Arms," Update Report 3 (United Nations, April 18, 2008), citing inter alia the Graduate Institute of International Studies, Geneva.

75. See Henryk J. Sokalski, *An Ounce of Prevention: Macedonia and the UN Experience in Preventive Diplomacy* (Washington: U.S. Institute of Peace Press, 2003). Secretary-General Kofi Annan has also described as preventive deployments—because taking place before the beginning of an armed internal or international conflict—the

United Nations Mission in the Central African Republic (MINURCA) and a succession of operations in Haiti. See Annan, *Prevention of Armed Conflict*, p. 45.

76. International Commission on Intervention and State Sovereignty, *The Responsibility to Protect* (Ottawa: International Development Research Center, 2001), p. 58, paragraph 7.6.

77. International Crisis Group, "Liberia: Security Challenges," Africa Report 71 (November 3, 2003), p. 13.

78. "Arms Shipment Meant for Zimbabwe to Return to China," *New York Times*, April 24, 2008.

Chapter Five

1. Lee H. Hamilton (President, Woodrow Wilson International Center for Scholars), "Helping a Troubled Continent," *Commentary*, July 5, 2005, available at www.wilsoncenter.org.

2. UN General Assembly, "World Summit Outcome 2005," Resolution A/RES/60/1 (October 24, 2005); available at www.un.org/summit2005/documents.html.

3. As noted in chapter 2, the situation was specifically characterized by Secretary-General Kofi Annan, Genocide Special Adviser Francis Deng, and others as a "responsibility to protect" one. On the outcome see AU, "Communiqué of the 115th Meeting of the Peace and Security Council," March 14, 2008 (www.iss.co.za/dynamic/administration/file_manager/file_links/PSC115COM.PDF); and on the dynamics of the negotiations and the unfinished business, see International Crisis Group, "Kenya in Crisis," Africa Report 137 (February 21, 2008). This and all other Crisis Group reports and briefings cited here are available at www.crisisgroup.org.

4. International Crisis Group, "Is Dayton Failing?: Bosnia Four Years after the Peace Agreement," Europe Report 80 (October 28, 1999). For an excellent account of the peace process by its primary architect, see Richard Holbrooke, *To End a War* (New York: Random House, 1998). For a critical discussion of the agreement, see also Richard Caplan, "Assessing the Dayton Accord: The Structural Weaknesses of the General Framework Agreement for Peace in Bosnia and Herzegovina," *Diplomacy and Statecraft* 11, no. 2 (2000): 213–32.

5. Rt. Hon. Lord Robertson of Port Ellen, launching Mark Laity's "Preventing War in Macedonia: Pre-emptive Diplomacy in the 21st Century," Whitehall Paper 68 (London: Royal United Services Institute, March 11, 2008); speech available at www.rusi.org/research/studies/european/commentary. For background on the Ohrid Agreement, see International Crisis Group, "Macedonia: War on Hold," Europe Briefing 21(August 15, 2001).

6. International Crisis Group, "Sudan's Comprehensive Peace Agreement: The Long Road Ahead," Africa Report 106 (March 31, 2006); "The Khartoum-SPLM Agreement: Sudan's Uncertain Peace," Africa Report 96 (July 25, 2005).

7. For a current list, see United Nations, "Other High Level Appointments" (www.un.org/Depts/dpko/SRSG/table). In mid-2008 there were—leaving aside

deputy-level positions, forty-one such special representatives working in specific geographical settings (twenty in Africa, seven each in the Middle East and Asia-Pacific, five in Europe, and two in the Americas), with another forty-one working on thematic issues (many on issues like HIV/AIDS, climate, and gender, but some very immediately security related, like the special adviser on the prevention of genocide and the special representative for children and armed conflict).

8. For details, see www.cartercenter.org, www.santegidio.org/en/pace, and www.hdcentre.org, respectively.

9. See www.theelders.org.

10. Extracts from video accompanying presentation to Ahtisaari at the International Crisis Group 2008 Award Luncheon, New York, April 30, 2008.

11. Dennis Ross, *Statecraft: And How to Restore America's Standing in the World* (New York: Farrar, Straus and Giroux, 2007), chaps. 9 and 11. His twelve rules for negotiators are: know what you want, know what you can live with; know everything there is to know about the decisionmaker(s) on the other side; build a relationship of trust with the key decisionmaker; keep in mind the other side's need for an explanation; to gain the hardest concessions, prove you understand what is important to the other side; tough love is also required; employ the good cop–bad cop approach carefully; understand the value and limitations of deadlines; take only calculated risks; never lie, never bluff; don't paper over differences; and summarize agreements at the end of every meeting. His eleven rules for mediation are: identify shared objectives; assess what can be negotiated, and frame the talks; sensitize each side to the other's concerns and grievances; think outside the box when forging critical compromises; make sure the parties demonstrate their seriousness; get each side to adjust to reality; set aside each side's principles and focus on practicalities; make agreements where you can; act swiftly to contain crises; use anger as a tool—but use it rarely; and put your drafts on the table.

12. See International Crisis Group, "Sri Lanka: The Failure of the Peace Process," Asia Report 124 (November 28, 2006); "Zimbabwe: A Regional Solution?" Africa Report 132 (September 18, 2007).

13. For a brief account, see Gareth Evans, "Achieving Peace in Cambodia," address to The Hague Centennial Peace Conference, February 20, 1999 (www.crisisgroup.org/home/index.cfm?id=2572&l=1); for a full-length study, see Ken Berry, *Cambodia: From Red to Blue—Australia's Initiative for Peace* (Sydney: Allen and Unwin, 1997).

14. This is one of a number of counterintuitive findings well documented in the *Human Security Report 2005: War and Peace in the 21st Century* (Oxford University Press, 2005), and its sequels in 2006 and 2007; specifically on peace settlements, see "How Wars End" in the *Human Security Brief 2006* (Human Security Center, University of British Columbia, 2006), pp. 18–20, all at www.hsrgroup.org.

15. International Commission on Intervention and State Sovereignty (ICISS), *The Responsibility to Protect* (Ottawa: International Development Research Center, 2001), p. 30.

16. See Galima Bukharbaeva, "Remember Andijan," *International Herald Tribune*, May 10, 2008; see also International Crisis Group, "Uzbekistan: Europe's Sanctions Matter," Asia Briefing 54 (November 6, 2006); Alain Délétroz, "Europe's Reasons without Reason," *European Voice*, February 8, 2007; International Crisis Group, "Political Murder in Central Asia: No Time to End Uzbekistan's Isolation," Asia Briefing 76 (February 14, 2008).

17. The study was later published as Keith Ovenden and Tony Cole, *Apartheid and International Finance: A Program for Change* (Ringwood: Penguin Books Australia, 1989).

18. See, for example, Robert A. Pape, "Why Economic Sanctions Do Not Work," *International Security* 22, no. 2 (1997): 90–136; Lord Robert Skidelsky and Edward Mortimer, "Economic Sanctions as a Means to International Health," in *Preventive Diplomacy: Stopping Wars before They Start*, edited by Kevin M. Cahill (New York: Basic Books, 1996), chap. 9.

19. Peter Wallensteen, Carina Staibano, and Mikael Eriksson, eds., *Making Targeted Sanctions Effective: Guidelines for the Implementation of UN Policy Options* (Uppsala University, 2003), p. iii. More information on the Stockholm Process can be found at www.smartsanctions.se.

20. The Kimberley Process doctrine can be found at www.kimberleyprocess.com; for background, see, for example, Andrew J. Grant and Ian Taylor, "Global Governance and Conflict Diamonds: The Kimberley Process and the Quest for Clean Gems," *Round Table* 93, no. 375 (2004): 385–401. For similar initiatives against illegal logging, see www.illegal-logging.info.

21. Examples of the use and potential use of targeted sanctions are discussed in International Crisis Group, "Zimbabwe: An End to the Stalemate?" Africa Report 122 (March 5, 2007); "Uzbekistan: Europe's Sanctions Matter"; "Liberia: The Key to Ending Regional Instability," Africa Report 43 (April 24, 2002); "Darfur: The Failure to Protect," Africa Report 89 (March 8, 2005); "A New Sudan Action Plan," Africa Briefing 24 (April 26, 2005); "Stopping Guinea's Slide," Africa Report 94 (June 14, 2005); "A Congo Action Plan," Africa Briefing 34 (October 19, 2005); "Zimbabwe's Continuing Self-Destruction," Africa Briefing 38 (June 6, 2006).

22. Other economic incentives include granting special trade status (for example, the United States giving most-favored-nation status to China), tariff reductions, direct purchases, reduction or elimination of export subsidies, export or import licenses, and investment guarantees. See David Cortright, "Positive Inducements in International Statecraft," paper presented at Fraser Institute Conference on Promoting Human Rights: Isolation or Investment, Calgary, May 2, 2000; available at www.fourthfreedom.org/Applications/cms.php?page_id=39. See also David Cortright and George A. Lopez, "Carrots, Sticks and Cooperation," in *Cases and Strategies for Preventive Action*, edited by Barnett R. Rubin (New York: Century Foundation Press, 1998), pp. 113–34.

23. See International Crisis Group, "Macedonia: War on Hold."

24. Other examples of such courts are the Crimes Panels of the District Courts of Dili and the "Regulation 64" Panels in the Courts of Kosovo; their common charac-

teristic is that, unlike the first generation international criminal tribunals (the Nuremberg and Tokyo Tribunals) and the second (the International Criminal Tribunal for the former Yugoslavia, International Criminal Tribunal for Rwanda, and now the International Criminal Court), they comprise mixed international and local judges and supporting personnel, and apply a compound of international and national substantive and procedural law. See Project on International Courts and Tribunals at www.worldlii.org/int/other/PICTRes/2004/1.html.

25. Also in this ad hoc category are the hybrid tribunals set up in Cambodia, East Timor, Kosovo, and Sierra Leone, in the creation of all of which the UN had a hand.

26. The Rome Statute is available at www.icc-cpi.int/library/about/officialjournal/Rome_Statute_120704-EN.pdf.

27. International Crisis Group, "The International Criminal Tribunal for Rwanda: Time for Pragmatism," Africa Report 69 (September 26, 2003).

28. The ICC's jurisdictional considerations are contained within the Rome Statute. To summarize, the ICC has jurisdiction where a crime is alleged to have taken place on the territory of a state party to the statute, where the accused is a national of a state party, where a country has specifically accepted the ICC's jurisdiction, and where a case has been referred to the ICC by the UN Security Council or by a state party. In addition to this, under Article 15, the prosecutor may seek to begin an investigation, *proprio motu*, if the court's pretrial chamber accepts such an investigation; the UN Security Council can block any investigation for a period of twelve months by the adoption of a resolution to that effect under Chapter VII of the UN Charter.

29. This is probably a problem without a solution in the real world, like the desirability of a volunteer international rapid reaction force under UN command, discussed in chapter 8, but a heroic attempt has been made to offer one by Richard Cooper, "Moving from Military Intervention to Judicial Enforcement: The Case for an International Marshals Service," in *The Responsibility to Protect: The Global Moral Compact for the XXIst Century*, edited by Richard Cooper and Juliette Voinov Kohler (Basingstoke, England: Palgrave Macmillan, forthcoming).

30. As this book was going to press, while General Ratko Mladic remained at large, former Bosnian Serb leader Radovan Karadzic was finally arrested by Serbian authorities on July 21, 2008, more than ten years after a warrant for his arrest was issued by the International Criminal Tribunal for the former Yugoslavia on charges including genocide, extermination, and deportation. See the ICTY Prosecutor's press statement welcoming the arrest, available at www.un.org/icty/pressreal/2008/pr1274e.htm. On the Bemba arrest, see the ICC's press release of May 24, 2008, available at www.icc-cpi.int/ press/pressreleases/370.html. On this and the Court's performance generally in its first five years, see Nick Grono, "The International Criminal Court: Success or Failure?" *openDemocracy*, June 9, 2008, available at www.opendemocracy.net/article/the-international-criminal-court-success-or-failure.

31. For the international crimes that can be tried by the ICC under the Rome Statute, see appendix A, "Treaty Definitions of Mass Atrocity Crimes." On the warrants for arrest sought, as this book was going to press, against President Omar al-Bashir for

genocide, crimes against humanity, and war crimes committed in Darfur, see the Prosecutor's press release, statement, and "Summary of the Case" available at www.icc-cpi.int/press/pressreleases/406.html. For the International Crisis Group's statement on the case, identifying both the positives and negatives involved in the Prosecutor's action, and recommending that the Security Council stay its hand before agreeing on any suspension of the prosecution under Article 16 of the Rome Statute, see "New ICC Prosecution: Opportunities and Risks for Peace in Sudan," media release, July 14, 2008, available at www.crisisgroup.org.

32. For the arguments for and against prosecutions and amnesty in Northern Uganda, see International Crisis Group, "Northern Uganda Peace Process: The Need to Maintain Momentum," Africa Briefing 46 (September 14, 2007); "Northern Uganda: Seizing the Opportunity for Peace," Africa Report 124 (April 26, 2007). Also see Nick Grono and Adam O'Brien, "Justice in Conflict? The ICC and Peace Processes," in *Courting Conflict? Justice, Peace and the ICC in Africa*, edited by Nicholas Waddell and Phil Clark (London: Royal African Society, 2008), pp.13–20; Adam O'Brien, "The Impact of International Justice on Local Peace Initiatives: The Case of Northern Uganda," presentation to the Conference on Building a Future on Peace and Justice, Nuremberg, June 26, 2007; and John Prendergast, "What to Do about Joseph Kony," Strategy Paper 8 (Washington: ENOUGH, October 2007). For these arguments in regard to Sudan and Darfur, see International Crisis Group, "Getting the UN into Darfur," Africa Briefing 43 (October 12, 2006); Nick Grono and Don Steinberg, "Future of the World Court in Balance," *YaleGlobal Online*, March 7, 2007 (http://yaleglobal.yale.edu/display.article?id=8875); David Mozersky and Nick Grono, "Sudan and the ICC: A Question of Accountability," *openDemocracy*, January 31, 2007 (www.opendemocracy.net/democracy-africa_democracy/sudan_icc_4301.jsp).

33. I have been much assisted in thinking and talking my way through these issues by my colleague Nick Grono; see Grono, "The Role of the International Criminal Court in Peace Processes: Mutually Reinforcing or Mutually Exclusive?" IPPR briefing paper (London: Institute for Public Policy Research, November 28, 2006); "What Comes First, Peace or Justice?" *International Herald Tribune*, October 26, 2006; and "The Role of International Justice in Preventing and Resolving Deadly Conflict," presented at the Law and Public Affairs Program, Princeton University, May 6, 2008. The relevant principles have been usefully discussed by others including Gary Bass, *Stay the Hand of Vengeance: The Politics of War Crimes Tribunals* (Princeton University Press, 2000); Paul R. Williams and Michael P. Scharf, *Peace with Justice? War Crimes and Accountability in the Former Yugoslavia* (Lanham, Md.: Rowman and Littlefield, 2002); Juan Méndez, "Accountability for Past Abuses," *Human Rights Quarterly* 19, no. 2 (1997): 255–82.

34. There are a number of very long-established, and still current, missions of this character, in particular those operating in Israel-Palestine, Kashmir, Cyprus, Lebanon, and the Golan Heights: they can be argued to have not so much kept or advanced the peace as simply participated in the freezing of decades-old postconflict situations.

35. Gareth Evans, *Cooperating for Peace: The Global Agenda for the 1990s and Beyond* (Sydney: Allen and Unwin, 1995), explains this and the other peace operations categories as they evolved, and lists and describes all the UN operations up to that date. The literature on peacekeeping is very large: see, for example, Alex J. Bellamy, Paul Williams, and Stuart Griffin, *Understanding Peacekeeping* (Cambridge: Polity, 2004); David M. Malone and Karin Wermester, "Boom and Bust? The Changing Nature of UN Peacekeeping," in *Managing Armed Conflicts in the 21st Century*, edited by Adekeye Adabajo and Chandra L. Sriram (London: Frank Cass, 2001), pp. 37–54; Virginia P. Fortna, "Does Peacekeeping Keep Peace? International Intervention and the Duration of Peace after Civil War," *International Studies Quarterly* 48, no. 2 (2004): 269–92; Department of Peacekeeping Operations, *Handbook on United Nations Multidimensional Peacekeeping Operations* (United Nations, 2003); Birger Heldt and Peter Wallensteen, "Peacekeeping Operations: Global Patterns of Intervention and Success, 1948–2000," Research Report 1 (Sandöverken, Sweden: Folke Bernadotte Academy, 2004).

36. *Report of the Panel on United Nations Peace Operations*, A/55/305-S/2000/809 (United Nations, 2000). For further background material on UN peacekeeping, see www.un.org/Depts/dpko/lessons.

37. International Crisis Group, "Sierra Leone: Time for a New Military and Political Strategy," Africa Report 28 (April 11, 2001); also Richard Connaughton, "The Mechanics and Nature of British Interventions into Sierra Leone (2000) and Afghanistan (2001–2002)," *Civil Wars* 5, no. 2 (2002): 77–95.

38. *Report of the Panel on United Nations Peace Operations*, Executive Summary, pp. ix–x.

39. Figures for the number of missions, troops, and civilian staff are as of April 2008; for monthly updated summaries of UN peacekeeping missions, see "Monthly Summary of Contributors of Military and Civilian Police Personnel" (www.un.org/Depts/dpko/dpko/contributors). In addition to these peacekeeping missions, there are three other special political or peacebuilding missions, with around another 2,000 personnel between them, supported by the UN's Department of Peacekeeping Operations: United Nations Assistance Mission in Afghanistan (UNAMA), United Nations Integrated Office in Burundi (BINUB), and United Nations Integrated Office in Sierra Leone (UNIOSIL); see Department of Peacekeeping Operations, "United Nations Political and Peacebuilding Missions," background note, April 30, 2008 (www.un.org/Depts/dpko/dpko/ppbm.pdf).

40. For an excellent analysis of this emerging new "coercive protection" peacekeeping role and its implications for military force structures, doctrine, and training, see Victoria K. Holt and Tobias C. Berkman, *The Impossible Mandate? Military Preparedness, the Responsibility to Protect and Modern Peace Operations* (Washington, D.C.: Henry L. Stimson Center, 2006).

41. High-Level Panel on Threats, Challenges and Change, *A More Secure World: Our Shared Responsibility* (United Nations, 2004), p. 68. See also Susan C. Breau, "The

Impact of the Responsibility to Protect on Peacekeeping," *Journal of Conflict and Security Law* 1, no. 3 (2006): 429–64.

42. In addition to the non-UN-commanded missions mentioned in this paragraph, an additional range of peacekeeping missions operates without any effective UN mandate but rather one contingent upon cease-fire agreements or other international organizations (such as the Organization for Security and Cooperation in Europe [OSCE]). Russian troops were mandated to keep the peace in Moldova and South Ossetia by Russian-brokered cease-fires. In Moldova and in South Ossetia, however, Russian peacekeepers are either seen as being backers of one party or not wanting a final settlement—at least not one that would involve Russia losing strategic influence, military position, or the ability to classify troops and matériel as peacekeepers.

43. International Crisis Group, "The Congo's Transition Is Failing: Crisis in the Kivus," Africa Report 91 (March 30, 2005). Crisis Group's Africa Report 64, "Congo Crisis: Military Intervention in Ituri" (June 13, 2003), dealt specifically with MONUC I and the EU force intervention in Ituri province. Artemis was authorized by UN Security Council Resolution 1484 and operated on the ground in the Democratic Republic of Congo from June to September 2003. Crisis Group, "Pulling Back from the Brink in Congo," Africa Briefing 18 (July 7, 2004), dealt with the incapacity of MONUC II to contain or prevent an upswing in violence around Bukavu in 2004.

44. For analysis of the Darfur missions, see International Crisis Group, "Darfur's New Security Reality," Africa Report 134 (November 26, 2007); "Getting the UN into Darfur"; "To Save Darfur," Africa Report 105 (March 17, 2006); "The AU's Mission in Darfur: Bridging the Gaps," Africa Briefing 28 (July 6, 2005).

45. See François Grignon and Daniela Kroslak, "The Problem with Peacekeeping," *Current History,* April 2008. The authors are Africa Program Director and Deputy Director, respectively, of the International Crisis Group. See also Crisis Group, "Congo: Four Priorities for Sustainable Peace in Ituri," Africa Report 140 (May 13, 2008).

46. James Goodby, "Collective Security and the European Case," in *Managing Global Chaos*, edited by Chester A. Crocker and Fen Osler Hampson (Washington: U.S. Institute of Peace Press, 1996), p. 239.

47. See chapter 1 for a description of the scarifying events in Bosnia in 1995.

48. For background, see International Crisis Group, "Congo Crisis: Military Intervention in Ituri"; "Maintaining Momentum in the Congo: The Ituri Problem," Africa Report 84 (August 26, 2004).

49. International Crisis Group, "The AU's Mission in Darfur: Bridging the Gaps"; "Sudan: Now or Never in Darfur," Africa Report 80 (May 23, 2004).

50. Examples are the embargo placed in 1991 in relation to all former Yugoslav republics by Security Council Resolution 713; Liberia, where an embargo was imposed in 1992 and tightened in 2001; and more recently the extension of the embargo preventing militias from acquiring arms in the Congo. See, respectively, UN Security Council, "3009th Meeting, Resolution S/RES/713," September 25, 1991 (www.nato.int/ifor/un/u910925a.htm); Human Rights Watch, "Liberia: U.N. Arms Embargo Failing," November 5, 2001 (http://hrw.org/english/docs/2001/11/05/

liberi3243.htm); "DR Congo: Security Council Extends Arms Embargo and Monitoring Group," UN News, March 31, 2008 (www.un.org/apps/news/story.asp?NewsID= 26148&Cr=drc&Cr1=sanctions). For further examples of past and present arms embargoes, the Stockholm International Peace Research Institute lists all arms embargoes at www.sipri.org/contents/armstrad/embargoes.html.

51. See Jamie F. Metzl, "Rwandan Genocide and the International Law of Radio Jamming," *American Journal of International Law* 9, no. 4 (1997): 628–51; Alexander C. Dale, "Countering Hate Messages That Lead to Violence: The United Nations's Chapter VII Authority to Use Radio Jamming to Halt Incendiary Broadcasts," *Duke Journal of Comparative and International Law* 11, no. 1 (2001): 109–31.

Chapter Six

1. Wole Soyinka, Nigerian Nobel Laureate for Literature, quoted in *Los Angeles Times,* May 11, 1994.

2. For the full text of the Preamble, see www.un.org/aboutun/charter.

3. Adlai Stevenson, address to the Chicago Bar Association, June 1945, quoted in Stephen C. Schlesinger, *Act of Creation: The Founding of the United Nations* (Boulder, Colo.: Westview, 2003), p. 261.

4. The figure of 200 is cited by Thomas M. Franck, "Some Observations on the I.C.J.'s Procedural and Substantive Innovations," *American Journal of International Law* 81, no. 1 (1987): 116–21. He notes that customary norms of nonintervention are "adhered to, at best, only by some states, in some instances, and have been ignored . . . with impunity in at least two hundred cases." Herbert K. Tillema counts 690 "overt military interventions" during roughly the same period. See Tillema, "Risks of Battle and the Deadliness of War: International Armed Conflicts," paper presented to the International Studies Association, San Diego, April 16–29, 1996. The disparity between the two is at least in part accounted for by the inclusion in the latter of interventions sanctioned by the state in which intervention occurred, interventions into non-fully-autonomous states, and interventions justified under the terms of Article 51, as well as cases of UN-sanctioned interventions. Neither figure was calculated on the basis of any minimum thresholds for casualties, as most published counts of interstate war are.

5. An attempt by the United States to rely on "collective self-defense" to justify using military force on behalf of El Salvador against Nicaragua was rejected by the International Court of Justice (ICJ), taking both a narrow view of Article 51 and a wide view of Article 2(4) and their respective customary international law counterpart principles. See Military and Paramilitary Activities in and against Nicaragua *(Nicaragua v. United States of America)*, Judgment, ICJ, June 27, 1986; available at www.icj-cij.org. This case amply demonstrated, if this was necessary, the limits of the enforceability of international law, even if the preliminary obstacle of nonacceptance of the ICJ's jurisdiction is overcome: the United States refused to comply with a court order to pay reparations and was able to block any enforcement resolution attempted by Nicaragua in the Security Council. It also simply ignored the nonbinding resolu-

tion (A/RES/41/31), passed 94-3 by the General Assembly on November 3, 1986, urging it to comply.

6. Thomas M. Franck, "What Happens Now? The United Nations after Iraq," *American Journal of International Law* 97, no. 3 (2003): 607–20.

7. Adapted from International Crisis Behavior (ICB) data set, updated through 2005 (www.cidcm.umd.edu/icb), from Michael Brecher and Jonathan Wilkenfeld, *A Study of Crisis* (University of Michigan Press, 2000).

8. The most sophisticated quantitative research on peacekeeping suggests that, all things being equal, the deployment of peacekeepers reduces the risk of another war by 70 to 85 percent. Virginia Fortna, "Peace Operations: Futile or Vital?" paper commissioned by the United Nations Foundation for the work of the High-Level Panel on Threats, Challenges, and Change (January 2004).

9. Figures in Peter Wallensteen and Patrik Johansson, "Security Council Decisions in Perspective," in *The UN Security Council: From the Cold War to the 21st Century*, edited by David Malone (Boulder, Colo.: Lynne Rienner, 2004); and David Cortright and George A. Lopez, *The Sanctions Decade: Assessing UN Strategies in the 1990s* (Boulder, Colo.: Lynne Rienner, 2000).

10. Security Council Resolution 1368, S/RES/1368 (September 12, 2001).

11. As the International Commission on Intervention and State Sovereignty pointed out: see ICISS, *The Responsibility to Protect* (Ottawa: International Development Research Center, 2001), paragraphs 6.16–18. The High-Level Panel on Threats, Challenges, and Change put the point similarly robustly in *A More Secure World, Our Shared Responsibility* (United Nations, 2004), paragraph 202: "Step by step the Council and the wider international community have come to accept that, under Chapter VII and in pursuit of the emerging norm of an international responsibility to protect, it can always authorise military action to redress catastrophic internal wrongs if it is prepared to declare that the situation is a 'threat to international peace and security,' not especially difficult when breaches of international law are involved."

12. The full text of Article 51 makes clear that the Security Council was still intended to play an important supervisory and backup role in these cases: "Nothing in the present Charter shall impair the inherent right of individual or collective self-defence if an armed attack occurs against a Member of the United Nations, until the Security Council has taken measures necessary to maintain international peace and security. Measures taken by Members in the exercise of this right of self-defence shall be immediately reported to the Security Council and shall not in any way affect the authority and responsibility of the Security Council under the present Charter to take at any time such action as it deems necessary in order to maintain or restore international peace and security."

13. See, for example, Gareth Evans, "When Is It Right to Fight?" *Survival* 46 (Autumn 2004): 59–82. For another account of the debate, see, for example, Tarcisio Gazzini, *The Changing Rules on the Use of Force in International Law* (Manchester University Press, 2005), pp. 117–79.

14. On the role of regional organizations generally within the UN framework, see Ademola Abass, *Regional Organisations and the Development of Collective Security: Beyond Chapter VIII of the UN Charter* (Oxford: Hart Publishing, 2004). NATO has in recent years engaged in Security Council–authorized missions (IFOR in Bosnia, KFOR later in Kosovo, and ISAF in Afghanistan) and could properly be described as a Chapter VIII arrangement even though until now, apparently fearful that this would imply additional UN obligations, it has preferred not to think of itself in those terms, but rather as a collective self-defense pact. See inter alia Ove Bring, "Should NATO Take the Lead in Formulating a Doctrine on Humanitarian Intervention?" *NATO Review* 47, no. 3 (1999): 24-7; Antonia and Abram Chayes, *Planning for Intervention: International Cooperation in Conflict Management* (The Hague: Kluwer Law International, 1999), p. 19; Rosalyn Higgins, "Peace and Security: Achievement and Failure," *European Journal of International Law* 6, no. 3 (1995): 445.

15. UN General Assembly Resolution 377 of November 3, 1950, resolving "that if the Security Council, because of lack of unanimity of the permanent members, fails to exercise its primary responsibility for the maintenance of international peace and security in any case where there appears to be a threat to the peace, breach of the peace, or act of aggression, the General Assembly shall consider the matter immediately with a view to making appropriate recommendations to Members for collective measures, including in the case of a breach of the peace or act of aggression the use of armed force when necessary, to maintain or restore international peace and security."

16. See, for example, Commission on Global Governance (cochairs, Ingvar Carlsson and Shridath Ramphal), *Our Global Neighbourhood* (Oxford University Press, 1995); Kemal Dervis and Ceren Ozer, *A Better Globalization: Legitimacy, Governance, and Reform* (Washington, D.C.: Center for Global Development, 2005).

17. Allen Buchanan and Robert O. Keohane, "The Preventive Use of Force: A Cosmopolitan Institutional Proposal," *Ethics and International Affairs* 18.1 (Winter 2004): 1–22.

18. ICISS, *The Responsibility to Protect*, paragraph 6.21. The High-Level Panel similarly thought it appropriate to "ask the permanent members, in their individual capacities, to pledge themselves to refrain from the use of the veto in cases of genocide and large-scale human rights abuses." See *A More Secure World*, paragraph 256.

19. See the discussion in Michael Byers and Simon Chesterman, "Changing the Rules about Rules? Unilateral Humanitarian Intervention and the Future of International Law," in *Humanitarian Intervention: Ethical Legal and Political Dilemmas*, edited by J. L. Holzgrefe and Robert O. Keohane (Cambridge University Press, 2003), pp. 177–203.

20. Michael J Glennon, "Why the Security Council Failed," *Foreign Affairs* 82, no. 3 (2003): 16–35.

21. See Evans, "When Is It Right to Fight?" p. 64. Thomas Franck is also trenchant: "What, then, is the proper role for the lawyer? Surely, it is to stand tall for the rule of law. What this entails is self-evident. . . . When the politicians seek to bend the law, the lawyers must insist that they have broken it. . . . When the powerful are tempted to dis-

card the law, the lawyer must ask whether someday, if our omnipotence wanes, we may not need the law. Lawyers who do that may even be called traitors. But those who do not are traitors to their calling." See Franck, "What Happens Now?" p. 620.

22. Quote from "The Secretary-General's Address to the General Assembly, September 23, 2003"; available at www.un.org/apps/sg/sgstats.asp?nid=517 .

23. ICISS, *The Responsibility to Protect*, paragraph 6.14. See also High-Level Panel, *A More Secure World*, paragraph 198; the full text of the panel recommendations on the use of force is set out in chapter 2.

24. Independent International Commission on Kosovo (cochairs Richard Goldstone and Carl Tham), *The Kosovo Report: Conflict, International Response, Lessons Learned* (Oxford University Press, 2000).

25. These are essentially the headings employed by the High-Level Panel, *A More Secure World*, paragraph 56, picked up in turn by Secretary-General Annan in *In Larger Freedom: Toward Development, Security and Human Rights for All*, A/59/2005 (United Nations, 2005), paragraph 126.

26. On "just war" theory and its contemporary application, see Charles Guthrie and Michael Quinlan, *Just War—The Just War Tradition: Ethics in Modern Warfare* (London: Bloomsbury, 2007). On other traditions, see, for example, Sohail Hashmi, "Interpreting the Islamic Ethics of War and Peace," in *Islamic Political Ethics*, edited by Sohail Hashmi (Princeton University Press, 2002); Oliver P. Ramsbotham, "Islam, Christianity and Forcible Humanitarian Intervention," *Ethics and International Affairs* 12, no. 1 (1998): 81–102; Norman Soloman, "The Ethics of War in Judaism" (pp. 39–80), Torkel Brekke, "Between Prudence and Heroism: Ethics of War in the Hindu Tradition" (pp. 113–44), and Tessa Bartholomeusz, "In Defense of Dharma: Just War Ideology in Buddhist Sri Lanka" (pp. 145–56), all in *The Ethics of War in Asian Civilizations: A Comparative Perspective*, edited by Torkel Brekke (London: Routledge, 2005); and Elizabeth J. Harris, "Buddhism and the Justification of War: A Case Study from Sri Lanka" (pp. 93–108), Francis X. Clooney, S. J., "Pain but Not Harm: Some Classical Resources toward a Hindu Just War Theory" (pp. 109–25), Gurharpal Singh, "Sikhism and Just War" (pp. 126–38), all in *Just War in Comparative Perspective*, edited by Paul Robinson (Burlington, Vt.: Ashgate, 2003).

27. Paragraph 126.

28. High-Level Panel, *A More Secure World*, annex 1, recommendation 56(a).

29. ICISS, *The Responsibility to Protect*, Synopsis, p. xii.

30. On good international citizenship, see, for example, Nicholas Wheeler and Tim Dunne, "Good International Citizenship: A Third Way for British Foreign Policy," *International Affairs* 74, no. 4 (1998): 847–70; Paul Keal, "Can Foreign Policy Be Ethical?" in *Ethics and Foreign Policy*, edited by Paul Keal (Canberra: Allen and Unwin, 1992), pp. 12–13.

31. ICISS, *The Responsibility to Protect*, paragraphs 4.41–43, quoted in full in chapter 3, where this argument is discussed in more detail.

32. Ibid., paragraphs 6.36–40. This was the formula on which Lee Hamilton and I were able to find eventual agreement, ensuring that consensus was maintained in the final report. See the Introduction in this volume.

33. Thomas Franck, "Interpretation and Change in the Law of Humanitarian Intervention," in *Humanitarian Intervention*, edited by Holzgrefe and Keohane, pp. 212–14.

34. Byers and Chesterman, "Changing the Rules about Rules?" pp. 198, 203.

Chapter Seven

1. One of the most comprehensive and useful efforts to define such a strategy may be found in the UN Security Council, *Twelfth Progress Report of the Secretary-General on the United Nations Mission in Liberia* (UNMIL), S/2006/743, September 12, 2006, pp. 18–21, available at http://daccessdds.un.org/doc/UNDOC/GEN/N06/517/11/PDF/N0651711.pdf?OpenElement. This spells out (in Annex 1, pp. 18–21) multiple benchmarks—divided into categories of security, governance and the rule of law; economic revitalization, and infrastructure and basic services—relevant to the drawdown and ultimate withdrawal of the UNMIL mission.

2. Former U.S. congressman Howard Wolpe, who is a strong and articulate advocate of this approach, and his team have done some outstanding work in this respect in Burundi, the Democratic Republic of the Congo, and Liberia: see Howard Wolpe and Steve McDonald, "Democracy and Peace-Building: Re-thinking the Conventional Wisdom," *Round Table* 97, no. 134 (2008): 137–45.

3. In Somalia a U.S.-led coalition succeeded an initial UN-led peacekeeping mission and preceded another one; in Haiti the UN mission followed a U.S.-led entry.

4. All these cases (together with the cold war examples of Germany, Japan, and the Congo), and the lessons to be drawn from them, are discussed in the excellent—and not at all U.S.-centric—Rand series produced under the leadership of the highly experienced and competent former U.S. diplomat James Dobbins: see James Dobbins and others, *America's Role in Nation-Building: From Germany to Iraq* (Santa Monica, Calif.: Rand Corporation, 2003); James Dobbins and others, *The UN's Role in Nation-Building: From the Congo to Iraq* (Rand Corporation, 2005); and James Dobbins and others, *The Beginner's Guide to Nation-Building* (Rand Corporation, 2007). *The Beginner's Guide* is misleadingly titled: it is is much more than that and has been drawn on extensively in the preparation of this chapter.

5. Not least with the noncooperation of the Khmer Rouge in the whole process and the fear that it would attack the election process. See Gareth Evans, "Achieving Peace in Cambodia," address to The Hague Centennial Peace Conference, Melbourne, February 20, 1999; available at www.crisisgroup.org. See also Ken Berry, *Cambodia: From Red to Blue—Australia's Initiative for Peace* (Sydney: Allen and Unwin, 1997), chaps. 9–11; Dobbins and others, *The UN's Role*, chap. 5.

6. Dobbins and others, *The UN's Role*, pp. 245, 246.

7. Ibid., p. 250.

8. Paul Collier, Lisa Chauvet, and Haavard Hegre, "The Security Challenge in Conflict-Prone Countries," Copenhagen Consensus Challenge Paper (Copenhagen Business School, 2008); available at www.copenhagenconsensus.com.

9. International Crisis Group, "Reforming Afghanistan's Police," Asia Report 138 (August 30, 2007). This and other Crisis Group reports and briefings cited here are available at www.crisisgroup.org.

10. International Commission on Intervention and State Sovereignty (ICISS), *The Responsibility to Protect* (Ottawa: International Development Research Center, 2001), pp. 65–66.

11. Figures obtained from Geneva International Center for Humanitarian Demining, 2006 (www.gichd.ch), as quoted in John C. Kostelnick and others, "Cartographic Symbols for Humanitarian Demining," *Cartographic Journal* 45, no. 1 (2008): 18–31, at p. 18.

12. See "Executive Summary," in *Landmine Monitor Report 2007: Toward a Mine-Free World* (Ottawa, 2007), pp. 39–40; available at www.icbl.org/lm/2007/executive_summary.

13. Donald Steinberg, "A Seat at the Table: The Role of Displaced Persons in Peace Talks and Peacebuilding," address at U.S. Institute of Peace, Washington, D.C., December 14, 2007, arguing the case for greater consultation with IDPs on this and other issues.

14. See, for example, Julie Kim, "Bosnia and the European Union Military Force (EUFOR): Post-NATO Peacekeeping," Report RS21774 (Congressional Research Service, Library of Congress, January 15, 2008); "Statement by Carla Del Ponte, Prosecutor, International Criminal Tribunal for the former Yugoslavia, to the Security Council," The Hague, December 10, 2007; Steven Woehrel, "Conditions on U.S. Aid to Serbia," Report RS21686 (Congressional Research Service, January 7, 2008). See also International Crisis Group, "Serbia: Spinning Its Wheels," Europe Briefing 39 (May 23, 2005). On the arrest of Karadzic on July 21, 2008, made as this book was going to press, see the ICTY Prosecutor's press statement at www.un.org/icty/pressreal/2008/pr1274e.htm.

15. For a specific discussion of DDR in Afghanistan, see International Crisis Group, "Disarmament and Reintegration in Afghanistan," Asia Report 65 (September 30, 2003); "Afghanistan: Getting Disarmament Back on Track," Asia Briefing 35 (February 23, 2005).

16. See, for example, International Crisis Group, "Congo: Four Priorities for Sustainable Peace in Ituri," Africa Report 140 (May 13, 2008); "Back to the Brink in the Congo," Africa Briefing 21 (December 17, 2004).

17. International Crisis Group, "Aceh: Post-Conflict Complications," Asia Report 139 (October 4, 2007); "Aceh: So Far, So Good," Asia Briefing 44 (December 13, 2005).

18. See João Gomes Porto and Imogen Parsons, *Sustaining the Peace in Angola: An Overview of Current Demobilisation, Disarmament and Reintegration*, Paper 27 (Bonn: Bonn International Center for Conversion, 2003).

19. See International Crisis Group, "Iraq: Building a New Security Structure," Middle East Report 20 (December 23, 2003). For the wider security implications of the badly planned demobilization process and suggestions how to rectify the situation, see Crisis Group, "Iraq's Civil War, the Sadrists and the Surge," Middle East Report 72 (February 7, 2008); "The Next Iraqi War? Sectarianism and Civil Conflict," Middle East Report 52 (February 27, 2006).

20. See, for example, International Crisis Group, "An Army for Kosovo?" Europe Report 174 (July 28, 2006); "What Happened to the KLA?" Europe Report 88 (March 3, 2000).

21. Dobbins and others, *The UN's Role*, pp. 78–79.

22. See, for example, International Crisis Group, "Dealing with Savimbi's Ghost: The Security and Humanitarian Challenges in Angola," Africa Report 58 (February 26, 2003).

23. For the 1999 UN Security Council discussions of the process, see "Security Council Discusses Disarmament, Demobilization and Reintegration of Ex-Combatants in Peacekeeping Environment" (www.reliefweb.int/w/rwb.nsf/s/42723E0E93ABCB39C12567A90048CA95). See also Dobbins and others, *The UN's Role*, chap. 6.

24. See Dobbins and others, *Beginner's Guide*, p. 31.

25. See, for example, John Williamson, "The Disarmament, Demobilisation and Reintegration of Child Soldiers: Social and Psychological Transformation in Sierra Leone," *Intervention* 4, no. 3 (2006): 185–205; David M. Rosen, *Armies of the Young: Child Soldiers in War and Terrorism* (Rutgers University Press, 2005).

26. See, for example, International Crisis Group, "Beyond Victimhood: Women's Peacebuilding in Sudan, Congo and Uganda," Africa Report 112 (June 28, 2006).

27. U.K. Department for International Development, *Understanding and Supporting Security Sector Reform* (London, 2002), p. 7.

28. For an assessment of recent literature on the failures of insitutional intelligence, see Simon Chesterman, "I Spy," *Survival* 50, no 3 (2008).

29. See Jane Chanaa, *Security Sector Reform: Issues, Challenges and Prospects*, Adelphi Paper 344 (International Institute for Strategic Studies and Oxford University Press, 2002); also Development Assistance Committee, "Security System Reform and Governance" (Paris: OECD, 2004).

30. See Michael Lund, *Preventing and Mitigating Violent Conflicts: A Guide for Practitioners* (Washington, D.C.: Creative Associates International, 1996), pp. 3:78, 3:90.

31. See International Crisis Group, "Rebuilding Liberia: Prospects and Perils," Africa Report 75 (January 30, 2004).

32. In part because of the success of the U.K. military adviser, the International Crisis Group recommended that "watchdogs" be placed in critical areas of government like customs and the health fund. Crisis Group, "Macedonia's Public Secret: How Corruption Drags the Country Down," Europe Report 133 (August 14, 2002).

33. See, for example, David Greenwood and Sander Huisman, *Transparency and Accountability of Police Forces, Security Services and Intelligence Services* (Geneva Center for the Democratic Control of Armed Forces [DCAF], 2004); available at www.dcaf.ch/publications.

34. The need for police reform was discussed for Afghanistan in International Crisis Group, "Reforming Afghanistan's Police," Asia Report 138 (August 30, 2007); for Haiti in "Haiti: Prison Reform and the Rule of Law," Latin America/Caribbean Briefing 15 (May 4, 2007), and in "Spoiling Security in Haiti," Latin America/Caribbean Report 13 (May 31, 2005); for Iraq in "Iraq: Building a New Security Structure"; for Timor-Leste in "Timor-Leste: Security Sector Reform," Asia Report 143 (January 17, 2008); and for Bosnia in "Bosnia's Stalled Police Reform: No Progress, No EU," Europe Report 164 (September 6, 2005).

35. For the case of Burundi, see Human Rights Watch, "Emptying the Hills: Regroupment in Burundi," June 2000 (www.hrw.org/reports/2000/burundi2/); Macedonia is discussed in International Crisis Group, "Moving Macedonia toward Self-Sufficiency: A New Security Approach for NATO and the EU," Balkans Report 135 (November 15, 2002), p. 7; for an evaluation of the Royal Ulster Constabulary, see Human Rights Watch, "To Serve without Favor: Policing, Human Rights, and Accountability," May 1997 (www.hrw.org/reports/1997/uk1); and for the Patten Report, see Independent Commission on Policing for Northern Ireland, *A New Beginning: Policing in Northern Ireland* (London: Northern Ireland Office, 1999); available at www.nio.gov.uk/a_new_beginning_in_policing_in_northern_ireland.pdf.

36. Dobbins and others, *Beginner's Guide,* pp. 135–38, and chap. 6 generally. Examples of the first category are Congo and Côte d'Ivoire; of the second, Kosovo and East Timor; and the third, Afghanistan and Iraq.

37. See ICISS, *The Responsibility to Protect,* p. 43; International Crisis Group, "Central African Republic: Anatomy of a Phantom State," Africa Report 136 (December 13, 2007).

38. Dobbins and others, *Beginner's Guide,* p. 189. For all the ambition of its title, chapter 6 is an excellent, balanced account of the pitfalls as well as opportunities for achieving improved general systems of governance in nation-building missions.

39. International Crisis Group, "Why the Bosnian Elections Must Be Postponed," Europe Report 14 (August 14, 1996).

40. Richard N. Haass, *The Opportunity: America's Moment to Alter History's Course* (New York: PublicAffairs, 2005), p. 73. The excellent Institute for Democracy and Electoral Assistance (IDEA), in its many publications devoted to making democracy and its electoral systems work better, has also made very clear the need for caution about elections being held too early. See, for example, Andrew Ellis, Paul Guerin, and Ayman Ayoub, "Effective Electoral Assistance—Moving from Event-Based Support to Process Support," conference report and conclusions (Stockholm: IDEA, 2006); *Electoral System Design: the New International IDEA Handbook* (2005); both available at www.idea.int.

41. Timothy Garton Ash, "A Little Democracy Is a Dangerous Thing—So Let's Have More of It," *The Guardian*, August 3, 2006.

42. Governor Al Smith, quoted in the *New York Times*, February 4, 1923, and many times since. On the South Asian cases, see International Crisis Group, "Elections, Democracy and Stability in Pakistan," Asia Report 137 (July 31, 2007); "Restoring Democracy in Bangladesh," Asia Report 151 (April 28, 2008).

43. William Maley, "Democratic Governance and Post-Conflict Transitions," *Chicago Journal on International Law* 6, no. 2 (2006): 683–701.

44. See ICISS, *The Responsibility to Protect*, paragraphs 5.25–31.

45. Tore Rose, "Integrating Conflict Prevention and Peacebuilding into United Nations Development Assistance Frameworks," International Peacebuilding Assistance Discussion Paper 2 (Geneva: WSP International, October 2005), p. 9; available at www.interpeace.org. This paper was commissioned by WSP International after a Lessons Learned workshop on Integrating Conflict Sensitivity into UN Planning and Programming, Turin, May 23–24, 2005.

46. Kofi Annan, "The Situation in Afghanistan and Its Implications for International Peace and Security, Report of the Secretary-General," A/56/875–S/2002/278 (United Nations, March 18, 2002), paragraph 98(d); available at www.unama-afg.org/docs/_UN-Docs/_repots-SG/2002/2002-278.pdf.

47. See House of Representatives, Committee on Foreign Affairs, Subcommittee on the Middle East and South Asia, "Strategic Chaos and Taliban Resurgence in Afghanistan," testimony by Mark L. Schneider, Senior Vice President, International Crisis Group, 110 Cong. 2 sess.(April 2, 2008); available at www.crisisgroup.org/home/index.cfm?id=5370. See also International Crisis Group, "Afghanistan: The Need for International Resolve," Asia Report 145 (February 6, 2008); "Countering Afghanistan's Insurgency: No Quick Fixes," Asia Report 123 (November 2, 2006); "Disarmament and Reintegration in Afghanistan," Asia Report 65 (September 30, 2003).

48. Samantha Power, *Chasing the Flame: Sergio Vieira de Mello and the Fight to Save the World* (London: Allen Lane, 2008), pp. 307, 313.

49. ICISS, *The Responsibility to Protect*, paragraph 5.13.

50. See, for example, Gareth Evans, *Cooperating for Peace* (Sydney: Allen and Unwin, 1995), p. 56; ICISS, *The Responsibility to Protect*, paragraph 5.14; Dobbins and others, *Beginner's Guide,* chap. 4.

51. Dobbins and others, pp. 102–07.

52. These different court options for prosecuting mass atrocity crimes are discussed in the context of prevention in chapter 4 and reaction in chapter 5.

53. Robert C. Johansen, "Peace and Justice? The Contribution of International Judicial Processes to Peacebuilding," paper prepared for the International Studies Association Annual Convention, Chicago, March 3, 2007.

54. For a wealth of material on this subject, see the website of the International Center for Transitional Justice, www.ictj.org. See also Edel Hughes, William A. Schabas, and Ramesh Thakur, eds., *Atrocities and International Accountability: Beyond Ttransitional Justice* (Tokyo: United Nations University Press, 2007); Mark A. Drumbl, *Atroc-*

ity, Punishment, and International Law (Cambridge University Press, 2007); Naomi Roht-Arriaza and Javier Mariezcurrena, eds., *Transitional Justice in the Twenty-First Century: Beyond Truth versus Justice* (Cambridge University Press, 2006); Steven R. Ratner and Jason S. Abrams, *Accountability for Human Rights Atrocities in International Law: Beyond the Nuremberg Legacy,* 2nd ed. (Oxford University Press, 2001).

55. Naomi Roht-Arriaza, "The New Landscape of Transitional Justice" (www.cambridge.org/catalogue/catalogue.asp?isbn=9780521860109&ss=exc). If the postponement course is taken it is crucial that steps also be taken, by those in a position to do so, to gather and preserve evidence, which can be very difficult years after the event.

56. Dobbins and others, *Beginner's Guide,* pp. 94–95.

57. Frank Meyer, "Complementing Complementarity," *International Criminal Law Review* 6, no. 4 (2006): 551.

58. See Roman David, "From Prague to Baghdad: Lustration Systems and Their Political Effects," *Government and Opposition* 41, no. 3 (2006): 347–72; Natalia Letki, "Lustration and Democratisation in East-Central Europe," *Europe-Asia Studies* 54, no. 4 (2002): 529–52; Mark Gibney, "Prosecuting Human Rights Violations from a Previous Regime: The East European Experience," *East European Quarterly* 31 (1997): 93–110.

59. Neil J. Kritz, "Coming to Terms with Atrocities: A Review of Accountability Mechanisms for Mass Violations of Human Rights," *Law and Contemporary Problems* 59, no. 4 (1997): 139.

60. "David Little argues that the role of reconciliation in restorative justice is rooted in the concept of forgiveness. He lists five features of forgiveness that are essential to restoring relationships and, thus, the process of reconciliation: 1) There must be a transaction between the 'forgiver' and the 'forgivee'; 2) There must be a common acknowledgement between the two parties regarding the wrongdoing and the penalty; 3) There must be contrition on the part of the 'forgivee'; 4) The 'forgiver' must annul the fitting punishment; and 5) The 'forgivee' must accept the obligations of the 'forgiver' by going out and restoring relations with others. The key to this model of restorative justice is that it is voluntary. It cannot be imposed by peace agreements, officials, or outside powers. Both the perpetrator and the victim must acknowledge the wrongdoing, accept the consequences that follow from it, and commit to moving forward together." David Little, "A Different Kind of Justice: Dealing with Human Rights Violations in Transitional Societies," *Ethics and International Affairs* 13 (1999): 65–80, as described in Craig Kauffman, "Transitional Justice in Guatemala: Linking the Past and the Future," paper prepared for the International Studies Association (ISA)-South Conference, Miami, November 3–5, 2005; available at www.isa-south.org/2005% 20Miami%20Papers_files/Craig_Kauffman.pdf. See also David A. Crocker, "Reckoning with Past Wrongs: A Normative Framework," *Ethics and International Affairs* 13 (1999): 43–64.

61. See Nick Grono, "Negotiating Peace and Justice: Considering Accountability and Deterrence in Peace Processes," presentation to the international conference on

Building a Future on Peace and Justice, Nuremberg, June 26, 2007; available at (www.crisisgroup.org/home/index.cfm?id=4922&l=2).

62. Kritz, p. 143.

63. The truth commission ended in October 2004 with the dissemination of its final report, although the special court continues to operate. See Hughes, Schabas, and Thakur, *Atrocities and International Accountability*, pp. 3–4.

64. See Citizens for Global Solutions, *"Q&A: What Is the International Criminal Court"* (www.globalsolutions.org/issues/international_criminal_court/Q_and_A).

65. *Final Report on the Implementation of the Japanese Canadian Redress Agreement, 1988* (Ottawa: Japanese Canadian Redress Secretariat and Canadian Heritage, November 1997), p. 5.

66. For the full text of Prime Minister Rudd's historic apology see Parliament of Australia, House of Representatives, "Apology to Australia's Indigenous Peoples" (www.aph.gov.au/house/Rudd_Speech.pdf). See also Australian Government, Culture and Recreation Portal, "Sorry Day" (www.cultureandrecreation.gov.au/articles/indigenous/sorry).

67. David Crane, "Dancing with the Devil: Prosecuting West Africa's Warlords: Building Initial Prosecutorial Strategy for an International Tribunal after Third World Armed Conflicts," *Case Western Reserve Journal of International Law* 37, no. 1 (2005): 5.

68. "Gacaca" roughly translates as "justice on the grass" because the courts met outdoors. The vast majority of gacaca investigations began only in 2005. The conventional justice system will still hear cases of category 1 prisoners: those suspected of organizing, planning, instigating, supervising, and leading genocide.

69. The community has the power to reduce penalties if the accused confesses and apologizes.

70. There are approximately 80,000 people awaiting trial in Rwanda's jails, and it is thought that, at the current slow pace, many could die before their cases are heard.

71. Since its inception in 1994, the tribunal has indicted eighty-one people for genocide-related crimes; twenty people have been convicted, and three have been aquitted. See also International Crisis Group, "The International Criminal Tribunal for Rwanda: Time for Pragmatism," Africa Report 69 (September 26, 2003).

72. See Amnesty International, "Rwanda: Gacaca: A Question of Justice," December 17, 2002 (http://web.amnesty.org/library/index/engafr470072002); International Crisis Group, "Rwanda at the End of Transition: A Necessary Political Liberalisation," Africa Report 53 (November 13, 2002), p. 26.

73. Richard Fanthorpe, Alice Jay, and Victor Kalie Kamara, "Sierra Leone: A Review of the Chiefdom Governance Reform Program, Incorporating an Analysis of Chiefdom Administration in Sierra Leone," internal paper (London: U.K. Department for International Development, November 2002).

74. See International Crisis Group, "Liberia and Sierra Leone: Rebuilding Failed States," Africa Report 87 (December 8, 2004), p. 24.

75. International Crisis Group, "Building Judicial Independence in Pakistan," Asia Report 86 (November 10, 2004), p. 18.

76. See International Crisis Group, "Timor-Leste's Displacement Crisis," Asia Report 148 (March 31, 2008).

77. See Dobbins and others, *Beginner's Guide*, pp. 125–26; also see David Romano, "Whose House Is This Anyway? IDP and Refugee Return in Post-Saddam Iraq," *Journal of Refugee Studies* 18, no. 4 (2005): 430–53.

78. See ICISS, *The Responsibility to Protect*, p. 42.

79. See, for example, International Crisis Group, "A Half-Hearted Welcome: Refugee Return to Croatia," Europe Report 138 (December 13, 2002).

80. As happened in the case of Croatia; see Human Rights Watch, "Broken Promises: Impediments to Refugee Return to Croatia," September 2003 (www.hrw.org/reports/2003/croatia0903).

81. On the issue of socially owned property, see, for example, International Crisis Group, "The Continuing Challenge of Refugee Return in Bosnia and Herzegovina," Europe Report 137 (December 13, 2002).

82. This problem was raised by the International Crisis Group, particularly in the Burundi context, in "Refugees and Displaced Persons in Burundi—Defusing the Land Time-Bomb," Africa Report 70 (October 7, 2003).

83. See as an example the website of the Bosnian Commission for Real Property Claims of Displaced Persons and Refugees, at www.law.kuleuven.ac.be/ipr/eng/CRPC_Bosnia/CRPC/new/en/main.htm, which also provides a link to the relevant section of the Dayton Agreement.

84. For background, see Daniela Heimerl, "The Return of Refugees and Internally Displaced Persons: From Coercion to Sustainability?" *International Peacekeeping* 12, no. 3 (2005): 377–90. More generally, on managing refugee return and the role of the UN High Commissioner for Refugees (UNHCR), see UNHCR, *Handbook for Repatriation and Reintegration Activities* (Geneva, 2004); available at www.unhcr.org/partners/PARTNERS/411786694.pdf.

85. This short section draws extensively, again, on Dobbins and others, *Beginner's Guide*, which in chapter 7 on "Economic Stabilization" and chapter 9 on "Development" identifies in short compass just about everything of which peacebuilders should be aware in planning and implementing their economic role.

86. See International Crisis Group, "Liberia and Sierra Leone: Rebuilding Failed States"; "Liberia's Elections: Necessary but Not Sufficient," Africa Report 98 (September 7, 2005); Mike McGovern, "The Fourth Leg," International Aid Report (Crisis Group, January 2006).

87. Dobbins and others, *Beginner's Guide*, p. 246.

88. International Crisis Group, "Beyond Victimhood: Women's Peacebuilding in Sudan, Congo and Uganda," Africa Report 112 (June 28, 2006). See also Jackie Kirk, "Promoting a Gender-Just Peace: The Roles of Women Teachers in Peacebuilding and Reconstruction," *Gender and Development* 12, no. 3 (2004): 50–59, in particular p. 52.

89. See, inter alia, Isabelle Roger, "Education for Children during Armed Conflicts and Post-conflict Reconstruction," *Disarmament Forum*, no. 3 (2002): 48, available at www.unidir.org/pdf/articles/pdf-art1731.pdf; David Hamburg, *Preventing Genocide: Practical Steps toward Early Detection and Effective Action* (Boulder, Colo.: Paradigm);

David A. Hamburg and Beatrix A. Hamburg, *Learning to Live Together: Preventing Hatred and Violence in Child and Adolescent Development* (Oxford University Press, 2004).

90. Roger, "Education for Children."

91. See UN General Assembly, "2005 World Summit Outcome," A/RES/60/1 (October 24, 2005), paragraphs 97–105; "The Peacebuilding Commission," A/Res/60/180 (December 30, 2005); S/Res/1645 (December 20, 2005).

92. See High-Level Panel on Threats, Challenges and Change, *A More Secure World: Our Shared Responsibility* (United Nations, 2004), paragraphs 261–69; recommendations 82–85.

93. The discussion in this section draws heavily on that thirty-one-page report, one of whose principal authors was a key High-Level Panel staffer, Bruce Jones. See NYU Center on International Cooperation (CIC) and International Peace Institute (IPI), "Taking Stock, Looking Forward: A Strategic Review of the Peacebuilding Commission" (April 2008); available at www.ipacademy.org/asset/file/305/PBCsrev08.pdf.

Chapter Eight

1. Quoted in Samantha Power, "United It Wobbles: Should We Blame the U.N. for Its Shortcomings, or the Countries That Make Up the World Body?" *Washington Post*, January 7, 2007; available at www.washingtonpost.com/wp-dyn/content/article/2007/01/05/AR2007010500116.html.

2. For UN core function employees, see UN General Assembly, "Composition of the Secretariat—Report of the Secretary-General," A/62/315 (August 31, 2007), p. 37, figure I; for costs see UN General Assembly, "Resolutions Adopted by the General Assembly—62/235. Programme Budget for the Biennium 2006–2007," A/RES/62/235 A–B (January 16, 2008), pp. 1–4. For New York Police Department personnel figures, see "Frequently Asked Questions" (www.nyc.gov/html/nypd/html/faq/faq_police.shtml#1), and for costs see Office of Management and Budget, *City of New York Executive Budget Fiscal Year 2009* (May 2008), p. 27; available at http://home2.nyc.gov/html/records/pdf/govpub/3900sum5_08.pdf. Excluded for present purposes from the "UN system" figures are the Bretton Woods institutions—the World Bank and the International Monetary Fund—which between them employ around 11,000 people and spend over $3 billion annually.

3. For total UN system cost, see United Nations, "Is the United Nations Good Value for Money?" in *Image and Reality: Questions and Answers about the United Nations* (May 2001); available at www.un.org/geninfo/ir/index.asp?id=150. For Wall Street figures, see David Ellis, "Wall Street Bonuses Down, but Not Out," *CNNMoney.com*, January 18, 2008 (http://money.cnn.com/2008/01/18/news/companies/bonuses/index.htm).

4. For total UN employees, see Chief Executives Board for Coordination, High-Level Committee on Management, "Headcount of Field Staff Available as of 31 December 2006 for the Cost-Sharing of Field Costs of the UN Security Management

System," UN document CEB/2007/HLCM/30 (November 6, 2007), p. 5. Disney, as of December 13, 2007, employed 137,000 people worldwide, 100,000 at its resorts and theme parks; see *The Walt Disney Company 2007 Annual Report* (Burbank Calif., 2008), pp. 9, 23; available at http://amedia.disney.go.com/investorrelations/annual_reports/WDC-AR-2007.pdf. Starbucks, as of September 30, 2007, employed 172,000 people worldwide (see http://media.corporate-ir.net/media_files/irol/99/ 99518/200710K.pdf, p. 7), although this number has since slightly reduced (see Alex Beam, "A Bitter-Tasting Jolt for Starbucks," *International Herald Tribune*, July 8, 2008). McDonald's employs some 1,600,000 systemwide in directly owned stores and franchises (see www.mcdonalds.com/corp/invest/pub/2007_annual_report.html).

5. For current peacekeeping numbers, see "Monthly Summary of Contributors of Military and Police Personnel" (www.un.org/Depts/dpko/dpko/contributors). See also the discussion of UN peacekeeping in chapters 5 and 7 of this volume. For the UN peacekeeping budget for 2007–08, see "Fact Sheet: United Nations Peacekeeping" (www.un.org/Depts/dpko/factsheet.pdf). The Iraq War is expected to cost the U.S. government $158.2 billion in fiscal year 2008: Amy Belasco, "The Cost of Iraq, Afghanistan, and Other Global War on Terror Operations since 9/11," Report RL33110 (Congressional Research Service, updated June 23, 2008), pp. 21, 24, available at www.fas.org/sgp/crs/natsec/RL33110.pdf.

6. Chapter 7, note 3.

7. See Human Security Center, *Human Security Report 2005: War and Peace in the 21st Century* (Oxford University Press, 2005), and its successor reports, *Human Security Brief 2006* (University of British Columbia, 2006) and *Human Security Brief 2007* (Human Security Report Project, Simon Fraser University, 2007), all available at www.hsrgroup.org.

8. James Dobbins and others, *The UN's Role in Nation-Building: From the Congo to Iraq* (Rand Corporation, 2005), p. 26.

9. For the recommendation to establish an ECPS (Executive Committee for Peace and Security) Information and Strategic Analysis Secretariat—EISAS—see the Brahimi Report: *Report of the Panel on United Nations Peace Operations*, A/55/305-S/2000/809 (United Nations, August 17, 2000), paragraphs 68–75. On the fate of the proposal, see William J. Durch and others, *The Brahimi Report and the Future of UN Peace Operations* (Washington, D.C.: Henry L. Stimson Center, 2003), pp. 38–40; available at www.stimson.org/fopo/pdf/BR-CompleteVersion-Dec03.pdf. See also Simon Chesterman, "Does the UN Have Intelligence?" *Survival* 48, no. 3 (2006): 154; Thorsten Benner and Philipp Rotmann, "Learning to Learn? UN Peacebuilding and the Challenges of Building a Learning Organization," *Journal of Intervention and State-building* 2, no. 1 (2008): 51.

10. Dobbins and others, *The UN's Role,* p. 26. On the problem of declining Western support for UN peace operations, see Alex J. Bellamy and Paul D.Williams, "The West and Contemporary Peace Operations," *Journal of Peace Research* (forthcoming).

11. See International Crisis Group, "Congo: Four Priorities for Sustainable Peace in Ituri," Africa Report 140 (May 13, 2008); "Congo: Bringing Peace to North Kivu," Africa Report 133 (October 31, 2007); and "Congo: Consolidating the Peace," Africa Report 128 (July 5, 2007), all available at www.crisisgroup.org.

12. See the lead to chapter 9 below.

13. Dobbins and others, *The UN's Role*, chap. 2, from which this account and assessment of the United Nations Operation in the Congo (ONUC) mission is immediately derived. See also, among many others, Brian Urquhart, *Ralph Bunche: An American Odyssey* (New York: W. W. Norton, 1993), and Marrack Goulding, "The Evolution of United Nations Peacekeeping," *International Affairs* 69, no. 3 (1993): 451–64.

14. Shashi Tharoor, "Is the United Nations Still Relevant?" speech delivered to the Asia Society, Hong Kong, June 14, 2004; available at www.asiasociety.org/speeches/tharoor04.html.

15. Among the most important recent packages of proposed reforms are those presented by the High-Level Panel on Threats, Challenges and Change, *A More Secure World: Our Shared Responsibility*, A/59/565 (United Nations, December 2, 2004); Low-Level Panel, *Practical Steps to a More Effective and Efficient United Nations* (United Nations, February 6, 2006), available at www.lowlevelpanel.org/uploads/report_internal_UN_reform.pdf; and Four Nations Initiative on Governance and Management of the UN, *Towards a Compact: Proposals for Improved Governance and Management of the United Nations Secretariat* (Stockholm: September 2007), available at www.the4ni.org.

16. Most important, recently those in High-Level Panel, *A More Secure World*, and Kofi Annan, *In Larger Freedom: Towards Security Development, and Human Rights for All*, A/59/2005 (United Nations, March 21, 2005).

17. See also the discussion of the veto issue, and the associated issue of possible new institutional arrangements to bypass the UN Security Council, in chapter 6 in this volume, text at footnote 14.

18. Robert Kagan, *The Return of History and the End of Dreams* (London: Atlantic Books, 2008); Senator John McCain, address on U.S. foreign policy, Hoover Institution, Stanford University, May 1, 2007; available at http://media.hoover.org/documents/McCain_05-01-07.pdf.

19. Good discussions of the weaknesses of the League of Democracies proposal include Morton H. Halperin and Ted Piccone, "Doomed to Fail?" *International Herald Tribune*, June 6, 2008, p. 6; Edward Luce, "The Neo-Cons' Black and White World," *Financial Times*, June 2, 2008, p. 10; Mark Mazower, "America Needs the United Nations," *Financial Times*, May 29, 2008, p. 11.

20. UN Charter, Chapter VI, Article 33(1) and Chapter VIII, Article 53(1). As already noted in chapter 6 of this volume, in relation to the military role of regional organizations, the authorization of the Security Council is required for any enforcement action.

21. As discussed in chapter 6, footnote 12.

22. On the League of Arab States, see its website (www.arableagueonline.org/las/english/level1_en.jsp?level1_id=1) and, for example, Joseph Mayton, "Is the Arab League Still Viable?" *Middle East Times*, March 12, 2008, available at www.metimes.com/International/2008/03/12/is_the_arab_league_still_viable/1219/; on the Organization of American States, see its website (www.oas.org) and, for example, Elizabeth Spehar, "The Role of the Organization of American States in Conflict Prevention," *International Journal on Minority and Group Rights* 8, no. 1 (2001): 61–70; on the Commonwealth of Independent States, see its website (www.cisstat.com/eng/cis.htm) and, for example, Roy Allison, "Regionalism, Regional Structures and Security Management in Central Asia," *International Affairs* 80, no. 3 (2004): 463–83; on the Association of Southeast Asian Nations, see its website (www.aseansec.org) and, for example, Helen Nesadurai, "The Association of Southeast Asian Nations (ASEAN)," *New Political Economy* 13, no. 2 (2008): 225–39; on the ASEAN Regional Forum, see its website (www.aseanregionalforum.org) and, for example, G. V. C. Naidu, "Multilateralism and Regional Security: Can the ASEAN Regional Forum Really Make a Difference?" *East-West Centre Asia Pacific Issues*, no. 45 (August 2000), available at www.eastwestcenter.org/fileadmin/stored/pdfs/api045.pdf; on the Pacific Islands Forum, see its website (www.forumsec.org.fj) and, for example, Asian Development Bank and Commonwealth Secretariat, *Toward a New Pacific Regionalism* (Manila, 2005), available at www.adb.org/Documents/Reports/Pacific-Regionalism; on the South Asian Association for Regional Cooperation, see its website (www.saarcsec.org) and, for example, Dwarika Dhungel, "South Asian Association for Regional Co-operation (SAARC): Prospects for Development," *Pakistan Development Review* 43, no. 4, part II (2004): 933–41, available at www.pide.org.pk/pdf/PDR/2004/4/PartII/Dwarika%20Dhungel.pdf; on the Shanghai Cooperation Organization, see its website (www.sectsco.org) and, for example, Henry Plater-Zyberk, "Who's Afraid of the SCO?" Central Asian Series 07/09 (Shrivenham, U.K.: Conflict Studies Research Center, March 2007), available at www.defac.ac.uk/colleges/csrc/document-listings/ca/07(09)HPZ.pdf.

23. See generally the Council's website, www.coe.int; for recent PACE activity, see "Council of Europe: Harsh Rhetoric Emerges from Summer Session," Radio Free Europe, June 26, 2008, available at www.rferl.org.

24. See, for example, Laurie Gorman, "The Implications of Regional Peace Operations on United Nations Capacity for Peacekeeping," *The Pearson Papers* 11, no. 1 (2008):1–19.

25. The EU's GDP ($16.8 trillion) and population (495 million) are higher than those of the United States ($13.8 trillion, 304 million); for current GDPs, see www.imf.org, and for populations, see https://www.cia.gov/library/publications/the-world-factbook/index.html.

26. Patten's comment was made on the occasion of the launch of the European Commission's "Wider Europe" communication, March 2003.

27. On the Göteborg Program, and the EU's role in conflict prevention more generally, see Benita Ferrero-Waldner (European Commissioner for External Relations

and European Neighborhood Policy), "Conflict Prevention: Looking to the Future," address to the Conflict Prevention Partnership Dialogue on "Five Years after Göteborg: The European Union and Its Conflict Prevention Potential," Brussels, September 12, 2006, available at http://ec.europa.eu/world/enp/speeches_en.htm; David Hamburg, *Preventing Genocide: Practical Steps toward Early Detection and Effective Action* (Boulder: Colo.: Paradigm, 2008), chap. 14, pp. 227–44; also Emma J. Stewart, "Capabilities and Coherence? The Evolution of European Union Conflict Prevention," *European Foreign Affairs Review* 13, no. 2 (2008): 229–53. On institutional arrangements across the whole crisis prevention and management spectrum, see Crisis Group, "EU Crisis Response Capability Revisited," Europe Report 160 (January 17, 2005); available, as are other Crisis Group reports and briefings cited here, at www.crisisgroup.org.

28. Jim Cloos, "Conflict Prevention as an Instrument in the EU's Security Toolbox," in *Development, Security and Conflict Prevention: Anna Lindh Programme on Conflict Prevention 2005*, edited by Anders Melbourn (Hedemora, Sweden: Gidlunds förlag, 2005), p. 14.

29. See Council of the European Union, "The European Consensus," 14820/05 (Brussels, November 22, 2005), available at http://ec.europa.eu/development/icenter/ repository/eu_consensus_en.pdf; "The Cotonou Agreement," June 23, 2000 (www.acpsec.org/en/conventions/cotonou/accord1.htm), and "Information Note on the Revision of the Cotonou Agreement" (http://ec.europa.eu/development/icenter/ repository/negociation_20050407_en.pdf). See also European Commission External Cooperation Programs, "Democracy: More than a Question of Choice" (http://ec.europa.eu/europeaid/what/governance-democracy/democracy/index_en.htm).

30. For more on the ESS, which was adopted at the Brussels Council in December 2003, see Council of the European Union, "A Secure Europe in a Better World—The European Security Strategy" (www.consilium.europa.eu/showPage.asp?id= 266&lang=en&mode=g).

31. On the ESS and mini-lateral engagement, see Antonio Missiroli, "Revisiting the European Security Strategy—Beyond 2008," Policy Brief (Brussels: European Policy Center, April 2008); available at www.epc.eu/TEWN/pdf/835822279_ Revisiting%20the%20ESS.pdf. On the special representatives, see http:// consilium.europa.eu/cms3_fo/showPage.asp?id=263&lang=en&mode=g.

32. This "Quartet Minus Three" description was coined by Arab League Secretary-General Amr Moussa. See Chris Patten, "Cousins and Strangers: America, Britain and Europe in a New Century," Brookings Center on the United States and Europe Briefing, Brookings Institution, February 3, 2006 (www.brookings.edu/~/media/Files/ events/2006/0203europe/20060203patten.pdf), p. 24; and "While Bush and Blair Fumble and Fiddle, Beirut Burns," *Financial Times*, July 19, 2006, p. 19. See also Crisis Group, "After Mecca: Engaging Hamas," Middle East Report 62 (February 28, 2007); Jonathan Steele and Jonathan Freedland, "Carter Urges 'Supine' Europe to Break with US over Gaza Blockade," *The Guardian*, May 26, 2008, available at www.guardian.co.uk/world/2008/may/26/israelandthepalestinians.usa1.

33. See Council of the European Union, "Guidelines on Implementation and Evaluation of Restrictive Measures (Sanctions) in the Framework of the EU Common Foreign and Security Policy," 6749/05 PESC 159 FIN 80 (Brussels, December 2, 2005), available at http://register.consilium.europa.eu/pdf/en/05/st15/st15114.en05.pdf; Joakim Kreutz, "Hard Measures by a Soft Power? Sanctions Policy of the European Union," Paper 45 (Bonn International Center for Conversion, January 2006), available at www.bicc.de/publications/papers/paper45/paper45.pdf. For a list of restrictive measures currently in force, see European Commission, "Sanctions or Restrictive Measures in Force" (http://ec.europa.eu/external_relations/cfsp/sanctions/measures.htm).

34. Germany's campaign was evidently motivated by its desire to maintain a military base in Termez, used to support its role in Afghanistan but of marginal military significance otherwise, and its unrealistic hope that Uzbek gas could somehow help diversify European energy supplies. See Andrew Stroehlein, "Europe's Soft Powerlessness," *Wall Street Journal*, May 20, 2008; available at http://online.wsj.com/article/SB121123410130105125.html; also Crisis Group, "Political Murder in Central Asia: No Time to End Uzbekistan's Isolation," Asia Briefing 76 (February 14 2008), p. 8, and "Uzbekistan: Stagnation and Uncertainty," Asia Briefing 67 (August 22 2007), p. 13.

35. On the U.K. intervention in Sierra Leone (Operation Palliser), see Richard Connaughton, "The Mechanics and Nature of British Interventions into Sierra Leone (2000) and Afghanistan (2001–2002)," *Civil Wars* 5, no. 2 (2002): 77–95; Paul Williams, "Fighting for Freetown: British Military Intervention in Sierra Leone," *Contemporary Security Policy* 22, no. 3 (2001): 140–68; and International Crisis Group, "Sierra Leone: Time for a New Military and Political Strategy," Africa Report 28 (April 11, 2001). On the French intervention in Côte d'Ivoire (Operation Licorne), see International Crisis Group, "Côte d'Ivoire: The War Is Not Yet Over," Africa Report 72 (November 28, 2003); Stephan Sjöberg, "The Evolution of the French Special Forces: Experiences from the Past, Adapted for the Future," FOI, Swedish Defence Research Agency, 2004, available at:http://montegen.com/Montegen/Nature_of_Business/INET-O/Intelligence-Net_Office/The_Intelligence_Process/Special_Forces.pdf; Lansana Gberie and Prosper Addo, "Challenges of Peace Implementation in Côte d'Ivoire," Report 08/04, Paper presented at the Expert Workshop by the Kofi Annan International Peacekeeping Training Centre (KAIPTC) and the Center for International Peace Operations (ZIF), May 31–June 2, 2004, available at www.zif-berlin.org/Downloads/Cote_d_Ivoire_08_04.pdf.

36. In addition to the Aceh mission, the EU has led police missions in Macedonia (2004–005 and 2006), DRC (2005–07), and Afghanistan, the Palestinian territories, and Bosnia (ongoing); rule of law missions in Georgia (2004–05) and Iraq and Kosovo (both ongoing); security sector reform missions to Guinea-Bissau and the Congo (ongoing); and two border assistance missions in Moldova/Ukraine and the Palestinian territories (ongoing). For a list of all current and completed missions, see Council of the European Union, "EU Operations" (www.consilium.europa.eu/showPage.asp?id=268&lang=en&mode=g).

37. The ESDP embraced the "Petersberg tasks" previously agreed upon in 1992 by the Western European Union, which included humanitarian and rescue tasks, peacekeeping tasks, and tasks for combat forces in crisis management and "peacemaking"— the last never formally defined but generally understood to extend to coercive military intervention. See Assembly of the Western European Union, Interparliamentary European Security and Defense Assembly, "The Petersberg Missions," Assembly Fact Sheet 4 (Paris, December 2007); available at http://assembly-weu.itnetwork.fr/en/documents/Fact%20sheets/4E_Fact_Sheet_Petersberg_Missions.pdf.

38. For the text of the Lisbon Treaty, see http://europa.eu/lisbon_treaty/index_en.htm. For a description of its potential effects on the CFSP, see Antonio Missiroli, *The Impact of the Lisbon Treaty on ESDP*, briefing paper requested by the European Parliament's Subcommittee on Security and Defence, January 2008, available at www.europarl.europa.eu/meetdocs/2004_2009/documents/dv/pe389028_/PE389028_en.pdf.

39. See EU Council Secretariat, "EU Battlegroups," Factsheet (February 2007); available at www.consilium.europa.eu/uedocs/cmsUpload/Battlegroups_February_07-factsheet.pdf.

40. See European Security and Defense Assembly, "European Land Forces in External Operations," Document A/1953 (Paris, December 19, 2006).

41. The Berlin Plus arrangements and preceding 2002 "NATO-EU Declaration on ESDP" are described in "NATO-EU: A Strategic Partnership" (www.nato.int/issues/nato-eu/evolution.html).

42. Missiroli, "Revisiting the European Security Strategy," p. 4.

43. Ibid.

44. I am indebted to Sara Tesorieri, of Crisis Action, Brussels, who has maintained a compilation of such statements by the EU's General Affairs and External Relations Council, for supplying this information.

45. Kishore Mahbubani, "Europe Is a Geopolitical Dwarf," *Financial Times,* May 22, 2008; Robert Kagan, *Of Paradise and Power: America and Europe in the New World Order* (New York: Knopf, 2003).

46. African Union, "Constitutive Act of the African Union," OAU Assembly, Lomé, Togo, July 12, 2000, entered into force on May 26, 2001; available at www.africa-union.org/root/au/AboutAU/Constitutive_Act_en.htm. On the evolution in thinking from the sovereignty-focused OAU to the much more overtly interventionist AU, see Michael Byers and Simon Chesterman, "Changing the Rules about Rules? Unilateral Humanitarian Intervention and the Future of International Law," in *Humanitarian Intervention: Ethical, Legal and Political Dilemmas,* edited by J. L. Holzgrefe and Robert O. Keohane (Cambridge University Press, 2003), pp.190–91, and the references there cited. The impotence of the OAU in the face of the Rwandan genocide was an important catalyst for change; see the OAU's own report: International Panel of Eminent Personalities, *Rwanda: The Preventable Genocide* (Addis Ababa, 2000).

47. African Union, "Protocol Relating to the Establishment of the Peace and Security Council of the African Union," Durban, South Africa, July 9, 2002.

48. African Union, "Solemn Declaration on a Common African Defence and Security Policy," Sirte, Libya, February 28, 2004; African Union, "Policy Framework for the Establishment of the African Standby Force and the Military Staff Committee," Addis Ababa, Ethiopia, July 8, 2003. For a cautious assessment of the size of the task involved in building this capability, see Vanessa Kent and Mark Malan, "The Africa Standby Force: Progress and Prospects," *African Security Review* 12, no. 3 (2003): 71–81.

49. Stephan Klingebiel, "How Much Weight for Military Capabilities? Africa's New Peace and Security Architecture and Role of External Actors," Discussion Paper (Bonn: Deutsches Institut für Entwicklungspolitik, 2005), p. 8.

50. See United Nations and African Union, "Declaration, Enhancing AU-UN Cooperation: Framework for the Ten-Year Capacity-Building Programme for the African Union," signed in Addis Ababa, November 16, 2006; on the U.S. program, see Moira Shanahan and Dara Francis, "U.S. Support to African Capacity for Peace Operations: The ACOTA Program," Peace Operations Factsheet (Washington, D.C.: Henry L. Stimson Center, 2005), available at www.stimson.org/fopo/pdf/ACOTA_BriefFinal_Feb05.pdf; on challenges confronting AU planners, see Theo Neethling, "Conducting Operations in the Realm of Peace and Security: Key Issues and Challenges in the African Context," *Small Wars and Insurgencies* 14, no. 2 (2003): 87–112, particularly pp. 95–96.

51. See Colin Warbrick and Zeray W. Yihdego, "Ethiopia's Military Action against the Union of Islamic Courts and Others in Somalia: Some Legal Implications," *International and Comparative Law Quarterly* 56, no. 3 (2007): 666–76, and Robert Spencer, "Somalia: Rise and Fall of an Islamist Regime," *The Journal of International Security Affairs*, no. 13 (Fall 2007), available at www.securityaffairs.org/issues/2007/13/spencer.php.

52. On numbers in uniform, see Stephen J. Flanagan and James A. Schear, eds., *Strategic Challenges: America's Global Security Agenda* (Herndon, Va.: Potomac Books, 2008), p. 213; on numbers of helicopters, see chapter 9, footnote 2 below.

53. Victoria K. Holt and Tobias C. Berkman, *The Impossible Mandate: Military Preparedness, the Responsibility to Protect and Modern Peace Operations* (Washington, D.C.: Henry L. Stimson Center, 2006), p. 58; Klaus Naumann, John Shalikashvili, Lord Inge, Jacques Lanxade, and Henk van den Breemen, *Towards a Grand Strategy for an Uncertain World: Renewing Transatlantic Partnership* (Lunteren, Netherlands: Noaber Foundation, 2007), pp.133–34; NATO, "Prague Summit Declaration," press release, November 21, 2002 (www.nato.int/docu/pr/2002/p02-127e.htm).

54. Holt and Berkman, *The Impossible Mandate*, pp. 126–28.

55. Ibid., p. 65.

56. See, for example, "Shortages Force NATO to Rethink Combat Strike Force," *International Herald Tribune*, September 20, 2007, and International Institute for Strategic Studies (IISS), "European Military Capabilities: Building Armed Forces for Modern Operations," London, July 2008. Also relevant are Sean Kay, "What Went Wrong with NATO?" *Cambridge Review of International Affairs* 18, no. 1 (2005): 69–83; Andrew Michta, "What Next for NATO?" *Orbis* 57, no. 1 (2007): 155–64; John R.

Schmidt, "Last Alliance Standing? NATO after 9/11," *Washington Quarterly* 30, no. 1 (2006–07): pp. 98–99; Crisis Group, "Countering Afghanistan's Insurgency: No Quick Fixes," Asia Report 123 (November 2, 2006), pp. 14–15.

57. The IISS strategic dossier, "European Military Capabilities: Building Armed Forces for Modern Operations," published on July 9, 2008, as this book was going to press, estimated that 71,000 military personnel were deployed abroad on crisis management missions in 2007, representing just 2.7 percent of all active service personnel (see www.iiss.org/publications/strategic-dossiers/european-military-capabilities/press-statement). See also David Cameron (MP, leader of the U.K. Conservative Party), "Crossroads for NATO—How the Atlantic Alliance Should Work in the 21st Century," April 1, 2008 (www.chathamhouse.org.uk/files/11280_010408cameron.pdf). I was told off the record by a senior German official a few years ago that of some 250,000 men and women then in uniform, only around 10,000 were deployable at any given time on international peace operation tasks.

58. Naumann and others, *Towards a Grand Strategy*, pp. 94 (on nuclear first strikes), 122 (on Security Council approval), 132–36 (on the three circles).

59. I explored the arguments for and against this scenario in "All Dressed Up with Somewhere to Go: NATO and Out of Area Peace Operations," address to the NATO conference on Securing Peace: NATO's Role in Crisis Management and Conflict Resolution, Brussels, October 16, 2003; available at www.crisisgroup.org. See also Hamburg, *Preventing Genocide*, chap. 16, "The North Atlantic Treaty Organization: An Instrument to Help in Preventing Genocide," pp. 256–62.

60. See www.osce.org. For general background, see Michael Bothe, Natalino Ronzitti, and Allan Rosas, eds., *The OSCE in the Maintenance of Peace and Security: Conflict Prevention, Crisis Management and Peaceful Settlement of Disputes* (The Hague: Kluwer Law International, 1997). On the OSCE's role in minority protection, see, for example, Jane Wright, "The OSCE and the Protection of Minority Rights," *Human Rights Quarterly* 18, no. 1 (1996): 190–205.

61. See Hamburg, *Preventing Genocide*, chap. 15, "The Organisation for Security and Cooperation in Europe: Its Potential for Preventing Genocide," p. 245. See also OSCE, High Commissioner for National Minorities, "Recommendations on National Minorities in Interstate Relations," June 20, 2008, available at www.osce.org.

62. OSCE Secretariat, "The OSCE Conflict Prevention Centre," factsheet (Vienna, January 10, 2008); available at www.osce.org/publications/cpc/2008/01/13558_57_en.pdf.

63. OSCE, "Factsheet of the OSCE Office for Democratic Institutions and Human Rights" (Warsaw, May 10, 2005); available at www.osce.org/odihr/item_11_13555.html.

64. See International Crisis Group, "Armenia: Picking up the Pieces," Europe Briefing 48 (April 8, 2008).

65. On the World Bank, see www.worldbank.org, and on the IMF, see www.imf.org/external/index.htm; see also "Report of the MDB Working Group: Toward a More Harmonized Approach to MDB Engagement in Fragile Situations,"

presented at 2007 Meeting of the Heads of Multilateral Development Banks and Multilateral Financial Institutions, October 2007; available at http://siteresources.worldbank.org/INTLICUS/Resources/Report_of_the_MDB_Working_Group.pdf. For a discussion of the institutions' role in conflict prevention and rebuilding, see, for example, James K. Boyce, "The International Financial Institutions: Postconflict Reconstruction and Peacebuilding Capacities," paper presented at the seminar on "Strengthening the UN's Capacity on Civilian Crisis Management," UN Secretary-General's High-Level Panel on Threats, Challenges and Change, Copenhagen, June 8–9, 2004; available at www.um.dk/NR/rdonlyres/462BD9E3-F919-4779-94E3-553E0A01F8A7/0/FinancialInstitutions.pdf. See also earlier mentions of the institutions' role in economic sanctions in chapter 4 and in economic development in chapter 7 of this volume.

66. On the ICJ, see www.icj-cij.org, and on the ICC, see www.icc-cpi.int; see also the earlier discussion in this volume of direct legal measures in chapter 4, and criminal prosecutions in chapters 5 and 7.

67. On the Commonwealth, see generally www.thecommonwealth.org, and for a discussion of its conflict prevention role, see, for example, Don McKinnon, "Conflict Resolution: A Commonwealth Perspective," *RUSI Journal* 149, no. 2 (2004): 16–20. Since the establishment of its Good Offices Section in 2003, the Commonwealth has increased the scope and depth of its work in this area, using a distinguished group of special envoys to work on good offices in Fiji, Lesotho, Swaziland, Zanzibar, Cameroon, The Gambia, Guyana, Kenya, Maldives, and Tonga. See Commonwealth Secretariat, "Conflict Prevention" (www.thecommonwealth.org/Internal/38129/156558/special_envoys). On l'Organisation internationale de la Francophonie, see www.francophonie.org. On the OIC, see www.oic-oci.org/oicnew; for a discussion of its limits and potential, see Shahram Akbarzadeh and Kylie Connor, "The Organization of the Islamic Conference: Sharing an Illusion," *Middle East Policy* 12, no. 2 (2005): 79–92.

68. World Summit Outcome Document, paragraph 139; see chapter 2, box 2-2, in this volume.

69. The United Kingdom has been a leader in pooling the conflict and prevention resources of traditionally fractious foreign affairs, defense, and development departments and agencies within a common conceptual agenda. See, for example, Foreign and Commonwealth Office (FCO), Ministry of Defence (MoD), and Department for International Development (DFID), *The Global Conflict Prevention Pool: A Joint UK Government Approach to Reducing Conflict* (London, August 2003), available at dfid.gov.uk/pubs/files/global-conflict-prevention-pool.pdf, and *The Africa Conflict Prevention Pool, an Information Document: A Joint UK Government Approach to Preventing and Reducing Conflict in Sub-Saharan Africa* (London, September 2004), available at www.dfid.gov.uk/pubs/files/acppinfodoc.pdf. As of April 1, 2008, these two pools became a single Conflict Prevention Pool (CPP); see www.fco.gov.uk/en/about-the-fco/what-we-do/funding-programmes/conflict-prevention-pools. In Canada, the Stabilization and Reconstruction Task Force (START), designed to coordinate disas-

ter preparedness, peacekeeping, and mediation/peacebuilding on a whole of government basis, was established in 2005 with substantial annual funding and personnel drawn from the major international departments and agencies, Defence, CIDA, and DFAIT: see www.international.gc.ca/START-GTSR/index.aspx.

In the United States, past failures in Iraq and elsewhere have led to a major new effort to better organize whole-of-government postconflict responses by establishing the Office of the Coordinator for Reconstruction and Stabilization, organizationally within the State Department but operating with the cooperation of the Defense Department and other agencies; see www.state.gov/s/crs. In the specific area of prevention and early response to mass atrocities, a Genocide Prevention Task Force was established in November 2007, with Madeleine Albright and William Cohen as cochairs, to generate practical recommendations to enhance the U.S. government's capacity to respond to such emerging threats; see www.usip.org/genocide_taskforce.

70. On the number of NGOs worldwide—including INGOs, BONGOs, GONGOs, ENGOs, QUANGOs, and TANGOs (respectively, international, business-oriented, government-operated, environmental, quasi-autonomous, and technical assistance NGOs)—see Helmut Anheier and Nuno Themudo, "Organisational Forms of Global Civil Society: Implications of Going Global," in *Global Civil Society Yearbook*, edited by Marlies Glasius, Mary Kaldor, and Helmut Anheier (Oxford University Press, 2002), p. 194. On their economic contribution, a recent study of nonprofit institutions by the Johns Hopkins Center for Civil Society Studies covering forty countries estimated them as producing nearly 50 million full-time equivalent jobs, with an economic value equivalent to the world's fifth-largest economy. See European Policy Center, "Demonstrating the Economic Value of the Non-Profit Sector for Society," Policy Dialogue, 12 June 2008, available at www.epc.eu/en/er.asp?TYP=ER&LV=293&see=y&t=2&PG=ER/EN/detail&l=&AI=822.

71. For detailed information on the role, structure, personnel, and programs of the International Crisis Group, assessments of its impact, and access to all its publications, see www.crisisgroup.org.

Chapter Nine

1. Jean-Marie Guehenno, Under-Secretary-General for Peacekeeping Operations, reporting to the UN Security Council on the deployment of the UN-AU Mission in Darfur (UNAMID), May 14, 2008; see "Darfur Mission Deployment Slowed by Deteriorating Security, Harsh Conditions; Must Be Considerably Strengthened to Carry out Mandate, Security Council Told" (www.un.org/News/Press/docs/2008/sc9330.doc.htm). Since the units mentioned each had six helicopters, he was referring to the need for a total of twenty-two helicopters. Seven other military helicopters have been pledged, but at the time of this writing, none had been delivered. I am indebted to Brendan Cox of Crisis Action (www.crisisaction.org) for his help in untangling the

question of military helicopter numbers and availability, both the numbers required for Darfur and those in the total global military inventory.

2. This figure comes from the following compilation by the Henry L. Stimson Center, March 2008, from country data in International Institute for Strategic Studies, *The Military Balance 2008* (London, February 2008).

Region	Attack helicopters[a]	Transport-utility helicopters[b]
Americas		
United States	1,049	2,042
Canada	0	131
Latin America–Caribbean[c]	82	798
Subtotal	1,131	2,971
Europe and Russia		
EU member states[d]	549	1,080
Other Europe[e]	268	331
Russia	661	643
Subtotal	1,478	2,054
Asia-Pacific		
China	31	93
India	20	298
Others[f]	489	1,644
Subtotal	540	2,035
Africa and Middle East		
Middle East and North Africa[g]	547	787
Sub-Saharan Africa	129	170
Subtotal	676	957
Total	3,825	8,017
NATO[h]	1,619	3,390

a. Defined as helicopters with an integrated fire control and aiming system, designed to deliver anti-armor, air-to-ground, or air-to-air weapons.

b. Defined as helicopters designed to transport personnel or cargo in support of military operations.

c. Mainly Colombia (31 attack, 225 transport-utility).

d. Mainly Germany (192, 219) and Italy (60, 199).

e. Mainly Turkey (37, 224).

f. Mainly Japan (85, 344), Republic of Korea (60, 370), and Taiwan (Republic of China; 101, 81).

g. Mainly Iran (50, 201), Israel (94, 113), and Saudi Arabia (12, 115).

h. The twenty-six NATO member states are the United States; Canada; EU member states excluding Austria, Cyprus, Finland, Ireland, Malta, and Sweden; and non-EU states Iceland, Norway, and Turkey.

A detailed Crisis Action Report on the issue was published on July 31, 2008. See Thomas Withington, "Grounded: The International Community's Betrayal of UNAMID," available at www.globefordarfur.org/docs/Grounded.pdf.

3. As noted in chapter 5, there are currently over forty SRSGs working in specific geographical settings: for a current list see United Nations, "Other High-Level Appointments" (www.un.org/Depts/dpko/SRSG/table). This summary is drawn from Connie Peck, "United Nations Mediation Experience: Practical Lessons for Conflict Prevention," in *Handbook on Conflict Resolution*, edited by Jacob Bercovitch, Victor Kremenyuk, and I. William Zartman (London: Sage Publications, 2008, forthcoming).

4. *Report of the Panel on United Nations Peace Operations,* A/55/305-S/2000/809 (United Nations, August 21, 2000), p. 16.

5. Connie Peck, *On Being a Special Representative of the Secretary-General* (Geneva: UNITAR, 2006), pp. 2–3. I am indebted to Dr. Peck, with whom I worked in Australia in the early 1990s, for her advice and assistance in the preparation of this section.

6. Connie Peck, "Special Representatives of the Secretary-General," in *The UN Security Council: From the Cold War to the 21st Century,* edited by David Malone (Boulder, Colo.: Lynne Rienner Publishers, 2004), p. 328.

7. *Report of the Independent Inquiry into the Actions of the United Nations during the 1994 Genocide in Rwanda,* A/54/549 (United Nations, December 15, 1999), p. 48.

8. Aldo Ajello, "Mozambique: Implementation of the 1992 Peace Agreement," in *Herding Cats: Multiparty Mediation in a Complex World,* edited by Chester A. Crocker, Fen Osler Hampson, and Pamela Aall (Washington, D.C.: U.S. Institute of Peace Press, 1999), pp. 619–20, quoted in Peck, *On Being a Special Representative,* p. 8.

9. UN Security Council, 4213th Meeting, S/RES/1325, adopted October 31, 2000.

10. See World Summit Outcome Document, paragraph 78, and the more detailed recommendations of the High-Level Panel on Threats, Challenges and Change, *A More Secure World: Our Shared Responsibility* (United Nations, 2004), recommendations 18–19.

11. See www.un.org/peacemaker.

12. For the work of the Department of Peacekeeping Operations (DPKO) Best Practices Section, including the *Report of the Secretary-General on Peacekeeping Best Practices,* A/62/593 (United Nations, December 18, 2007), see www.un.org/Depts/dpko/lessons/.

13. See UNITAR, "Programme in Peacemaking and Conflict Prevention" (www.unitar.org/peacemaking/PPD1.htm).

14. See website at www.cscap.org; for an analysis, see, for example, Sheldon W. Simon, "Evaluating Track II Approaches to Security Diplomacy in the Asia-Pacific: The CSCAP Experience," *Pacific Review,* 15, no. 2 (2002): 167–200.

15. For their respective websites, see http://cppf.ssrc.org and www.idea.int.

16. See, for example, "The Hague Recommendations Regarding the Education Rights of National Minorities and Explanatory Note" (Vienna: OSCE, October 1, 1996), available at www.osce.org/documents/hcnm/1996/10/2700_en.pdf; "The Oslo Recommendations Regarding the Linguistic Rights of National Minorities and Explanatory Note" (OSCE, February 1, 1998), available at www.osce.org/documents/hcnm/1998/02/2699_en.pdf; and Foundation on Inter-Ethnic Relations, "The Lund Recommendations on the Effective Participation of National Minorities in Public Life and Explanatory Note" (OSCE, September 1, 1999), available at www.osce.org/documents/hcnm/1999/09/2698_en.pdf.

17. Ahmedou Ould-Abdallah, *Burundi on the Brink, 1993–95: A UN Special Envoy Reflects on Preventive Diplomacy* (Washington, D.C.: U.S. Institute of Peace Press, 2000), p. 97. See also, on the general issue of coordination in this context, Connie

Peck, *Sustainable Peace: The Role of the UN and Regional Organizations in Conflict Prevention* (Lanham, Md.: Rowman and Littlefield, 1998).

18. *Report of the Secretary-General on the Relationship between the United Nations and Regional Organizations,* S/2008/186 (United Nations, April 7, 2008), paragraph 78. This proposes the opening of a new regional office for Central Africa and the Great Lakes region to support the preventive efforts of the Economic Community of Central African States (ECCAS) and the Executive Secretariat of the Great Lakes Conference.

19. See http://www.un.org/unowa/unowa/bckgrdnew.pdf.

20. See www.un.org/depts/dpa/whatsnew.html; also "UN Regional Centre for Preventive Diplomacy in Central Asia Set to Open," UN News Service, December 7, 2007 (www.un.org/apps/news/story.asp?NewsID=24967&Cr=central&Cr1=asia).

21. On U.S. Institute of Peace programs, see generally www.usip.org; on its Genocide Prevention Task Force, established in November 2007, with Madeleine Albright and William Cohen as cochairs, see www.usip.org/genocide_taskforce. On Swisspeace programs, see generally www.swisspeace.ch.

22. Teresa Whitfield, *Friends Indeed: The United Nations, Groups of Friends and the Resolution of Conflict* (Washington, D.C.: U.S. Institute of Peace Press, 2007).

23. See Ken Berry, *Cambodia from Red to Blue: Australia's Initiative for Peace* (Sydney: Allen and Unwin, 1997), chapter 9.

24. The European Gendarmerie Force (EGF) is a multinational initiative of five EU members—France, Italy, Netherlands, Portugal, and Spain—designed to strengthen international crisis management capacities. It aims to provide a consistent and coordinated deployment of EU police forces with a military status and full police powers. It possesses an initial rapid reaction capability up to 800 persons within 30 days that can be reinforced. Although first and foremost at the disposal of the EU, the EGF can also be utilized by the UN, OSCE, NATO, other international organizations, or ad hoc coalitions. It was first deployed as part of the EUFOR "Althea" mission in Bosnia in December 2007; see www.eurogendfor.org.

25. Graham Day and Christopher Freeman, "Operationalizing the Responsibility to Protect—The Policekeeping Approach," *Global Governance* 11, no. 2 (2005): 139–46, at p. 142.

26. UN Security Council "Postconflict Peacebuilding," S/PV.5895 (May 20, 2008), p. 7, available at http://daccessdds.un.org/doc/UNDOC/PRO/N08/347/04/PDF/N0834704.pdf?OpenElement.

27. For the number of international military personnel currently deployed in UN peacekeeping missions, see DPKO, "United Nations Peacekeeping Operations," background note, April 30, 2008 (www.un.org/Depts/dpko/dpko/bnote.htm); for numbers of police and other civilians currently engaged in EU European Security and Defence Policy (ESDP) missions, see Zentrum für Internationale Friedenseins_tze (ZIF), "International and German Personnel in EU, UN, OSCE, NATO and Other Field Missions" (Berlin, April 2008), pp. 6–7, available at www.zif-berlin.org/Downloads/Mission_Update_April_2008III.pdf.

28. See Joshua G. Smith, Victoria K. Holt, and William J. Durch, "From Timor-Leste to Darfur: New Initiatives for Enhancing Civilian Policing Capacity," Issue Brief (Washington, D.C.: Henry L. Stimson Center, August 2, 2007), p. 1, available at www.stimson.org/fopo/pdf/Stimson_UNPOL_Issue_Brief.pdf.

29. See EU Council Secretariat, "European Security and Defence Policy: The Civilian Aspects of Crisis Management," Background (Brussels: May 2007), p. 2, available at www.consilium.eu.int/uedocs/cmsUpload/Background_JPO_2007-Civilian_aspects_compressed.pdf; for a comprehensive discussion of the EU's civilian rapid reaction capability, see Peter Viggo Jakobsen, "The ESDP and Civilian Rapid Reaction: Adding Value Is Harder than Expected," *European Security* 15, no. 3 (2006): 299–321. These targets were set in the context of the 2008 and now 2010 Civilian Headline Goal; as to the latter, see www.consilium.europa.eu/uedocs/cmsUpload/Civilian_Headline_Goal_2010.pdf.

30. See U.K. Prime Minister Gordon Brown, "Speech to the UN Security Council on Africa," April 16, 2008 (http://www.number-10.gov.uk/output/Page15286.asp).

31. See High-Level Panel, *A More Secure World*, paragraph 223; and "First Officers from UN Specialized Police Unit Deploy for Chad to Start Key Training Role," UN News Service, November 21, 2007 (www.un.org/apps/news/story.asp?NewsID=24750&Cr=chad&Cr1).

32. "Under the new budget proposal, the CRS [Coordinator for Reconstruction and Stabilization] nucleus would grow to a 250-person Active Response Corps pulled from agencies, including Agriculture, Commerce, Justice and Treasury. It would include city planners, economists, port operators and correction officials. . . . Their mission would be to deploy within the first 72 hours of a U.S. military landing. As much as 80 percent of the team [200] would be dispatched for as much as one year. . . . The second group would be a roughly 2,000-strong Standby Response Corps, again pulled from all branches of government and having the same diverse skills. They would train for two or three weeks a year and would be the second group to deploy in a crisis. Between 200 and 500 would deploy within 45 to 60 days of a crisis onset. . . . The third group is the Civilian Reserve Corps of about 2,000 that would be pulled from the private sector and state or local governments, much like the military reserve. Its members would sign up for a four-year commitment, which would include training for several weeks a year and an obligation to deploy for as much as one of the four years." Robin Wright, "Civilian Response Corps Gains Ground," *Washington Post*, February 15, 2008, p. A19.

33. Judy Dempsey, "Europe Lagging in Effort to Train Afghan Police," *International Herald Tribune*, May 28, 2008.

34. Ibid.

35. Center on International Cooperation, "Annual Review of Global Peace Operations 2008," Briefing Paper (New York University, March 2008), p. 9. The authors comment that "the contemporary practice of authorizing broad multidimensional mandates has not been matched by efforts to increase the availability of the necessary

human resources, especially qualified civilian personnel for crucial tasks in the area of the rule of law."

36. The following discussion draws on Jakobsen, "The ESDP and Civilian Rapid Reaction"; Smith and others, "From Timor-Leste to Darfur"; Security Council Report, "Building Sustainable Peace: Post-Conflict Stabilisation," Update Report no. 2, May 9, 2008 (www.securitycouncilreport.org).

37. "The UN has traditionally recruited and deployed its police personnel for peacekeeping missions as individuals, a labor-intensive effort. More recently, the UN turned to *formed police units* (FPUs), groups of roughly 120–140 armed officers specially trained in unique skillsets, such as crowd control. Known initially as Specialized Police Units, they were authorized for the UN operation in Kosovo (UNMIK) in 1999, and then became a more regular feature of operations with the UN mission in Liberia (UNMIL) in 2003. By early 2007, there were 35 FPUs (roughly 4,000 officers) deployed in UN peace operations in Côte d'Ivoire, the DRC, Haiti, Kosovo, Liberia, and Timor-Leste." Smith and others, "From Timor-Leste to Darfur," pp. 3–4.

38. UN Security Council, "Security Council Hears 60 Speakers, Asks Secretary-General to Advise Organization within One Year on Best Ways to Support National Peacebuilding Efforts," 5895th Meeting, SC/9333 (May 20, 2008). The summary record of the debate is available at www.un.org/News/Press/docs/2008/sc9333.doc.htm.

39. UN Security Council, "Statement by the President of the Security Council," S/PRST/2008/16 (May 20, 2008).

40. This is the terminology employed by Victoria K. Holt and Tobias C. Berkman, *The Impossible Mandate: Military Preparedness, the Responsibility to Protect and Modern Peace Operations* (Washington, D.C.: Henry L. Stimson Center, 2006). I have drawn extensively in this section on this study, which was sponsored by the Canadian Government explicitly as a follow-up to ICISS and is an excellent account of all relevant issues.

41. Sir Brian Urquhart, "For a UN Volunteer Military Force," *New York Review of Books* 40, no. 11(1993): 3–4.

42. See Scott F. Feil, "Preventing Genocide: How the Early Use of Force Might Have Succeeded in Rwanda," Report to the Carnegie Commission on Preventing Deadly Conflict, April 1998, available at www.wilsoncenter.org/subsites/ccpdc/pubs/rwanda/frame.htm. Based on research including the proceedings of a meeting sponsored by the Carnegie Commission, the Institute for the Study of Diplomacy at Georgetown University, and the United States Army in 1997, the author concluded that "a modern force of 5,000 troops, drawn primarily from one country and sent to Rwanda sometime between April 7 and 21, 1994, could have significantly altered the outcome of the conflict."

43. Netherlands Ministries of Foreign Affairs and Defense, "A UN Rapid Deployment Brigade–A Preliminary Study" (The Hague, January 1995), as quoted in Carl Conetta and Charles Knight, "Vital Force: A Proposal for the Overhaul of the UN Peace Operations System and for the Creation of a UN Legion," Research Monograph 4 (Cambridge, Mass.: Project on Defense Alternatives, Commonwealth Institute, Octo-

ber 1, 1995), p. 68; among other commentators see Lukas Haynes and Timothy W. Stanley, "To Create a United Nations Fire Brigade," *Comparative Strategy* 14, no. 1 (1995): 7–21; for the Ford-Schmidt-Gorbachev quote, see Haynes and Stanley, p. 9. Canada in 1995 released its own recommendations for decreasing deployment times and increasing the effectiveness of UN peace operations, focusing on existing resources rather than an entirely new mechanism; see Amanda Lieverse, "A Rapid Reaction Capability for the United Nations: Past Failures and Future Possibilities," University of Manitoba, Department of Political Studies, 2006 (http://mspace.lib.umanitoba.ca/bit-stream/1993/254/3/Lieverse_Thesis_v2.pdf), p. 33.

44. "World Publics Favor New Powers for the UN," a survey conducted by the Chicago Council on Global Affairs and WorldPublicOpinion.org (2007), available at www.globalpolicy.org/security/peacekpg/reform/2007/0509newpowers.pdf.

45. Charter of the United Nations, Chapter VII, Articles 46–47.

46. These are points I have myself made in the past: see "A UN Volunteer Military Force: Four Views," *New York Review of Books* 40, no. 12 (1993), available at www.nybooks.com/articles/2521.

47. Brian Urquhart, "A Force behind the UN," *New York Times*, August 7, 2003.

48. For a very thorough account of the standing force debate, and the subsequent evolution of standby arrangements, see H. Peter Langille, "Conflict Prevention: Options for Rapid Deployment and UN Standing Forces," in *Warlords, Hawks and Doves: Peacekeeping as Conflict Resolution*, edited by Oliver Ramsbotham and Tom Woodhouse (London: Frank Cass Publishing, 2000), available online at www.glob-alpolicy.org/security/peacekpg/reform/canada2.htm.

49. For a useful short summary of these various developments, see Tim Pippard and Veronica Lie, "Enhancing the Rapid Reaction Capability of the United Nations: The Options," UNA-UK Briefing (London: United Nations Association of the United Kingdom, July 2004), available at www.una-uk.org/Enhancing%20the%20Rapid%20Reaction%20Capability%20of%20the%20UN_July%202004.pdf.

50. For a comprehensive assessment of the state of the armed forces in Europe, published as this book was going to press, see International Institute for Strategic Studies (IISS), "European Military Capabilities: Building Armed Forces for Modern Operations," London, July 2008; its main themes are summarized at www.iiss.org/publications/ strate-gic-dossiers/european-military-capabilities/press-statement. For a summary in English of the French white paper on defense and national security, see French Embassy in the United Kingdom, "New French White Paper on Defence and National Security" (www.ambafrance-uk.org/New-French-White-Paper-on-defence.html#sommaire_3); for specific references to R2P in the original, see Ministère de la Défense, *Défense et Sécurité nationale: le Livre blanc* (Paris, June 17, 2008), pp. 74, 76, 115, 116, available at www.defense.gouv.fr/defense/articles/discours_du_president_de_la_republique_sur_la_strategie_de_defense_et_de_securite_de_la_france.

51. On the global numbers, see International Institute for Strategic Studies, *The Military Balance 2008*, p. 448, table 37; for UN numbers see DPKO, "United Nations Peacekeeping Operations," available at www.un.org/Depts/dpko/dpko/bnote.htm.

52. Quoted in "U.S. Proposes Worldwide NATO Strike Force," *Globe and Mail*, September 24, 2002.

53. On these timings, see generally Holt and Berkman, *The Impossible Mandate?* p. 74. On NATO's NRF, see "Questions and Answers on the NATO Response Force (NRF)" (www.arrc.nato.int/brochure/q_a.htm); on the EU battlegroups, see EU Council Secretariat, "EU Battlegroups," Factsheet, (November 2006), available at www.consilium.europa.eu/ueDocs/cms_Data/docs/pressData/en/esdp/91624.pdf.

54. ICISS, *The Responsibility to Protect* (Ottawa: International Development Research Center, 2001), p. 67.

55. Holt and Berkman, *The Impossible Mandate?* pp. 114 (in regard to Canada and the United Kingdom) and 126 (in regard to multilateral organizations).

56. Ibid., pp. 133–54, 188–91.

57. Ibid., chap. 5; for ROE 1.7, see p. 95, for the MONUC mandate, see p. 205.

58. See ICISS, *The Responsibility to Protect,* paragraphs 7.15–17 on mandates, and 7.26–29 on rules of engagement.

59. U.K. Military Joint Doctrine Publication 3-90, as quoted in U.K. Joint CIMIC Group, "Contemporary Civil-Military Co-operation in the Field," in *Comparative Perspectives on Civil-Military Relations in Conflict Zones,* edited by Michael J. Williams and Kate Clouston (Royal United Services Institute, 2007), p. 54, available at www.rusi.org/downloads/assets/Cusps_Report.pdf.

60. ICISS, *The Responsibility to Protect,* paragraph 7.25.

61. See International Crisis Group reports, "Afghanistan: The Need for International Resolve," Asia Report 145 (February 6, 2008), and "Countering Afghanistan's Insurgency: No Quick Fixes," Asia Report 123 (November 2, 2006), both available at www.crisisgroup.org. See also Kate Clouston, "Comparative Perspectives on Civil-Military Relations" (pp. 1–9); Michael Aaronson, "An Outsider's View on the Civil-Military Nexus in Afghanistan" (pp. 10–19); and UK Joint CIMIC Group, "Contemporary Civil-Military Co-operation in the Field" (pp. 54–59), all in *Comparative Perspectives,* edited by Williams and Clouston, and articles by LaRose Edwards, Rietjens, and Cornish in the collection "NATO and Militaries as Trusted Partners in Civil-Military Interaction," *The Pearson Papers* 11, no 1 (2008): 1–86

Chapter Ten

1. International Commission on Intervention and State Sovereignty (ICISS), *The Responsibility to Protect* (Ottawa: International Development Research Center, 2001), p. 75.

2. Samantha Power, *"A Problem from Hell": America and the Age of Genocide* (New York: Perennial, 2002), especially chap. 14, pp. 504–06.

3. For the Clinton quote, see Power, *"A Problem from Hell,"* p. 386; for the National Security Archive report, see William Ferroggiaro, "The U.S. and the Genocide in Rwanda 1994, Information, Intelligence and the U.S. Response" (Washington, D.C.,

March 24, 2004); also William Ferroggiaro, ed., "The U.S. and the Genocide in Rwanda 1994, Evidence of Inaction" (Washington, D.C., August 20, 2001), both available at www.gwu.edu/~nsarchiv/NSAEBB.

4. Don Cheadle and John Prendergast, *Not on Our Watch: The Mission to End Genocide in Darfur and Beyond* (New York: Hyperion, 2007). Their appendix, "Taking Action: Things You Can Do Immediately," is a particularly useful checklist for activists. See also William F. Schulz (former executive director of Amnesty International USA), "Spread Wide the Word: Organizing the Grassroots to End Atrocity Crimes," in *The Responsibility to Protect: The Global Moral Compact for the XXIst Century,* edited by Richard Cooper and Juliette Voinov Kohler (Basingstoke, England: Palgrave Macmillan, forthcoming); and appendix D in this volume.

5. See Paul Slovic, "Genocide: When Compassion Fails," *New Scientist,* no. 2598, April 7, 2007, p. 18, citing the study by Deborah A. Small, George Loewenstein, and Paul Slovic, "Sympathy and Callousness: The Impact of Deliberative Thought on Donations to Identifiable and Statistical Victims," *Organizational Behavior and Human Decision Processes* 102, no. 2 (2007): 143–53. This reality reinforces the point made in chapter 4 in this volume about the vital importance of human rights education, or education for tolerance, which can instill not only general respect for human rights but an empathetic response for those who suffer human rights abuses.

6. See, for example, Ian Buruma, "'Asian Values' in Burma," *Los Angeles Times,* June 3, 2008.

7. See Peter Singer, *The Expanding Circle: Ethics and Sociobiology* (New York: Farrar, Straus and Giroux, 1981), cited in Steven Pinker, "The Decline of Violence," *New Republic,* February 21 2007.

8. These arguments are developed in ICISS, *The Responsibility to Protect,* paragraphs 8.8–8.23, which were based in turn on earlier speeches and writings by the author, in particular "Preventing Deadly Conflict: The Role and Responsibility of Governments and NGOs," lecture to London School of Economics, February 2, 2001, available at www.crisisgroup.org.

9. BBC Broadcast, September 27, 1938, referring to the Czechoslovakia crisis, reported in *The Times,* September 28, 1938, p. 10.

10. The author's concept of good international citizenship is developed, for example, in Gareth Evans and Bruce Grant, *Australia's Foreign Relations,* 2nd ed. (Melbourne University Press, 1995), pp. 40–41, and discussed in Nicholas Wheeler and Tim Dunne, "Good International Citizenship: A Third Way for British Foreign Policy," *International Affairs* 74, no. 4 (1998): 847–70.

11. Jack Straw, "Failed and Failing States," speech to European Research Institute, University of Birmingham, September 6, 2002, available at www.eri.bham.ac.uk/events/jstraw.htm.

12. Amy Belasco, "The Cost of Iraq, Afghanistan, and Other Global War on Terror Operations since 9/11," Report RL33110 (Congressional Research Service, Library of Congress, updated June 23, 2008), pp. 21, 24, available at www.fas.org/sgp/crs/natsec/RL33110.pdf.

13. Personal communication, June 2008, from Donald Steinberg, who was at the relevant time Senior Director for African Affairs at the U.S. National Security Council.

14. Chicago Council on Global Affairs and WorldPublicOpinion.org, "World Public Opinion 2007" (June 25, 2007), p. 24; available at www.thechicagocouncil.org/past_pos.php#. The survey in its entirety involved interviews in China, India, United States, Russia, France, Thailand, Ukraine, Poland, Iran, Mexico, South Korea, Philippines, Australia, Argentina, Peru, Armenia, and Israel, as well as the Palestinian territories, but not all questions were asked in all countries. The China figures are based on a sample of 1,964 respondents interviewed face-to-face, representing both rural and urban areas.

15. See Human Security Center, *Human Security Report 2005: War and Peace in the 21st Century* (Oxford University Press, 2005), and its successor reports, *Human Security Brief 2006* (University of British Columbia, 2006) and *Human Security Brief 2007* (Human Security Report Project, Simon Fraser University, 2007), all available at www.hsrgroup.org.

16. A long-time advocate of such centers has been David Hamburg, who describes the efforts he has largely personally led (with support, in particular, from the Stockholm conferences on genocide) to establish such focal point operations in the UN and Europe in *Preventing Genocide: Practical Steps toward Early Detection and Effective Action* (Boulder/London: Paradigm, 2008), chapter 14, "International Centres for the Prevention of Genocide."

17. The full membership of the Advisory Committee, appointed in 2006, is David Hamburg of the United States, Monica Andersson of Sweden, Zackari Ibrahim of Nigeria, Romeo Dallaire of Canada, Gareth Evans of Australia, Roberto Garretón of Chile, Juan Méndez of Argentina, Sadako Ogata of Japan, and Desmond Tutu of South Africa; see "Secretary-General Appoints Advisory Committee on Genocide Prevention" (www.un.org/News/Press/docs/2006/sga1000.doc.htm). Francis Deng and special adviser on R2P matters Edward Luck also participate.

18. Secretary-General's letter (S/2004/567) to the President of the Security Council, quoted in "Report of the Secretary-General on the Implementation of the Five Point Action Plan and the Activities of the Special Adviser on the Prevention of Genocide to the Human Rights Council," A/HRC/7/37 (Geneva: United Nations, 2008); also the equivalent 2006 report to the Human Rights Commission (E/CN.4/2006). See also Payam Akhavan, "Report on the Work of the Office of the Special Adviser of the United Nations Secretary-General on the Prevention of Genocide," *Human Rights Quarterly* 28 (2006): 1043–070.

19. For full details about GCR2P, housed at the Ralph Bunche Institute in the Graduate Center of the City University of New York, see www.globalr2p.org. The global NGOs who initiated it were the International Crisis Group, Human Rights Watch, OXFAM International, Refugees International, and the World Federalist Movement–Institute for Global Policy; it has initial pledged financial support from the governments of Australia, Belgium, Canada, France, Netherlands, Norway, Rwanda, and the United Kingdom, and from the John D. and Catherine T. MacArthur Foun-

dation, Open Society Institute, and Scott Lawlor; its International Advisory Board is cochaired by Gareth Evans and Mohamed Sahnoun; its inaugural patrons are Kofi Annan, Lloyd Axworthy, Romeo Dallaire, Jan Eliasson, Joschka Fischer, David Hamburg, Lee Hamilton, Prince El Hassan bin Talal, Sadako Ogata, Fidel Ramos, Mary Robinson, and Desmond Tutu; its Interim Executive Director is Professor Tom Weiss; and its initial group of associated centers includes the Asia-Pacific Center for the Responsibility to Protect, Fundación para las Relaciones Internacionales y el Diálogo Exterior (FRIDE), the Kofi Annan International Peacekeeping Training Center, and the Norwegian Institute for International Affairs.

20. Sudanese-born Dr. Mo Ibrahim, one of Africa's most successful business leaders, established the Mo Ibrahim Foundation with the main goal of promoting good governance in sub-Saharan Africa by developing objective criteria by which citizens could hold their governments to account and by recognizing exemplary leadership. His extraordinarily generous and innovative annual Prize for Achievement in African Leadership is the world's biggest individual award, with winners getting US$5 million over ten years and US$200,000 annually for life thereafter, plus up to another US$200,000 a year for ten years toward the winner's public interest activities and good causes. See www.moibrahimfoundation.org.

Index